Population
versus
Liberty

Population
versus
Liberty

JACK PARSONS

Pemberton Books

First published 1971 by Pemberton Books
(Pemberton Publishing Co Ltd), 88 Islington High Street
London N1

SBN 301 71051 1

Set in ten on twelve point Intertype Times
Printed in Great Britain by
The Garden City Press Limited, Letchworth, Hertfordshire, SG6 1JS

To
Dr F. Kräupl-Taylor
and
Dr W. W. Roberts
Two friends in need

Contents

Part Four: FREEDOM TO CHOOSE

List of diagrams

Note: Many statistical tables have blank spaces for later years in case readers wish to complete them when the data become available.

Foreword 1

DOUGLAS HOUGHTON MP

THE LIBERALISATION of the law on abortion has speeded up the acceptance of family planning. The revulsion of many people against the possibility of abortion becoming a form of family planning has brought about a significant change of attitude. When Sir Keith Joseph, Secretary of State for Social Services, announced an expansion of government-aided local family planning services, it was welcomed (by a Catholic MP) 'particularly by those who think it is a crazy social policy to make abortion easy and family planning difficult'.

Yet, Sir David Renton's attempt to link the new measures with population control was quickly brushed aside by the Secretary of State, who said: 'I would not like my Rt Hon and Learned Friend to delude himself into thinking that the increase in family planning is intended for population policy reasons. It is intended to increase family happiness and as such has an important contribution to make.'

The aim of government-blessed contraception is for family planning and not for family limitation. The emphasis is upon individual and family happiness by the avoidance of unwanted pregnancies. This is probably the beginning of contraception for all on the Health and Welfare Services provided the emphasis is kept the same.

Family limitation for personal or family reasons may be admitted as part of it, but population control may not; not yet. This is what must come under increasing and persistent challenge.

The reason for this growing acceptance of birth control as a 'contribution' to 'increase family happiness' but not to increase national happiness lies in attitudes towards individual freedom. The fear of State intervention, directly or indirectly, in personal and private life is the root of it.

What is not realized is that the exercise of one freedom may curtail or even destroy many more. What is so surprising and so depressing is that mounting social and economic problems of this country (in common with some others) are so timidly related to population growth. The pollution of the environment, the destruction of the countryside under the bulldozers of new roads, housing estates, new towns, airfields, the extraction industries and the rest are all problems aggravated by the growth in population.

The social tensions of urban congestion and the industrial tensions of large-scale units of production are not unconnected with the human condition in a populous community. The more we are together and the more of us there are together, the more inevitable will be the erosion of individual liberty. There will be no escape from it. That is the message of this important book and it simply must be understood.

In almost every other field of human activity except procreation of children is the concept of the public interest boldly put across—from litter to inflation, and from marriage to divorce. The saving of life, the prolongation of life, the treatment of disease and all forms of death control are regarded as the concern of people as a whole, and all are heavily if not exclusively financed out of public funds.

Birth control is different. Population control is more different still. This is the gap in thought and action which has to be overcome.

This book will add to the indictment of the complacency and prejudice which at present stand in the way.

Douglas Houghton is Member of Parliament for the Sowerby Division of Yorkshire; and Chairman of the Parliamentary Labour Party since 1967.

Foreword 2

SIR DAVID RENTON MP

EXCESSIVE POPULATION is generally thought of in terms of scarcity of land, food, resources, as part of the pollution problem, as causing poverty and urban congestion or endangering the peace of the world.

In this fascinating and readable work, however, Mr Parsons breaks new ground by examining in detail how over-population interferes with personal freedom, that treasured possession which we too often take for granted. When we do at last wake up and defend it, however, we do so with relish.

Although in high places there is much concern for freedom, the suggestion of a freedom preserving population policy is sometimes met with the excuse that it is too difficult and would mean interfering with the discretion of parents and even with freedom itself. That is of course complete nonsense for the population could be stabilized entirely by voluntary methods, that is to say by making family planning advice and help freely available and with a modicum of Government advice as to the advantages of reducing the birth rate.

It is only if such voluntary methods were not attempted or were to fail that more stringent methods might be needed later on.

Let us hope that through prompt action now a later generation will not be faced with the dilemma of having to sacrifice freedom to breed, in order to preserve the freedom to live.

Sir David Renton is a former Minister of State at the Home Office; and Conservative Member of Parliament for Huntingdon.

Foreword 3

LORD BEAUMONT

EXPERTS differ on projections and forecasts of population and resources, and it is all too easy to get bogged down in argument about the accuracy of individual prophecies. There is one basic fact which is incontrovertible: it is that man is multiplying and that he is doing so in a finite world. We may be conquering space but to think that the moon is going to solve man's population difficulties is to cry for it.

This is a finite world with only so many resources. We may discover more of them, grow more of them, we may recycle more of them, but however fast we do so we are populating this world faster than we can produce the resources and the resources must come to an end.

This is to speak merely in terms of subsistence. It has been calculated that for a standard of living which we in the Western World do not consider excessive for ourselves, the world has four times too many people in it already. So much for our pious talk about helping the developing countries!

I do not know whether the limiting factor in population growth will be found to be food or raw materials or our production of waste materials, that is pollution. I rather suspect that the last may be as important as the first. But that there is a limiting factor and that we are quickly running up against it, if we have not run up against it already, is undeniable.

In this position we have some urgent tasks. We must increase our resources. We must recycle our resources. But we must also halt the increase of population. There are only three ways of doing that that I know: starvation, the bomb or the pill—and I know which of these I prefer.

When I suggested in the House of Lords recently that if we did not manage to limit population growth voluntarily we would be forced to limit it compulsorily, it was clear that some highly intelligent people were not prepared even to consider that these were the two alternatives. But they are. And it is for this reason that we must welcome—and I certainly welcome very warmly—this serious study of the whole problem of liberty in this context.

This must be a seminal book (to use a slightly unfortunate expression) in a subject which will be moving more and more into the centre of national and international politics.

Lord Beaumont of Whitley is former Chairman and President of the Liberal Party; and Liberal spokesman on Education in the House of Lords.

Preface

The case presented in this book is that the population problem is probably the greatest challenge mankind has so far had to face, greater even than that presented by the H-bomb, which may never go off, or by chemical and bacteriological warfare, which may never be unleashed. The population bomb is already exploding in our faces, we ignore it at our peril and this necessitates our accepting the fact, studying its nature and implications, and shaping our malleable social institutions and values to cope with it in exactly the same sort of way we approach, or should approach, other social problems. To paraphrase Marx in another context, the problem is not to understand the population threat but to *change* it.

If it is argued that population presents a biological not a social problem I would accept that there is a fundamental biological component—along with spiritual, religious, moral, psychological, economic, political, military, physical, and chemical components—while insisting on adding, however, that the biological drive to reproduce is not modifiable, except in the very long run, whereas its expression and outcome are largely under social control, as we can see by studying the social matrix enveloping the reproductive process in all cultures. This means that it is social and cultural variables—beliefs, norms, institutions, role-definitions, goals, and so forth which we must readjust to bring about the inevitable outcome, a balance between man and nature, assuming we manage not to eliminate ourselves and leave nature to strike a balance without us.

The great weakness about nearly all discussion of population problems is parochialism. Many of us seem unwilling or unable to look more than a year or two into the future and even distinguished scholars can be found talking about AD 2000—less than half a life-span away—as though it were ineffably remote. We seem to want to believe that the population problem, if there is one at all, does not affect *us*—at least not *here,* or not *now,* but the ostrich approach will not make it go away any more than the problem of the H-bomb or biological warfare. We have to start looking on human development in a panoramic way, taking the long view, and this means we ought to be trying to look into the future at least as far as we can see into the past; two or three hundred years in some detail, and several thousand years in rough perspective. For this reason I want to explore a wide area, sweeping backward and forward in time and space so that we do not get lost in the forest with our demographers, unable to see the wood because of the trees.

At the very least we ought to look one lifespan into the future, say seventy-five years. Even this would take us into the 2040s, by which time the population of the world could easily be 15 billion, against today's 3.6 billion, and that of the United Kingdom 100 million, against the 56 million of today, with both growing more rapidly still. Growth rates of this order are physically impossible for more than an eye-blink of historical time, let alone evolutionary time. They must and will be halted and we must see to it that the brake is applied early and by social rather than physical or biological means.

I hope to prove that population control is necessary by making three basic points which in turn raise three basic questions.

The three basic points

1. The population explosion started over three centuries ago.
2. It presents a world problem and embraces Europe and the United Kingdom, both directly and indirectly.
3. It cannot possibly go on much longer because the Earth is finite.

The three basic questions

1. When will population be controlled?
2. By what means will it be controlled?
3. How much suffering will be involved in the control process?

Readers must work out the answers to these questions for themselves but the view presented here is that in order to answer 'as little as possible' to question 3 (How much suffering will be involved), we must answer question 1 'as soon as possible', and question 2 'by intelligent, democratic, and humane means'. If we fail to answer question 2 in this way, population may be controlled by unintelligent, undemocratic, and inhumane means, or finally, and worst of all, by the blind and amoral forces of nature.

The typical response to a proposed discussion of population control is to reject it as a violation of individual liberty, and this book—starting off as *The Population Challenge* and originally intended as a systematic demolition of the popular population fallacies—was going to have one or possibly two chapters on the 'fallacy of individual liberty'. However, as work progressed it became increasingly obvious that liberty is the central issue. This theme eventually took over completely, the whole thing had to be restructured around it, and the project grew into two books[1] with the liberty tail wagging the population dog. It became necessary to analyse the meaning of 'liberty', to spell out its implications, and, finally, to offer a working definition.

In brief the argument became that 'liberty' standing alone is meaningless, so that talk of population control—or any other sort of control—as a reduction of 'liberty' is not much more than verbiage unless and until a particular interpretation of the meaning of liberty is put forward and defended. A simple method of helping to make discussion of this sort more practical is proposed and the case argued that only in these or similar terms can a productive debate about population control—or any other issue touching on human liberty—take place, though of course it certainly is not claimed that this analysis is exhaustive.

The object of a population policy in conditions approaching saturation must be to define and work towards an 'optimum' population and if individual liberty is prized above all other things then it must be maximized at their expense. If it is not *the* most desirable factor but only one of a number of desirable things, which is the point advocated here, then it must be optimized rather than maximized, which is to say that we must so organize our social system that individual liberty attains a maximum value *consistent with the development or preservation of other desirable values*, such as equality of opportunity, conservation of the environment, or survival of the species. I hope to show that the way to optimize

---

[1] The first now renamed *Population Fallacies*, was largely completed before the birth of this volume. If all goes well it will appear not too long after it.

liberty is not necessarily to abolish existing controls or to oppose new ones but to balance them very carefully against each other, the forces in the system, and our social goals.

About 80,000 of my countrymen alive in 1970 have seen the population of England double. In my middle age I have seen the population of the world double and I could easily live to see it double again. The case I found myself presenting is that explosive population growth is itself the greatest single threat to individual liberty so that population control—far from destroying individual liberty—is needed in order to preserve it. This is not put forward as a gimmick, or as a paradox to stimulate the intellect, but as a matter of commonsense and a sound basis of practical policy.

Without going all the way with Hegel, who claimed that 'Freedom is necessity transfigured',[2] we can agree that true freedom can develop only from a clear understanding of the areas of experience in which the human will can and cannot prevail—vagueness and evasion of unpleasant facts prostitute the noble concept of liberty. However, if we do not shrink from a realistic appraisal of the human situation and if we then take the necessary steps, there is no reason why humanity cannot surge forward to a life of a quality as yet unimaginable. We can 'invent our own future', to paraphrase the distinguished physicist, Dennis Gabor.

If we fail—if we try to retain both death control and unrestricted fertility—the result must be chaos.

Population control is essential for the preservation of all that we hold most dear, including individual liberty, and I hope the facts and arguments put forward here add up to a satisfactory intellectual and moral basis for its acceptance by libertarians. In the final analysis there can be no question whether we have population control but only when and by what means.

2 *Logik.* § 158.

Acknowledgements

I want to offer my grateful thanks to a number of people who have helped and encouraged me in this project. First perhaps should be my old friend John Hands who painstakingly read voluminous and straggly earlier drafts and made many wise comments, then David Chambers of the London Graduate School of Business Studies who brought his keen academic mind to bear on an almost complete draft, the unknown publisher's reader who sandwiched some very sensible criticisms and suggestions among his fair and generally encouraging report, and my two colleagues at Brunel with legal qualifications, John Burnett and Keith Devlin, who read the first draft of the Law of Liberty chapter and whose genial head-shaking caused me to delete a few sections, re-write some of it, re-order most of it, and make it much clearer that I am not trying to interpret the law for the layman, much less teach lawyers their business, but merely to raise some important questions on which I hope they will bring their expertise to bear.

Alastair Service kindly read Chapter 15 on population policies and gave me his expert views. Ray Thomas, then of PEP, now at the Open University, helped with a number of points to do with transport—though he has not seen the MS and is consequently even less responsible than others for what finally appears in print. My colleague Max Petterson helped with some biological points, and Mr Birch of the Central Council for Physical Recreation told me a lot in my initial inquiries into this field and kindly gave me copies of some of his own papers, and Hector Hawton and Christopher Macy of Pemberton Books have been so unfailingly helpful and patient whilst one book grew into two—nearly three— that they have restored my faith in publishers.

Mrs Durrant in charge of the typing staff in the School of Social Sciences at Brunel has been very sympathetic and helpful in dovetailing typing from dictation on tape into a very full order-book, as it were, and Miss Tina Firmin—now gone off to New Zealand—did a great deal of the typing of the earlier draft, when reduced pressure of other work made this possible.

Richard West kindly took time off during his final year at Brunel to check all the tables and calculations and a number of other acknowledgements are made in the text. I hope that any missed—if any there are—will be forgiven.

Lastly I must thank my wife Barbara who—having taught herself touch-typing for one of my earlier projects—has hammered her way through perhaps as many as half a million words as draft succeeded draft, and my two young children Miranda and Toby for being more understanding and patient with their much sequestered father than anyone could reasonably have expected of two such small citizens.

Introduction

Most of us cannot fully grasp the impact of the scientific and technological revolution we are living through. We are able to understand how it is affecting our lives and our society only bit by bit as results emerge. Most of its influence becomes apparent only in retrospect so that only later will we see why we can no longer ascribe finality to many of the truths now held to be self-evident.

In the field of science the natural 'laws' thought by earlier scientists to be immutable are now known to be merely useful generalizations fitting particular local conditions. Grudgingly we have accepted the relativity—as they relate to the physical and biological worlds—of what men once conceived to be the laws of God. As it becomes apparent that we benefit practically from this new conception of nature and 'Nature's God' we begin to build a rationale to defend our new ways of doing and thinking. However, there remains a widespread belief that all these changes can take place without any effect in what we call the 'moral' or 'spiritual' realm. It is assumed that we have learned this part of what we know by means different from those used to give us our knowledge of the physical and biological worlds. Even though we have found scientific methods so effective in understanding and controlling the practical aspects of our lives most of us assume they have no relevance for our system of values and that in this sphere there are no better ways than those of the ancients. Accordingly we hold fast to these values and pursue them in the order of priority our forebears believed desirable without any consideration of the fact that in so doing we produce results differing enormously from theirs.

In spite of this, however, many of our day-to-day actions—the consequences of which we make little effort to foresee—undermine the old value-system we try to adhere to. Disparity between what we have been taught to believe is right or good and what experience shows will best serve the emerging hierarchy of values has grown until our moral rhetoric seems to be a hypocritic device to delude the young rather than a means of perpetuating what ought to be. The citadels of revealed truth yield only after their incapacity to provide rallying points for a new generation has been demonstrated. The young abandon outmoded values and seek new ones more likely to realize the ends they now see to be necessary.

However, the evolution of a new ethic or religion is at best a slow and crisis-ridden process and the long delay in the emergence of a system for guiding our behaviour effectively may prove fatal. A society requiring a new value-system to ensure its survival may delay until it becomes incapable of accepting and maintaining one even if its thinkers manage to indicate values capable of averting disaster if only they are adopted in time. There are numerous instances of the abuse of new technology but evidence of an emergent set of values capable of dealing with them and the physical and biological world as a whole whilst at the same time creating the social conditions necessary for a good life is much harder to come by and the likelihood of societal breakdown increases.

Nowhere are the omens more apparent than in the sphere of population growth. In the early part of this century most of the leaders in the governmental, business, and intellectual spheres were concerned with the *decline* of population growth in the 'civilized' world. Race suicide was widely feared and those who saw the threat of over-population were given short shrift. Warren Thompson, a young American professor who had come to the conclusion that Malthus was essentially right, found few colleagues who would recognize his competence, let alone accept his conclusions. Luckily his work came to the attention of the emerging press tycoon, E. W. Scripps, who was so convinced of the soundness of Thompson's views that he took him for a two-year voyage on his yacht to study population changes around the world. In 1922 he followed this by establishing the Scripps Foundation for Research in Population Problems which has done a good deal to stimulate work in this field, one now enjoying considerable academic prestige.

More revealing than early academic opposition and neglect was the action of people actively involved in effecting population changes. A great charitable foundation set out to improve health, particularly in 'industrially backward' areas, and when Thompson approached them with the idea that it might be a good thing to examine the likely consequences in terms of population growth he was treated with scorn and disgust—the thought that anyone might question the desirability of prolonging human life was totally abhorrent.

People's interest in the survival of their children, and often of their parents, upon which innovators in public health could build, was found high among value-systems almost everywhere. Even so early efforts to interfere with 'natural' death were often resisted— as they still are to some extent—with the consequence that those who accepted the new system outlived those who did not and per- petuated the new beliefs. Opponents often did not survive to pass on the old values and in time the results of the public health move- ment have sanctioned its widespread adoption.

Unfortunately there has not been a similar modification of values relating to births, indeed, far from death control leading to support for birth control, the desire to see more children survive has served to support the idea that more should be born. It is much easier to take health measures such as purifying water supplies and getting rid of mosquitoes—because they require little active co-operation from most of the people—than it is to affect the sex act, almost universally the most intimate of human experiences and requir- ing an exceptional degree of co-operation for its regulation. What birth control *was* practised provided no immediate feedback from experience to justify departure from practices originally sanctified in conditions where early death threatened the survival of par- ticular families or even society itself. Moreover in many places large numbers of workers or soldiers were seen as advantages justifying the high value placed on fertility. Many actively seeking to control the advent of death continued to oppose birth control.

The results of public health movements, many of them spon- sored by the Foundation referred to earlier, are now evident all over the world. Support for the kind of work originally promoted has now been largely abandoned by this Foundation so that it may engage itself more fully in learning how to increase food supplies with the object of averting the immediate threat of starvation for those people—plus their descendants—who, without the Founda- tion's efforts, might never have lived to reproduce. Thus a value once held to be infinitely worthwhile, without reservation, is now seen to have directed our efforts so as to produce a threat to all the other values of human society. Yet even today belief in the 'sacredness of human life' is widely held to be a supreme good, regardless of the consequences of actions stemming from it.

Mr Parsons has dealt insightfully with the threat posed by this juxtaposition of pre-scientific judgment and the results of scientific practice, arguing that only as men come to see the extent and significance of this threat can they effectively act to reduce it. His concentration on the population problem of his own country is justified for two reasons. In the first place most informed observers are already agreed that there is a world problem, whereas few are persuaded that the United Kingdom is threatened in this way. In the second place few intellectuals and men of affairs in Africa or the East, among the areas with the greatest rates of population growth and most extreme poverty, are going to be convinced by the preachings of western writers about the population threat so long as they are always about other peoples' problems. The implications of indefinite population growth are universal, the same basic criteria apply to East and West, and we must put our own house in order first.

An appeal to fear, however rational that fear might be, will not in itself establish new priorities but there are many good reasons why numbers should be limited. Population pressure threatens complete extinction of human society but even if that does not come about it greatly impairs the creation of a new, more humane world which science and technology would otherwise make possible. Given a limited and stable population the freedom of men can be enhanced through the employment of new knowledge and new instruments, but a pre-requisite is an ethical system that puts emphasis on something more than simple biological survival. Through its concentration on that end traditional wisdom ordains behaviour inimical to the full achievement of the possibilities latent in new knowledge. If freedom means pursuing goals set in the past by people living in different conditions and with limited knowledge of the world around them, then freedom will often be destructive of the world that might be. Socialization based on traditional wisdom internalizes old attitudes and values so that we feel free when we obey the rules laid down by our elders even though they grossly limit our ability to think, communicate, and act. Doing what we think makes us free often enslaves us.

There *are* traditional values which seemingly should guide men in all societies at all times, but mingled with this true 'wisdom of the ages' is a multitude of beliefs, held in equal esteem and with equal authority to be good, which if followed in urban industrial conditions will destroy society. Clearly each generation must continue to give such priority as will provide biological reproduction adequate to sustain their society in their specific circumstances. They must also ensure that the experience of children and parents are such as to produce human beings who give to one another— freely, for preference—that which is required to make truly human beings out of creatures genetically programmed only with human potentiality. Without a tremendous amount of nurture this potential will not be adequate to assure man's survival in most modern environments—values ensuring the provision of that nurture are a must.

It is extremely difficult to discover which elements from the past will contribute to survival and which will impede or destroy it. Certainly the knowledge and rationality of the average man are inadequate to make a proper judgment between them. The idea that pure reason will automatically guide men to select for retention that which is best and to reject that which, if followed, will retard, blind, fetter, or even destroy society is obviously false, as the sorry calendar of fallen civilizations bears witness.

Science and technology, advancing much of the time against traditional authority and wisdom, have freed many of us from starvation and undue proneness to disease, granted us tremendous mobility, and emancipated our minds from much of the superstition and fear that hobbled and haunted them. Together they have granted for the common man a range of choices not open even to great rulers of the past. Their contribution to freedom can be shown merely by listing the things he can *do* for which his grandfather lacked the means. In preceding eras the expansion of mind common among us was vouchsafed only to a very few.

However, science and technology create not only new freedoms but a need for new restraints on their would-be users. If old fears vanish, new nightmares haunt our sleep and we *must* discover what new disciplines are required of us. Romantic insistence on the 'natural rights' which once permitted men to break the fetters of dying institutions not only fails to guide us along the right path but gives us a false sense of freedom and security as we go astray. Among the new imperatives with which we must comply is learning to understand both spirit and substance of the science and technology we seek to harness to our social ends. An increasingly large number of people must be freed from other work to fulfil these tasks. We must teach our children not only what biological and physical science and technology require, but also—having first taught ourselves—what kinds of effective social arrangements are compatible with their use.

Uncovering the nature of emerging social systems is a costly enterprise, as is the socialization required to induce individuals to adopt the necessary social roles. If so many children are born that most of our resources must be spent in giving them the bare necessities of life we can have little left over for educating them to the levels demanded by a complex industrial society. The multitude of unprepared people will be unable to shoulder the mounting burden being thrust upon them. Only if we can prevent the misuse of scarce resources can we be free even to explore the potentials of human personality. Uncontrolled breeding may not only deprive us of freedoms already won but may deny us many new freedoms potentially within our grasp.

The mere physical presence of a dense population limits freedom. The most horrendous result would be the kind of response generated in lower animals crowded too closely together, but long before that point it limits the mobility necessary for freedom. A case in point is the result of excessive use of automobiles in densely populated areas, as Mr Parsons shows. The presence of a second driver on the road limits the freedom of the first, and limits multiply geometrically as more drivers are added. What is lost is not merely the immediate satisfaction that comes from controlling one's own mobility, but also much of our productive potential because skilled people cannot be quickly and efficiently deployed where and when they are wanted. Over-population distorts and complicates the already complex ramifications of transportation, production, and services.

Mr Parsons presents the picture of the threats offered by over-population in detail, with adequate evidence that they are not chimerical, and vividly portrays the probable future of Britain, and, by implication, that of the United States and the world as a whole. His argument should be widely read and quickly heeded.

F. Cottrell

Fred Cottrell is Professor of Government and Sociology and Chairman of the Department of Sociology and Anthropology at Miami University, Oxford, Ohio; and Director of the Scripps Foundation for Research in Population Problems.

Part 1

Freedom from ignorance

Chapter 1

A cautionary note

All populations behave differently at different times. However, despite this fact, it is not impossible to make generalizations to some degree about how they must behave and there are certain basic questions which can be asked to help to understand them.

The questions needing answers are:

1. What is the population now?
2. How does it differ from what it was?
3. What changes are taking place now, if any?
4. Why are these changes taking place?
5. What is likely to happen in the future?
6. What is the significance of the present facts, the present changes, and probable future developments?
7. In what direction ought these trends to be modified, if at all?
8. What should actually be done to bring about these modifications?
9. How can appropriate policies be adopted?
10. How can the effectiveness of these policies be measured and re-inforced?

Demographers normally stop short at question 5 but the argument presented here is that not merely demographers but our whole society must go on to ask and answer questions 6, 7, and 8, and then *do something constructive* in accordance with 9 and 10.

However, this is not so easy as it may appear, and we must sound a cautionary note. Human populations are so complicated and difficult to understand fully that something approaching a complete analysis and description may never be attained. Precise mathematical models may prove impossible to formulate and the ideal of near perfect understanding—giving the possibility of really accurate prediction—seems utterly utopian for the foreseeable future.

Demographers and their statistical allies have developed an impressively sophisticated body of mathematical technique in this field but the factors relevant to a full treatment of population dynamics are so numerous and varied that it would be a bold man who claimed he had identified them all, let alone measured their values and linked them to a coherent body of tested theory.

Births and deaths, the two central issues, are influenced by physical, chemical, biological, psychological, spiritual, and social factors; and all of these can be broken down into sub-categories. For example, social factors can be separated out into sociological, economic, political, military, religious, and historical influences, at least. A population theory would somehow have to take note of all of these regions, evaluate them, and explain their interaction.

Because of this tremendous complication there is as yet no basic population theory other than almost simple-minded formulations such as that about the weight and the spring quoted from Sir James Stewart at the beginning of Chapter 2, that populations always grow when there is no positive force to stop them.[1] Nor is there any sign of such a theory on the horizon. What the expert knows in this essential region is what we all know—that virtually all human populations at all times expand except when obvious social controls or environmental constraints such as starvation, violence, and disease temporarily hold them back. What is likely to be the effect of more subtle influences such as a slump, increased family allowances, automation, changes of government, an international monetary crisis, new methods of birth control, a shift in dogma or policy in a powerful religious body, exploration of space, or the crowding of hundreds of millions into huge conurbations can only be guessed at.

The questions are endless and the answers hard to seek. We would expect—other things being equal—that an increase in family allowances would tend to increase fertility, but by how much, and when, and for how long, we would be very loth to say—and how often do other things remain equal? We would expect the emancipation of women to lead to a lowering of fertility as women begin to use their hitherto buried talents in industry, commerce, science,

---

[1] This is borne out by the latest contribution to this field from the distinguished scholar Professor Wynne-Edwards. See Chapter 9.

medicine, politics, and the arts, but we know few of the answers to the questions that spring immediately to mind about this one issue, let alone what would happen if this emancipation was accompanied by increases in family allowances, improvements in the health services, and the threat of nuclear war.

After reflecting, perhaps despondently, upon this vast arena of ignorance, conflict, doubt, hope, and fear, we can draw a few scraps of comfort from at least a few near-certainties—a few Gibraltar-like rocks of fact in the sea of uncertainty. Alfred Sauvy has commented that demography:

> ... includes fearfully certain areas of knowledge ... as well as fearful mysteries.[2]

The first of the certainties is that we must all be born as a result of the same biological process and that the stuff of our bodies and our needs while we live must be drawn from Mother Earth with the help of energy from the sun.

The second is that we must all die and permit our substance to return to the environment to enable the physical and chemical cycles of life and death[3] to roll majestically on.

The third is that though the universe as a whole may be infinite, our country, our space-ship Earth, and the Earth's environs are only too finite, so that growth of population—or any other expanding physical process—must one day stop, absolutely and irrevocably.

The fourth is that populations always explode when conditions permit.

The fifth is that notwithstanding the complexity of biosocial systems our wealth of practical experience enables us to deal with them after a fashion even though we may not only fail to understand the underlying causal mechanisms but have hopelessly incorrect theories about them. Primitive societies which believe that the success or failure of their crops is determined by a battle between good and evil spirits—in which they can sometimes effectively intervene by means of sacrifices, dancing, or other rituals—also take the trouble to cultivate the soil, plant the seeds, scare off pests, and generally behave, within limits, like scientific agricultura-

---

[2] (1961) *Fertility and Survival* (p 9).

[3] Religions teaching corporeal resurrection have a problem here; to explain what is to happen to molecules which have formed part of more than one body, perhaps very many bodies, at different times.

lists. In our more complex societies of the West, though we have only a primitive understanding of the mechanisms underlying the 'Deterrent', money markets, general elections, the action of many important drugs, the motivation of criminals and judges, and a whole host of other things, we nonetheless deal with them in a more or less workmanlike way so that the related social mechanisms continue to function for the time being—until we find out more and invent a better way. We can draw comfort from the fact that most of the really big questions about human life are so intractable that no black or white answers are forthcoming.

Though a bookmaker would be hard put to it to write a thesis on the mathematics or philosophy of probability, the psychology of jockeys or punters, the physiology of horses, the effect of climate or terrain on the 'going', and so forth, nonetheless he observes, judges, acts, and generally grows rounder and redder as the years roll by. Insurance companies—dealing with extraordinarily complex systems, and still longer odds—do even better.

Despite the difficulties, the same sort of situation is to be found in the population field and with reasonable confidence we can formulate a working principle going something like this; 'This monumentally complicated system has been behaving in this sort of way for a very long time. Although we do not understand *why*, let us make the assumption it will not change its behaviour drastically in the fairly near future unless important new factors—which we can reasonably hope to know about—enter the situation. Let us proceed by rule of thumb, exercising our best judgment and due care, until we have more knowledge and better methods.

It is by no means impossible to ask sensible questions about populations, get sensible if not perfect answers, and use them to make sensible political and social decisions. It is becoming increasingly urgent for decision-makers to have at least the beginnings of an understanding of population trends because they are rapidly becoming a key political issue like productivity, industrial discipline, education, and the state of the pound.

The facts of population not only justify but require that non-experts in this field, as an act of responsible citizenship, should inform themselves and act as best they can through our democratic machinery.

If war, as Talleyrand is said to have observed, is too serious a matter to be left to the generals, then population can by no means be entrusted solely to the hands of demographers.

Chapter 2

The arithmetic of growth

'The generative faculty resembles a spring loaded with a weight which always exerts itself in proportion to the diminution of resistance; when food has remained for some time without augmentation or diminution, generation will carry numbers as high as possible; if then food comes to be diminished, the spring is overpowered; the force of it becomes less than nothing. Inhabitants will diminish, at least in proportion to the over charge. If, upon the other hand, food be increased, the spring, which stood at 0 will begin to exert in proportion as the resistance diminishes; people will begin to be better fed; they will multiply, and in proportion as they increase in numbers the food will become scarce again.'[1]

Malthus explicitly accepted Stewart's formulation and stated as a general principle that the number of living creatures tends to grow in a geometrical progression, whereas production of food tends to grow in an arithmetical progression, so that there is a tendency for the two to separate and for a gulf to appear between them. We might say in everyday language that population tends to grow with compound interest whereas food production tends to grow with simple interest.

In fact Malthus over-simplified and we now know that productivity tends to increase with compound interest, too. Nonetheless his essential point remains valid because population increases effortlessly whilst productivity, despite constant nurture and great endeavour, often fails to keep up with population growth, sometimes slips backward, and, in any case, often becomes subject to the law of diminishing returns.[2]

[1] Sir James Stewart (1767) *Principles of Political Economy.*
[2] For a simple but striking example of the operation of this law see the tug-o-war team experiment in Chapter 14.

It is important to specify exactly what is meant by 'tend' here. The *Shorter Oxford Dictionary* defines the word as follows:

1. To have a motion or disposition to move toward. To have a natural inclination to move (in some direction)

'Tendency' is defined as:

1. The fact or quality of tending to something; *constant disposition to move or act in some direction or toward some point, end or purpose;....*

The italics are added to illustrate the essential biological property of all known living things, to increase in numbers and occupy more space wherever and whenever the environment permits. A population as a whole probably cannot have tendencies[3] in the strictest sense of the word—we have to relate the meaning of the word and the dynamics of the *process* of 'tending' to individual members of the species making up the population we are interested in.

In the case of man it must mean that enough of us enough of the time have an urge to behave in a way which would lead to an increase in numbers if controls were not operating. The activity appropriate to this function is heterosexual intercourse and most of us, expert and laymen alike, seem to agree that the urge, need, and capacity for this activity are very strong in most of us for most of our lives. Where the natural consequences of the sex act are not deliberately averted by means of birth control, the flood of babies continues unabated.

Actual babies are not needed here to make Malthus' point about 'tending'. The basic biological fact is that even where the babies themselves are not wanted the activity which would normally produce them is still wanted very much.[4] The following evidence demonstrates this pretty conclusively and we know that one of the fundamental areas of social control in all societies is the regulation of sexual activity, who can connect with whom, when, and in what circumstances—even the 'how' of it is often specified by the culture. This 'tendency' of population to grow is a primeval force, the

[3] Malthus clearly recognized this. See Bonar, J (1966) *Malthus and His Work* (p 66).
[4] No distinction is made here between the sex urge and a possible reproductive urge. Let it suffice that the sex urge is very potent and that its natural outcome is reproduction.

foundation of the evolutionary process and of the whole of living nature, as Benjamin Franklin argued:

> There is, in short, no bound to the prolific nature of plants or animals, but what is made by their crowding and interfering with each other's means of subsistence. Was the face of the earth vacant of other plants, it might be gradually sowed and overspread with one kind only, as, for instance, with fennel; and were it empty of other inhabitants, it might in a few ages be replenished with one nation only, as, for instance with Englishmen.[5]

Charles Darwin expressed himself similarly, in *Origin of Species.* as did Malthus, Rousseau, and many other distinguished commentators.

Sex and evolution

Charles Darwin accepted the key role of sex in evolution and Desmond Morris in his scintillating book *The Naked Ape* (1967) —particularly in the chapter on 'Sex'—elaborates this thesis:

> ...There is much more intense sexual activity in our species than in any other primates, including our closest relations.

> ...It could be said that the advance of civilization has not so much moulded modern sexual behaviour, as that sexual behaviour has moulded the shape of civilization.

The range and power of the sexual urge is demonstrated in several ways:

> ...The female orgasm in our species is unique amongst primates.

> ...The species [has] the largest erect penis of any living primate...

> ...By the age of twelve 25 per cent of boys have experienced their first ejaculation and by fourteen, 80 per cent...

> ...It is estimated that 58 per cent of females and 92 per cent of males masturbate at some time in their lives...

---

[5] (1751) *Essay on the Increase of Mankind.* Quoted by Haney, LH (1921) *History of Economic Thought* (p 230).

... Approximately 90 per cent of the population becomes formally paired ... (and) 50 per cent of females and 84 per cent of males will have experienced copulation before marriage. By the age of forty, 26 per cent of married females, and 50 per cent of married males will have experienced extra-marital copulation ...

... The adult male achieves an average of about three orgasms a week, over 7 per cent experience daily or more than daily ejaculations ... (and) ... 70 per cent are still sexually active at the age of seventy....

... So we can sum up by saying that with both appetitive and consummatory behaviour, everything possible has been done to increase the sexuality of the naked ape and to ensure the successful evolution of a pattern as basic as pair formation, in a mammalian group where it is elsewhere virtually unknown.

Sex and mental illness

Desmond Morris' thesis is strongly supported in the field of psychopathology by Freud's teaching and similar views can be found in the works of more recent writers. For example, Wilhelm Reich[6]:

My contention is that every individual who has managed to preserve a bit of naturalness knows that there is only one thing wrong with neurotic patients; the *lack of full and repeated sexual satisfaction* ...

The severity of any kind of psychic disturbance is in direct relation to the severity of the disturbance of genitality.

The prognosis depends directly on the possibility of establishing the capacity for full genital satisfaction.

He quotes with academic humour a comment from the Viennese physician Chrobak who, along with Charcot and Breuer had profoundly influenced Freud:

We know only too well what the prescription for such cases [neurosis in married women] is, but we cannot prescribe it. It is *Rx Penis normalis, dosim. Repetatur.* [original italics]

Sex and the law

It is clearly recognized in law that sex is an extremely powerful

[6] (1942) (1968) *The Function of the Orgasm* (pp 108/9) Panther edition.

urge which must be kept rigorously under control to preserve the fabric of our social life.

An enormous amount of time and energy has been expended under the aegis of the law in an effort to dam up all sexual expression other than that between married couples in the privacy of their own bedrooms. Liberals arguing in favour of a relaxation of the sexual code to permit homosexual behaviour between consenting adults in private, heterosexual relationships between the unmarried, and extra-marital sex for those in wedlock, also exemplify —from their very different standpoint—an equal conviction of its importance in our lives.

A distinguished liberal in this sphere, Professor H. L. A. Hart, Professor of Jurisprudence in the University of Oxford, has recently said:

> ... Interference with individual liberty ... is of particular importance in the case of laws enforcing a sexual morality. They may create misery of a quite special degree. For both the difficulties involved in the repression of sexual impulses and the consequences of repression are quite different from those involved in the abstention from 'ordinary' crime. Unlike sexual impulses, the impulse to steal or to wound or even kill is not, except in a minority of mentally abnormal cases, a recurrent and insistent part of daily life. Resistance to the temptation to commit these crimes is not often, as the suppression of sexual impulses generally is, something which affects the development or balance of the individual's emotional life, happiness, and personality.[7]

The function of sexual power

What is the purpose of the stupendous urge implanted in us by Mother Nature, this power to increase at a rate that would gladden the heart of any investor or manufacturer if he could only harness it?

Desmond Morris argues at the lengths described earlier to show that our tremendously heightened sexuality, greater than that of any other species, is no biological accident nor

---

[7] (1962) *Law Liberty and Morality*, the Harry Camp lectures at Stanford University, Oxford University (1963) (p 22).

... some kind of sophisticated, decadent out-growth of modern civilization, but a deep rooted, biologically based, and evolutionary (*sic*) sound tendency of our species.

All this has evolved because of the fundamental need for what he calls 'pair bonding' in order to ensure stable relationships between parents during the long period of helplessness typical of infants of our species. Sex is not only the means for bringing new human beings into the world but the lure, the fulfilment, and the reward for the long and painful process of socializing and protecting them on the hazardous road to adulthood.

Georgine Seward bears out Desmond Morris' thesis in several ways. She refers to data which tend to show that

... sexual intercourse provides an important outlet for tensions in groups whose recreational resources are limited ...

... intercourse may be demanded by a domineering husband as his male prerogative or as a test of his potency. A wife may seek coitus as a means of reassurance of her husband's love.

Perhaps the strongest piece of evidence she adduces is that

Unhappy couples, even those on the point of divorce, indulge almost as often as and sometimes even more often than happy pairs.[8]

In addition to the intensity of the urge to reproduce implanted in us by nature the mechanism of reproduction itself is prodigally over-endowed. A single male ejaculation contains some 226 million sperms,[9] each normal female is equipped at birth with 750,000 potential ova,[10] and Professor A. S. Parkes has quoted a recent estimate that 'coitus now results in pregnancy only once in 2,000 times.'[11]

If we put the figures for sperms and coitus together and multiply we see that over 450 billion sperms are released per conception. We can multiply this by a factor of at least 4, I would guess, to allow for sperms available in frustrated urges towards coitus, and another 2 for miscarriages, infant mortality, and other deaths

[8] (1946) *Sex and Society* (p 23).
[9] Carr Saunders (1922) *The Population Problem.*
[10] Bell, *et al.* (1969). *Textbook of Physiology and Biochemistry.*
[11] (1968) *Biology and Ethics*, a Symposium of the Institute of Biology, London. Not published at the time of writing.

before adulthood, giving us over 3,600 billion sperms—about a thousand times greater than the 1969 population of the whole world—per adult produced.

Another way of looking at it is in terms of the ratio between 'urge' and the 'need'. If we assume the 'need' (for conceptions to maintain a stationary population) is now exactly met—of course it is much more than met—we see that the 'urge' is 8,000 times stronger, making the same rather stingy allowance for unsatisfied urges as before.

If the gigantic machine we have built for the social control of sexual expression were to jam suddenly so that every urge towards coitus in either male or female was more or less immediately met, without any social hindrance from morality, law, convention, considerations of privacy, or anything else, we can dimly begin to imagine this stupendous power for procreation which nature has put in our hands, or, rather, our loins.

As Desmond Morris puts it:

> Thanks to medical science, . . . and hygiene, we have reached an incredible peak of breeding success. We have practised death control and now we must balance it with birth control. It looks very much as though, . . . we are going to have to change our sexual ways at least. . . . *Not because they have failed, but because they have succeeded too well.* (Italics added)

A Roman Catholic view

> There persists in the [Roman Catholic] Church a certain pessimistic, negative attitude regarding human love, not to be attributed either to scripture or to tradition but to philosophers of past centuries. The council should state, without fear or reticence, that the two ends of marriage, procreation and conjugal love, are both equally good and holy.[12]

This view ties in very well with that of Desmond Morris. If it is correct, it makes nonsense of the official Roman Catholic position on birth control as stated by Pope Pius XI, for example:

> . . . since therefore the conjugal act is destined primarily by nature for the begetting of children, those who in exercising it

12 Cardinal Leger, of Montreal, at the Vatican Council, October, 1964. Quoted in *Oxfam Bulletin*, No 9, Spring, 1965.

deliberately frustrate its natural power and purpose, sin against nature and commit a deed which is shameful and intrinsically vicious.[13]

If sex has a dual function, that of reproduction plus that of welding couples together in a loving relationship for life, or at least for substantial periods so that they can provide a stable background for infant development, then it follows inexorably that though all forms of birth control—including the mechanical and chemical means—frustrate the first 'natural' function of sex they powerfully reinforce its second and equally important 'natural' function.

The whole Roman Catholic position[14] on birth control—weak enough in all conscience—crumbles to dust under the impact of this new biological teaching.

The power of compound growth

Many people seem to find it hard to grasp—or at least to accept—what compound growth means in the field of human population. I find in public lectures on these topics that it helps to give examples of compound growth in quite different spheres and then switch back to population once the point is imaginatively seized. Anyone with mathematical knowledge can of course ignore this section.

(1) Growth of a water lily on a pond

I suppose in our schooldays most of us are asked the question: 'If a water lily doubles its size every week and covers its pond after one year, how long does it take to cover half the pond?' or words to that effect. Most of us dutifully reply '6 months' instead of the correct answer, '51 weeks', the water lily doubling its size in the last week as it has done every week since the beginning, only this time from half-size to full-size.

Figure 2/1 shows the size of the waterlily at various stages and brings out the basic point; the same rate of growth gives ever-increasing additions to size as time goes on.

The water lily is too small to show at all for the first 7 or 8

[13] (*Encyclical No 4*, Pius XI, Casti connubii—On Christian Marriage, *31 December, 1930*). Also see Canon 1013.1.

[14] The traditional Roman Catholic position is argued at length by St John-Stevas, N in, "A Roman Catholic View of Population Control" in *Law and Contemporary Problems*, Vol XXV, No 3, Summer, 1960 (p 446).

Fig 2/1

Examples of geometric growth: Water lily doubling its size each week for one year

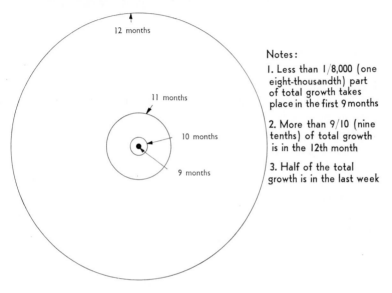

Notes:

1. Less than 1/8,000 (one eight-thousandth) part of total growth takes place in the first 9 months

2. More than 9/10 (nine tenths) of total growth is in the 12th month

3. Half of the total growth is in the last week

Fig 2/2

Examples of geometric growth: Folding over a sheet of paper once each generation

Generation and fold	Year	Thickness
0	AD	0.001 in
1st	25	0.002 in
3rd	75	0.008 in
5th	125	0.032 in
10th	250	1 in
20th	500	>cricket pitch
40th	1000	>circum of earth
60th	1500	14,000 m miles
80th	2000	2,460 light years[1]

[1] 1 light year = distance travelled in 1 year at 186,000 miles per second

months of its year's growth and the black dot in the middle illustrates the size at the end of the 9th month.

The other circles show the size at the end of the 10th and 11th months, whilst the outside circle represents the size of the pond and, by definition, the size of the water lily, at the end of the 12th month.

(2) *Folding over a sheet of paper once each generation since the year AD.*

Imagine that some woad-stained old eccentric dying in the year 0 left his belongings to his descendants on the understanding that once every generation they folded[15] over a thin sheet of magical substance he gave them, his own invention, which he thought would later be of great importance to mankind. It was one thousandth of an inch thick and he proposed it should be called 'paper'.

Figure 2/2 shows the result of each new folding-over as the generations roll by.

(3) *One penny invested in the year AD at 1 per cent per annum, compound interest*

This again is a problem we often get as children, not perhaps related to the year 0 but this makes a useful starting point.

Figure 2/3 shows the fortunes of the penny as time passes.

(4) *Growth of a baby in the womb*

To bring our arithmetical explorations back into the area we are really interested in, the behaviour of living things, let us look at the growth of any normal human being from conception to birth.

We all start off as two cells, one from each parent, but these fuse into one cell and from this point a new potential individual exists.

Figure 2/4 shows the baby's growth as measured by the number of cells comprising its body.

(5) *Growth of a human population with the 'ideal size' family of four children*

This final example brings us back to our central topic, human population.

---

[15] Folding more than 6 to 8 times is physically impossible in real life, of course.

Fig 2/3

Examples of geometric growth: One new penny invested at 1% per annum compound interest

Year	Generation (approx)	Amount
AD	0	1p
70	3rd	2p
140	6th	4p
210	8th	8p
280	11th	16p
350	14th	32p
420	17th	64p
490	20th	£1.28
700	28th	£10.24
980	39th	£164
1400	56th	£10,486
1680	67th	£168,000
1890	75th	£1,342,000
1960	78th	£2,684,000
2100	84th	£10,750,000

Notes:

1. At 1% per annum compound interest capital (or a population) doubles every 70 years

2. In the 1st 1,000 years (approx) the penny grows by about £164. In the 2nd 1,000 years (approx) it grows by about £4,000,000

3. In the next 1,000 years it would grow to about £80 billions

4. After 2,000 years at 1% simple interest it would come to 21p

On the birth of Prince Edward the *Guardian* said:

When Prince Andrew was born in 1960 we said how much nicer a family of three was than a family of two, and a family of four is surely nicer still. The new prince will have a very big brother to look up to, as well as a little brother who will, in time, be not too old to play with, and a sister who will be just the right age to attract admiring affection before she vanishes irretrievably into the company of the grown-ups.[16]

If *The Guardian* eulogy is thought a trifle unscientific—bare

[16] Editorial, March 11, 1964. According to one report this reflected the feelings of the parents. When the fourth royal pregnancy was announced, the *Daily Herald* claimed that the Queen had '... often told friends that she would like four children—"an ideal size family." ' (September 7, 1963).

Fig 2/4

Examples of geometric growth: Development of a human embryo from conception to birth

Months	No of cell doublings (approx)	No of cells in embryo
Conception	–	I cell
	5	
I		32
	10	
2		1,024
	14	
3		16,384
	18	
4		262,144
	23	
5		8,400,000
	27	
6		134,000,000
	32	
7		4,000,000,000
	36	
8		69,000,000,000
	40	
9		1,000,000,000,000 (= 1,000 billion)

Notes:

1. By maturity, at 20 years, there are 25 thousand billion cells after a total of 45 doublings

2. This table distorts reality to some degree by smoothing out the growth process which in real life goes in surges.

assertion about the personal predilections of laymen—it is by no means impossible to find backing from experts.

In a talk on the Third Programme[17] Dr Eversley, then Reader in Population Studies in the University of Sussex, said:

. . . I have four children myself, as my wife and I planned, . . . I am a great believer in the value of the family. Three or four is in itself a good number. . . .

In a letter to *The Times*[18] Mr D. R. Hughes of the Duckworth

[17] Reported in *The Listener*, July 27, 1967.
[18] April 21, 1964.

Laboratory of Physical Anthropology, University of Cambridge, wrote:

Sir,

As a university teacher with six children and a splendidly indefatigable wife, I was dismayed to read your report that the Earl of Huntingdon believes that I and people like me should be looked upon as indulging themselves in a luxury which possibly was in the interests of neither the children nor the country. . . .

. . . I believe that the joy of creating and rearing a large family should be unrestrained for all who are willing and able to accept the responsibilities involved and who desire this kind of enrichment. . . .

Figure 2/5 shows what it means in practice if as a society we decide that four children is the ideal size for a family and make sure it is realized in practice.

Fig 2/5
Population growth with 'ideal size' family (4 surviving children)

Year	Generation	Great-grandparents dying	Grand-parents	Parents	Newborn infants	Total population (approx)
AD	0	0	0	0	2[1]	2
25	1st	0	0	2	4	6
50	2nd	0	2	4	8	15
75	3rd	2	4	8	16	30
100	4th	4	8	16	32	60
200	8th	64	128	256	512	900
500	20th	232,144	462,288	924,576	1,849,152	3.7 million
600	24th	1978 population of Britain				58 million
750	30th	1967 population of whole world				3.4 billion
1150	46th	More than one person for each sq yard of the earth's land surface				245,000 billion
2000	80th	About 40 times[2] the mass of the whole earth				4,210,000 billion billions

1. Starting at year AD with two newly born infants, one male, one female, as total population
2. Taking 20 people to the ton

To simplify, let us assume for a moment that we have magical powers enabling us to bring about the painless removal of the whole existing human population of the globe except for two newborn infants—a little prince and princess—and implant an instinct telling them they must have four surviving children. We shall have to let them reproduce incestuously, of course, but this need not trouble us too much as it is only a paper exercise.[19]

Figure 2/5 shows what would happen to a population given these conditions.

Summary

From the foregoing evidence we see the almost unbelievable powers of increase inherent in geometric or compound interest growth patterns in all fields, including human populations which now have to deploy ever-increasing resources to hold it at bay.[20] It follows that the popular idea of our ancestors rearing large families must be wrong; it is true they used to beget many children, but no less true that they failed to rear them for very long, otherwise the Earth would have been solid with human flesh a long time ago.

As a final illustration of the utter impossibility of our species having appreciably larger than replacement-size families for more than the briefest of historical periods let us take a concrete example. Assume that our species started from one couple only 75,000 years ago, that the length of a generation is 25 years, giving us 3,000 generations, that life expectancy equals the generation, and that each person produces on average one-hundredth of a child more than is needed for replacement. Couples produce 2.02 children by the age of 25 and then die.

---

[19] There are good historical precedents, in any case. Rameses II left behind rather more than the huge stone likeness which has just been moved to make way for the Aswan High Dam. He cohabited with his wives and daughters to such good effect that with a hundred sons and fifty daughters he was able to start a new social class from which Egypt's rulers were chosen for over a century after his death. Durant, W (1935) *Our Oriental Heritage* (p 214).

[20] In 1968 world consumption of contraceptive devices was as follows:

Aerosol foam	4.25 million cans (4 gms. each).
Condoms	23 billion.
Diaphrams	350,000 new fittings.
IUDs	10 million new fittings.
Orals	230 million complete months.

Estimated retail value about $500 million.

After Sollins and Belsky, Reports on Population/Family Planning No 4. June, 1970.

By January 1, 1969, 5 million sterilizations had been carried out under national family planning programmes in only 10 countries. After Presser, HB, Reports on Population/Family Planning, No 5. July, 1970.

A very simple compound interest equation[21] shows that this would have given us nearly 16,000 billion by now, more than 5,000 times the actual world population in 1970, and a present numerical rate of growth of about 300 billion per generation.

Figure 2/6 illustrates this growth process and demonstrates that our families cannot on average be even one ten thousandth of one per cent above replacement size in the long run. They must be the right size, no more and no less, unless we are prepared to tolerate great fluctuations in the size of both families and populations.[22]

Fig 2/6
Growth of world population with very small families

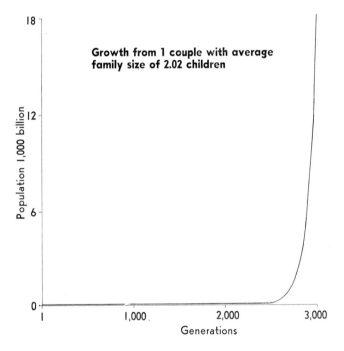

21 $P_2 = P_1 (1 + I)^g$ where P_2 = later population, P_1 = earlier population (2) I = interest per generation, expressed as a fraction (0.02), and g = the number of generations (3,000).   (0.01)

22 Fred Hoyle has argued that this is the likeliest outcome. See *A Contradiction In the Argument of Malthus*, a lecture delivered at the University of Hull, May 17, 1963. Published in pamphlet form by University of Hull Publications.

We must recognize the enormous power and significance of the sexual urge and provide wholesome and fulfilling means of expression. We must also impose upon it constraints sufficient to ensure that one of its two main outcomes, the flow of progeny, is a force for stability, peace, plenty, and the fullest possible flowering of the human spirit, instead of a threat to the continued existence of civilization.

Chapter 3

Numbering the people: I. World population

For the King David said to Joab the captain of the host, ... go now through all the tribes of Israel . . . and number ye the people, that I may know . . .[1]

Nobody knows how many people there are in the world and we can safely surmise that if perfect precision is sought no one ever will.[2]

Although statistics itself and statistical services have improved greatly in the last few decades there still remain many shortcomings in the picture we have of the population of certain regions and, consequently, of the world as a whole.

Quite apart from the inherent problems of sorting out how many people live in particular areas and their marriage, birth, and death rates, for example, the complications superimposed upon them by political considerations in some areas make the outcome very doubtful indeed.

It is very difficult to get an accurate idea of the size of the population of China, for example, or its rate of increase. The Chinese, for reasons best known to themselves, keep their population figures secret. When I wrote to the Foreign Languages Publishing House in Peking in 1968 to find out what material was published in English on population questions, I was sent the *Thoughts of Chairman Mao*.

[1] II Samuel 24. 2–8.
[2] See, for example, Krzywicki, L (1934) *Primitive Society and its Vital Statistics,* or, more recently, McArthur, N, 'The Demography of Primitive Populations'. *Science,* **167**, 3921, February 20, 1970.

Similarly population dynamics are very important at the present time in both South Africa and Southern Rhodesia where black fertility is much higher than that of the whites and is obviously a potent factor in the present explosive political situation. The 'whites'[3] want to play down the size of the coloured population and decrease its fertility while the coloureds want to stress and increase their numerical strength.

The upshot of all this is to make population figures uncertain, and a special problem is that of 'under-enumeration'. It is far easier to miss people out than to count them twice, especially if they think there may be a link between the enumerator and the tax man.

Situations such as those described can play havoc with statistics and make it very difficult indeed to get an accurate picture of what is going on. However, these special factors apply only to limited areas for limited times and do not have a very large effect on world population figures as a whole. In the case of China—the largest single problem—we have a very good idea of the probable upper and lower limits of the population so that—even though China accounts for nearly one quarter of the world's population—an error as large as a hundred million, which is unlikely, would change the world figure by less than 3 per cent.

The changes in human life and numbers have been so great that there can be little doubt about the overall picture. One writer, Ralph Thomlinson, has exemplified this in a rather poignant way by dedicating a book[4] to Mozart, the man he would:

> ... most like to have given another twenty years of life:
> One of seven children, five of whom died within six months of birth;
> Father of six children, only two of whom lived six months;
> Himself a survivor of scarlet fever, smallpox, and lesser diseases,
> Only to die at the age of thirty-five years and ten months
> From a cause not diagnosable by the medical knowledge of his time;
> Thus making his life demographically typical of most of man's history.

---

[3] Probably more than half the 'whites' in South Africa are of coloured ancestry. See Findlay, G (1936) *Miscegenation.*

[4] (1967) *Demographic Problems.*

The evolutionary background

Manlike creatures have lived on the Earth for a million years or more, perhaps two million, possibly even four. The latest evidence seems always to push the dawn of man a little further back. Our picture of world population in the past has been built up like a gigantic jigsaw puzzle, there is no one piece or source of evidence which tells us that world population was this, that, or the other. It has been built up from a very large number of snippets of information which sometimes appear to contradict each other but more often than not dovetail and amplify, though from time to time estimates have to be changed in the light of new knowledge or new techniques of interpreting old knowledge.

Kinds of evidence

The techniques of greatest use in producing evidence are those of physical and cultural anthropology and archaeology, all of which are making ever greater use of the new techniques in the physical sciences, for measuring age of specimens, for example, and for analysing large amounts of information by computer. From their studies of teeth, bits of skull, slivers of bone, and remains of food, coupled of course with an extensive knowledge of the structure of the skeletons of modern man, the other primates, and the wider fossil record, physical anthropologists have built up a very convincing mosaic of the evolution of man.

Archaeologists can dig up the remains of a settlement and, within limits, tell us the probable population from the line of the boundary, the area of the settlement, the number and size of the dwellings, and similar facts. This can be reinforced by evidence from cooking fire sites and rubbish tips about what food was eaten and how it was obtained, whether by collecting, hunting, or by agriculture, and a deduction can be made from this of roughly how many people such a culture in such an environment could have supported, which can be compared with the figure from the settlement size. Evidence from graves gives further support; objects buried with the bodies give information about religious beliefs which may have implications for fertility and population.

A computer has been used to analyse the styles of pottery produced by the Beaker Folk of Britain and thereby produce a coherent picture of its evolution over time and provide further evidence of sequences and dates.

The radio-carbon system of estimating the age of pottery, bones, ash from cooking-fire sites, and so on, has produced a great improvement in chronology and this will now be supported by the new method of dating by means of thermo-luminescence,[5] a method of finding out how much radiation a body has received since it was last heated, giving directly the time which has elapsed since a pot, for example, was fired by the potter, who thereby set this particular 'clock' at zero.

Apart from the buried record and experimental results, evidence from comparable contemporary sources is readily available from people living in Stone Age cultures in New Guinea, Australia, and elsewhere. Australian Aboriginals, insofar as they have not been affected by the dominant European culture, have found that their harsh environment, without the assistance of agriculture, will support about two-and-a-half persons to the square mile and a number of authorities have put forward estimates of this order based upon evidence from other areas.[6]

A new source of evidence on the carrying capacity of earlier 'socio-technic' systems is provided by the new discipline of experimental archaeology—the modern technique of recreating ancient artefacts and measuring their efficiency and durability. Research is now going on into the rate and kind of weathering suffered by various types of earthworks, the protective capacity of primitive underground grain storage systems, quality control in Roman pottery kilns, the efficiency of iron smelting furnaces operated at Ashwicken in Norfolk in the second century AD, and many other fascinating topics.[7]

Even in this sphere of pure science there may be a most unlikely spin-off as the Intermediate Technology Development Group—formed to help the poor countries to help themselves—is seriously investigating the potential of modernized Roman blast furnaces in the remoter regions of India and similar places.

Evidence of this sort can be reinforced from many other directions. Agricultural scientists can show what yields there will be from different sorts of crops in different environments and climates and thereby give a good indication of how much food is available. Physiologists and nutritionists can provide evidence on the needs

[5] (1968) *Nature*, August 3 (219, 442).
[6] Cipolla, C (1962) *The Economic History of World Population* (p 73) for example. Other writers put it a good deal lower.
[7] For an introductory discussion see Proudfoot, VB, 'Experiments in archaeology'. *Science Journal*, November, 1967.

of people of different body weights doing various amounts of work in different temperatures and humidities. This evidence, coupled with the knowledge of the amount of food available, provides reasonable upper and lower estimates of the number of people given environments and cultures can support.

The really important thing to remember about earlier populations is that simply huge errors in measuring and describing them are of very little significance in the light of what has happened since the middle of the seventeenth century—a time when our studies of population and society were beginning to be more reliable.

A pictorial history of world population

Figure 3/1 gives a simplified picture of world population over a period of about 10,000 years, 8000 BC up to nearly AD 2000. The graph is represented by a dotted line for the greater part of its length because no precise figures are known, as we have seen. The graph turns through almost 90° in the middle of the seventeenth century and it is shown as a continuous line from there, although of course there was no sudden change from imprecise to precise knowledge. However, the rate of change is so enormous that very large errors would make little or no difference.

Where the graph begins, about the end of the Old Stone Age, it is very probable that the world population was below 5 million. One writer,[8] estimates that population doubled four times between 8000 and 4000 BC—increased by a factor of 16, that is, bringing it up to somewhere in the region of 80 million by 4000 BC.

The United Nations experts believe that world population was between 200 and 300 million in the year AD and over 500 million by the middle of the seventeenth century when the 'explosion' started.

Figure 3/2 carries on from where Fig 3/1 left off; it is to the same scale and shows the expected growth of world population in the remaining years between 1970 and the year 2000. It will be seen that the increase in the height of the graph over those remaining thirty years is the same as over the previous 10,000 years, the base line of the graph.

In fact the picture is even worse than this because the graph in Fig 3/1 is open-ended. To represent world population accurately

[8] Deevey, ES, 'The Human Population', *Scientific American* (September, 1960) CC. 111:3, 195–204.

the base line of the graph would have to be not 10,000 years but at least a million years long. Representing this in graphical terms is difficult, but if the base line of the graph on the page in front of you is 4 inches long then the point of origin—the place where it should start—would be 11 yards to your left. This is the graph which, in your mind's eye, you must compare with Fig 3/2 in order to get a true picture of the relationship between past and present growth.

The graph in Fig 4/2 in the next chapter compares the populations of Britain and the world over a thousand-year period, approximately, from AD 1000 up to 1969. This much shorter baseline shows the period when the 'explosion' started in more detail and demonstrates that though the world curve did start a rapid upward movement in the middle of the seventeenth century it did not suddenly turn through approximately 90°. On this expanded

Fig 3/I
World Population (1):
Growth over past 10,000 years

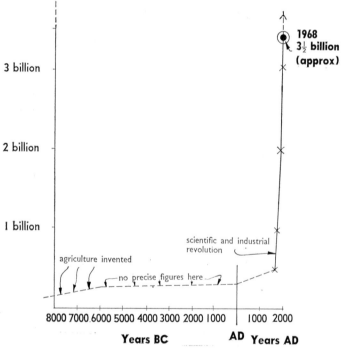

scale about two centuries elapse before the line becomes nearly vertical, as it was on the graph with the 10,000-year base-line in Figs 3/1 and 3/2.

Serial billions

Figure 3/3 shows the history of world population in terms of the numbers of billions of humans and the time which each took to produce. The left hand column shows the serial order of the billions; first, second, third, and so on. The middle column shows the approximate dates, and the right hand column approximate times taken.

Fig 3/2
World Population (1): continued
Expected growth over 32 years
following 1968

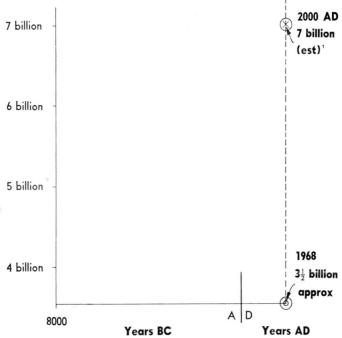

7 billion

2000 AD
7 billion
(est)[1]

6 billion

5 billion

4 billion

1968
3½ billion
approx

8000

A D

Years BC

Years AD

[1] Based on UN 'High' projection, which seems the likeliest.
UN, (1966) World Population Prospects as Assessed in 1963.

There is a certain arbitrariness in the choice of the figure representing the time taken to produce the first billion; it depends where you start to count. The table is labelled 'Time taken by the Earth to evolve each billion human beings' so that it is legitimate to write in beside the first billion, in 1830, the age of the Earth, now taken to be about 4½ billion years.

Perhaps we ought not to start counting at least until life appeared on Earth. Nobody knows when this was as the earlier forms of life were soft bodied and left no fossil trace but it could perhaps be as much as 3 billion years ago. This again is arbitrary,

Fig 3/3
World Population:
Time taken by the earth to evolve
each billion humans

Human billions	Year AD	Time taken (years)	
1st	1830	4.5 billion	Time taken for each billion up to 1968
2nd	1930	100	
3rd	1960	30	
4th	1975	15	Time taken for each billion up to AD 2000
5th	1987	12	
6th	1995	8	
7th	2000	5	
8th			
9th			Times taken for next 5 billion
10th			
11th			
12th			

perhaps we should start when the mammals appeared, possibly 70 million years ago, the origin of the primates a little later, the 'superfamily', the *hominoids*—perhaps 40 million years ago, the 'family', the *hominids,* say 15 million years back, the *genus homo*, possibly one million years ago, or our species *homo sapiens*, for which we need go back only some 50 to 150,000 years.

Taking the smallest of these figures, 50,000 years, for the top of the right hand column in Fig 3/3, we see there was a truly gigantic drop between the times taken to produce the first and second billion human beings, from 50,000 years down to 100 years, 1/500th of the time.

There is a further large drop from the second to the third billion, the third to the fourth, and so on. The times taken by the later billions are so small that the differences seem insignificant. Nonetheless, considered as a proportion there is still a large drop for each one.

If present trends were to continue it would not be long before the latest billion appeared in less than a year and this is a figure to conjure with. Imagine the task of providing in one year the resources needed to equip one billion new human beings with what the same number has now, between a quarter and a third of the total wealth humanity has accumulated so far.

Population doubling times

Figure 3/4 shows rate of increase of human populations as measured by the concept 'doubling time', not much used by modern demographers. This simply means the time it takes for a population, whatever its size, to become twice as big, to increase from x to 2x, where 'x' is the population at a particular instant.

The table shows that up to the beginning of the New Stone Age,

Fig 3/4
World Population:
Decreasing doubling-times

Epoch	Time taken
before 8000 BC	75,000 years
8000 BC–AD	abt 2,000
AD −1650	1,650
1650 −1830	180
1830 −1930	100
1930 −1975	45
as at 1970	35
as at 2000	35
as at 2050	?
as at 2100	?

approximately, the population took about 75,000 years to double. This rapidly fell to about 1,600 years between the year 0 and the year 1650, down to 180 years between 1650 and 1830, and so on. At present it is running somewhere in the region of thirty-five years for the world as a whole and Fig 3/5 shows how this varied from country to country in 1968. The doubling time in the UK is about 130 years on this graph, a little under two lifespans.

The present world doubling time is twice the theoretical minimum, about $17\frac{1}{2}$ years. Of course populations could double in less time than this in somewhat unusual local circumstances—given massive immigration for example—but for consistent and sustained growth it is hard to see how the doubling time could be less than this as it involves each fertile couple producing more than four surviving children by the age of $17\frac{1}{2}$.

Fig 3/5
Population doubling-times:
Various countries in the 1960s

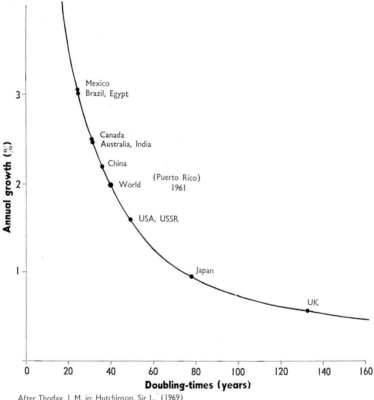

After Thoday, J. M. in: Hutchinson, Sir J.,ˊ (1969)
Population and Food Supply, p7

We see, therefore, that humanity as a whole has reached 50 per cent of the theoretical maximum efficiency of reproduction.

These figures are influenced by differing beliefs about the origins of mankind. Colin Clark, a well known student of population problems, believes that the human race

> ... started from only two people, which Christians are bound to believe. . . .[9]

This means the doubling time has to be somewhat shorter to enable the population to climb from two up to the accepted level by the year 0, or whatever datum point is taken, and Clark's figure for our early history is 37,000 years, taking

> 500 years to increase by 1 per cent.

Population growth as an annual percentage

Figure 3/6 shows rates of growth of human population as measured in percentages. The left hand column shows the period under consideration, the middle one the rate of population growth each year, expressed as a percentage, and the third column the increase in the rate of growth expressed as a ratio of the current rate as against the 'normal' rate.

[9] (1967) *Population Growth and Land Use* (p 62).

Fig 3/6
World Population:
Rate of growth as an annual percentage

Epoch	Rate of population growth (% each year)	Increase in rate of growth
Before agriculture (up to about 8000 BC)	0.001%	—
AD to 1650	0.040%	40 times
1650–1830	0.380%	380 times
1830–1960	0.700%	700 times
1968	2.000%	2,000 times
1968–2045	?	?
2045 onwards	?	?

Based on data from Clark, C.,(1967) **Population Growth and Land Use**

In the top right hand no figure is expressed as there is nothing earlier to compare it with. We see that from the year 0 to about 1650 the rate of growth had increased 40 times, from 1650 to 1830, 380 times, from 1830 to 1960 about 700 times, while at the present time it is running 2,000 times greater than the norm during the greater part of human evolutionary history.

How many people have ever lived on the Earth?

This account is based on a most interesting article by Annabelle Desmond[10] who says her figures should be regarded as

... no more than a reasonable guess. ...

We have already seen it is to some extent arbitrary when one starts to count 'man' from, and she takes what she admits is 'obviously a compromise...', about 600,000 years ago. She estimates that up to 1962 about 77 billion babies had been born so that the population at the time she was writing, about 3 billion, was 4 per cent of the grand total. Bringing this information up to date would give us about 78 billion babies born and those alive now, 3.6 billion, represent something over $4\frac{1}{2}$ per cent.

On this reckoning only 12 billion people lived before 6000 BC but Desmond also computes the figures for a starting point 1,000,000 years earlier. Her estimate of the number of births before 6000 BC then becomes 32 billion, making the grand total, up to the time she was writing, about 96 billion. Taking this basis, about $3\frac{3}{4}$ per cent of human beings who have ever lived were living in 1969.

Summary

Taking his history, somewhat arbitrarily, to span a million years, we have seen that for 99 per cent of his existence man has been a primitive food gatherer living in small scattered bands adding up to several hundred thousand, or at most a few million, and expanding at a rate giving a doubling time of between 37,000 and 75,000 years.

At the beginning of modern times, say 10,000 years ago, there

[10] 'How many people have ever lived on earth?', *Population Bulletin* (February, 1962), Population Reference Bureau. Reprinted in Mudd, S (ed) (1964) *The Population Crisis and the Use of World Resources*.

may have been 5 million of us and numbers began to expand rapidly as agriculture and urban life were invented and diffused, giving perhaps 250 million by the year 0, and 500 million by the middle of the seventeenth century when the explosion proper started.

By 1975 we shall have reached 4 billion, after three doublings in about 350 years, and our present doubling time, at 2 per cent per annum compound interest, has fallen to thirty-five years. As the doubling time drops, so the size of each doubling goes up by equally massive amounts. If this were to continue for a few more centuries the surface of the Earth would be completely covered with humans.

On Desmond's shorter reckoning, from the 6000 BC deadline, more than five-sixths of all human beings have lived in historic times and even on the longer timespan the figure is still two-thirds. It is equally clear that man as a mass phenomenon is extremely new in world history and that the rates of growth demonstrated here cannot possibly go on long. Something must give.

However, the problems presented for Britain by the world explosion are not dealt with here as they are becoming very familiar. Indeed they appear to be over-emphasized by many commentators in order to obscure the need to examine Britain's population problems.

Let it suffice to say that a world both inflicting and suffering from ever-greater pressure on its environment, with rapidly increasing numbers living in poverty, with more and more severe competition for food and raw materials—including most of those we have to import in order to survive—will not prove a very promising milieu for the peaceful flowering of our small country's national genius.

Chapter 4

Numbering the people: II. Population of the United Kingdom

Part (A) Population past

First we must be sure we agree on what areas we are talking about because the data is often very confusing. The expression 'Great Britain' refers to England, Wales, and Scotland. 'United Kingdom' has meant these three plus Northern Ireland (the 'Six Counties') since the Irish Treaty in 1921, before which the term 'United Kingdom of Great Britain and Ireland' was used.

The terms 'Britain', 'Great Britain', 'United Kingdom', and 'England' are used very loosely and the situation is complicated by the fact that population statistics of England and Wales are given as a combined figure by the Registrar General of England, and those of Scotland and Northern Ireland separately from each other and from England and Wales. The population, areas, and densities of these territories differ considerably which means that comparisons between 'Britain' and other countries are often fruitless or misleading even when they are not wrong.

To avoid having to spell everything out in quasi-legal form I shall leave certain ambiguities in the early historical discussion but become progressively more specific as we approach modern times. All offshore islands are included, excepting the Channel Islands.

As in the case of world population our firm knowledge peters out as we go back in time. We cannot speak with any precision about numbers before, say, the fourth census in 1841, but once again, this matters little for two reasons. The first is that although we have not got exact figures we have a very good idea from many sources of the probable margin of error on the estimates made by recognized authorities. The second reason is that even if both estimates and margins of error are wrong by simply huge amounts the basic picture would change very little because the greatest and fastest population growth has been in recent times, just as our techniques and knowledge in this field were being so greatly improved that they now approach perfection, that is.

For example, the Domesday Survey gives us good grounds for believing that the population of England was about 1.1 million. If the Domesday figure is too large this will minimize the explosive appearance of population growth and so for the purpose of this argument the error can be ignored. If, on the other hand it is too small, even by as much as 75 per cent—an unthinkably large error —the correct figure would still be between only four or five million and there would still remain a huge increase—some 43 million— between then and now.

Let us now take a brief look at numbers from pre-historic times.

Prehistoric population

Our firm knowledge of the 'British' population in this epoch can be expressed in very small compass, as in the case of the world. Problems of definition are superimposed on awkward geological facts. How meaningful is it to talk of the population of England, or even Britain, before either existed as political entities, when the territory destined to become England was still joined to that now called the Continent, with the 'Thames', a tributary of the 'Rhine', the 'Rhine' a tributary of the 'Elbe', and the last Ice Age only just ending?

Much of the information we have comes from archaeologists as we saw in Chapter 3, and the picture generally accepted is of a population of up to 20,000 by the end of the New Stone Age, about 1900 BC, building up to 100,000 or so during the Bronze Age, 1000 BC to 500 BC, possibly reaching 400,000 at the time of the Roman conquest. With Roman technology and organization the 'carrying capacity' of the environment increased markedly and one authority[1] thinks numbers may have reached the 2 million mark, but there was a considerable drop after this, as we shall see.

[1] Frere, S (1967) *Britannia, A History of Roman Britain.*

Medieval population

We are fortunate in having a source of information unique for that period in history as we have already seen, the Domesday Survey, conducted in 1086, from which documentary evidence still exists. Unfortunately it did not cover the whole area; London was excluded, together with Scotland and Wales, and of course 'enumeration' in the areas that were covered was imperfect. However, it was a very workmanlike job as far as it went and careful analysis of the Domesday figures in the light of other evidence shows that the population of England was something under $1\frac{1}{4}$ million, as we have seen, rather less than at the end of the Roman occupation seven centuries earlier, and the reason for the decline in numbers was the breakdown in organization and communications following the departure of the Romans.

Population was very unevenly distributed then, as now. According to W. G. Hoskins,[2] an admirable commentator, only six counties had over 50,000 people; Norfolk 95,000; Lincs, 90,000; Suffolk and Devon, 70,000 each; and Essex and Somerset 50/60,000. Kent, Hants, Sussex, and Wilts had 40/50,000 and Yorkshire—much devastated since the Conquest—had less than 30,000. Northern England averaged less than four to the square mile while East Anglia, the most densely populated region in the whole country, had 40/50 to the square mile.

In 1279 the 'Hundred Rolls' were completed and though few of these survive they provide fairly full information on some midland counties. The poll taxes in 1377, 1379, and 1381 were much more comprehensive.

The great plagues of the fourteenth century struck first in 1348, and then again in 1360, 1369, and 1374, reducing the population by between a third and a half, from $3\frac{3}{4}$ to $2\frac{1}{4}$ million approximately. Figure 4/1 illustrates this graphically and shows that the population took 250 years, until 1600, to recover to the 1348 level.

Catastrophic though this was, it may have been a blessing in disguise, a much needed breathing space, as Britain had by that time become grossly over-populated *vis-à-vis* its current level of technology and organization. The manpower shortage led to agricultural and social reform, liberating the serfs, raising wages, and

---

[2] (1959) *Local History in England.* A much fuller treatment will be found in a standard work: Russell, JC (1948) *British Medieval Population.*

setting the country on the road towards agricultural and, later, industrial revolution.

One writer describes the situation as follows:

> The economy ... rested on a razor edge, yet the population continued to grow and the size of holdings began to fall. ...
>
> Only catastrophe could rescue the medieval peasantry and it came in the form of a drastic pruning of peasant households as a result of the Black Death.[3]

The great subsidy of 1524–5 required assessments for which, in rural parishes, almost completely comprehensive records exist, and parish registers, started in 1538, were the beginnings of the

Fig 4/1

Population of England, AD 1000-1600

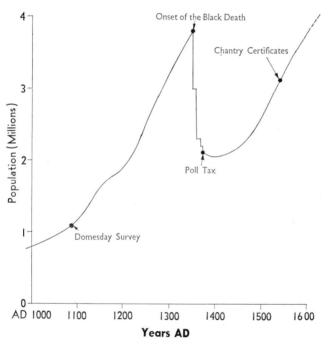

Data from Russell, J. C. (1948) **British Medieval Population**, p219

[3] Chambers and Mingay (1900) *The Agricultural Revolution 1750–1880* (p 6). This contention is supported by Robertson JM (1912) *The Evolution of States* (p 384) and other authorities.

first 'registration', a systematic and continuous check on numbers. These were improved from 1558, when Elizabeth I ordered them to be copied and henceforth kept in parchment books for their better preservation.

Hoskins says that if the average number of baptisms (births) over ten years is multiplied by thirty it will give a good guide to the total population of the parish.

Ecclesiastical sources provide a good deal of information on numbers. Chantry certificates of 1545 give the number of communicants of that time, and in 1563 the bishops of England and Wales made returns of all families and individual communicants, nonconformists, and Catholic recusants, at the request of the Privy Council.

The Public Records Office still contains 'Muster Rolls', for various dates in the sixteenth century, of all men between sixteen and sixty years able to serve in a military capacity, usually specifying each man's weapon. The muster of 1569 is said to be particularly full and useful. Hoskins offers a 'somewhat rash' multiplier of six or seven to obtain total population from the number of able bodied men.

The seventeenth century is better documented. The *Protestation Returns* of 1642, now in the library of the House of Lords, are said to be the best. These contain the names of every male of eighteen years or more in every parish who signed or failed to sign the Oath of Protestation.

In 1600 Parliament introduced a tax based partly on social rank and wealth, leading to a poll of all persons of sixteen or more and many detailed assessments from this still exist.

The Hearth Tax was levied from Michaelmas Day 1662 to Lady Day 1689 and the return of 1664 is particularly full, listing all persons chargeable and non-chargeable. This tax provided the basis for the first proto-demographic survey in Britain—published by Gregory King late in the seventeenth century.

In 1676 *The Compton Return*, the complete copy of which is in the William Salt Library in Stafford, listed for every parish in England the number of persons over sixteen who were conformists, or Roman Catholics.

Modern times

Paradoxically the eighteenth century is said to be worse documented than the seventeenth and little remains for study except ecclesiastical documents such as those referring to Bishop Wakes's visit to the Lincoln Diocese in 1705 and the Bishop of Exeter's questionnaire, including the number of families, in 1744.

The reasons given for this 'particularly unfortunate gap' by Hoskins are: (*a*), that nonconformism was spreading rapidly so that Church of England records were progressively less complete, and (*b*), that large areas were being industrialized. Hoskins does not amplify (*b*) but the large new conurbations required new forms of social organization which developed on an *ad hoc* basis without any mechanism for keeping an eye on the huge population movements then taking place.

The absence of firm knowledge about population was keenly felt by many legislators and commentators and an attempt to introduce a national census in 1753 was passed by the Commons only to be violently rejected by the Lords.[4]

About this time the Reverend Thomas Malthus (1766 to 1834)

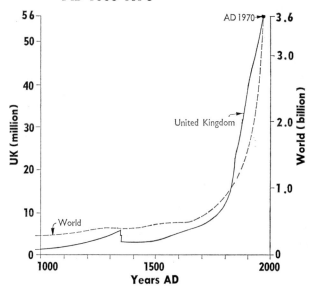

Fig 4/2
**World and United Kingdom:
Population Growth compared
AD 1000-1970**

4 See quotation on p 345.

came on the scene and his demographic battering ram, *An Essay on Population*, published in 1798, seems to have broken through the last political barriers so rapidly that the first national census was taken in 1801. Since then a census has been taken every ten years,[5] with progressive improvements in coverage, detail, and accuracy.

The 1,000-year graph in Fig 4/2 shows that the population has 'exploded' here, as in the world as a whole, and that in Fig 4/3 shows the history of our populations separately. The plural is used deliberately as the various territories comprising the United Kingdom are shown separately and it is immediately apparent that their trends have differed very considerably. England has led the field by a very large margin, partly because of migration from the other territories, and Northern Ireland has actually gone down.

Figure 4/4 shows the growth of our total population in serial tens of million.

Fig 4/3
Population of the United Kingdom: Growth over 1000 years

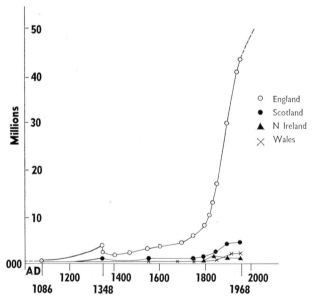

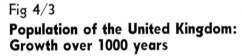

Fig 4/4
Population of the United Kingdom:
Serial tens of millions

Population (tens of millions)	Date (approx)	Years taken (approx)
1st	1797	1 million
2nd	1847[1]	50
3rd	1882	35
4th	1911	29
5th	1951[2]	40
6th	1982 (est)	31
7th	2004 (est)	24
8th	?	?
9th	?	?
10th	?	?
11th	?	?
12th	?	?

1. About 20 millions, mainly in the reproductive age-groups, emigrated in the century before 1914

2. Two world wars occurred between these dates, plus further emigration, though there was some immigration also

3. The Registrar General's current projection, 68.2 million for AD 2000

* (1969)

Population structure

The four population 'pyramids' for England and Wales in Fig 4/5 illustrate the point that population structure, as well as overall size, has changed appreciably in the past century. The stepped pyramid shows in each case the actual population and the smooth beehive lines drawn over the top show what the 'stationary'[6] population would have been on each date with the current number of births and mortality.

In 1901 the pyramid has a much wider base than in 1841, indicating a much larger number of births, but both of these are truly pyramidal.

By 1931 the 'pyramid' has caved in at the base—the numbers in the 0–5 year group being appreciably smaller than in the 5–10 year, 10–15 year group, and so on, up to 30–35 in the case of males and 40–45 in the case of females—and it was this temporary cut back in births which worried the demographers of the day. Quite unnecessarily as we have seen.

[6] A population remaining a constant size. Normally called a 'stable' population, a term having a special (and different) meaning for the demographer.

Fig 4/5

Population Pyramids England and Wales

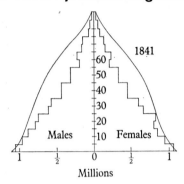

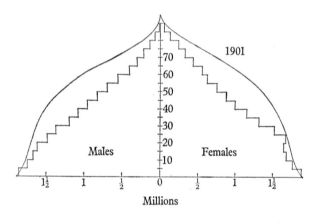

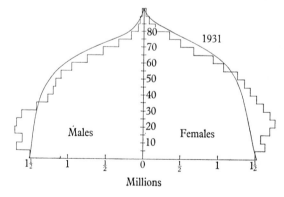

The 1965 'pyramid'—more like a botched beehive—shows a further squaring off of its sides, which reflects our greatly increased life-expectancy, the large bite out of each side is the result of the lower birth rate in the 1930s and early part of the war. The famous post-war 'bulge' is clearly visible on each side in the 5–10 year age group. A pyramid for 1970 would show that it had crept up to the 20–25 year group.

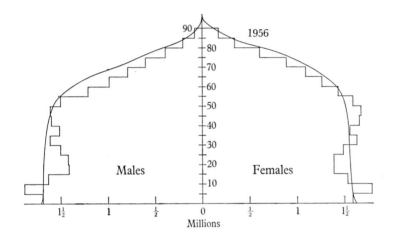

Britain's population 'crisis' in the 1930s: what went wrong?

Many worthy citizens are deeply puzzled by what happened in Britain in the 1930s. The 'great population scare', as it has been called, was very unsettling at the time and has begun to upset people again in more recent years—though for very different reasons. In the 1930s the fear was that the population of Britain was declining—perhaps catastrophically. In the 1970s the fear is certainly not that the population is declining—nor yet that it is rising—but that if demographers could be hopelessly wrong in the 1930s when they were predicting catastrophe from a declining population, can they not be just as wrong in the 1970s as they predict rapidly increasing populations, even if they refrain from crying woe about it this time?

The 1930s debacle is one of the main factors making people suspicious of the whole business of dealing with population statistically, often reinforcing the uneasy feeling about statistics in general which people in our society often harbour. Those who do have this attitude are rendered incapable of looking at the population problem objectively and constructively and it is essential to clarify the events of the 1930s to remove this stumbling-block.

What people thought was happening

There is a very good discussion of the 1930s scare in the PEP publication, *World Population and Resources,*[7] still one of the best introductory books on population available, which the reader should consult for a more detailed description. However, in brief, what happened was as follows. During and after the great depression, birth rates in the United Kingdom fell to levels which came to be thought by a few experts too low for the replacement of the population. This view gradually caught on, was popularized through the BBC and the press, and became a received truth.

What really happened

i Natural increase

At no time did the birth rate fall below the death rate. Every year there was a surplus of births over deaths, giving a 'natural increase'. At no time did the population cease to grow rapidly. It was not an *actual* decline in population which worried some of the demographers, but a *potential* decline some time in the future and this fact must be heavily stressed.

ii Immigration

A factor complicating the situation was the migration into Britain of large numbers of refugees from Hitler, and others, but even without this immigration there would have been a substantial increase in population.

iii Increase in life-expectancy

A further complication at this time was the increase in life-expectancy throughout this whole period because of the improvement of medical science and health services. In a manner of speaking death rates were artificially reduced so that more and more people stayed alive up to the biological maximum, roughly speaking, their three score years and ten. Seventy per cent of the increase in population

[7] (1955).

in Britain in the first half of this century was due to the increase of life-expectancy.[8]

Fig 4/6 shows by means of simple arithmetic what happened. We see that not only did our population not go down; it never ceased to rise at an annual rate of at least $\frac{1}{4}$ per cent per annum, giving a doubling time of about $3\frac{1}{2}$ lifespans, a dangerous, indeed impossible, rate in the long run. Even if numbers had started to go down it would have been some time later and at a very slow rate so that there would have been plenty of opportunity to study the

Fig 4/6
United Kingdom:
Population growth in the 1930s,
Period 1931–1941

Population at mid-1931:	46,038,000
Total births:	6,930,000
Total deaths:	5,770,000
Natural increase:	1,160,000
Immigration:	650,000
Total increase:	1,810,000
Population at mid-1941:	47,848,000

Average annual natural increase: $\dfrac{1,160,000}{10} = 116,000$ persons per annum

Average annual natural increase as a percentage of the 1931 population: $\dfrac{116,000}{46m} = \frac{1}{4}\%$ pa

This is equivalent to a doubling-time of about $3\frac{1}{2}$ lifespans

Adapted from Royal Commission Report on Population, pp9–10

problem and work out appropriate counter-measures *if* they appeared necessary because, within limits, a declining population confers considerable advantages in some spheres, notably education. As the Royal Commission pointed out:

> The reduction in the numbers of children under fifteen years from 12.6 million in 1911 to 10.4 million in 1947 has helped in raising standards in education and other services for children. The increase that has recently taken place will operate the other way . . .[9]

[8] WHO. *Epidemiological and Vital Statistics Report,* Vol V, No 4 (April, 1952).

[9] (*Op cit*) (para 642).

The whole 1930s scare was a storm in a teacup and, taking the wider perspective, the fact leading to it, a substantial fall in birth rate down to somewhere near replacement level, was very unusual in the absence of harsh environmental constraints and/or population control.

Justice for demographers

This account must be further qualified. In the first place the 1930s scare was centred on Britain—there was no suggestion that world population was about to decline. There had been some academic speculation on the theme that the population of the USA would rise to a peak[10] much higher than the figure in the mid-1930s[11] and then level out but this did not cause a public outcry as in Britain. In addition there has been a good deal of concern about population problems in France whose population really did decline, if barely perceptibly, during this period.

In the second place it is not demographers who are calling attention to the possibility of over-population in Britain, or, in the main, of the world as a whole. By and large demographers are emulating the Wise Old Owl. It looks as though they feel that their profession and, in some cases, they personally, burned their fingers very badly in the 1930s so that they are chary of putting themselves at risk again.

In Britain, all the warnings about our own population problem are coming from physical scientists, engineers, journalists, conservationists, and public spirited citizens in general, and this puts the demographers in a paradoxical situation. If they come out now and commit themselves on this issue they have got to climb on the band-wagon, belatedly calling out 'me too', or condemn as misinformed or alarmist the still small but influential and rapidly growing group of non-experts (non-expert in the population field, that is) who have been warning society of the danger. The painfulness of this choice has led to a resounding silence on the part of demographers so far, which—if something unexpected occurs to cure or remove the population problem—they can break with rather virtuous expressions on their faces, even if they desist from remarks about fools rushing in.

---

[10] 200 million by AD 2060. Lotka, A (1956) *Elements of Mathematical Biology.*
[11] About 130 million.

The only demographer in the public eye in Britain to commit himself on this issue, Mr David Eversley,[12] chose the second strategy, abusing those who have uttered warnings on this issue, especially members of the then newly formed Conservation Society[13] ridiculing most of their alleged opinions, insinuating that their motives are selfish, and truculently questioning the right of anyone not qualified as a demographer to have any opinions at all on population questions:

> The eminent scientists [supporting the Conservation Society and its policy of a stationary population in Britain] ... are not demographers. I would not presume to tell a nuclear physicist whether Culham Laboratory should be kept open; I do not know why botanists or archaeologists ... should know about population growth.[14]

Criticism of warnings about present or future population problems in Britain must in all fairness be aimed at those who have made them, which means that in the main demographers can continue to observe from the sidelines, above the hurly-burly of public debate, hoping it is all a bad dream, and it is sad that they have been pushed into this position. The population explosion is a serious scientific and moral challenge to them,[15] as to society as a whole, and their concern in the 1930s showed that they were second to none among social scientists in the depth of their commitment to the issues of the day. Although aware of the advantages conferred by hindsight we cannot refrain from criticizing the serious errors made in the 1930s by ignoring both biological and historical perspectives, but we must hope that our demographers will cautiously emerge as the crisis increases in severity and lend us their much-needed expertise. We shall not do too well without them.

[12] Reader in Population Studies, University of Sussex, in the first two talks on the Third Programme, reported in *The Listener*, July 20, 1967.

[13] *The Listener*, July 20, 1967 (pp 78–9).

[14] Letter, *The Listener*, July 27, 1967, in reply to criticisms of his talks by Dr Michael Watts, of Nottingham University, then Press Officer of the Conservation Society. The present writer was then Hon Education Officer of this Society and is therefore an interested party.

[15] It is a challenge to all social scientists, which, in Britain, is almost universally ignored.

Part (B) Population present

Numbers

The graph in Fig 4/3 gives an overall impression of the numbers in the various regions comprising the United Kingdom but, as many people seem to be somewhat unsure of the details, the following figures are given for mid-1970.

Fig 4/7

United Kingdom:
Population, mid-1970

Total	
England	46,500,000
Wales	2,750,000
Scotland	5,220,000
N Ireland	1,530,000
United Kingdom	56,000,000
Sub-totals[1]	
England and Wales	49,250,000
Great Britain	54,470,000

[1] Author's estimates for sub-totals, official figures are not readily available

Densities

Population density is often used as a measure for the purpose of comparison, frequently to indicate over-population, and the figures are given in full in Fig 4/8 for the United Kingdom as a whole and for each of the regions separately as there are very wide differences. Unless these are known, comparisons between the densities of population in 'Britain' and in Holland, say, are misleading to the point of uselessness.

The densities vary from the moderate figure of 170 per sq. mile in Scotland to the very high one of 920 for England. In contrast[16]

[16] Comparisons are misleading to some extent if they do not allow for the different terrain. Japan, for example is much more mountainous than Britain. However, even if one cannot farm or build on a mountain it remains an important part of one's living space.

the densities of Japan, India, and China—often thought of as grossly over-populated countries—are about 710, 360, and 170 per sq. mile, respectively. Only Holland is more densely populated than England, at 1,000 per sq. mile, while the USA has about 55 per sq. mile, Canada 6, and Australia 3.

Fig 4/8
United Kingdom:
Areas' and population densities
Sq miles

Country	Land Area	Water Area	Totals	1970 densities[2] (per sq mile [3])
England	50,056	276	50,332	920
Wales	7,967	49	8,016	340
Scotland	29,798	616	30,414	170
GB	87,821	941	88,762	610
N Ireland	5,206	246	5,452	280
UK	93,024	1,187	94,214	590

[1] Based on Annual Abstract of Statistics

[2] Author's estimates, rounded

[3] 1 sq mile = 640 acres (approx) = 2.59 sq km, or 259 hectares

Sex ratio

The sex-ratio is simply the number of males over the number of females × 100 and it is a crucial factor in population dynamics, especially as it varies a great deal in different age-groups. Normally more males than females are born—apparently the result of natural compensating mechanism for the inherently greater survival-power of females. About 106 boys are born for every 100 girls and higher male mortality steadily erodes this numerical superiority. At present the numbers of males and females reach approximate equality about the age of 45 and beyond this the numerical superiority of women rapidly increases. At the age of 85 and over there are two and three-quarter times as many women as men.

Until recently there have normally been many surplus females in the marriageable age group, 15–49 years but by 1966 approximate equality had been reached. In 1980 there will be half a million surplus marriageable males and by the year 2000 the number will have reached three-quarters of a million, about 5% of the male age group (1969 projection).

These facts can hardly fail to have far-reaching consequences. The shortage of marriageable women should do a lot to raise the

general status of the sex, producing sexual equality at long last—perhaps rather more than equality—and the custom of older men marrying younger women ... total population will come under pressure. Our traditional persecution of male homosexuals will probably have to cease—it is already on its way out—as male homosexuals could come to be regarded as public benefactors. On the other hand, and regrettably, our past tolerance of female homosexuality may come under considerable strain as the horde of partnerless males increases. It seems likely that we shall have to experiment freely, both scientifically and socially, to get the sexes back into balance by 'sexing'[17] conceptions, perhaps, and/or to cope with the imbalance as well as may be.

Our thinking should be flexible enough at least to consider the feasibility of 'marriage' allowances for male homosexual households, group marriage, polyandry, social approval of lovers for married women, state brothels[18] staffed by attractive, well paid, and highly regarded ladies, and so on. It would be rather unwise to make no provision at all.

Life-expectancy

Life-expectancy at birth has increased enormously since the beginning of the last century and to a great extent has eroded the really huge differences in this respect between social classes, occupation groups, and geographical regions, though surprisingly large discrepancies remain.[19] Life-expectancy at birth in Preston in the period 1837–47, broken down by social class, is shown in Fig 4/9.

More than half the 'operatives' died before five years and their life-expectancy was about that of the population as a whole in the Bronze Age.

Things have improved so much since then that there is not a lot of scope for further increases, unless there is some really fundamental breakthrough in medical science leading to a 'cure' for the ageing process itself.[20] It is expected that the increase will go on for a number of years but the annual increments will probably get smaller and smaller.

[17] Dr Shettles of the Columbia Presbyterian Medical Centre has proposed a very simple method. *The Guardian* April 6, 1970 and *Look* magazine.

[18] Municipal brothels have already been seriously proposed for Birmingham. See *The Guardian*, July 7, 10, 19, 1967.

[19] See Howe, GM (1970) *National Atlas of Disease Mortality*.

[20] Some American biologists think they will have made this breakthrough within two decades.

The Biblical 'three score years and ten' was a surprisingly good generalization, considering the high mortality of those days, and children born in Britain in 1961 could expect to live, at 1961 mortality rates, for sixty-eight years if they were male and seventy-three if they were female.

Fig 4/9
Life expectancy at birth:
Preston 1837–1843[1]

	Average age at death	Percentage dying under 5 years
Gentry	47.4 years	17.6%
Tradesmen	31.6 years	38.2%
Operatives	18.3 years	55.4%

[1] Adapted from Knowles, L. C. A. (1947) Industrial and Commercial Revolutions, p81

Mortality rates are expected to continue to improve, however, as we have seen, and these children can in fact expect to live seventy-three and seventy-nine years,[21] respectively. .

Increases in life-expectancy distort population statistics for a time by 'artificially' lowering death rates as we saw in the section on the 1930s, but this effect should not be serious from now onward.

Family size

It is common knowledge that family size has gone down a great deal since Victorian times but this is nonetheless misleading because there is an important ambiguity in the concept of 'family size'. The most obvious index is simply the number of live births per family, regardless of how long they live, and the other is the number of children reared to maturity.

Figure 4/10 illustrates the enormous drop in the proportion having large families since Victorian times. It would be very interesting to know what the proportions are now but this information is difficult to gather as a woman is normally fecund for thirty-five years and the demographer has a long wait to find out her 'completed' family size, even though fertility is about 98 per cent completed after twenty years.

[21] Figures kindly supplied by the Registrar General's Department.

Fig 4/10
Population of England and Wales: Change in percentage of large families[1]

Family size	Marriages in	
	1860	1925
Up to 4 children	37%	89%
5 or more children	63%	11%
	100%	100%

[1] Adapted from HMSO (1949) **Report of Royal Commission on Population,** p26

However, estimates are made of average completed family sizes and for 1955 marriages this was 2.34; 2.51 for 1964; and for 1984 marriages 2.67.[22] No figures are calculated for the average size of family required for a stationary population—an odd omission—but this is known to be somewhere in the region of 2·1/2·2. Families seem to be having a third to half a child too many.

There is plenty of scope for reduction, however, without doing violence to family life with any reasonable definition of that term. The 1961 census showed that more than three-quarters of a

Fig 4/11
United Kingdom: Family size at 1961 census[1]

No of children	No of families
0	2,324,704
1	3,020,076
2	3,093,631
3	1,524,728
4	707,298
5 to 10	737,307
11 to 15	25,279
16 to 20	827
Over 20[2]	10

[1] Source: Registrar General's Office

[2] Including one family with 30 children

[22] Registrar General's Office, March 15, 1968.

million families had five or more children, including over 26,000 with eleven or more, and a further three-quarters of a million, very nearly, had four. (See Fig 4/10.)

If inducements can be given in the future to bring large families down to medium-size families, and family-planning extended to avoid illegitimacies and other unwanted pregnancies, we could be getting very near to the goal so forcefully advocated by the Royal Commission in 1949, '. . . a replacement-size family'.

Migration

In our national preoccupation with coloured immigration we are in danger of forgetting that migration is a two-way process and that in most years we are left with a net loss, emigrants exceeding immigrants. If Britain is already over-populated, as many think, this could be no bad thing but we must be aware of the demographic, economic, and social structure of the migrant populations and be ready to take appropriate action to avoid unduly costly, lopsided or indeed dangerous situations arising. The USA, for example, has gained more from the brain drain (from other countries, of course), despite the huge sum involved, $4 billion, than she has paid out in foreign aid.[23] Zanzibar appears to have been the first country to give practical recognition to the capital value of its mature citizens by claiming a duty of 56,000 Tanzanian shillings[24] on Tanzanian brides of foreigners if they are taken out of the country.

There is no better reason why Britain should spend £10,000 or more in rearing and educating an engineer for the American labour market than why Pakistan should train a doctor to keep our National Health Service going. Both are needed more in their countries of origin than of adoption and if we in Britain had to pay cash on the nail at the true going rate for an incoming lawyer, carpenter, or nurse, we would take a second look at technological potentials and the pay and conditions in London Transport and the Southern Region of British Rail, for example, who so abysmally fail to recruit enough native manpower to keep them going.

Apart from economic factors, demographic pressures in Britain are strongly against further immigration as we are already seriously

[23] See Titmuss, RM, 'Trading in Human Capital', *Science Journal*, June, 1967.
[24] £3,300. Reported *The Guardian*, October 11, 1969.

over-populated. The natives are already finding it hard to put up with each other, let alone with the added pressure from immigrants and their descendants and this will be regardless of pigmentation, although, of course, coloured citizens have to bear the brunt of our frustration and hostility as they are more easily recognized as 'extras'. If the Irish had some readily recognizable visual 'identity card', as it were, they would probably be suffering as much persecution as our coloured friends. Even Israel, with what is probably the highest powered immigration scheme the world has ever seen and the tremendously strong binding force of Judaism, reinforced by Zionism, centuries of persecution, and dangerous military pressure from the Arab states, treats some of its immigrants badly— all Jews, of course—especially those with dark skins.

Fig 4/12
United Kingdom:
Post-war migration[1]

Year	Net total for year	Net running total
1946–50	− 226,900	− 226,900
1951	− 90,200	− 317,100
52	− 50,800	− 367,900
53	− 24,900	− 392,800
54	+ 18,500	− 374,300
55	+ 76,600	− 297,700
56	+ 55,400	− 242,300
57	− 38,200	− 280,500
58	+ 48,200	− 232,300
59	+ 71,500	− 160,800
1960	+ 122,000	− 38,800
61	+ 170,000	+ 131,200
62	+ 77,900	+ 209,100
63	− 15,100	+ 194,000
64	− 24,300	+ 169,700
65	− 13,800	+ 155,900
66	− 15,900	+ 140,000
67	+ 31,800	+ 171,800
68	− 11,000	+ 160,800
69		
1970		
1971–75		
1976–80		
1981–85		
1986–90		
1991–95		
1996–2000		

[1] Source: Registrar General's Office

It would be more desirable and morally better in my judgment if the British were not prejudiced on such matters as race, if we had room for anyone who wanted to come here, and, more generally, if everyone was free to go anywhere at any time. None of these conditions obtain, however, and this seems to be less rather than more likely to be the case in the foreseeable future as population pressure increases. We can afford these refinements of morality and the spirit only in a situation of spaciousness and plenty. If we define free migration, regardless of race or creed, as one of the liberal values, we have already seen how these can suffer under the pressure of numbers, even, sad to relate, under a semi-radical government.

However, it would obviously be wrong to panic and lash out on the immigration issue—as on any other—and Fig 4/12 shows that migration since the war has not been as unfavourable, demographically speaking, as many have feared, in terms of quantity at least. We could have no informed opinion about the quality aspect—using such indicators as health, economic potentiality, criminality, and so on—without a lot of research, some of which is now under way.

Part (C) Population future

Present rate of growth

Our crude birth and death rates in 1968 were 16.9 and 11.9, respectively, giving a natural increase of 5.0 per thousand each year, equivalent to 0.5 per cent p.a. and a doubling time of 140 years, a little less than two life-spans.

In terms of numbers rather than rates there were 947,000 births and 656,000 deaths giving a natural increase of 291,000. Of these births probably half were unplanned[25] and perhaps a quarter to a third of them unwanted. A 1968 figure of 250,000 unwanted preg-

[25] See Fraser and Watson, 'Family Planning—A Myth?', *The Practitioner*, **201**, August, 1968, pp 351–3.

nancies, 100,000 abortions, and 150,000 unwanted births is accepted by the Family Planning Association.[26]

Preventing these unwanted births would go a long way towards curing the population problem in Britain but we cannot afford to be complacent because of the inroads now being made by medical science into the present involuntary infertility of a large number of couples. Estimates of the extent of sub-fertility vary between three-quarters and one million affected couples[27] at any given time and a medical breakthrough here could present a serious demographic threat even without the very high proportion of multiple births produced by treatment with such drugs as gonadotrophin.

Official projections for AD 2000

Taking the year 2000 as the target date, the Registrar General's projections for the United Kingdom have been going down since the peak in 1965, as Fig 4/13 shows.

Another mention may not be out of place that the open spaces in the tables are left for two purposes, to enable readers who feel like it to fill them in for themselves and as a gentle reminder that the process of dealing with population must go on as long as the species lasts. Projections are given for dates other than AD 2000, and those of 1969, in more detail, are shown in Fig 4/14.

Of course we cannot speak with certainty about our future population and the Registrar General's figures have fluctuated considerably over the years, as we have seen, partly because the official approach, despite computerization, is somewhat archaic, unscientific, and misleading. In the first place we are told that the figures presented are not forecasts but 'projections'—statements about what will happen *if the trends continue*—despite the fact that everybody must take them as forecasts, people who have to plan for housing, schools, power supplies, and the rest. In the second place they are not given with a stated margin of error, which ought to be at least plus or minus 10 per cent, judging by recent performance.

What we need is not one projection but three, with the assump-

[26] Brook, C, 'The Cost-Effectiveness of Family Planning', *Family Planning Miscellany,* July, 1968.

[27] See Potts, Dr M, Conservation Society Newsletter, February, 1969. Sandler, B, *The Guardian,* April 13, 1965. Brook, C (*Op cit*).

Fig 4/13
United Kingdom:
Population projections[1] for
AD 2000

Year projection published	Projected population in 2000 AD (thousands)
1959	60,100*
1960	60,300*
61	63,822
62	67,500*
63	71,100*
64	71,581
65	74,660
66	74,574
67	72,059
68	70,339
69	68,190
1970	
71	
72	
73	
74	
75	
76	
1981	
1986	
1991	
1996	

Sources: HMSO Annual Abstract of Statistics

[1] For a useful treatment of the technique of forecasting by the Government Actuary's Department, see 'Projecting the Population of the United Kingdom', **Economic Trends** No 139, May 1965

Projections asterisked estimated by author from official figures for target dates between 1998 and 2002

tions made explicit, a 'high', 'medium', and 'low', in accordance with the practice of the United Nations. It is as unrealistic to put forward figures known to be subject to huge errors of extrapolation as though they were accurate to the nearest thousand, and without a stated tolerance, as it is to pretend that people are not obliged to take projections as forecasts.

Figure 4/16 shows what will happen to our numbers if the 1969 rate of increase, 0.5 per cent per annum—giving a doubling time of 140 years, continues for 840 years. This is a little less than the time separating us in 1970 from the Norman Conquest and in this

period our population would have doubled six more times to about
3.6 billion, the 1969 population of the whole world.

This shows how utterly impossible—even on this short time-
scale—is the present rate of increase.

Fig 4/14

United Kingdom:
1969 Population projections at
5-year intervals up to AD 2000

For	Projection	(rounded)
1975	57,590,000	
1980	59,260,000	
1990	63,170,000	
2000	68,200,000	

The figure for AD 2000 is made up as shown in Fig 4/15

Fig 4/15
United Kingdom:
Composition of population by
generations in AD 2000[1]

Survivors of those alive at mid-1968:	33.6 million
Children of those alive at mid-1968:	26.8 million
Children of these children:	7.8 million
Total	68.2 million

[1] The Government Actuary's Office kindly computed these
figures, which are not normally available in this form

Fig 4/16
United Kingdom:
840 years of population growth
at the 1969 rate, 0.5% per annum

Year	Population (millions)
AD 1970	56
2110	112
2250	224
2390	448
2530	896
2670	1,792
2810	3,584

Summary

Until very recent times the territories now comprising the United Kingdom were peopled only by small bands of primitive men totalling a few tens of thousands. By the Roman Conquest there may have been close on half a million inhabitants who rapidly grew to some 2 million under the Romans.

After the departure of the Romans numbers probably declined, picked up to about $1\frac{1}{2}$ million by the time of the Domesday Survey, and once more increased rapidly to a peak of about 5 million by the time the Black Death struck in the middle of the fourteenth century. The population of England was reduced by some 30 per cent to 40 per cent and took 250 years to catch up on the pre-Plague level. From 1600 numbers continued to rise steadily for another century and an explosion similar to that of the world population was well under way by the middle of the eighteenth century. We saw that it was an English rather than a British phenomenon.

Since about 1700 our population has doubled three times, the last one within living memory, to its 1970 level of 56 million and the next doubling is expected in just under two life-spans. This is equivalent to an annual increase of 0.5 per cent, adding between a quarter and a third of a million every year—about one fair-sized new village of 800 to 900 inhabitants every day. We have gained another 6 million (12 per cent) since the Royal Commission announced in 1949:

> ... the uncertainties of the future regarding world supplies of food and the opportunities for British export trade give us good reason to be thankful that no further large increases in our population are probable.[28]

We are due to have another $12\frac{1}{4}$ million by AD 2000, making an extra 18 million, 36 per cent, since the Royal Commission, and at this rate of growth there would be a thousand million of us about eight lifespans from now.

We have seen that there is considerable scope for reducing fertility by the elimination of unwanted births but that under the continuing impetus of medical science there are powerful tendencies in the opposite direction which could more than compensate. The only safe policy is to assume that our population will always

28 Para. 638.

rise unless something is done to stop it. We must plan for the worst while hoping for the best, and we must never lose sight of the facts that for the formulation of effective social policies it is not necessary to know the exact whys and wherefores of population and that an increase of only one ten thousandth of 1 per cent per annum is impossible in the long run.

Part 2

The meaning of liberty

Chapter 5

The 'philosophy' of liberty

Licence they mean when they cry liberty, for who loves that must first be good and wise.

Milton, Sonnet XII

It is true that liberty is precious—so precious that it must be rationed.[1]

attributed to Lenin

Liberty, too, must be limited, in order to be possessed.[2]

Burke

Headstrong liberty is lashed with wo . . .[3]

William Shakespeare

The point of discussing the population problem in terms of individual liberty, as explained in the Preface, is that this is the issue which looms in front of us and tends to block our path whenever population control is brought up for discussion. The word 'philosophy' is in quotation marks at the head of this chapter as it does not contain a treatment of liberty that would satisfy any recognized philosopher. A truly philosophical examination of the concept of liberty would have to dwell at length on the notions of free will and determinism but this topic is really for professionals and will play no part in this discussion. Liberty is considered only at the simple, matter of fact, everyday level, without going into the linguistic or metaphysical niceties of whether what appears to be free behaviour—that is to say behaviour without fairly obvious

---

[1] *Penguin Dictionary of Quotations.*
[2] Ibid.
[3] *Comedy of Errors*, Act II, Sc 1.

internal or external constraint—is *really* free. The possibility is ignored that the whole of a person's heredity, past growth, and experience is one vast constraint—possibly operating without his knowledge—which makes his seemingly free behaviour the mere by-product of an inexorable causal chain, as the determinist would assert.[4]

By the same token no attempt is made to deal with the idea of freedom as the capacity to act in the light of reason or morality, expressed by Spinoza and Kant, respectively:

> A free man ... is one who lives according to the dictate of reason alone.[5]

and

> Freedom is '... independence of anything other than the moral law alone'.[6]

Kant's categorical imperative bases the whole of morality on freedom. His argument was neatly summarized by the sociologist Simmel as follows:

> Only when we cease being a mere product and cross point of external forces and become a being that develops out of its own ego, can we be *responsible*. Only then can we acquire the possibility of both guilt and moral value.

Not only is it true that:

> ... only the man who is free is moral, but also, only the man who is moral is free. ...[7]

The justification of the title is that the idea of liberty in relation to population control is subjected to a critical appraisal from a standpoint which, it is hoped, will not cause too much discomfort to a pragmatist, a logical positivist, or a linguistic analyst. Perhaps 'pragmaticism' is the best label for the approach adopted, defined by C. S. Peirce as follows:

> In order to ascertain the meaning of an intellectual conception one should consider what practical consequences might con-

---

[4] My own tentative answer to this problem of free will, for what it is worth, is that acquiring a belief in free will leads to a physiopsychological modification of our bodies which might create conditions capable of generating free will, but this must remain a bare assertion in this context.

[5] *Ethics*, Pt IV. Prop LXVII.

[6] *Critique of Pure Reason*.

[7] Wolff, KH, (1950) *The Sociology of Georg Simmel* (p 72).

ceivably result by necessity from the truth of that conception and the sum of these consequences will constitute the entire meaning of the conception.[8]

It is the practical consequences of our understanding of the concept of liberty and our attempts to realize it in practice that we are chiefly concerned with.

The great bulk of important writing on the theme of liberty is not dealt with here—partly because of lack of space, of course—but largely because it has little or no relevance to the operational approach I have adopted as the only practical one in an overcrowded world.

To give just one example of the approach referred to, I will quote F. Hayek's recent scholarly work, *The Constitution of Liberty*.[9] In this he starts by saying:

> We are concerned in this book with that condition of men in which coercion of some by others is reduced as much as possible in a society. This state we shall describe throughout as a state of liberty or freedom ... (p 1)
>
> ... In this sense 'freedom' refers solely to a relation of men to other men, and the only infringement on it is coercion by other men ...
>
> ... The range of physical possibilities from which a person can choose at a given moment has no direct relevance to freedom ... (p 2)

Professor Hayek explicitly rejects the operational approach adopted here. None of the 'confusions' of the meaning of the word liberty is as 'dangerous' as its use:

> ... to describe the physical 'ability to do what I want', the power to satisfy our wishes, or the extent of the choice of alternatives open to us ...
>
> Once this identification of freedom with power is admitted, there is no limit to the sophisms by which the attractions of the word 'liberty' can be used to support measures which destroy individual liberty. ... (p 16)

It is often objected that our concept of liberty is merely negative. This is true in the sense that peace is also a negative

---

[8] Quoted in Runes, DD (Undated) *Dictionary of Philosophy*. See Gallie, WB (1952) *Peirce and Pragmatism* for an interesting discussion of this topic.

[9] (1960). First English edition.

concept. . . . It is to this class of concepts that liberty belongs: it describes the absence of a particular obstacle—coercion by other men . . . (p 19)

While informed discussion, classification, and exhortation within this extremely limited field are no doubt valuable contributions to civilization, they also completely fail to safeguard liberty in the round. According to Professor Hayek's conclusions we would all be in a state of liberty even if there were a thousand billion of us crammed cheek by jowl, provided only that we agreed not to 'restrain' or 'constrain' each other by deliberate actions, the facts that we were totally immobilized and possibly starving to death having no relevance. Professor Hayek also fails to allow that voluntary co-operation made necessary by environmental exigencies is an invasion of individual liberty and I fear his weighty tome is beside the point when it comes to population control.

The meaning of 'liberty'. The commonsense approach

There is a quite remarkable amount of misunderstanding about liberty in social life. Many people seem to believe that if society—most obviously in the form of the policeman—is not actually flagging their car down in the street, tugging them along to the police station by means of handcuffs, refusing them permission to build their new bungalow on the site they desire, or carrying out one of the many other official activities which obviously and immediately impinge on their freedom, then they are free individuals.

This approach, this philosophy of liberty, is quite out of step with the facts. We are all restricted, hemmed in on every side by a mass of regulations, both official and unofficial, which when added up drastically reduce our freedom of behaviour—even our thought—and it is surely obvious that life in huge, highly complex, technologically based societies requires an enormous amount of co-ordination of human activity simply in order to make the myriad pieces of jigsaw fit in and the whole society work.

In addition to the constraints on individual liberty brought about by legal and other compulsion and essential co-operative activities, there are many others, more or less binding through public opinion and improper use of positions of authority, which reduce it still further. The result is that in a modern society surprisingly little liberty is left.

Of course there are some individualists, people who think for themselves, do what they want to do or believe is right, regardless of social pressures and the norms of their society, but the fact is that most of them meet a lot of opposition. Most of us, far from welcoming such independence and originality, will actually try to damp it down, cut it out if possible. This is quite obvious in our society at the present time in the quite frenetic attitudes adopted by many people towards fashions in dress, hair styles,[10] hygiene, and so forth, quite apart from the more important areas of behaviour and belief in sexual morality and art. The permissive society is a libertarian society and the anti-permissives are anti-libertarians. The Lord's Day Observance Society, Mrs Whitehouse's censorship campaign, and many other movements are for the sole purpose of reducing other people's freedoms.

The sad fact seems to be that many of our compatriots *hate* liberty, as instanced by one of the mouldier scraps of information spewed out of Warwick University's confidential files. In a letter to the Vice-Chancellor, Major-General Leakey, Director of the Wolfson Foundation, is reported to have said:

> I was very interested to see round this wonderful new university.... However, I can't say that I was impressed by your students. How sad it is to see these long-haired louts flopping around in such splendid surroundings.
>
> What a pity you can't order them to have some sort of uniform —if only a cap and gown.[11]

Apart from Gilbert & Sullivan characters like the Major-General, how many of us—at any rate in the older generations—can readily accept the fact that some men want to grow their hair long? The fact that women are allowed to do it, that men in many other societies do the same, and that eminently respectable men in our own society in the recent historical past have done likewise is not considered relevant to the question. Until very recently in our society men in general simply were not free to grow their hair long if they so desired and many still are not, the pressures against it are still too great. It is only now that a sufficiently large minority of pioneers have come forward to permit fairly coherent sub-groups

[10] Hair is the subject of powerful taboos in many cultures and there may be very deep reasons for these explosive attitudes. See Frazer, Sir J (1950) *The Golden Bough*.

[11] Reported anonymously in Thompson, EP (ed) (1970) *Warwick University Ltd.* Attributed in full in *The Guardian* report, March 3, 1970.

to emerge that this has become possible for at least some of the individuals who feel that way inclined. They can now grow their hair long and take shelter, as it were, with the growing, though still small, minority groups which give them moral support.

Maurice Cranston, a modern philosopher, has made a point which goes a long way towards explaining our bewilderment and frustration in understanding and dealing with the concept of liberty. According to him (liberty and freedom being synonymous):

> ... while the descriptive meaning of 'freedom' ... varies, the emotive meaning tends ... to be constant.[12]

This emotional connotation he defines '... for English-speaking people ...' as a '... strong laudatory ... meaning.'

The point of this is that we are driven to accept a constantly changing descriptive content of the word 'liberty', as society evolves and its needs change, while we maintain—or at least attempt to maintain—a constant approval for what it stands for, an obvious source of confusion and frustration.

The meaning of 'liberty'. The analytical approach

Montesquieu wrote in the eighteenth century:

> ... There is no word that admits of more varied meanings, and has made more different impressions on the human mind. Some have annexed this name to one form of government exclusive of others; those who have republican tastes applied it to this form of polity; those who lived under a monarchical government gave it to monarchy. They have all applied it to the form of government best suited to their customs and inclinations.[13]

Since his day the word has become so overworked and misused as to mean practically anything, superficially, and practically nothing when the attempt is made to analyse it in detail. In the political sphere in particular the word is bandied about with an almost limitless number of implicit definitions and connotations. This abuse is typified in the present state of international affairs in which the communist and anti-communist blocs each think them-

---

[12] (1953) *Freedom, A New Analysis* (p 21). A very good book to start with for anyone wishing to study liberty more philosophically.

[13] Montesquieu (C 18) Quoted Inge, WR (1949) *The End of An Age.*

selves 'liberated' and the others 'enslaved'. The stage has been reached at which the word liberty is quite useless to a thinker or even the practical man unless it is qualified, and its use as a plain noun should surely be taboo. It should be specified and given an explicit reference wherever possible.

The Shorter Oxford Dictionary defines 'liberty' as follows:

1. Exemption or release from captivity, bondage, or slavery.

2. Freedom from arbitrary, despotic, or autocratic rule or control.

3. Faculty or power to do as one likes.

4. Free opportunity or scope to do something; hence leave, permission. . . .

5. Unrestrained action, conduct or expression, licence etc.

Let us consider (3), (4), and (5) above, the 'power' and 'opportunity' for '. . . unrestrained action . . .', which combine brevity and comprehensiveness; the inner power to do things and an absence of external restraints which might frustrate it, a definition which would probably satisfy an anarchist.

A little reflection shows that we cannot have absolute liberty, for restraints are imposed upon us by the natural physical laws. In a state of perfect anarchy one would not have the liberty to eat a ton of steak at one sitting—however much one liked it—nor yet to subject oneself with impunity to an acceleration of more than about four times the force of gravity. From the outset, we must recognize the natural physical barriers to absolute liberty.

In addition to external barriers there are internal constraints of a physiological and psychological kind hemming all of us in to some degree.

In addition to physical laws and internal obstacles restricting our liberty there are the external constraints of man-made laws, both formal and informal, because liberty to do, say, or think as one pleases is incompatible with social life. In other words liberty is hemmed in from all sides and to be understood it must be *specified* with explicit references as above. Different societies spell it out differently and the task falls to the lot of legislators, moralists, philosophers, priests, poets, judges, and society as a whole. They must together decide what they shall be free to do and be free from and then evolve and apply a system of rewards and punishments in order to enforce the resulting code of behaviour.

A suggested working definition of liberty is put forward for your consideration at the end of Chapter 6 after the sociological discussion.

Population control and the fallacy of individual liberty

When the topic of population control comes up, unusual though this was until the very recent past, it is often dismissed—sometimes out of hand, sometimes with regret—as an invasion of individual liberty. Discussion is often completely blocked by this allegedly conclusive argument, or at least vitiated by emotional overtones implying that anyone who wants to discuss it is an authoritarian, if not a budding fascist.

The fallacy of individual liberty can be expressed in a form akin to the classical syllogism:

1st premise	We now have 'Liberty of the Individual'.
2nd premise	Reductions in 'Liberty of the Individual' must be opposed.[14]
3rd premise	Population control would necessarily reduce or even destroy this 'Liberty'.
Conclusion	Proposals to control population must be opposed.

If it is legitimate to infer the meaning of a word from the way it is used, it is instructive to spell out the definition of liberty implied by these anti-population control arguments:

> All couples, stable or unstable, married or unmarried, responsible or irresponsible, affluent or in poverty, healthy or sick, old or young, have the inalienable liberty to produce as many children as they want, or conceive by accident, regardless of the possible or even likely consequences for each new child, for children born earlier into the family, for the parents themselves, for other parents and children in the same region, for society at large, and for the future of the human race.

This implied judgment is further reinforced by three implicit assumptions in the minds of those rejecting any dialogue about population control. These are as follows:

1. 'Liberty of the individual' could never be reduced by population growth *itself*.

2. The adoption of a population policy would not only be a

---

[14] Many would want to add: 'at all costs'.

violation of individual liberty but a radical departure from long established norms of democratic government hitherto completely excluding population policies.

3. All the above arguments are self-evident so that discussion is not needed.

Once it is conceded that any one of these points does not have the status of a revealed truth or that population growth itself might conceivably reduce individual liberty then we are inexorably committed to a reappraisal—to a dialogue with those holding different views. Once we agree that successive governments have for years had more or less explicit population policies designed—in what was thought the national interest—to reduce our freedom *not* to have children by means of propaganda, a refusal to make family planning and abortion fairly readily available, and substantial allowances in cash and kind amounting to fertility bonuses, we have to admit that what is required is not the radical departure of adopting a population policy where none existed before, but merely a revision of the goals and mechanisms of partially implicit population policies of long standing and almost universal acceptance, as the Royal Commission on Population strongly recommended in 1949.

Taking the broad anthropological perspective, population policies—more often restrictive than expansionist—have been the norm[15] rather than the exception.

With respect to the third point, regarding self-evident truths, it is hoped that most people, when pressed, would accept that—with the possible exception of those in the sphere of religion, and probably not even there—there are no statements so unshakeably valid that discussion with sincere, informed, and reasonable opponents is a waste of time.

If we accept that there is an iota of doubt on any of these scores we land ourselves with the obligation to look again at the problems and possible solutions with an open mind, as far as is humanly possible.

The point we are concerned with—in the form of a question rather than a statement—does population control reduce individual liberty, can be answered off the cuff—at least superficially—in the sense that it removes a liberty that was previously enjoyed, reproduction at will. All control reduces liberty in this sense and population control is no exception. However, to escape the label 'superficial' we must go deeper than this and ask if it is possible that a

[15] See Chapter 15 for a fuller discussion.

reduction of liberty in one sphere can possibly increase it in another, either by increasing an existing liberty or creating an entirely new one. If it can then we have to compare the gains and losses in both amount and kind and see whether *on balance* there is a gain or a loss.

To deal with the topic adequately at this deeper level we must bring into the open a further implicit assumption in addition to the four mentioned earlier and still more fundamental. This is that control and liberty are enemies, polar opposites, that the more there is of one the less there must be of the other.

This can be formulated strictly as a classical syllogism:

1st premise	All social control decreases individual liberty.
2nd premise	Population control is a form of social control.
Conclusion	Population control would decrease individual liberty.

It is contended here that this again is a fallacy but the only way to prove the point is to undertake further analysis from a sociological standpoint and this is attempted in Chapter 6. Meanwhile we can revert to the four earlier points and attempt to resolve those. If the possibility is admitted that population growth itself could reduce individual liberty then the implication is that the central question must be reformulated; it should be changed from:

(*a*) 'Does population control reduce individual liberty?'

to:

(*b*) 'Does population control reduce individual liberty more than unrestricted population growth?'

The second question is radically different from the first and cannot be answered fully without a great deal of thought and empirical evidence of a sort which may not be available without research. It certainly cannot be answered off the cuff and the central contention here is that while we can say without hesitation that a new control must *change* individual liberty in some way we cannot say whether it will decrease or increase it without inquiry, and possibly experimentation, and the remainder of this book is devoted precisely to these activities. Of course it is not possible to do experiments on paper but a kind of experimentation is attempted through the rearrangement of existing knowledge, some of it obtained by true experiments.

Those who reject these arguments may as well close the book at this point. Those who do not reject them I hope will accompany me through a detailed examination of the concept of liberty in society—not with the object of being led to *the* answer but to explore some of its intricacies, pitfalls, and possible ways out of the maze from which our society must, in the final analysis, choose her path.

Summary

Despite the fact that for centuries it has been recognized by thinkers that liberty is an elusive idea which needs a great deal of care in its understanding and use, the man in the street continues to feel sure that it is a clear and definite property and that he possesses it —or did possess it until recently when insidious governmental action, often called 'creeping socialism', robbed him of it.

A great deal of the richness of its meaning was not pursued here, neither is the bulk of the literature on the topic, and the 'commonsense' view was also rejected.

The view was put forward that although we profess to love liberty many of us seem to fear it—in some cases even hate it— and Maurice Cranston's explanation of some of our perplexity was accepted, that the emotional 'meaning' of the word liberty tends to remain constant while its practical meaning, its content, must change (only sometimes being reduced) as society changes.

The 'fallacy of individual liberty' as applied to population control was attacked and the question raised whether unrestricted population growth might not itself reduce individual liberty. If this could happen then the question must be:

'Does population control reduce individual liberty more than unrestricted population growth?'

I pointed out that though a policy of population stabilization would be an innovation, policies attempting to influence population —i e control it—have been commonplace for years. Therefore fertility control would be a modification of population policy rather than a radical innovation, the introduction of a population policy where none existed before.

At a deeper level of analysis it was argued that the plain man's idea of liberty and control as polar opposites is mistaken—that liberty is in fact *produced* by control. A proof of this point is attempted in the next chapter.

Chapter 6

The sociology of liberty

These people were extremely fond of liberty; but seem not to have understood it very well.[1]

C. H. Cooley

David Hume

It is freedom to be disciplined in as rational a manner as you are fit for.[2]

C. H. Cooley

In Chapter 5 it was argued that an important fallacy often underlying the rejection of population control is that all control reduces liberty. In this chapter this fallacy is examined further and the paradoxical case argued that social[3] control, far from reducing individual liberty, is its source, mainstay, and guarantor. Social control and liberty are not enemies but the best of friends.

This, like most important ideas, is by no means new. Aristotle argued over two millennia ago that 'constitutional control' is the 'salvation' of man in society.

Under 'Pathology of the State' Aristotle says:

Extreme democracies—those, mainly, which are considered patterns of the democratic type—have adopted a policy which runs counter to their real interests; and this is due to a false idea of liberty. Two principles are generally regarded as characteristic

[1] Speaking of the ancient Greeks, in the essay 'On the Populousness of Ancient Nations'.

[2] (1964) *Human Nature and the Social Order*.

[3] The word 'social' is used in its wide technical sense here, denoting the processes by which a society controls itself. When the social sciences come of age the word 'social' may well be dropped, in this context and 'control' used by itself.

of democracy: the absolute sovereignty of the masses and individual liberty. Justice is believed to consist in equality, equality in mass supremacy, and liberty in doing exactly what one likes. In extreme democracies, therefore, everyone lives as he pleases, or, as Euripides says, 'for any end he happens to desire'. But this is an altogether unsatisfactory conception of liberty. *It is quite wrong to imagine that life subject to constitutional control is mere slavery; it is in fact salvation.* (Italics added.)

Such in general are the causes leading to the changes in constitutions; such also are the means to their preservation and stability.[4]

Sociological theories of liberty: I. Liberty as a product of social control

Although the germ of the idea was clearly present in the writings of Aristotle, as we have seen, it was not until the late nineteenth century—as far as the present writer is aware—that it was argued explicitly and cogently that liberty is the *product* of social control.

Emile Durkheim, one of the great pioneers of scientific sociology, argued in a very striking passage that, far from reducing our liberty, social control is a necessary *precondition* if we consider liberty of the majority rather than that of powerful individuals or minorities.

[If] . . . nothing restrains the active forces of society and assigns them limits they are bound to respect, they tend to develop haphazardly, and come into collision with one another, battling and weakening themselves. To be sure, the strongest succeed in completely demolishing the weakest, or in subordinating them. But if the conquered, for a time, must suffer subordination under compulsion, they do not consent to it, and consequently this cannot constitute a stable equilibrium. Truces, arrived at after violence, are never anything but provisional, and satisfy no one. Human passions stop only before a moral power they respect. If all authority of this kind is wanting, the law of the strongest prevails and latent or active, the state of war is necessarily chronic.

That such anarchy is an unhealthy phenomenon is quite evident, since it runs counter to the aim of society, which is to

4 *Politics*, Book 5, Everyman's edition (p 156).

suppress, or at least moderate, war among men, subordinating the law of the strongest to a higher law. To justify this chaotic state, we vainly praise its encouragement of individual liberty. Quite on the contrary, *liberty (we mean genuine liberty, which it is society's duty to have respected) is itself the product of regulation. I can be free only to the extent that others are forbidden to profit from their physical, economic, or other superiority to the detriment of my liberty. But only social rules can prevent abuses of power. It is now known what complicated regulation is needed to assure individuals the economic independence without which their liberty is only nominal.'*[5] (Italics added)

Even so single minded and passionate a devotee of individual liberty as Herbert Spencer has agreed that restraints are a necessary foundation for liberty:

> Every man is free to do that which he wills, provided he infringes not the equal freedom of any other man.[6]

II. Population and liberty

The American sociologist David Riesman, with his colleagues, has proposed a conceptual scheme[7] relating to individual liberty and society, though without dealing with the concepts 'liberty' and 'freedom' explicitly. His view, especially interesting in this context, is that there are three typical kinds of socio-cultural submissiveness, each of which is associated with a particular stage of population growth.

The first of these types is the *tradition-directed* character to be found in societies of high population growth potential, i e simple agricultural societies with high birth and death rates. This type of character lacks liberty because it is dominated by tradition.

The second type, to be found in societies in which rapid population growth is taking place (i e retaining high birth rates whilst death rates are lowered), is the *inner-directed* man who is enslaved by non-traditional internal goals implanted in his childhood because his society is having to change rapidly under the pressure of population growth.

The third type is the *other-directed* man who is enslaved by

---

5 Durkheim, E (1964) *The Division of Labour in Society* (pp 2 and 3).
6 Quoted in Elliot, H (1917) *Herbert Spencer* (p 201).
7 Riesman, D, Glazer, N, Denney, R (1950) *The Lonely Crowd.*

current social pressures, whatever they may be. This one, the socio-logical Vicar of Bray, is said to be produced when a population is in a state of 'incipient decline'. In 1950, when the book was first published, Riesman and his collaborators said that the United States was already largely peopled by the 'other directed'.

It is not clear what the massive and continuing increase in the US population has done to the theory of 'incipient decline'. How-ever, from our point of view this matters little. The central issue is his three types of socio-cultural enslavement relieved by only one kind of liberty enjoyed by a few *autonomous* individuals:

> ... those who on the whole are capable of conforming to the behavioural norms of their society ... but are free to choose whether to conform or not.

It is impossible in this small compass to do justice to Riesman's arguments which are by no means crude or simplicist. He readily admits that his types are to be found virtually nowhere in their pure form—we are all admixtures of the various ingredients listed —he claims only that there are tendencies towards the predomin-ance of one of these characteristics at particular stages of popula-tion growth.

The central fact from our point of view is that various types of conformity are the norm and the autonomous individual is the exception. He is the only one who can claim to enjoy individual liberty in any strong sense.

III. Objective versus subjective liberty

> *Stone walls do not a prison make*
> *Nor iron bars a cage;*
> *Minds innocent and quiet take*
> *That for an hermitage;*
> *If I have freedom in my love,*
> *And in my soul am free;*
> *Angels alone, that soar above,*
> *Enjoy such liberty.*

> Richard Lovelace 1618–1658
> To Althea, From Prison

Pitirim Sorokin, the distinguished American sociologist, has given Lovelace's poetical theme a scientific treatment and drawn a useful distinction[8] between objective and subjective or outer and inner liberty, describing the two types as 'sensate' and 'ideational' liberty, respectively.

His definition of liberty is:

> ...a human being is free when he can do whatever he pleases, need not do anything he does not wish to do, and does not have to tolerate what he does not want to tolerate. Consequently his freedom becomes restricted when he cannot do what he would like to do; has to do what he would prefer not to do; and is obliged to tolerate what he would like not to endure.[9]

He goes on to say:

> Without a knowledge of the individual's desires, observing his overt activity only, we cannot pass any judgment as to whether or not he is free.

From this he deduces a formula for the freedom of a particular individual as:

$$\text{Freedom} = \frac{\text{Sum of means}}{\text{Sum of wishes}} = \frac{\text{SM}}{\text{SW}}$$

'Means' signifies, of course, ways or possibilities of satisfying wishes.

If SM is equal to or greater than SW, whatever their absolute values, then the individual is free. If SW is greater than SM, however, the individual is not free and from this it follows that an individual can increase his freedom either by increasing the means of satisfaction or by decreasing his wishes.

This, though illuminating, is unsatisfactory as a critical part of the freedom equation is entirely subjective. It seems to follow that a person who has been brought up as slave and knows no other way of life could be free even in his condition. The libertarian would like to subject the slave[10] to a 'revolution of rising expectations' and so widen his notion of freedom that he was dissatisfied with his state, and aspired to a greater humanity, thus making SW greater than SM.

I do not think Sorokin takes us very far on our quest.

[8] (1957) *Social and Cultural Dynamics* (p 488).
[9] (*Op cit*) (p 487).
[10] Epictetus, the Greek philosopher who lived as a slave for some time, claimed that he was freer than his master.

IV. Environmental imperatives. A physical and biological approach

F. Cottrell has argued that our approach to liberty in the West is crippled by the fundamental misconception that freedom automatically ensures survival of the system professing and practising it.

> In our culture with its individualistic orientation we hold that freedom exists only where controls are exercised with the consent of the controlled. In the long run, we say, the only patterns which will persist are those which so operate that they engender this consent. It is [also] presumed ... that if a social system meets this test, if in fact it induces men freely to choose that course which it sanctions, it will necessarily survive. But ... disaster has often struck societies in which men were absolutely devoted to their ... way of life. The fact remains then that if they are to survive, social systems must meet not only psychological but also physical and biological imperatives.

> We have spent far more time in learning and teaching our children how *ideas* were related to our freedoms than in how ... our special geographic, demographic, and historic situation was also related to the technology through which in turn many of those freedoms were assured.

> Man *can* be free only if he has learned to choose freely to do what he must for the survival of his society.

> The 'must' may be found in the basic nature of the human being. ... From the technology ... in the kind of social organization required ... so that the technology can function. Unless we know that men in the west will be taught to choose freely that which the operation of the system requires we cannot know whether they are to remain free.

> ... where the physical elements of the system are inadequate to maintain it, no amount of effort to preserve by purely psychological manipulation will suffice, traditional wisdom will itself have become the source rather than the cure for disaster. In such a culture men who are free to do as they wish will by their free choice destroy freedom.[11]

This argument seems completely unchallengeable; to survive, a society—or even a whole species—must meet not only social

[11] (1966) *The Future of Freedom* (pp 8, 10, and 11).

requirements but biological and physical imperatives. If it fails the society or species must go under.

The social mechanics of liberty

The mechanism modifying virtually all behaviour—and therefore both free behaviour and its opposite—is called 'social control', as we have seen, a basic social process by which societies cohere and manage themselves so as to ensure their continuance.

We might say, along with the cyberneticians, that society is a 'goal-seeking' system—it controls itself in pursuit of the goals set in part by its present citizens, and in part by their ancestors. Although the goals of different societies can differ greatly, nearly always the same two will appear at the apex of the goal 'hierarchy':

1. Survival of the society as a whole.
2. Preservation of its essential identity.

Socialization

The most important mechanism of social control is called 'socialization'. This is the process by which each new individual born into a society, each baby in other words, is moulded by that society to accept its norms and values. In order to survive, the child must speak the appropriate language, like those kinds of food which happen to be available, and co-operate with the people in its immediate environment.

This much is obviously essential, but the smallest acquaintance with films, TV, or newspaper reports, let alone historical or anthropological studies, shows that human infants have been and still are socialized in radically different ways at different times and places. This implies that the freedoms they are trained to expect, enjoy, and grant to others differ also, as must the restrictions they learn to live with. The essential aspect of this socializing process is not so much that people learn to do the right things, as defined by their society at that time, but that *they do not learn that other choices are possible.*

In other words the values, customs, expectations, and norms of a culture are taught as universals. They are taken into each individual in such a way that he finds it hard, if not impossible, even to *think* of behaving in different ways, let alone doing it. It is like an actor learning his part—not an ordinary actor learning his part in the ordinary way, but a 'method' actor trying in some sense to actually *become* the character for the duration of the play. To extend the metaphor, the duration of the play for most of us is life, as Shakespeare recognized.

We learn to conform more or less continuously without ever realizing we conform at all, indeed, priding ourselves on our individualism and self-discipline. But the reality for most of us most of the time—and of course I include myself in this category—is that we are little better than slaves to a particular socio-cultural system at a particular time and place.

This outcome is very useful for the society concerned. If it can get what it wants by persuading people, not merely to produce the required behaviour under pressure but to *want* to produce it, a society saves itself a great deal of trouble.

However, it is impossible to get everybody to do all the right things all of the time simply by socializing them in the right way in the first place—not least because societies change and need different forms of behaviour later. What is required in addition to socialization, is a monitoring and remedial process and this is the wider process of social control.

Social control in the wider sense

Just as each individual is socialized into the appropriate role by means of rewards and punishments as well as upbringing and education, so must he be kept from deviation after the socialization process is largely completed. (Of course, strictly speaking, it never stops. We are constantly being resocialized into new social roles as change comes along, either in society as a whole or in our place within society, through ageing, for example.)

To keep behaviour within tolerable limits societies set up elaborate mechanisms for observing, assessing, reviewing, and judging it, administering rewards and punishments as the occasion arises. In simple societies this is done by time-honoured customs, reinforced perhaps by decisions of the elders of the tribe sitting in formal conclave from time to time. In more elaborate societies specialized organs of control are gradually built up, the law, churches, unions and professional associations, political parties, police, military, government, and state. The larger and more complicated the society, the more separate and institutionalized are the means of control and the more they tend to be written down rather than handed down.

The object of the control process is to produce, within limits, what is normally called 'conformity' of behaviour, but to avoid the undesirable moral overtones of that expression a technical term is used in the social sciences, 'compliance', which is contrasted with 'non-compliance'—behaviour which is broken down into two sub-categories: 'variant' and 'deviant' activities.

Compliant behaviour is in accordance with the most acceptable norms of the society, *variant* behaviour is that which neither 'toes the line' nor yet 'oversteps the mark', whereas *deviant* behaviour is that which does overstep the mark, is therefore unacceptable, and must be prevented or punished.

Counter-control

A further general process tending to increase individual liberty—although it seems to go against Durkheim—is called 'counter-control'.[12] In Britain, for example, just as we have an organized control system, the organs of government, we have an organized counter-control system—the opposition and its various supporting bodies—and this is true of many other states. Once these are in being, government and opposition, then individuals have a degree of freedom to join the one or the other. In Britain they are also free to join a third or a fourth party or even start a new one all of their own, but in so doing they relinquish most of their already limited freedom to have any real say in the running of the country. In deciding to vote Liberal, for example, you also make the decision to waste a substantial part of your political power because of the way voting is organized. However, having the freedom to join only two parties is much greater than the freedom (for some) to join only one, as in the Soviet Union.

How much is this real freedom? How far are we really free to join the one party or the other in the light of our own judgment? The answer to this seems to be that we are not very free, the great majority of us support the party our fathers supported before us. We are generally brought up in a particular political belief and by and large we tend to remain true to it and this must mean that the individuals concerned are not really free to choose. Children

[12] For a useful introduction to this topic see Wolff, KH, 'Social Control', in Roucek, JS (ed) (1961) *Readings in Contemporary American Sociology.*

brought up in working-class families will tend to vote Labour, and those from middle-class families will tend to vote Conservative. This of course is the statistical picture, the average, it is not true in all cases.

This means that even where the formal mechanisms for counter-control do exist within society, the earlier socializing processes have operated in such a way as to remove much of our freedom to use them. Does this mean that we are all condemned inextricably and permanently to cultural slavery, glued to the values instilled in us in our earlier childhood?

The answer to this, fortunately, is 'no'. The fact that some of us know or at least have heard of individuals who do not conform to the customs and beliefs that society tried to drum into them, proves that there is a certain element of true freedom left when everything has been said about the pressures tending to produce conformity and therefore to reduce individual liberty.

Socio-cultural determinism

What is going on in the social control process is called, in the jargon of the social scientist, a process of 'socio-cultural determinism'. In order to keep itself going, society is producing new individuals in its own image and 'keeping going' means not merely continuing in existence but maintaining its basic identity. The idea of state-controlled seminaries producing tens of thousands of Jesuits in the Soviet Union, or droves of Marxist Leninists in Spain is quaint, to say the least of it.

John Locke, the English philosopher, said that each individual is born with a *tabula rasa*—a clean slate[13]—on which society writes what it will. Society 'programmes' its budding citizens to believe, like, say, and do the right things—writing its instructions on the 'clean slate', just as scientists programme their computers.

Another way of looking at it is to picture human beings as units in a socio-cultural 'field of force', rather like iron filings in a magnetic field. The filings take up a particular position and direction automatically, quite without volition or awareness. This is not strictly true of human beings but there is a very strong parallel,

[13] It is perhaps not quite a clean slate. See (*a*) Andreski, I, 'The Baby as Dictator', *New Society*, March 30, 1967, and (*b*) Wrong, D, 'The Over-socialised Conception of Man', *American Sociological Review*, XXVI, pp 184–193. Reprinted in Coser and Rosenberg (eds) (1964) *Sociological Theory*.

nonetheless, because of the large measure of automatism in the way we orientate ourselves to our society's unique needs.

Even where there appears to be strong awareness of voluntarism the 'voluntariness' itself is often specified by the social system. A young man born into a poor, ill-educated family in the West who, through innate ability, determination, and ambition becomes a well paid and influential scientist, say, is seeking a socially approved goal in a socially approved way and not 'being himself' in any very striking fashion.

Are we all equally enslaved?

It is not argued here that everybody is equally enslaved at all times and places. This is manifestly untrue. There are crucial differences in 'liberty of the individual' in Britain, on the one hand, and the Soviet Union, Portugal, or Rhodesia, say, on the other.

To make this statement meaningful we would have to specify in precisely what way 'liberty' differs in these states, and there is no difficulty in listing particular freedoms present in Britain and absent from the other states: freedom of assembly, of speech, conscience, religion, and so forth. Of course these are relative, not absolute terms but we should have little difficulty in defining them operationally and finding measurable differences in the amount of each of these freedoms present in each case. Among the things we would find would be the fact that the Briton's freedoms are hedged and qualified in all sorts of ways so that, very likely, they add up to a very much smaller freedom than many of us like or would have expected.

Conversely we would find that some freedoms we lack are enjoyed by the Russians, freedom from unemployment, and from exploitation by landlords and advertisers, for example. It would not be a one-sided revelation.

In addition to differences between systems we also find important differences within them, of course; not all individuals conform to the same degree.

Control, liberty, and conformity

What is the solution to this paradox—does social control produce cultural slaves or individual liberty? Examining this with even passable adequacy would need a whole book but a partial answer can be given by first going back to some notional pre social-control situations—perhaps like those depicted in the Icelandic Sagas—and examining the state of affairs there with respect to liberty.

What we would expect to find would be not a condition of no liberty (except for that enjoyed by the powerful), but one of rapidly varying and unstable liberties. One day you might rob or murder with complete impunity in broad daylight, another rape some passing innocent on the whim of the moment and get away with it, but only moments after your successful crime it might be your turn to fall beneath the cudgel of some sturdy villain.

In such a situation many people would live in fear and trembling —a mere animal existence as in a state of nature—every further hour of life depending on the whim of the stronger and the potential victims' skills in evasion, placation, and defence. Others would have more security and liberty and others again the absolute freedom of absolute tyrants. However, all of this would rest on insecure foundations and be unstable and unpredictable—none would know where he would be in a couple of weeks, let alone in ten years' time; even the most powerful and therefore the most free, the tyrant himself, would be almost certain to fall as he became overconfident and more oppressive, or simply older and weaker. Liberty in the sense of stability, continuity, predictability, and security, would be missing and all of these would be provided if social control were to be introduced, thereby justifying Durkheim's claim, up to a point.

However, there are degrees of social control, the process can go and often has gone too far—social control has been used not to create liberty but to reduce or even destroy it. Hitler and Stalin used the control mechanisms of modern states as ruthlessly as the Inquisition or any tyrant of ancient days to root out the last vestiges of individual liberty in matters affecting the wider society. There is a very great danger that the modern technology of information handling and communication will be used by aspiring totalitarians of the future to exercise a more rigorous and efficient control than has ever been possible in the past because of the sheer inefficiency of the tyrant's instruments. George Orwell's Big Brother with his two-way television in every room and public place, coupled to automatic surveillance mechanisms, is technologically only just round the corner and we must work hard to prevent its realization. The price of liberty is eternal vigilance.

To sum up so far we can say that in a state of zero social

control, anarchy, there is not much reliable liberty except for the few powerful individuals because of the instability and unpredictability of the system. Where 'might is right' we can also say 'force is freedom'. In a state of tyranny or excessive social control there is little or no liberty because the mechanism is used for the express purpose of ironing it out as far as possible.

What is the situation in a system with a moderate amount of social control, one which has progressed beyond anarchy but not gone so far as tyranny? Clearly, in such a system there would be a lot of liberty, as Durkheim argued. People would be free to think for themselves to a certain degree, to plan ahead—because of their society's stability—and carry out their plans with confidence when the time came, so how can the earlier claim that we are little better than cultural slaves be justified?

The answer lies essentially in the fact that Durkheim's liberty is relative whereas the meaning implied here 'strives towards the unconditional', as Goethe put it. In any society with a moderate machine for social control the citizens are tacitly agreeing (without their conscious knowledge or consent) to a 'package deal' of liberty: their society says to them, in effect,

> You must give up absolute freedom and particular freedoms a, b, and c, in return for a guarantee of freedoms x, y, and z. If you don't want to we shall compel you, we shall punish you for failing to agree (or at least to act as though you agree) by taking your money, goods, liberty, or life. You have a certain freedom to persuade us to change our definition of your liberty but this is limited and granted only on our terms.

Some societies permit those who reject the package deal to leave and seek another, elsewhere, but many—such as Portugal, South Africa, and the Soviet Union—normally refuse even this; citizens have to stay and like it or lump it. The biggest snag about this package deal of rights and duties is not that it is presented with this take it or leave it attitude but that it is insidiously introduced to us as we lie gurgling in our cradles, when we are not in the slightest degree aware of what we are letting ourselves in for. There is no real opportunity for reading the small print in the 'social contract', as Rousseau labelled it, until it is very nearly too late.

What this all adds up to is that particular societies provide particular sets of freedoms and the more open, moderate, and undogmatic they are, the greater is the citizen's total freedom.

However, all known societies, present and past, have withheld many freedoms they could by other more liberal standards have granted freely, for the simple reason that no society has yet taken seriously or worked hard at the notion of maximum individual liberty, and this means that liberty in Durkheim's sense can still be a variant of cultural slavery.

The pathology of liberty

It is this anomic state that is the cause, as we will show, of the incessantly recurrent conflicts, and the multifarious disorders of which the economic world exhibits so sad a spectacle.[14]

Emile Durkheim

Social scientists recognize a pathology of freedom and the social condition exemplifying this is called 'anomie',[15] after Durkheim, or 'anomy'. This is a condition of normlessness, analogous to the state of weightlessness experienced by astronauts in their space-ships. Human beings have evolved in a gravitational field and nor-mally live in one, using its energy in many ways for their life processes. Gravity encompasses and conditions all our activities, we are thoroughly habituated to this and live accordingly. In orbit, however, gravitational forces are missing.[16] Human beings float freely to and fro, completely weightless, just like any inanimate object released in the spacecraft.

Coping with this condition is quite a problem. If we want to drink on Earth we fill a vessel with the aid of gravity, convey it to our lips, pour, and gravity causes the liquid to flow into our mouths. We then swallow and it is pumped down through the oesophagus into the stomach, the last part being the only one not depending on gravity. In space, however, you cannot fill a vessel; even if you did manage it, conveyed it to your lips, and poured, nothing would happen; the apparently childishly simple task of drinking a glass of water has become impossible.

The condition of anomy is a situation in which the analogue of the gravitational field, the social 'field', is either:

(a) missing, owing to some drastic changes   in   social

---

[14] *The Division of Labour in Society.* Preface to 2nd edition.

[15] See (1951) *Suicide*, Bk 2 Ch 5.

[16] Strictly speaking they are not missing entirely. The weaker gravita-tional forces at that distance are exactly compensated by the centrifugal forces of rotation. It is just as though they were missing, however.

organization, through conquest, civil war, a great natural catastrophe, or some comparable agency; or

(b) though it is not destroyed, the social field is in some way compensated or cancelled out by other social fields so that instead of having just one set of social values and norms to live with there are two or more, conflicting in some respects. Individuals are thereby thrust into the difficult situation of having no clear indication which of the two or more sets of values to observe.

Both of these conditions add up to a state of normlessness; (a) in which there are no norms at all, or (b), in which there are no *effective* norms because those that do exist conflict with each other and give no guidance on which are the 'correct' or best courses to follow. This means that our social actions, akin to the astronaut's attempt to drink a glass of water, become difficult—perhaps even virtually impossible—because we become disorientated, unrelated to the individuals around us and to the social system as a whole.

A few individuals, it is true, welcome this state of affairs as a heaven-sent opportunity for doing what they want to do, all too frequently exploiting their fellow men in the process.

For most individuals, however, the condition of anomy is extremely painful. Not knowing 'where you stand', as we say, or 'what is expected of you' is a very trying and demoralizing situation for most people. Statistics for suicide can be used to illustrate this effect, and Durkheim showed that where there is a threat to a society from the outside, as from a potential conqueror, members of a society tend to draw together,[17] their norms become stronger. they feel more integrated, a greater 'solidarity', and suicides go down markedly. Where there is a threat to the society from the inside, however, from civil war, revolution, or a financial crisis, the opposite occurs. Suicide rates go up markedly and the explanation of this appears to be in the fact that an internal disruption of this kind breaks down social norms, leaving people in a state of confusion and helplessness; their world 'tumbles about them' as we say, and a significantly larger number take their own lives in consequence, the uncertainty being more than they can stand.

The upshot of all this seems to be that freedom is something of a mixed blessing. We need a certain amount of it, of certain kinds, but not too much, or of the wrong kind, either of which can be very bad for individuals and, consequently, for the system. This

[17] The British felt this very strongly during the 1939–45 war.

does not mean that in the future people could not be trained to accept, even to demand, much greater degrees of freedom, possibly even to the point desired by anarchists—a state in which everyone is completely free and self-governing and no one attempts, or even wishes, to curtail the freedom of others. It also means we must avoid the more or less automatic response in our society at this time to any proposed modification or reduction of an existing freedom, which is to say, 'we must reject it'—often in a manner which suggests 'we must reject any discussion of the matter'.

The correct response is surely to say:

> *What* new reduction of freedom, why, when, and how? What do we lose, what do we stand to gain in compensation, if anything?

Only when these questions are asked and the answers compared can we come to any sensible decision whether to accept or reject a proposal to modify an existing freedom.

The desire for liberty

A question we must now ask is how much individual liberty do we really want? The answer, far from being, 'As much as possible as soon as possible' seems to be more like, 'Not too much and not too soon'.

In the West we pay lip-service to the *idea* of liberty, we are prepared to support it in principle—provided it does not degenerate into permissiveness, i e letting individuals actually pursue their individual notions of liberty—but many of us not merely lack the substance of liberty, we are afraid of its name, not only are we not free, we have a fear of freedom, of being thrust into situations where we not only can but must exercise it.

This is the essence of the existentialist paradox, not only that man is free but that he is *compelled* to be free. He is compelled by circumstances to make choices, to take responsibility for himself, to seek his own future. He cannot escape this except by choosing not to choose, itself a choice of course, and letting himself be swept along by the social forces surrounding him. In either case he must make the choice, either overtly, or by default.

The paradox is expressed in the image of man sitting in a cage with the door wide open, not wanting to come out, preferring to squat in his cage of authority, habit, and convention to avoid the pain and problems of stepping through the open doorway into the wide open spaces of freedom outside.

Erich Fromm, the distinguished American psychologist has discussed the psychological implications of freedom. He asked:

> Can freedom become a burden, too heavy for man to bear, something he tries to escape from? Why then is it that freedom for many is a cherished goal and for others a threat?[18]

Is there not also, perhaps, besides an innate desire for freedom, an instinctive wish for submission?

In his cogent and moving analysis Fromm also says:

> ... A premise necessary for the understanding of the analysis of freedom in modern society ... [is] ... the concept that freedom characterizes human existence as such and furthermore that its meaning changes according to the degree of man's awareness and conception of himself as an independent and separate being.

He argues that, historically, western man has evolved to a sort of halfway house of freedom from the binding forces of medieval society, a process he calls 'individuation'. As this process took place in society it also takes place in every developing individual:

> ... We can also say that the *one side of the growing process of individuation is the growth of self-strength*. The limits of the growth of individuation and the self are set, partly by individual conditions, but essentially by social conditions.
>
> ... Every society is characterized by a certain level of individuation beyond which the normal individual cannot go.
>
> The other aspect of the process of individuation is *growing aloneness*.

Fromm develops his argument by postulating that this release from the ties of the family group, whilst being liberating, is also a threat to many individuals.

> This separation ... is ... often threatening and dangerous, [and] creates a feeling of powerlessness and anxiety. ...
>
> ... When one has become an individual, one stands alone and faces the world in all its perilous and overpowering aspects.
>
> Impulses arise to give up one's individuality, to overcome the feeling of aloneness and powerlessness by completely submerging oneself in the world outside.

[18] Fromm, E (1942) *The Fear of Freedom.*

Fromm argues that this insecurity may lead to a drive to submit oneself to authority, which, if succumbed to, may well result in the very opposite of what was intended:

... Submission increases the child's insecurity and at the same time creates hostility and rebelliousness, which is the more frightening since it is directed against the very persons on whom the child has remained—or become—dependent.

Fromm then points out that submission is only one of the ways of avoiding this aloneness and anxiety:

The other way, the only one which is productive and does not end in an insoluble conflict is that of *spontaneous relationship to man and nature,* a relationship that connects the individual with the world without eliminating his individuality. This kind of relationship—the foremost expressions of which are love and productive work—are rooted in the integration and strength of the total personality and are therefore subject to the very limits that exist for the growth of the self.

Fromm's analysis is based upon what he calls a 'dialectic process . . .' as individuality develops and the potential for freedom increases.

The child becomes more free *to* develop and express his own individual self unhampered by those ties which were limiting it ... [and] ... also ... more free *from* a world which gave it security and reassurance.

Fromm stresses the potentiality within this process of acquiring new strength, vigour, harmony, and integration but points out that the individual may become:

... Alone and free, yet powerless and afraid. The newly won freedom appears as a curse; he is free *from* the sweet bondage of paradise, but he is not free *to* govern himself, to realize his individuality.

'Freedom *from*' is not identical with positive freedom, with 'freedom *to*'.

Fromm stresses the great temptation of people in this frame of mind to seek radical and authoritarian solutions to their problems, to submerge themselves in religious or political ideologies which, it is hoped, will remove the nagging sense of aloneness and fear of responsibility. But this is the wrong answer, he says:

> ...There is a positive answer, ...the process of growing freedom, does not constitute a vicious circle, ...man can be free and yet not alone, critical and yet not filled with doubts, independent and yet an integral part of mankind. This freedom man can attain by the realization of his self, by being himself....
>
> [This] ... is accomplished not only by an act of thinking but also by the realization of man's total personality, by the active expression of his emotional and intellectual potentialities. These potentialities are present in everybody; they become real only to the extent to which they are expressed. In other words, *positive freedom consists in the spontaneous activity of the total, integrated personality.*

Unfortunately, Fromm, writing in 1942, was not demographically informed. The postwar impetus to the population explosion had not arrived and he gave no consideration to the problems of controlling fertility. It may be a tragic truth that pursuit of this positive self-expression and full flowering of the personality may for some people be attainable only—or most readily—through the process of loving and reproducing, giving oneself wholly to another person in the full knowledge that biological creation will be the natural outcome. I suppose most of us at some time or other have met or read about and been warmed by women so overflowing with *joie de vivre* that they blurt out their urge to have ten children.

Fromm's analysis, profound and sensitive though it is, gives us no guidance in this crucial field. It may be that as *homo sapiens* comes of age, spontaneity in some of the most important fields of human expression and self-realization may have to go by the board in the interests of the greatest good of the greatest number and in pursuit of the very goal which Fromm so admires, harmony between man and nature.

Self-knowledge

The first step on the road to true individual liberty is knowledge, including a large component of self-knowledge. Before an individual can become free, he must have knowledge of what he is now, how he got like that, what he might have been, and what he might yet become. He can get this through studying other societies—not necessarily academic study. Simply by reading science fiction or even listening to news bulletins we can find out a lot about how other societies are, have been, or might in future be organized.

The next stage must be that of insight. Having acquired knowledge about his own society, himself, and about other societies and the individuals they produce, the person concerned must have the flash of insight that the whole system, including himself as a part of it, could have been different. 'He' could have been born at another time and place, could have had different experiences, which as a consequence would have made him a different person.

On these two solid foundations the third stage now becomes possible. This is choosing, deciding to pursue a course of action in the future different from that which would have been pursued had the same old habits of thought and behaviour continued.

Anyone who has gone through these three critical stages is no longer a complete slave to his society. He is now in some sense an independent individual—or at least has sown the seeds of independence. He can begin to break away from the forces which have made him what he is and become more truly, more spontaneously, himself: become one of David Riesman's 'autonomous' persons, or acquire freedom *to*, as Fromm put it. But of course none of these activities will take the individual very far if his society is not fairly permissive, unless he is satisfied by internal liberty as described by Sorokin.

However, if social reality is studied from the vantage point of the social scientist, as we have seen, it is quite clear that few of us go through the three stages: most of us, most of the time, are little better than slaves to particular societies at particular times and places simply by accident of birth.

The question we end up with—why have only basically conformist societies evolved so far and whether an appreciably less conformist society would be viable—are imponderables at this stage of knowledge. However, we do know enough to make our discussions of freedom and control much more informed and fruitful, than they normally are, to recognize where constraints are necessary, and to increase our range and variety of freedoms to some degree at least where existing constraints are unnecessary.

By far the best discussion of liberty by a social scientist I have so far discovered, that by B. Malinowski the anthropologist, has not been dealt with here, despite its excellence. The reasons for this are threefold: in the first place because he was concentrating mainly on political/social liberty under the threat of Fascism, secondly he did not consider 'ecological' liberty, my main theme, and thirdly because he insists that 'Freedom is one and indivisible'.

However, his 'pragmatic' definition of liberty is as well worth quoting as his book is worth reading.

> Freedom is determined by the results of action as well as by its prerequisites. The individual's freedom consists in his ability to choose the goal, to find the road and to reap the rewards of his efforts. . . .
>
> All claims for freedom remain idle and irrelevant unless planning and aiming can be translated into an effective execution . . .[19]

This dovetails very well into the arguments presented here and equally undermines attempts by such writers as Hayek to explain liberty in *vacuo*.

Liberty, a practical definition

The definition of liberty proposed here is simply *the sum of all particular actual freedoms*. These must in principle be specifiable and in some sense measurable and they are equivalent to an infinity of potential activities less the sum of all actual restraints, which again must be specifiable for 'liberty' to be a meaningful concept.

Borrowing two terms now very popular in the social sciences, 'micro' and 'macro',[20] we might air the concepts 'microfreedom' and 'Macrofreedom' and write a little equation as follows:

Liberty = Macrofreedom = the sum of all microfreedoms.[21]

$$L = Mf = \sum_{o}^{n} mf$$

It must be stressed that the freedoms to be added up to form the definition of liberty must be *actual* and not merely *potential* freedoms. Clashes between potential microfreedoms occur both within

[19] (1947) *Freedom and Civilisation* (p 25).

[20] From the Greek for 'small', and 'long' or 'large', respectively, as in 'microeconomics' and 'macroeconomics'.

[21] If anyone from a popular newspaper happens to comment on this notion it is almost bound to be translated into popular terms, so the job may as well be done here. Liberty = Maxifreedom = the sum of all minifreedoms.

and between individuals—the same applying to groups—we recognize this in the everyday expression 'you can't have your cake and eat it'. For an individual, having his cake and eating his cake are two potential microfreedoms, only one of which can be enjoyed at a given time and place. Similarly, where there are two or more people and only one cake, only one individual can enjoy the microfreedom to have or to eat it. So, although it is quite proper to talk about the two potential microfreedoms—having your cake and eating your cake—it is obviously wrong to add both of them up to find the macrofreedom, the sum of the microfreedoms, for a given person at a given time and place.

To take one small practical example. Some people want the microfreedom to blare out pop music from portable radios in public places whilst others want the microfreedom not to have to suffer unnecessary noise. These freedoms are obviously incompatible, a decision must be made between them and one group forced to give up a valued microfreedom.

It is hoped that these concepts may prove of some use in the great debate which is about to begin on the question of population control versus individual liberty by helping to direct attention away from the mere slogan 'LIBERTY!' and focusing it on the complicated reality of multiple human freedoms and restraints and their attendant array of right and duties.

Summary

The basic problem here was to demonstrate that individual liberty is produced by social control—that without it we would have not liberty but anarchy, which most of us reject, with freedom for the powerful, and uncertainty, fear, and trembling for everybody else.

Evidence from writings of the ancients and modern scholars was presented and the social process of control examined, socialization of new recruits plus control mechanisms for the purpose of regulating non-compliance. I argued that socialization is a process of 'programming' human beings—much as computers are programmed—and that this process of socio-cultural determinism curtails individual liberty very severely as alternatives are not presented: we are taught *the* form of behaviour expected by our society. Counter-control was discussed as a means of increasing liberty and this can be reinforced by pluralism—permitting or encouraging the formulation of a number of sub-cultures which have an influence on some aspects of the socialization process and provide a number of different havens permitting cultural mobility later in life.

Several sociological theories of liberty were briefly examined and two of them—those of Riesman *et al*, and Sorokin—rejected, not as incorrect but as unhelpful in this context. Durkheim's view that liberty is produced by social control was largely accepted, and the pathology of liberty discussed with the aid of his concept of *anomie*. The question was raised how much liberty do we want and can we stand and Fromm's view that freedom can be a burden was related to the existentialist paradox and his concepts freedom *from* and freedom *to* accepted.

F. Cottrell's point that social systems must meet physical and biological imperatives in order to survive was accepted, the road to individual liberty was charted—via self-knowledge and insight into one's ecological and cultural milieu—and what, it is hoped, will be a useful way of discussing and to some extent measuring liberty was proposed.

Liberty equals Macrofreedom equals the sum of all microfreedoms equals an infinity of potential activities less all actual constraints.

Chapter 7

The arithmetic of liberty

... this multiplication and daily extension of forms of association brings with it a multiplicity of restrictive laws and regulations in many departments of human life. As a consequence, it
narrows the sphere of a person's freedom of action. The means
often used, the methods followed, the atmosphere created, all
conspire to make it difficult for a person to think independently
of outside influences, to act on his own initiative, exercise his
responsibility and express and fulfil his own personality.[1]

Pope John XXIII

The facts emphasized by Pope John—somewhat surprisingly in
view of the Roman Catholic position on fertility control and population problems in general—had not of course escaped the attention
of social scientists. One example of a more technical formulation
of the problem is provided by the sociologist, Georg Simmel, who
wrote:

Qualitatively speaking, *the larger the group is, usually the
more prohibitive and restrictive the kinds of conduct which it
must demand of its participants* in order to maintain itself: the
positive ties, which connect individual with individual and give
the life of the group its real content must (after all) be given over
to these individuals. The variety of persons, interests, events
become too large to be regulated by a center; *the center is left
only with a prohibitive function, with the determination of what
must not be done* under any circumstances, *with the restriction
of freedom, rather than its direction*[2] (Italics added)

[1] (1961) *Mater et Magistra* (para 62).
[2] Wolff, KH (1950) *The Sociology of Georg Simmel* (pp 397/8).

In developing his classic *'Iron Law of Oligarchy*, Robert Michels wrote:

> As organization develops, not only do the tasks of administration become much more difficult and . . . complicated, but, . . . enlarged and specialized to such a degree that it is no longer possible to take them all in at a . . . glance . . .
>
> . . . *democratic control . . . is eventually reduced to a minimum. . . .*
>
> . . . *the struggle for great principles becomes impossible . . .* in the democratic parties . . . the great conflicts of view are fought out to an ever decreasing extent with the weapons of . . . theory . . . and degenerate more and more into personal struggle and invective. . . .[3] (Italics added)

This offers a possible line of thought for explaining some of the disaffection of present day youth from the established politics of modern mass societies.

Colin Clark, the indefatigable protagonist of ever-increasing numbers, has argued the opposite case to that put forward by Pope John, Simmel, and many others. He believes that increased populations almost invariably bring increased freedom, although—as is often the case in his arguments—he refrains from considering incompatible evidence, or the differing view of other scholars, defining his central concept, or specifying means of measuring how much of it there is. Clark contents himself with a *mélange* of highly selected historical data which demonstrates, he claims:

> . . . population growth is generally beneficial . . . toward a more productive economy, . . . better and freer political forms, . . . better education, science and culture . . . as communities become larger . . . government control of economic life is found to be both impracticable and undesirable. . . .
>
> . . . The logical connection between 'planned population' and 'planned economy' was stated clearly and directly by Lord Stamp, . . .
>
> Those peoples . . . who courageously and intelligently face the challenge of population increase, will be rewarded by economic, political, and cultural progress to an extent beyond any limits that we can now foresee.[4]

[3] (1915) *Political Parties* (Collier edn. (1962) pp 71/2).
[4] 'Do Population and Freedom Grow Together?' *Fortune* Magazine, December, 1960.

Clark's thesis is rejected as over-simplified and tendentious and the case put forward here rests on three basic points:

1. There is no simple, obvious, or fixed relationship between numbers and liberty. In some spheres an increase in numbers tends to increase microfreedoms; in others—or beyond a certain point in the same sphere—the reverse occurs.

2. In many cases there are clashes between particular microfreedoms related to numbers, and, where this occurs, some sort of decision-making mechanism must choose between them.

3. Beyond a certain critical point, further increase in numbers, though continuing to increase some microfreedoms, progressively reduces other and more basic microfreedoms and thereby reduces macrofreedom—the total liberty of the individual.

We can take the argument several stages further by looking at a few microfreedoms and their relation to numbers.

Increase in certain microfreedoms with increase in numbers

A person who wishes to have the microfreedom to ride on railway trains should not live in a very sparsely populated area, unless by some chance it is attached to and subsidized by another area with sufficient surplus wealth and the will to use it to provide the service required.

In many of the less densely populated areas of Britain people who thought they had just this relationship with the more heavily populated regions are now finding that they were mistaken. The railways they have grown up to accept as part of the natural landscape, almost, are being systematically destroyed. To be sure of getting your railway you must live in an area with enough people to build it and then keep it going by using it.

Similarly, if a person wants to join a pop group or a philosophy society, work in a factory making scientific instruments, or send his children to a school, there must be enough other people about with similar interests, plus the necessary resources, with whom he can co-operate in order to attain mutual fulfilment.

The more unusual the desire the greater is the possibility of satisfying it as numbers increase, because a greater 'division of labour' is possible. If your particular bent is towards reading the Norse sagas in the original before an appreciative audience, before you could indulge it there would have to be a very large number of people with highly developed communications to provide a sufficient minority sharing this taste who could come together and form the appropriate society. The larger the population the greater the number of microfreedoms of this kind which will be generated.

Microfreedoms of many other kinds will increase also. Pregnant unmarried women from the provinces very frequently lose themselves in London to avoid moral censure and anyone who wants the microfreedom to be himself, to be unconventional, to get away from it all, to become a dropout, will find it the more readily obtainable as the size of the group increases. He will gain anonymity and relative freedom from informal social control, with a corresponding increase in the microfreedom to behave differently. He will also, incidentally, gain some microfreedoms perhaps he had not intended, freedom to be lonely and unwanted, but that may be a price he is prepared to pay. This may be the basic reason underlying the higher crime rates in the larger cities, in which the informal constraints on individual behaviour operating in smaller groups, from people who know you, are absent.

It can therefore be accepted at the outset that increases in the number of others in one person's environment tends to increase his microfreedoms indefinitely in some directions and up to a point in others; this is not in dispute. What we have to look at is the other side of the coin: whether certain microfreedoms tend to be *reduced* with an increase in numbers and we must pay particular attention to the question, whether some of those which tend to be reduced are *basic* microfreedoms. If there are such tendencies— and this is what one would expect from a commonsense approach —then a careful analysis must be made of the microfreedoms in the system. We must find out to what degree they are present and then assess how desirable they are in relation to each other in order to permit our Macrofreedom to be optimized.

Microfreedoms reduced by increases in numbers

Freedom from beaurocracy
Sir Geoffrey Vickers has pointed out in detail what a phenomenal growth there has been in co-ordinating activities in our own society in the last century or so, though of course it would not be correct to claim that this has been caused solely by an increase in numbers:

> In 1850 the central government had eight departments of which four dealt wholly and one partly with external affairs. Five more

departments were added in the next fifty years, eleven more in the first years of this century, four more in the last three years. By 1956 more than one in five of the entire labour force were working for the central government, local government, or public bodies. Eight years later it is nearer one in three. It would be naive to dismiss these figures as an example of Parkinson's law. They record a massive and accelerating increase in the scope and volume of deliberate regulation of the national life; it has grown despite strong ideological resistance, ... [and] ... grows ever faster, but few, I would think, would question that it fails ever further to keep up with its problems.[5]

In an interview with a *Guardian* correspondent, Lord Snow, Chairman of the GPO's 'think tank', said in response to a criticism of our telephone services:

> ... the difficulties of a service increase roughly by the square of the number of people using it.[6]

This fact is being brought home to telephone subscribers in all sorts of ways, quite apart from the indifferent service. For instance, the change from the easy-to-remember letter codes to numbers, and the proposal to break the London Telephone Directory into sixteen separate volumes which raised such an extraordinary protest. All of these are straws in the wind.

Chester Barnard,[7] an original contributor in this field, pointed out in 1938 how complexity increases geometrically as the size of a group increases arithmetically. Figure 7/1 shows this growth with one of the simplest possible examples of a social relationship; people 'knowing each other'. As the size of the group increases from 1 to 50 the increase in the number of 'knowing' relations increases from 0 to ~~1,035~~. 1,225.

If we begin to consider, let alone take into account, some of the other possibilities, asymmetrical relationships—A knows B while B does not know A, dominance and submission, compliance, variance, and deviance, friendliness and hostility, intelligence, knowledge, mental health, and so forth, we see how easily the enormous complexity of social systems as we know them, is built up.

---

[5] BBC sound broadcast, 'The end of free fall'. Reprinted in *The Listener*, October 28, 1965.

[6] 8 September, 1970.

[7] (1938) *The Functions of the Executive*.

Fig 7/1

Increase in complexity with increase in numbers. Based on the simple relationship of 'knowing each other'

No in group	No of relationships [*]	Increase in size of group	Increase in relations with increase in size of group
0	0	0	–
1	0	1	0
2	1	1	1
3	3	1	2
4	6	1	3
5	10	1	4
6	15	1	5
7	21	1	6
8	28	1	7
9	36	1	8
10	45	1	9
15	105	5	60
20	190	5	85
50	1,225	30	1,035

Based on Barnard, C. (1938) **The Functions of the Executive**, p108 (modified)

[*] Note: Number of pairs knowing each other

Freedom from social conflict

We tend to think of conflict in our society as a visitation of evil more or less out of the blue and of course this sometimes does occur. Occasionally, bloodthirsty hordes do descend on peace-loving peoples and involve them in conflict not of their seeking, but this is the exception rather than the rule. Paradoxically, most conflict is not brought about by such visitations but arises as a by-product of co-operation. The more we are thrown together the more we must co-operate and while it is obvious that compulsion involves loss of liberty it is not generally realized that co-operation does the same. While we co-operate—however freely we do it— we lose the microfreedoms to manifest certain sorts of behaviour not desired by our partner or partners in the co-operative activity. Until we place ourselves in social contact with each other to carry out some kind of co-operative activity we are not in a position to develop conflict, which is a social relationship, and all our experience teaches us that we cannot co-operate for long without generating a certain amount of it.

The pioneer sociologist Cooley has said:

> ... the more one thinks of it, the more that he [*sic*] will see that conflict and co-operation are not separable things but phases of one process that always involves something of both.[8]

The anthropologist Malinowski—using the psychological term 'aggression' instead of the sociological term 'conflict'—put it like this:

> Aggression, like charity, begins at home ... [it] ... is a by-product of co-operation. ...[9]

A third writer, E. T. Hiller, pointed out:

> Co-operation produces dependence, and withholding co-operation provides each party with a means of coercion and opposition against the other.[9]

The relevance of this fact to the population problem may not be immediately obvious but there is a two-fold connection. The first is that the more people there are on the Earth or a given part of it, within a particular nation, for example, the more they must interact with each other and the more they must co-operate to keep out of each others' hair. More co-operation, more conflict.

The second strand of the relationship is through the fact that many people, recognizing that there is a serious problem of over-population relative to the world's resources, at the present time at least, advocate a cure by rolling up our sleeves and co-operating with each other and the under-developed countries on a scale and intensity never before seen in history so as to produce more food and a more equitable sharing out of our environmental resources. These people are prescribing precisely those conditions in which more and more conflict must be generated, and already we see—according to all reports—that some of the most vicious politicking and in-fighting to be found anywhere in the world is generated in 'do-gooding' agencies, such as the United Nations. An ominous sign if it is alleged that our salvation from the crisis of over-population is to be sought through more and better co-operation.

---

[8] Coser, A (1956) *The Functions of Social Conflict* (p 18).
[9] Both of these are quoted in Coser, (*Op cit*).

If the theory of Thomas Hobbes, the influential English philosopher, is correct, that individuals are drawn together in society from self-interest—this being the reason for the formation of villages, towns, cities, and whole societies—each person realizing that his own selfish ends may be met more fully by a certain amount of calculated co-operation with his fellow men, then we see that such co-operation is not even well motivated. This theory has it that citizens A, B, C and so on co-operate with each other, not from any fellow-feeling or desire to serve, but simply to get as much as they can for themselves. This leads to what another American sociologist, Sumner, has called '...antagonistic co-operation...', and insofar as this is the motivation of individuals in co-operative groups it is hardly surprising that a lot of conflict is generated.

Freedom from crime

The American psychologist Cattel did a study of the dimensions of various cultures correlating significant variables. Krech, *et al*, summarize this, as follows:

> In the first factor—size—it is of interest that many political assassinations, riots, and local rebellions, and a high ratio of divorces to marriages are positively associated with size of country. Cattel interprets this finding as indicating that 'sheer size is connected systematically with difficulty of organization and movement.'[10]

Figure 7/2 illustrates this point from the work of other investigators. A more recent writer, Leopold Kohr, has invented the concept 'critical size'.[11] He claims that size is the chief factor in producing crime, even alleging that if several thousand criminals from a large town were put together to live in a small town they would in the main become indistinguishable from ordinary citizens.

Freedom from poverty

> The independence of India has no meaning unless and until it is translated into better sanitation, food, and education, until the village is lifted up so as to make independence a reality for the masses.[12]

[10] Krech, *et al*. (*Op cit*) (pp 364/5).
[11] 'Critical Size', *Resurgence*, July/August, 1967.
[12] Quoted Mitrany, D (1954) *Food and Freedom* (p 8).

Fig 7/2

Increase in crime rates with increase in size:
Urban crime rates per 100,000 population 1957

		Size of cities		
		over 250,000	50,000 to 100,000	under 10,000
Criminal homicide	Murder, non-negligent manslaughter	5.5	4.2	2.7
	Manslaughter by negligence	4.4	3.7	1.3
Rape		23.7	9.3	7.0
Robbery		108.0	36.9	16.4
Aggravated assault		130.8	78.5	34.0
At this point the scale changes				
Burglary, breaking or entering		574.9	474.6	313.3
Larceny-theft		1,256.0	1,442.4	992.1
Auto theft		337.0	226.9	112.9

Adapted from Federal Bureau of Investigation, **Uniform Crime Reports**, Annual Bulletin 1957 (Washington DC, US Government Printing Office 1958), p92

Raab and Selznick (1959) **Major Social Problems**, p139

This was said by Shri Mavalankar, Speaker of the Indian Parliament, a few years after India had regained her political liberty and it further illustrates the basic point made earlier that 'liberty' by itself means nothing. India has certainly gained her liberty as defined in the conventional sense but an attempt to translate political liberty into microfreedoms for half a billion individual Indians, freedom from hunger, freedom from poverty, from ignorance, squalor, disease, illiteracy, and so on shows it to be little more than an empty slogan.

This is not to say that the liberty of India after her independence from the British Raj is totally without meaning or value. India became a nation state with a voice in the United Nations and the councils of the world but the increase in real individual liberty—

as measured in terms of particular microfreedoms—for the hundreds of millions of semi-starving peasants was negligible.

Numbers and economic microfreedoms
(i) ECONOMIES OF SCALE

A piece of received wisdom in our society at the present time is that economists have proved material well-being and economic health can be achieved only if there is a steady growth of population. This works, it is thought, by means of increasing the size of the market which permits larger-scale production, greater division of labour, higher capitalization, and consequent savings in the cost per unit of whatever is produced.

> In the case of Britain, a great deal of unwarranted fuss and anxiety is now made about what is really a very modest rate of population growth. It seems probable that considerable economies of scale ... would be realized if the population were to increase to 100 million ... without leading to any severe problems of land availability.[13]

This was taken for granted by the Royal Commission on Population,[14] by Mr Harold Wilson, when he was Prime Minister, in his correspondence with Sir David Renton, by Mr David Eversley, the eminent demographer referred to earlier,[15] and is frequently put forward as one of the main justifications for joining the Common Market.

While this view reflects reality up to a point it is fallacious in the sense in which it is mostly used, i e to justify continuously expanding populations. Any elementary textbook or dictionary[16] of economics will point out that beyond a certain size, other things being equal, *dis*economies of scale begin to manifest themselves so that scale of production must be optimized rather than maximized.

This question formed the topic of a conference of the International Economic Association entitled 'Economic Consequences of the Size of Nations' (size being measured by population, of course). The proceedings were published under the same title and the Chairman, Professor E. A. G. Robinson, summed up as follows:

---

[13] Anonymous reviewer of *Population Growth and Land Use,* by Colin Clark, in *The Economist,* July 15, 1967.

[14] Para 261.

[15] 'Is Britain being threatened by over-population?', *The Listener,* July 27, 1967.

[16] *Everyman's Dictionary of Economics* (1965), for example.

... The outcome of our discussions ... was a belief that it was easy to exaggerate the importance of scale among the many factors that influence productivity.

... outside of a few exceptional industries most technical economies are exhausted by firms of quite moderate size. Even relatively small and poor countries can have a number of firms of the minimum size to give full, or almost full, technical efficiency ...

... most of the major industrial economies of scale could be achieved by a relatively high income nation of 50 million; ...[17]

Many other studies support these findings; even Colin Clark has written:

... rates of economic growth do not show any discernible correlation, positive or negative, with rates of population growth ...[18]

Even if economies of scale were inexhaustible we would soon have to forego them as the Earth is finite. As they are not we need no longer allow ourselves to be driven towards ever-increasing congestion and saturation of our resources[19] by pseudo-scientific arguments.

(ii) DECLINE IN FOREIGN TRADE WITH INCREASE IN POPULATION

There appear to be economic forces which reduce the proportion of foreign trade as population size increases. Figure 7/3 shows that the top two groups of nations have a median proportion of foreign trade of 33 per cent and the middle-size groups 52 per cent, against 68 per cent for the two groups of small nations.

It seems unlikely that it is absolutely impossible for a large nation to have a large proportion of foreign trade but it could well be that it becomes progressively more difficult as size increases. If in this sense there is a true economic law it bodes ill for the United Kingdom and her balance of payments if our numbers continue to rise.

(iii) INCOME AND INVESTMENT

... Nothing would so powerfully contribute to the advancement of rational freedom as a thorough knowledge generally

---

[17] Robinson, EAG (ed) (1963) p xviii).
[18] *Population Growth and Land Use* (p 258).
[19] Or, indeed, towards the Common Market.

Fig 7/3

Decline in foreign trade with increase in population

Columns:					
1	2	3	4	5	6
Groups of 5 nations	Average size (pop millions)	Average income per capita (US dollars)	Average foreign trade (US dollars)	Column 4 as % of Column 3	Median % for each pair
1st	69.0	653	142	21.8%	33%
2nd	15.0	399	176	44.1%	
3rd	10.2	429	252	58.8%	52%
4th	6.2	360	234	65.0%	
5th	3.9	579	306	52.9%	68%
6th	1.3	447	374	83.6%	

Adapted from S. Kuznets, ' Economic Growth of Small Nations '.
See chapter II in Robinson, E. A. G. (ed) (1963) **Op cit**

circulated of the principal cause of poverty; and that the ignorance of this cause, and the natural consequences of this ignorance, form, at present, one of the chief obstacles to its progress.

The pressure of distress on the lower classes of people, . . .
appears . . . to be the rock of defence, the castle, [and] the
guardian spirit of despotism. It affords to the tyrant the fatal and
unanswerable plea of necessity. . . .

A mob, which is generally the growth of a redundant population goaded by resentment for real sufferings, but totally ignorant of the quarter from which they originate, is of all monsters
the most fatal to freedom.

In this striking passage Malthus repeats a truism well known to
the ancients. In the Old Testament, for example, we find:

And Abraham went up out of Egypt, he, and his wife, and all
that he had, and Lot with him, into the south. . . . [and]

The land was not able to bear them, that they might dwell
together; for their substance was great . . .

And there was a strife between the herdmen of Abraham's
cattle and the herdmen of Lot's cattle . . .

And Abraham said unto Lot, 'Let there be no strife, I pray
thee, between me and thee, . . . for we be brethren . . .

. . . separate thyself, I pray thee, from me: if *thou wilt take* the
left hand, then I will go to the right; or if *thou depart* to the right
hand, then I will go to the left.[20]

The modern concepts 'critical population density', and 'carrying
capacity' (of an environment) dealt with in Chapter 14, are present

[20] Genesis xiii, 1–9.

in this passage, *in embryo*. The difficulty for most modern equiv-alents of the tribes of Israel is that there is little room, either to right or left, for a departure from over-populated regions.

Perhaps it might be useful to append a further reference for readers of the Christian persuasion who are not convinced of the need to restrain population growth.

In Ecclesiastes we read:

> To every *thing there is* a season, and a time to every purpose under the heaven:
> 2. A time to be born and a time to die; a time to plant, and a time to pluck up *that which is* planted.
> 3. A time to kill, and a time to heal; a time to break down and a time to build up;
> 4. A time to weep, and a time to laugh ... [and so on, to:]
> 8. A time to love, and a time to hate; a time of war, and a time of peace.[21]

Would it be irreverent or out of place to add:

> A time to give birth and a time to refrain from giving birth and to cherish those who are already born and safeguard the inheritance of those yet to be born.[22]

In a recent radio talk called 'Poverty amidst Wealth',[23] Mr J. H. Adler, Director of the World Bank, gave further evidence that over-population produces poverty and other studies have shown that poverty is strongly correlated with violence, as we shall see.

> ... In the fifteen years from 1950 to 1965 the world economy grew at an unprecedented rate. World production just about doubled and per capita income increased by more than 50 per cent. . . . [however]
> It is disturbing, though not surprising, that the poorest countries ... those with an annual per capita income of £125 have not done well and that the countries in the lower half of this income bracket show a growth record which is substantially worse than that of the rest.

[21] Ch 3.
[22] Verse 5 actually contains the words '. . . a time to embrace and a time to refrain . . .' and if this is given the strong connotation of sexual embrace the point is already made.
[23] BBC Third Programme, March 10, 1969. Not reprinted in *The Listener*. Text kindly supplied by World Bank.

The picture is getting considerably worse, ... if, instead of comparing the rise in total production and income, we focus on income per head. The most disconcerting aspect of the record of the world economy since 1950 has been the high, and rising rate of population growth. This is not, of course, a new discovery; ... But what is new in the picture is the heavy concentration of high rates of population growth in the poorest countries in the world. ...

These growth rates are alarming, ... because of the limitations ... they impose on economic advancement. ...

... We find that there is an inverse relation between population growth and growth in total as well as per capita income.

Mr Adler put concrete values on the amount by which population growth holds back economic growth.

... A reduction in population in the poor countries by one tenth of 1 per cent is equivalent to an increase in capital formation—or foreign aid—of £250 million per annum. So when we speak about the burden which high rates of population growth impose on the poor countries, we are not just talking about marginal adjustments, but about a major factor which bears directly on their growth prospects.[24]

(iv) RETURNS TO FERTILITY CONTROL

Unnecessary population growth robs all producers of a good slice of their hard-earned wealth, thereby increasing relative poverty, in two ways. In the here and now we must all pay extra taxes and consume less to provide for the 'demographic investment', the amount which has to be invested simply to keep society's wealth at the same per capita level as population grows. Later, we are robbed again—and of a very much larger sum, because if the same wealth that went into the demographic investment had been channelled into anything other than population growth, it could hardly have failed to increase our incomes very considerably later on.

Many studies have demonstrated this. For example one writer, Goran Ohlin, has shown that:

[24] For a sombre narration of the extra problems caused by excessive population growth in developing states see: Andreski, S: (*a*) (1966) *Parasitism and Subversion. The Case of Latin America.* (*b*) (1968) *The African Predicament.*

... Per capita income would ... be increased sixty times more by population control than by the alternative. [Non-control that is.][25]

He quotes another writer, Demeny, who has written:

... The gain from preventing a birth is of the order ... of two per capita incomes. ...

Two other writers, Enke and Zind, have shown that in a poor country an infant surplus to requirements—requirements being those needed for a stationary population—has:

... A negative value to the economy of almost $300—twice the current income per head.[26]

A third writer, Ansley J. Coale, a distinguished contributor in this field, has made comparative studies at the US Office of Population Research, based on the economic and demographic data of India and Mexico, of the income per capita after 150 years if on the one hand fertility continues unchanged, and if on the other hand it declines steadily until it is reduced by 50 per cent over twenty-five years: He reports:

... The estimated proportionate gains resulting from reduced fertility were almost identical in the two countries ...
... The difference is small at first but amounts to 40 per cent after thirty years and more than 100 per cent in sixty years. After 150 years the low fertility population would have an income per consumer six times as high as the faster growing population with unchanged fertility.[27]

Perhaps this should be explained a little further. He is not claiming that per capita wealth is six times greater than it was at the beginning of the period but *six times greater than the higher per capita income that would have been achieved* after 150 years despite continuing high fertility.

It is obvious that in all areas not manifestly under-populated, and there are very few of these left at the present day, everybody

---

25 (1967) Paris. *Population Control and Economic Development*, Development Centre of the OECD.
26 'Effect of fewer births on average income', *J. Biosocial Science*, **1**, No 1, January, 1969.
27 'Population and economic development'. In Hauser, MP (ed) (1963) *The Population Dilemma*. Copyright The American Assembly.

Fig 7/4
Demographic Investment:
Proportion of Gross National Product needed for investment each year to prevent per capita income dropping

Over 10%	Colombia, India, Morocco, Brazil, Ghana, Tunisia
7.5–10%	Malaysia, Peru, the United Arab Republic, Thailand, Mexico, Philippines, Turkey
5–7.5%	The Sudan, Pakistan, Nigeria, Indonesia, South Korea, Chile, Ethiopia
Less than 5%	United States, Norway, France, Sweden, Denmark, Finland, West Germany, Italy, the United Kingdom, Belgium, Austria, Greece, Portugal

Note:

Population growth figures are for 1967. The incremental capital–output ratio is for the period 1960–65. Countries included are those that had the necessary data, and they are classified in descending order

—except perhaps the baby food manufacturers—will be vastly better off if population growth ceases, and as wealth confers a number of valuable microfreedoms, we shall all be much freer.

Figures 7/4 and 5 show the ratio and total amounts absorbed by the demographic investment in various countries in the 1960s.

Michael Young[28] has calculated that each child born in Britain costs the taxpayers—in addition to what parents spend—something over £2,500 by the age of sixteen. Every school year after sixteen costs the taxpayer nearly another £300, and each undergraduate year, for those lucky enough to get to university, costs well over £1,000. None of these figures include the costs of welfare and health services, which he says are difficult to apportion by age group, but these can hardly be less than £20 a year on the average, adding another £300, say, by the age of sixteen.

This makes a total cost to the nation of some £2,800 per

[28] 'An anti-natal policy: rewards for smaller families'. *What?*, Autumn, 1969.

Fig 7/5

**Demographic Investment:
Poorer Countries only;
Amount of extra wealth needed
for investment each year
to prevent per capita income
dropping**

(Figures are in million US dollars at 1964 prices)

India	5,070
Brazil	2,060
Mexico	1,510
Colombia	720
Pakistan	680
Turkey	580
Philippines	380
Peru	340
Thailand	300
Malaysia, Morocco	250
Ghana	180
Tunisia, the Sudan	90

Note:

The investment proportions required to keep
per capita income at a constant level are
those in Fig 7/4. The GDP estimates are for
1966 at 1964 prices

After Zaidan, G. C. 'Population Growth and Economic
Development', **Studies in Family Planning**, No. 42, May 1969

sixteen-year-old, £175 for each year of his life, and as we are now
rearing getting on for a third-of-a-million children each year more
than we need for a stationary population the extra annual cost to
the taxpayer must be something over £50 million, allowing nothing
for higher education and many other public costs, or the large sums
the parents must spend, some of which would otherwise have gone
into savings and thus stimulated investment and the creation of
more wealth.

Freedom from violence

One of the causes of the Crusades was over-population, poverty,
and internal violence. Pope Urban II,[29] in urging men to set off on
these wars of aggression, said:

[29] (1042–1099). Quoted in Hutchinson, Sir J (1969) *Population and Food
Supply* (p 1).

... the lands which you inhabit, shut in on all sides from the sea and surrounded by mountain peaks, are too narrow for your large population; nor do they abound in wealth; they furnish scarcely food enough for their cultivators. Hence it is that you devour one another and that frequently you perish from mutual wounds. Let therefore hatred depart from among you; let your quarrels and your wars cease ... let none of your possessions detain you, no solicitude for your family affairs, ... Enter upon the road to the Holy Sepulchre; wrest the land ... which, as the Scripture says, 'floweth with milk and honey', ..., from the wicked race and subject it to yourselves.

Robertson gives further evidence from Scandinavia:

All the Scandinavian groups alike practised piracy as against the more civilized states of Northern Europe; and piracy showed them the way to conquest and colonization. At home their means of subsistence were pasturage, fishing, the chase, and agriculture which cannot have been easily extensible beyond the most fertile soil; hence a constant pressure of population, promoting piracy and aggressive emigration ...

There is testimony, going back to the eighth century, and occurring as late as the twelfth, to the effect that a certain number of men were periodically sent away by lot when the mouths had visibly multiplied beyond the meat.[30]

To relate these arguments to modern times we can quote Monsieur Pierre Trudeau, the Prime Minister of Canada, who recognized the threat posed by over-population elsewhere to a country itself by no means over-populated and rich in resources of many kinds:

We must recognize that, in the long run, the overwhelming threat to Canada will not come from foreign investments, or foreign ideologies, or even—with good fortune—foreign nuclear weapons. It will come instead from the two-thirds of the peoples of the world who are steadily falling farther and farther behind in their search for a decent standard of living. This is the meaning of the revolution of rising expectations. I repeat, this problem is not new. But its very size, involving some $2\frac{1}{2}$ billion people, makes it qualitatively different from what it has been in the past ...[31]

[30] Robertson, JM (1912) *The Evolution of States* (p 270).
[31] FAO Review, *Ceres*, Vol 1 No 5, September/October, 1968 (p 14).

Studies by the US Defense Department have shown that there is a striking correlation between poverty and violence in contemporary society. Mr Robert MacNamara, the US Secretary for Defense, speaking in Quebec on May 18, 1966, reported the results of this survey[32] covering 164 outbreaks of violence under eighty-two governments.

Figure 7/6 shows the outcome and we see that only 4 per cent of the 'rich' countries (with an income of $750 or more per head per year) were involved in major violence whereas 84 per cent of the very poor countries (income less than $100 per head per year) were in this category.

Fig 7/6

**Poverty and Violence:
Number of major outbreaks of
violence 1958–1966 related to
per capita income**

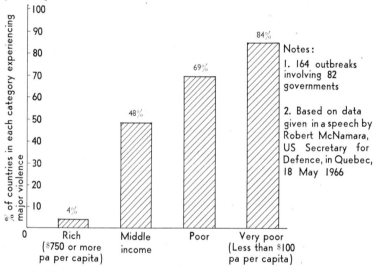

World Bank Income categories (US dollars)

If we want the microfreedom to live in a world free from poverty and violence we must drastically reduce population growth in the very near future and eventually stabilize populations at their optimum level.

[32] The Defense Department declines to publish or supply details of this study but has pointed out in a private communication that an article on this topic in the *New York Times*, May 22, 1966, is 'reasonably accurate'.

Freedom for our descendants. The implications for democratic government

If Thomas Jefferson was right and democracy is government of the people, by the people, and for the people, we need some fairly clear idea of who the 'people' are in order to understand him. The problem of the writer on the population explosion is to persuade the people of today that it will grow into a vastly increased people of tomorrow unless something is done about it. Some constituent members of today's people will be dead, it is true, but many of them will not and the descendants of both quick and dead will combine to generate and comprise the vastly extended people of tomorrow unless we regulate ourselves today so as to prevent it.

The point is that the way we behave now creates the boundary conditions within which those coming later must live. If we allow the country or the world to become grossly over-populated the people of later epochs will not have the freedom to do anything constructive about it.

Translating this into the terminology of majorities and minorities we accept that the majority will rule—provided 'tyranny of the majority' is avoided by institutionalizing basic rights for minorities —and that our political machinery shall enable present minorities to grow, change, and coalesce to form the new majorities of the future and govern in their turn. In conditions of rapid population growth, present-day majorities will become increasingly small minorities in relation to numbers only one or two generations later, so that there is a gross breach of the basic principle of democratic government in that the minority has legislated for the majority in an onerous and irreversible way.

This also violates, in a sense, a cardinal principle of our constitution, the sovereignty of parliament, which stipulates that no parliament shall be bound by the acts of its predecessors. Of course no parliament has passed a law saying 'population will be increased by x millions in the next y years' (though the French Chamber of Deputies has come very near), but all governments are passing laws on migration, differential taxation, housing, family-allowances and so forth, and failing to pass laws making contraceptive information and services and abortion readily available, for instance, which inevitably increase the population. As the Royal Commission pointed out, peoples and governments cannot escape responsibility for their action *or inaction* in this sphere any more than for that which lands their successors in epidemics without health services, economic crises with inadequate resources, or wars without weapons.

In 'pressure-group' terminology we have a society governed under the preponderating influences of a large number of groups competing with each other, in pursuit of their own interests, within a rough framework of Queensberry rules. This *is* democracy and it works tolerably well in most spheres, but the problem with this system, from the population standpoint, is that there are very few pressure groups operating on behalf of the unborn billions of the future.

With the exception of the family planning agencies, only a handful of dedicated scientists, intellectuals, unusually altruistic citizens, and a sprinkling of fanatics, few show any sign of constructive concern.

To illustrate how inequitable this might be let us compare the figures for the 1959 election in Britain and that of the year 2000, about half a lifespan later, assuming the system continues to function in roughly the same way. In 1959 there were 35 million voters and of these $13\frac{3}{4}$ million voted for the winning party, $12\frac{3}{4}$ million for its main rival, 2 million for the also rans, while 7 million stayed at home. This meant that 39 per cent of the voters were governing both themselves and the other 61 per cent, a somewhat inefficient form of democracy as the Liberals and other supporters of proportional representation frequently remind us.

Even if it seems equitable for a minority to govern a majority already one and a half times its size, does it still appear so when it makes decisions which cannot fail to affect in crucial ways the lives of possibly 50 million electors—not to mention 20 million non-electors—of the year 2000, more than $3\frac{1}{2}$ times the majority being governed in 1959?

Clearly governments must continue to govern and make decisions affecting the future, what has gone before is not intended to gainsay this. What *is* implied is that much more foresight must be developed and used so that decisions made now are less likely to be burdensome to, or irreversible by, the citizens of tomorrow. We see awful warning all about us, the results of failure to act or ill-starred decisions of earlier days, the black-hearted cities of the industrial revolution, endless miles of raw suburbs, polluted atmosphere and waterways, disfigured landscapes, ruined coastlines and many others. Let us not fail again, even more crushingly, in the sphere of population.

In practical terms this means that some attention should be given to the small if growing pressure groups endeavouring to speak now on behalf of the potential big battalions of the future. They could be right.

This does not relate to an entirely new and possibly fantastical sounding principle of government. We already accept—albeit in a bumbling and half-hearted sort of way—the idea that posterity has certain rightful demands, that in some way we are accountable to our successors for our stewardship of the nation's resources at least, and possibly even world resources too. We are also aware to some extent in some spheres that the future will have certain needs which can be met only by action initiated much earlier. For instance, the course of the 'bulge' in births in 1946/7 was plotted with some care if much ballyhoo. Nothing like enough was done to provide the necessary schools and teachers but the responsibility was to some extent recognized and some sort of provision was attempted.

The nationalized electricity supply industry, for example, has to work in the framework of the future to quite a considerable extent because the 'lead-time'—the time which must elapse between the initiation and completion of a new power station—is seven years. At the time of writing the Electricity Generating Board is responsible in an immediate and practical way not merely to the consumers of 1971 but to those of 1978 and beyond and things will be made hot for them indeed, if they fall down on the job.

What democrats must now do is take hold of this principle and comprehend, develop, preach, and practise it in ways hitherto not thought of. If they fail to do this democracy will surely perish and the frightful force of an exploding population could well prove to be the agency for its destruction.

Summary

Evidence has been presented that larger populations create a disproportionately greater complexity and require more control and of course this applies all the more as they are increasingly crowded together because of limitations of physical space. However, the converse is not necessarily true—that the smaller a population becomes the freer are its citizens. Small 'primitive' tribes often have a rigid social code which prescribes behaviour for every possible occasion and most of us have had experience in a small community—possibly a village or small town—in which 'everybody knows everybody's business' so that one's freedom of action is curtailed.

The implication of these facts is not that we should make our whole society or any of its units as small as possible—though we must certainly prevent them from getting too big—but that we should make them the *right* size—in other words work out and realize *optimum* sizes.

We have seen that some microfreedoms are added as numbers increase, while others are diminished, and I have argued that there must come a time when those which are diminishing are the most important ones, the most important one of all being dealt with later under 'ecology of liberty'.

The microfreedoms we gain as size increases are variety, anonymity—and therefore a certain freedom from informal controls—economies of scale in production, up to a point.

All this is at the cost of a continually increasing pressure on the social system and the environment, acting, as Clark stresses, as a force towards social and technological change, though without any guarantee that the change will be in a beneficial direction.[33]

Microfreedoms totally lost or diminished to some degree include freedom from undue control and bureaucracy, freedom from relative poverty, freedom from care about shortages of raw materials, including food—especially important to us here in Britain as we have to import half of what we consume—freedom to pursue foreign trade, from violence caused by poverty caused in turn by excessive population growth, and so forth.

A lost microfreedom worthy of special stress, as it is almost invariably overlooked, is freedom from co-operation where this is not entered into spontaneously but rendered necessary by external forces. Co-operation of this kind is no less an invasion of our liberty than compulsion, even though we may see its necessity and work together ungrudgingly.

Another worthy of being singled out because it is so widely canvassed and universally believed is that increasing populations are a prerequisite of economic health. This, though true up to a point in some circumstances, is no less untrue in others as pressure

[33] See Mishan, EJ (1967) *The Costs of Economic Growth.*

on resources becomes more acute and '*dis*economies of scale' begin to make themselves felt.

It was argued that if population continues to increase, decision-makers now—including voting majorities—will be only a small minority compared with later numbers but they will nevertheless, by their actions and inaction, have legislated for them in possibly extremely repressive ways, grossly limiting their freedom of action in bringing about the type of society they would like to enjoy, unless by some chance what they want is overcrowding and bureaucracy, shortage of raw materials, strict rationing of all amenities, poverty—absolute or relative—and, possibly, violence.

We must as an elementary matter of survival learn and practise the idea that democracy in the fullest sense, i e the system which provides maximum liberty of the individual, coupled with individual responsibility for the actions of government and the state of society, is extended in time as well as in space and that numbers are of the essence—they must be limited at some stage if liberty is to be maximized.

Chapter 8

The law of liberty

The end of law is not to abolish or restrain but to preserve and enlarge freedom: for in all states of created beings capable of laws: where there is no law there is no freedom.

John Locke[1]

With respect to population control and the law there appear to be four regions of interest.

1. The relationship between law and individual liberty in general.
2. The nature of rights and duties.
3. Existing legal regulation of sexual behaviour.
4. Existing legal concepts possibly adaptable to population control.

However, before these are dealt with four general points must be made. The first is that the law is a complex study with a history as old as civilization and a vast body of knowledge, empirical, theoretical, and normative, and it would be presumptuous in the extreme for an outsider to claim to understand it, let alone lay down the law either to lawyers or to future generations. Nonetheless the legal aspects of liberty in general and fertility control in particular are so important and so inextricably interwoven with the interests of social scientists, philosophers, practical politicians, and the man in the street, that it seems legitimate to try to untangle some of the threads and identify some of the more important questions which society, with the aid of its legal experts, may be called upon to answer.

The second point is that the law, if it is to be useful and respected, must be related to practicalities; it is pointless either to

[1] (1690) *Second Treatise of Civil Government* (Bk 2, Ch. 6, para. 57).

prescribe or proscribe the impossible. In this particular question of fertility control it would be quite useless for the law of England or any other authority to grant complete freedom of procreation to all people at all times, because the Earth is finite. The only situation in which this would be meaningful is one in which constraints in addition to the legal ones are operating, within or on individuals, and preventing sufficient numbers from procreating to allow room for the remainder to exercise to the full their lawful powers in this direction. Though the law may sometimes be an ass it is generally firmly rooted in reality and does not legislate for a dream world in which all things are possible.

The third point is that population has never been controlled by law in any direct way in advanced societies although some legislation has been designed to achieve demographic goals—family allowances to stimulate fertility, for example—and a good deal more has had unintended demographic consequences. A deliberate and explicit policy of bringing about a population which is stationary somewhere near a defined optimum level will therefore be a significant innovation.

The fourth and final point is that though the law in Britain does not at present and has not in the past regulated fertility it is in no sense fixed for all time but evolves in the same way as society as a whole.

The origins of law

The three main types of law are:

1. 'Divine' law,
2. 'Natural' law,
3. 'Positive' law.

Obviously the origin of divine law is in some supernatural being—God in the case of Christians, Jews, and Muslims—which provides inspiration, authority, and a test of the legitimacy of man-made laws.

Divine law is not dealt with here as it does not normally play a part in legal discussions; the majority of Christians see nothing wrong with birth control, the great bulk of Roman Catholics, even, practise methods condemned by the hierarchy—even the most orthodox accept some forms—and many are coming round to population control proper. There is sanction in the Bible for controlling numbers as well as an injunction to 'increase and multiply', the instruction to 'fill the earth' obviously set Christians a finite task, and a recent pope has even decreed that: '... it is certain that public authorities can intervene. ...'[2] in population problems.

Even if there were an explicit and inescapable order from God that the highest possible form of devotion is to continue producing as many children as possible, regardless of the situation or the consequences, it would make little difference as there is not much in the way of precedent—martyrs always excluded—for actually carrying out the higher spiritual duties imposed by the Christian religion when they conflict with expediency.

Liberty and law

The status of liberty under the law depends on which philosophy of law is favoured, the 'naturalistic' or the 'positivist'. These two main schools of thought are very different and fundamentally opposed to each other on the origin and validity of law, other than divine law, the essence of the difference being that sometimes asserted between 'justice' and 'legality'.

The naturalistic school is the older of the two, being as old as law itself. In embryo, in the folkways of ancient tribes, it probably long preceded any coherent notion of law. Natural law evolved and became more explicit with the development of western civilization and was influenced by the Christian religion, of which it became one of the pillars.

The first clear statement of the distinction between the two is attributed to the English philosopher, Thomas Hobbes, writing in the seventeenth century:

> Another division of lawes is into *Naturall* and *Positive*. Naturall are those which have been Lawes from all Eternity; and are called ... also *Morall* Laws; consisting in the Morall vertues, as Justice, Equity, and all the habits of mind that conduce to Peace and Charity ...
>
> Positive are those which have not been from Eternity; but have been made Lawes by those that have had the Soveraign Power over others ...[3]

---

[2] Paul VI (1967) *Populorum Progressio* (para 37). See p 136 for further discussion.

[3] Hobbes (1651) *Leviathan*. Everyman's edition (p 140).

Lawes are the Rules of Just and Unjust, nothing being reputed Unjust, that is not contrary to some Law ...

... none can make Lawes but the Common wealth: ...[4] and

... *the liberties of subjects depend on the silence of the law.*[5] (Italics added)

The Sovereignty of Parliament

One expression of the doctrine of legal positivism is in the principle of the sovereignty of Parliament. The great authority Blackstone said in his 'Commentaries...'

The power and jurisdiction of Parliament, says Sir Edward Coke, is so transcendent and absolute, that it cannot be confined either for causes or persons, within any bounds. ...

It hath sovereign and uncontrollable authority in the making, confirming, enlarging, restraining, abrogating, repealing, reviving, and expounding of laws, concerning matters of all possible denominations, ecclesiastical or temporal, civil, military, maritime, or criminal:...

All mischiefs and grievances, operations and remedies that transcend the ordinary course of the laws, are within the reach of this extraordinary tribunal. It can regulate or new-model the succession to the Crown; ... It can alter the established religion ... It can change and create afresh even the constitution of the kingdom and of parliaments themselves: ... It can, in short, do everything that is not naturally impossible: ...[6]

In Britain we feel so strongly that there are certain bounds beyond which the law must not step that it is as well for Blackstone that in addition to lauding the limitless powers of Parliament he also wrote:

No human laws are of any validity if contrary to the law of nature; and such of them as are valid derive all their force and ... authority mediately or immediately from this original.[7]

In spite of the forcefulness of these assertions of the sovereignty of Parliament they are little better than legal fictions; in sociological

[4] *Ibid.*   [5] *Ibid* (p 151).

[6] (1765/9). *Commentaries on the Laws of England.* Dicey supports this view. (*Op cit*) (pp 37/38).

[7] Quoted in Wedgewood, JC (1940) *Forever Freedom* (p 119).

terms these are the 'formal' powers of Parliament. According to the book, as it were, Parliament can pass any law whatever, but the social facts of opinion, tradition, and so on—the 'informal' controls in our society—restrain its legislative activities fairly rigorously in most cases though as we have recently seen in the case of capital punishment, Parliament can legislate in a way which is out of keeping[8] with the great body of public opinion.

If, on the other hand, Parliament attempted to legislate so as to raise income tax to 50 per cent, to forbid people to buy their own houses, to compel everyone between the ages of twenty and twenty-five to emigrate, or make everyone over seventy submit to euthanasia, there would be such a cry of protest as would bring down not only the government, but probably—for the second time—the Palace of Westminster itself.

It follows directly from these legal dicta and the sociological gloss put on them, that there is no legal or constitutional difficulty about legislating for fertility control in Britain though there could be practical, i e political, snags. If a law were to be passed it would be a perfectly good law and should be enforced by the courts.

To most laymen in the West, however, the positivist view is repugnant. In Britain, in particular, we feel that our liberty does not stem from the law but in some sense precedes it. So strong is our conviction that some of our liberties are inalienable that if a law which attempted to take them away was passed we feel we would have not only a right but a duty to break it, or at least force its repeal. Examples of such constituents of our individual liberty are freedom of speech, religion, and assembly, and from arbitrary arrest or imprisonment. It has been said that the price of liberty is eternal vigilance and we guard these particular liberties jealously indeed, though not so much that we are not prepared to relinquish them temporarily—or in some areas permanently—for a good cause, such as national security, especially in time of war. This, basically, is the 'natural law' approach.

Rousseau wrote:

> ... If natural law were written only on the tablets of human reason it would be incapable of guiding the greater part of our action; but it is also graven on the heart of man in characters

---

[8] Some, the present writer included, would say in advance of public opinion.

that cannot be effaced, and it is there that it speaks to him more strongly than all the precepts of the philosophers . . .[9]

According to one authority, J. Roland Pennock,[10] and in somewhat less passionate terms, natural law is:

> . . . The law peculiar to rational beings . . . made evident to them by their reason.

Either by holding, with Plato, that:

> . . . Reason in its highest form includes the faculty of perceiving *a priori* truth, of direct insight into the eternal verities. . . . [or] . . .

> . . . By deriving it from the physical and psychological nature of man and especially from observed *tendencies* of human nature. Just as it is the nature of an acorn to become an oak tree, so it is the nature of man to develop wisdom and virtue, . . .

A third school of thought on the origin and legitimacy of natural law is the *empirical*, involving the possibility of finding out by experience:

> . . . Certain rules of conduct that lead to the most satisfactory life, or the most happy and harmonious society, . . .

A fourth possible source of natural law for many theologians, who have identified it with the law of God, is revelation, the source of divine law.

As there are many schools of thought about the origin of law, even of natural law, so there are great divergencies of opinion on its content. Pennock puts forward the following propositions:

1. Human life is to be protected and forwarded.
2. No one should injure another.
3. All men are born free and equal.

He says that modern thought tends to boil this 'age old formula' down to the contention that:

> . . . There is a presumption in favour of freedom, and likewise of equality. In other words, any infringement on man's freedom or equality must be justified.

[9] 'The State of Law', an unfinished essay referred to in Everyman's edition of *The Social Contract*.
[10] In Gould and Kolb (eds) (1964) *Dictionary of Social Sciences*.

To the central question regarding natural law in this context—whether it sanctions unlimited procreation—the answer appears to be no. Although it is hard to prove a negative case, none of the historical discussions on natural law examined by the present writer have stated that this is an essential ingredient of individual liberty, with one important exception, possibly, that of the Roman Catholic Church.

The well known Roman Catholic apologist, the Rt Hon Norman St John-Stevas, MP, has expressed the position as follows:

> Scriptural texts apart, the Roman Catholic Church has based its condemnation of contraception on the natural law. The nub of the Roman Catholic position is contained in canon law, where it is stated that the primary end of marriage is the procreation and education of children.[11] Pius XI, in his encyclical on Christian Marriage, stressed the 'unnatural' character of contraception: since therefore the conjugal act is destined primarily by nature for the begetting of children, those who in exercising it deliberately frustrate its natural power and purpose, sin against nature and commit a deed which is shameful and intrinsically vicious.[12]
>
> The Pope thus restated the traditional teaching of the Roman Catholic Church, basing his pronouncement on the doctrine elaborated by St Thomas Aquinas.
>
> The Roman Catholic natural law tradition accepts as self-evident that the primary purpose of sexual intercourse is procreation and relegates as secondary such ends as fostering the mutual love of the spouses and allaying concupiscence. This conclusion is based on two propositions—that man by the use of his reason can discover God's purpose in the universe, and that God makes known his purpose by certain 'given' physical arrangements.[13]

The Roman Church seems to be the sole repository of this interpretation of the natural law tradition and the behaviour[14] of the great bulk of Roman Catholics, coupled with the demographic, political, social, moral, and theological pressures on that institution,

[11] Canon 1031.1.

[12] Pius XI, *Casti connubii—On Christian Marriage* (*Encyclical No 4, December 31, 1930*).

[13] St John-Stevas, N, 'A Roman Catholic View of Population Control' in *Law and Contemporary Problems,* Vol XXV, No 3, Summer, 1960 (p 446).

[14] In using forbidden forms of birth control.

seem likely to demolish this redoubt in the very near future.[15] If this turns out to be the case there should be little opposition from the natural law camp to the necessary fertility control of the future.

To return to the more general question, that of law and individual liberty, the concensus appears to be that there are few or no absolutes under the law and that individual liberty is the resultant of a complex interaction of historical precedents, legal principles, public policy, public opinion, commonsense, and practical necessity, as the following case illustrates very well.

A modern compromise

In a recent work called *Freedom, the Individual and the Law*, Harry Street—a libertarian concerned to define and preserve our traditional individual liberties—puts this point, the relativity of law and liberty, very well.

> ... Any evaluation of the limits on our liberties must always balance the competing interests at stake.[16]

This is in keeping with what the present writer believes to be the great tradition of liberty as expressed by John Stuart Mill and many others, that liberty is a question of judgment, balance, and mutuality, generated and exercised only within a social context.

> As soon as any part of a person's conduct affects prejudicially the interests of others, society has jurisdiction over it, and the question of whether the general welfare will or will not be promoted by interfering with it, becomes open to discussion ...

Street analyses the case of the reporters Foster and Mulholland, prosecuted in 1963 for refusing to disclose sources of confidential information concerning state security which they had used as a basis for articles in the press, and comments:

> The press ... used all its power to protest ... it ... made telling points ... contrasting the privilege of solicitors with the rightlessness of journalists; it ... represented the affair as an interference in the freedom of the press and as another triumph for bureaucracy against the individual. Against all this other factors must be weighed. ...
> ... In some circumstances closely and directly affecting

[15] See the attack mounted by Cardinal Leger (referred to on p 13).
[16] (1966) (p 19).

national security the need for a court to know the source of a journalist's information in order to test for possible leaks in our security outweighs the freedom of a journalist not to reveal the sources of his news. This is how English law goes about its job of defining limits on our freedoms....

... Whenever such a prohibition is made, the reason will be that some other interest is rated more important than that freedom on which it impinges. The reader will make up his own mind as he progresses whether the line has always been drawn at the right point, ...[17] (Italics added)

Rights and duties

Our understanding of human rights must be conditioned by our leaning towards either the natural or positive origin of law. Jeremy Bentham, the great utilitarian philosopher, was perhaps one of the most forceful advocates of the positivist view:

... Right is the child of law; from real laws come real rights, but from imaginary law, from 'laws of nature' come imaginary rights....

... Natural rights is simple nonsense, natural and imprescriptable rights, ... nonsense upon stilts.[18]

Whatever the orientation in positivist or naturalistic terms the great bulk of writing on this theme both historical and modern has stressed the rights of the individual to the exclusion of virtually everything else. The underlying philosophy seems to be that rights can be conjured up out of thin air or, at least, if they cannot be so produced, then the government or some other outside entity must generate and guarantee them. It is 'they' who must guarantee 'our' rights, a distinctly lopsided understanding of the problem.

The notion of rights has meaning only in a social context. We cannot have rights against our environment or against forces produced inside our own persons by the interaction of our heredity and past choices and environments, which may now limit our freedom. Rights and duties are two halves of the same equation and this has meaning only in social contexts. A's rights are produced by B's duties, and only by those duties, and vice versa. In a

[17] (*Op cit*) (pp 9/10).
[18] Anarchical Fallacies, Being an Examination of the Declaration of Rights issued during the French Revolution. *Works*, (1843) Vol II.

context in which nobody has any duties, nobody can have rights, as we saw in the sociological discussion of liberty.

F. Cottrell has written of the USA:

> ... our people are taught that they have 'inalienable rights' but not 'unavoidable duties' which are the concomitants of those rights ... but ... those rights must be alienable because they are not enjoyed by most men in the world ... we ourselves have come to enjoy them only as we have ... sufficient power. ... [19]

The French Revolution provides a good example of the one-sidedness of much thinking in this field. The National Assembly published in 1793 a *Declaration of the Rights of Man and of Citizens* which listed seventeen rights of the citizen against the state but paid no attention to his duties. This omission was repaired to some degree by the new *Declaration of Rights and Duties* in 1795 to which had been added a charter of nine 'Duties'. Herman Finer, the political scientist, comments that these duties were:

> The indispensible basis of the rights if these were to be more than paper promises, but [they] fell with a leaden weight after the optimism of the earlier years. [20]

The generous minded Tom Paine thought the addition unnecessary, as:

> A Declaration of Rights is also, by reciprocity, a declaration of duties. Whatever is my right ... is also the right of another; and it becomes my duty to guarantee as well as to possess. [21]

However, in modern democratic societies, the great majority of us seem to want the first without the second.

Universal Declaration of Human Rights

The General Assembly of the UN proclaimed the *Universal Declaration of Human Rights* in 1948 as:

> ... a common standard of achievement for all peoples and all nations to the end that every individual and every organ of society, keeping this Declaration constantly in mind, shall strive ... to promote respect for these rights and freedoms and by

[19] Cottrell, F (1966) *The Future of Freedom* (p 10).
[20] (1950) *The Theory and Practice of Modern Government* (p 14).
[21] (1791) *Rights of Man*, Everyman's edition (p 98).

progressive measures, national and international, to secure their universal and effective recognition and observance, . . .

Article 1 stated :

All human beings are born free and equal in dignity and rights. They are endowed with reason and conscience and should act towards one another in a spirit of brotherhood.

Though the motives behind these activities were no doubt praise-worthy their value is greatly undermined by a marked lack of realism. The first part of this article is manifestly untrue as F. Cottrell pointed out. Many human beings are not born 'free and equal in dignity', nor yet do they all have the same 'rights'. The great majority of mankind is condemned by accident of birth to a kind of slavery to hardship, poverty, hunger, illiteracy, and many other deprivations. The second part of Article 1 is more reasonable in that it recognizes that we '*should* act towards one another in a spirit of brotherhood'—it is aspiration rather than assertion. But even here the first part of the second sentence is only tenuously related to biological and social reality. Judged by the record, our endow-ment with reason is somewhat niggardly and if our conscience is measured by a practical index, such as the amount of our resources we of the wealthy societies devote to foreign aid, it is seen to be almost vanishingly small.

These are noble aspirations but surely it would be better to direct such exhortations towards the setting up of societies in which human beings really can be born 'free and equal in dignity and rights' and these must be societies which are in balance with their environment and each other—they must be societies which are not over-populated and consequently competing unduly for the scarce necessities of life.

It is pleasing to be able to report that the *Universal Declaration of Human Rights* is not completely unrealistic; it does wind up with a short section on the duties which must be borne in order to generate the catalogue of rights with which the Declaration largely concerns itself.

Article 29 (1)   Everyone has duties to the community in which alone the free and full development of his personality is possible.

(2)   In the exercise of his rights and freedoms, everyone shall be subject only to such limitations as are determined by law solely for the purpose of securing due recognition and a respect

for the rights and freedoms of others and of meeting the just requirements of morality, public order and the general welfare in a democratic society.

It is very striking that the rights part of the rights/duties equation is spelled out in such detail, whereas the duties part merits only a short postscript. Nonetheless this clause does recognize the limitations on individual liberty required by the process of '... securing due recognition and respect for the rights and freedoms of others ...', and, equally importantly, '... of meeting the just requirements of morality, public order, and the general welfare ...'

The right to procreate

Our response to a question on this topic would be automatic. Of course we have the right to procreate, otherwise the species would disappear in a century or so apart, possibly, from a handful of yoghurt-fortified Georgians. This cannot be in dispute but it is legitimate to call into question whether this right is absolute.

The *Universal Declaration of Human Rights*, already referred to, states in article 16 (1):

> Men and women of full age, ... have the right to marry and to found a family. ...[22]

It is interesting to see that while the right to reproduce without marriage is not granted or recommended, no limits are set, upper or lower, in the much more fundamental area of *amount* of reproduction and there is no reference to the needs of the existing family, if any, or of society as a whole, or to encourage *responsible* parenthood.

Clause (3) under article 16 says:

> The family is the natural and fundamental group unit of society and is entitled to protection by society and the state.

Article 25 asserts in clause (1):

> Everyone has the right to a standard of living adequate for the health and well being of himself and his family including food, clothing, housing and medical care and necessary social services, ...

[22] The Royal Commission on Population also accepted this principle.

and in clause (2):

> Motherhood and childhood are entitled to special care and assistance. All children, whether born in or out of wedlock, shall enjoy the same social protection.

It is interesting to observe that these rights are unconditional and state no corresponding duties. Article 25 appears to grant people the right to have more children than they can possibly cope with and then demand of the state, that is to say their fellow citizens, the duty of carrying the burdens they have irresponsibly produced. In 1968 U Thant said:

> The *Universal Declaration of Human Rights* describes the family as the natural and fundamental unit of society. It follows that any choice and decision with regard to the size of the family must irrevocably rest within the family itself, and cannot be made by anyone else.[23]

The *Declaration on Social Progress and Development,* adopted by the General Assembly on December 11, 1969, asserted:

> Parents have the *exclusive* right to determine freely and responsibly the number and spacing of their children (Article 4). (Italics added)

The word 'responsibly' occurs here but so do the words 'exclusive right'.

It is understandable that the IPPF and other worthy bodies came to adopt the stance indicated by U Thant in order to counter the sabotage in international bodies of discussion of, and dissemination of information about, birth control, by the Communists and the Roman Catholics. The momentum generated seems to be carrying them too far, however, and causing the baby to be thrown out with the bath water. This gross error must surely be put right; what appears to be needed is some force to redress the balance and hammer home the reciprocity of rights and duties and the emptiness of the gesture of 'guaranteeing' rights which are physically impossible of fulfilment. What we need is a Universal Declaration of Human Responsibilities and Duties.[24]

---

[23] *International Planned Parenthood Federation News,* No 168, February, 1968 (p 3).
[24] A resolution adopted by the Economic and Social Council of the UN at the 1673rd plenary meeting on April 3, 1970, read:

Incredibly enough a pronouncement on this topic by a recent pope was more realistic, although it also illustrated a conflict between incompatible rights and the agonized moral state of the Roman Catholic church. Paul VI wrote, in *Populorum Progressio*:

> *Where the inalienable right to marriage and procreation is lacking human dignity has ceased to exist....* In all this they (the parents) must follow the demands of their own conscience, enlightened by God's law authentically interpreted, and sustained by confidence in Him. (Italics added) (para 37)

Having granted this virtually unqualified right to parents, potential and actual, Pope Paul granted an equally potent but incompatible right to governments to regulate fertility:

> It is true that too frequently accelerated increase in population adds its own difficulties to the problems of development; the size of the population increases more rapidly than available resources, and things are found to have reached...an impasse...

and:

> *...It is certain that public authorities can intervene,* within the limit of their competence, by favouring the availability of appropriate information, by adopting suitable measures, provided that these be in conformity with the moral law and that they respect the rightful freedom of married couples...[25] (Italics added)

President Nixon, following President Johnson, is very concerned about over-population in the USA. He has been bluntly told by Garett Hardin, a distinguished biologist, that in the long run 'voluntary birth control is insanity...the result will be uncontrolled population growth.[26]

...efforts...to promote long term economic and social development...could be frustrated by...present high rates of population growth...
...national policies aimed at the achievement of more desirable rates of population growth and at the *acceptance by parents on a voluntary basis of smaller families* should be regarded as among the essential aspects of development strategy...

Reported *UN Population Newsletter* No 8, March, 1970 (p 26).
[25] 1967.
[26] Quotation as reported in the *The Guardian*, September 22, 1969. Professor Hardin has developed this argument at length in: 'The Tragedy of the Commons', *Science*, December 13, 1968.

In other words, if Professor Hardin is right, if it is left to individual consciences, as Pope Paul exhorted, the result will be catastrophe, and the right of government to intervene must have substance; it is hard to envisage what possible form, effect, or value it could have without infringing this alleged inviolable right of parents. The only bridge between these two extreme positions seems to be the somewhat remote possibility that all individuals would acquire such perfect knowledge, understanding, and conscientiousness that all their decisions—or at least a sufficient majority of them—would be in the interests of society as a whole.[27] If: 'population increases more rapidly than ... resources [and] things ... have reached ... an impasse', what possible intervention can the public authorities make which will not infringe or restrain in some way the 'inalienable right to ... procreation ... ?'

Even this equivocal assertion of the right of society to have a say in decisions on parenthood is totally rejected by many leading spokesmen for the Roman Church. For example, Dr Heenan, Archbishop of Westminster:

> If a man and woman decide to have ten children what business can it possibly be of yours or anyone else's?[28]

Even if the Vatican takes Pope Paul's tentative proposals to their logical conclusion there will be much opposition within the hierarchy.

In the historical avalanche of words on rights without duties the writings of the pious Mazzini strike a lonely chord:

> ... all your rights are summed up in one: *the right to be absolutely unfettered and to be aided within certain limits, in the fulfilment of your duties.*[29]

Your liberty will flourish, protected by God and men, so long

[27] Herbert Spencer thought that biosocial evolution would eventually produce the 'ultimate' man:

... who will be one whose private requirements coincide with public ones. He will be that manner of man who, in spontaneously fulfilling his own nature, incidentally performs the functions of a social unit; and yet is only enabled so to fulfil his own nature by all others doing the like.

The word to emphasize here is 'eventually'. Quoted in Elliot, H (1917) *Herbert Spencer* (p 180).

[28] On being interviewed in a teenage forum. BBC Home Service, December, 1963.

[29] (1907) (tr) *The Duties of Man.* Everyman edition (p 68).

as you regard it ... as the right to *choose freely and according to your special tendencies a means of doing good*.[30] (All italics original)

Four of Mazzini's twelve chapters deal solely with duties; to 'Humanity'—the most important one of all—to 'Country', 'Family', and to 'Yourself', respectively, and much of the material in the other chapters is on the same theme. A twentieth century Mazzini, if perhaps a trifle one-sided, would be a useful counterbalance to the steady spate of words about our rights with scarcely a syllable about our duties.[31]

In a democracy the aim should be to have mutuality of rights and duties where possible and equity where it is not; that is to say that A and B owe and enjoy the same duties and rights to and from each other. Of course not all relationships can have this simple symmetry, policemen have more rights for arresting citizens than vice versa, government and local authorities have the right to exact taxation which citizens do not. However, the citizen has the right to demand many services in kind for which his taxes have helped to pay, collection of his refuse, schools for his children, parks, museums, and so forth.

The essential point is that rights and duties are inextricably inter-linked, A enjoys his rights only insofar as B carries out his duties, and vice versa. In a democratic society, in order to persuade B to carry out his duties A must grant to him the same rights, which means undertaking similar duties. However, it is no use A and B granting each other symmetrical rights which in the long run are impossible of fulfilment, as we try to do at the moment in the sphere of procreation.

Generally speaking, the more symmetrical are these rights and duties the more democratic a society will be, but even in the case of a very unsymmetrical relationship, such as slavery, there are still rights and duties on both sides. The most overbearing slave-master has the duties of providing his slaves with enough food and shelter to keep them alive, at least.

[30] (*Op cit*) (p 82).
[31] Canon Hugh Montefiore, Bishop Designate of Kingston-upon-Hull, speaking to the Anglican Church Assembly in February, 1970, condemned the assumption that people '... have a right to have as many children as they wish. The Church should challenge this ...'
The Bishop of Norwich also condemned the selfishness of large families.

Existing regulation of sexual relations

Since procreation is the result of sexual intercourse[32] then population control by means of the regulation of fertility—there are other ways, as we have seen—involves regulation of the sex act, or its outcome, at least, which many seem to find unacceptable. For this reason it may be useful to draw attention to the numerous ways in which our society, in common with all others in their very different ways, already regulates our behaviour in this sphere.

Sexual urges and their expression are a matter of primary concern to the agencies of the law and their servants as we saw when dealing with the explosive power of sex in Chapter 2. Indeed it might not be unfair to say that the law at this time and place suffers from an obsession with sexual matters, though there are signs that a healthier attitude is beginning to hold sway. Welcome though the latter is most of us would agree that sexual urges—leaving aside population control for the moment—cannot be allowed completely free expression, at the present stage of our biocultural evolution, at any rate. This leaves us with an acceptance of the principle of sexual regulation and in Britain at the present time we exercise this in no uncertain way.

In the first place we not only regulate stringently actual sexual behaviour—although there has been a considerable loosening-up lately—we still restrict communication on sexual themes in many ways, in speech and gesture, in writing, drama, the plastic arts, photography, films, and other fields and few take it amiss.

In the second place we regulate sexual intercourse between humans and other species though this is acceptable in some other cultures. Bestiality is one of the deadliest crimes in the book, although it is hard to see what tangible harm it could do.

Until recently we regulated the sex of participants in sexual acts; one male and one female was the partnership required by law, two females being tacitly acceptable, while two males were strictly taboo. Though male homosexuality is now permitted, the circumstances and details of the age, venue, and number of the participants are still strictly regulated.[33]

The potential sexual aspects of clothing are strictly regulated, topless dresses did not come 'in' because they were forbidden,

---

[32] Strictly speaking, of course, this is not always true. We already have artificial insemination and may one day arrive in Brave New World.
[33] Sexual Offences Act, 1967, Ch 60, for example.

though they are the norm in many other cultures, and failure to cover up certain portions of the anatomy can lead to prosecution of males, not females, for 'indecent exposure', whether or not any harm is done.

The law lets a man have only one wife and specifies her minimum age at marriage, forbids us to have children without notifying the State, or to prevent an unwanted birth by means of induced abortion, except in State-approved clinics for State-approved reasons.

The law also regulates sexual behaviour even in the matrimonial chamber, defining conjugal rights, forbidding some forms of intercourse (sodomy), deciding whether a marriage has been consummated or not, whether the sexual behaviour of one of the partners constitutes cruelty and affords grounds for divorce, what the male may do with his semen (in the sphere of artificial insemination), not to mention sitting in judgment over extra-marital sexual expression.

It also forbids many treatments of sex as a commodity while permitting its flagrant exploitation in other spheres. A woman may not politely offer her services for profit in public places, a male may not live off a woman's 'immoral' earnings however fond they are of each other or whatever the circumstances, and no one may run a brothel no matter how well or how great the need.

It forbids most sexual relations among relatives, arbitrarily defining the permissible degree of consanguinity or kinship much more remotely than many other cultures—even forbidding a widower to marry his former wife's sister.

Before prospective adoptive parents can acquire a child they must pass through an extremely onerous selection process and as a rule wait a considerable time into the bargain—often longer than it would take to bear one in the ordinary way.* The irony of this is that people who are so unsuitable as parents that they would not stand a chance of getting a child from an agency can have twenty of their own, provided only that they have the requisite biological equipment. In addition our society condemns well over a million

---

* This assertion was subsequently strikingly borne out by the 18 month struggle by Hilary and David Chambers—parents admirably qualified in every conceivable way—to adopt a coloured baby (for whom there is a great shortage of adoptive parents) in London, which probably has the best supply of potential adoptees in this category in the whole country. See their article 'Hard to place' in *The Listener*, March 4, 1971.

children to live in poverty[34] and squalor, even singling out for especially harsh treatment some of the poorest of the poor by the application of the wage-stop.[35]

If this list is not formidable enough the law has given its servants the power—as we saw so dramatically illustrated in Jeremy Sandford's *Cathy Come Home*—to take a child by force from the arms of its mother and father and put it into an institution even though the mother and father have done nothing wrong, are duly married, and doing their level best—albeit in unfortunate circumstances—and the members of the family love and need each other. Compared with powers like these, preventing surplus births in an overcrowded island such as ours seems a paltry thing.

There is nothing inherently different about sexual behaviour which renders it an improper or otherwise unsuitable sphere for legislation or other forms of control.

Legal concepts ready made for population control

If it is true that harm could come to a society through the exhaustion of natural resources, pollution of the environment, stress, poverty, hunger, and violence, because of over-population, could the law have anything to say about it? Although the law is not at present, and, as it stands, probably could not be used for the purpose of population control, there seems little reason to doubt that the potential is there. The positivist answer would be simply to extend the criminal law and make it an offence to have children without a permit or more than the permitted total, say, four. Another approach, however, might be to take existing legal concepts and principles and extend them by new interpretations, developing their inherent logic and meaning to apply to new social situations, in accordance with time-honoured practice. Let us examine the potential of some of these concepts, italicized for identification, to a situation requiring the introduction of fertility control.

Over-population is produced by excessive procreation and this results from two causes. The first of these is having more children

---

[34] In 1966 345,000 families with 1.1 million children had initial resources below supplementary benefit level. HMSO (1967) *Circumstances of Families* (p 80).

[35] Some 25,000 families with probably more than 75,000 children were 'wage-stopped' in December, 1967. See White Paper *Administration of the Wage Stop*, HMSO, December 4, 1967 and *The Guardian*, December 5, 1967.

than necessary as a result of a deliberate choice—or at least a choice not to take contraceptive precautions—coupled with a conscious willingness to accept the possible consequences. The second cause is failure to take precautions because of irresponsibility or carelessness, or having taken precautions which failed. This makes three possible reasons for pregnancy; choice, irresponsibility, and failure of precautions.

In the case of the first two of the possibilities we can ask whether the concept *duty of care* could be extended to apply to the sexual act—whether we have a duty to our fellow citizens not to produce too many children. In the case of the last mentioned, a birth due to faulty precautions, the relevance of the related concepts *standard of care* and *negligence* could be considered. How careful were the parents, did their behaviour at the material time constitute *negligence*, are they liable for any *damage* done by the birth?

These questions raise further issues, those of *foreseeability*, the *remoteness* of the consequences of the act producing the birth, and *natural consequences*. Could potential parents as reasonable as 'the man on the Clapham omnibus' be expected to foresee that excessive fertility constitutes a danger to society, or, knowing that it does, that their contribution will make a significant difference. The answers appear to be that any reasonably educated and intelligent person should know by now of the danger from over-population, that practically everyone should soon be in this position, and that the causal chain is very clear. Irresponsible or careless intercourse leading to the birth of an unwanted or otherwise surplus child, creates a need for extra space, raw materials, and social services, and causes a worsened balance of payments, to mention only a few of the consequences.

The *quantum of damage* caused can be given a fairly precise price tag by means of a straightforward manipulation of existing economic concepts, for example, cost of congestion, diseconomies of scale, and the demographic investment.[36]

Questions which arise also are whether sexual intercourse is or could be a '*dangerous activity*' in the eyes of the law insofar as it tends to lead to over-population, and/or, are human infants '*dangerous things*'. Stated thus, both questions seem ludicrous but the fact is that very innocent looking things can be extremely dangerous in some contexts as many parents discover to their cost.

[36] The amount of investment consumed by a rising population in the prevention of a decline in per capita wealth. Dealt with in Ch 7.

A child may kill itself with a plastic bag, for example, and this fact was recognized in a famous judgment[37] by Lord Justice Scrutton:

> ... I do not understand the difference between a thing dangerous in itself, as poison, and a thing not dangerous as a class, but by negligent construction dangerous as a particular thing. The latter if anything, seems the more dangerous of the two; it is a wolf in sheep's clothing ...

This was borne out in a more recent case in which Lord Singleton approved counsel's argument as follows:

> The true question is not whether a thing is dangerous in itself but whether, by reason of some extraneous circumstances it may become dangerous. There is really no category of dangerous things; there are only some things which require more care and some which require less.[38]

It requires a certain stretch of the imagination to see a dainty, fragrant, atom of humanity lying back in a perambulator cooing and wiggling its toes as a threat to Britain, much less to the world, or an object which could be dangerous in any way, but where the '... extraneous circumstances ...' include eight thousand million other babies lying side by side—about 26 million tons of them—the inexorable physical logic, which the law has clearly recognized and set forth, is made apparent.

These points are raised as questions rather than statements, in the hope that others better qualified will take them up. However, the concept of *nuisance* is discussed at greater length.

Human beings as nuisances

At first sight it is hard to accept that human beings as such can be nuisances; the two words 'human' and 'nuisance' don't seem to go too well together. The *Shorter Oxford Dictionary* defines nuisance as:

> 1. Injury, hurt, harm, annoyance.

and we recognize only too readily that human beings can do things which injure, hurt, or otherwise harm others—in other words they can *become* nuisances, but our normal understanding would be

[37] Hodge and Sons v Anglo American Oil Co (1922), 12 Ll L Rep. 183, 187.
[38] Read v Lyons and Co Ltd (1947) AC 156.

that the activity is the nuisance rather than the human being producing it.

As we begin to open out the debate in this way we see that in some situations human beings can *be* nuisances in some rather more fundamental sense. Under 2b the *Oxford Dictionary* further defines nuisance as:

> Anything obnoxious to the community or individual by ... causing obstruction or damage, etc.

From this we see that humans can be nuisances simply by existing in certain places at certain times. A queue is an obvious example. If you want to buy a newspaper and you find thirty other people with the same intention there already, they are a nuisance to you as obstructions. However valuable they may be as citizens their simple physical presence in front of you at the shop constitutes a nuisance and you wish they were anywhere but there at that moment. This situation is becoming the norm on the roads.

Nuisance under the law

The legal meaning of 'nuisance' is merely an extension of that given in the *Shorter Oxford Dictionary*. One legal dictionary gives this definition:

> Inconvenience materially interfering with the ordinary comfort physically of human existence, not merely according to elegant or dainty notions among the English people ...
>
> A public or common nuisance is an act which interferes with the enjoyment of a right which all members of the community are entitled to, such as the right to fresh air, to travel on the highways, etc. ...
>
> A private nuisance is a tort [wrong] consisting of:
>
> 1. Any wrongful disturbance of an easement or other servitude appurtenant to land;
>
> 2. The act of wrongfully causing or allowing the escape of deleterious things into another person's land: e g water, smoke, smell, fumes, gas, noise, heat, vibrations, electricity, disease germs, animals, and vegetation.
>
> Nuisance is commonly a continuing injury, and ... there must be actual damage to the plaintiff.[39]

[39] Osborn, PG, 1954. *The Concise Law Dictionary*, 4th edn.

In a well-known judgment Lord Wright said:

> The forms which nuisance may take are protean. Certain classifications are possible, but many reported cases are not more than illustrations of particular matters of fact which have been held to be nuisances. . . .
>
> Negligence, moreover, is not a necessary condition for a claim for nuisance. What is done may be done deliberately, and in good faith and in a genuine belief that it is justified. Negligence here is not an independent cause of action but is ancillary to the actual cause of action, which is nuisance . . .

Lord Porter added:

> . . . It is clear that an occupier may be liable though he (1) is wholly blameless, (2) is not only ignorant of the existence of the nuisance but also without the means of detecting it, . . .[40]

Collective versus individual responsibility for nuisance

The law in its wisdom recognizes that activities not harmful in themselves can become so when conjoined with other activities either of a like or different nature, whether or not the person carrying on the first activity is acting with the other person—or even with knowledge of his activity.

The terms used are 'joint' versus 'several' 'tortfeasors'. The 'tort' is simply a wrong—in this case a nuisance—the 'tortfeasor' is the wrongdoer, and 'joint', 'several', and 'concurrent' tortfeasors are the people doing the wrong who may be subject to a joint action for damages. The meanings of 'joint', 'several', and 'concurrent' seem to be so subtle that lawyers themselves are unable to agree and we can leave the nuances to them, provided we note that in the eyes of the law there is no doubt that people doing things adding up to a nuisance are all responsible, no matter how small their individual contribution, as the following cases show.

Lambton v. Mellish and Cox[41]

This is a well-known case in which the plaintiff Lambton com-

---

[40] Sedleigh-Denfield v O'Callaghan. House of Lords (1940) AC 880; (1940) 3 All ER 349; 56 TLR 887. Quoted Wright, CA (1963) *Cases On The Law Of Torts.*

[41] Chancery Division. [1894] 3 Ch 163; 63 LJ Ch 929; 10 TLR 600; 71 LT 385.

plained about noise made by both Mellish and Cox separately, which disturbed his peace and quiet. The case has been reported[42] as follows:

> The defendants Mellish and Cox were rival refreshment contractors who catered for visitors and excursionists [to Ashsted Common in Surrey] ... both ... had merry-go-rounds on their premises, and were in the habit of using organs as an accompaniment to the amusements. ...
>
> ... These organs were for three months or more in the summer continuously being played together from 10 or 11 a m till 6 or 7 p m, ... the noise ... was 'maddening'.
>
> The organs used by Mellish had been changed, and it was alleged by him that the organ (now) in use ... was a small portable hand organ making comparatively little noise. That used by Cox was a much larger one provided with trumpet stops and emitting sounds which could be heard at the distance of one mile.
>
> The plaintiff Lambton had moved separately against each of the defendants for an injunction restraining him from playing these instruments so as to cause '... a nuisance or injury ...' to himself or his family. And the essence of the judgment was as follows.

Mr Justice Chitty said:

> 'I consider that the noise made by each defendant taken separately amounts to a nuisance. But I go further. It was said for the defendant Mellish that two rights cannot make a wrong—by that it was meant that if one man makes a noise not of a kind, duration, or degree sufficient to constitute a nuisance, and another man, not acting in concert with the first, makes a similar noise at the same time, each is responsible only for the noise made by himself, and not also for that noise made by the other. ... It is said that that is only so much the worse for the inhabitant. On the ground of commonsense it must be the other way. *Each of the men is making a noise and each is adding his quantum until the whole constitutes a nuisance. Each* hears the other, and *is adding to the sum which makes up the nuisance.* In my opinion each is separately liable, and I think it would be contrary to good sense, and, indeed, contrary to law, to hold other-

---

[42] Wright, CA (1963) *Cases On The Law Of Torts.*

wise. It would be contrary to common sense that the inhabitants of the house should be left without a remedy at law.' (Italics added)

The learned judge went on to argue that the point fell within the principle laid down by Lord Justice James in *Thorpe v Brumfitt* (1873), 8 Ch 650... a case of obstructing a right of way,... he says:

'Then it was said that the plaintiff alleges an obstruction caused by several persons acting independently of each other, and does not shew what share each had in causing it. It is probably impossible for a person in the plaintiff's position to shew this. Nor do I think it necessary that he should.... The amount of obstruction caused by any one of them might not, if it stood alone, be sufficient to give any ground of complaint, though the amount caused by them all may be a serious injury. Suppose one person leaves a wheelbarrow standing on a way, that may cause no appreciable inconvenience, but if a hundred do so, that may cause a serious inconvenience, which a person entitled to the use of the way has a right to prevent; and it is no defence to any one person among the hundred to say that what he does causes of itself no damage to the complainant.'

Mr Justice Chitty continued:

'There is in my opinion no distinction in these respects between the case of a right of way and the case, such as this, of a nuisance by noise.
'*If the acts of two persons, each being aware of what the other is doing, amount in the aggregate to what is an actionable wrong, each is amenable to the remedy against the aggregate cause of complaint.* The defendants here are both responsible for the noise as a whole so far as it constitutes a nuisance affecting the plaintiff, and each must be restrained in respect of his own share in making it.'[43] (Italics added)

Duke of Buccleuch v. Cowen (1866), 5 *March* (*Ct. of Sess*), 214.
In this case the plaintiff sued several millowners for an injunction to prevent them from polluting a stream flowing past his premises

---

[43] Wright (*Op cit*) (p 405/7).

and as the action came to an end the trial judge directed the jury as follows:

> ...It is not indispensable for each of the pursuers to prove that any of the mills would do itself, if all the other mills were stopped, be sufficient to pollute the river to the effect of creating a nuisance to him; ... it is sufficient to entitle the pursuer to a verdict on any one of the issues, to prove that the river is polluted by one of the mills belonging to the defenders generally, to the effect of producing a nuisance to him, and that the defenders in that issue materially contribute to the production of the nuisance to him.

The jury found for the plaintiff and this eventually went to appeal, at which the judge's direction was upheld. In the words of Lord Benholme:

> Now, in this world there are but few important effects, I take it, either in physics or in morals, that may not be said to have been occasioned by several causes. It is in general from a combination of causes that most great events are produced; and where you are merely considering the extent of an effect, it is quite obvious that every contributing cause must be held to be a cause of that resulting combined effect. If it were not so, you would be in this position, that there are many important effects that have no cause at all, although they are certainly produced by a combination of causes. ...
>
> ...A says—'My mill is not enough to pollute this stream and therefore you cannot reach me'; B says the same thing... but the fact is, that the mills of A and B together have polluted the stream. And the result is that there is no remedy, because you cannot say that either of them has polluted the stream!

The noble lord dismissed the arguments of counsel for the defence which were that if A the first transgressor had not polluted the stream so much as to cause injury he could not be attacked, whereas when B afterwards erects a mill:

> Although it may be a much smaller and less pernicious mill, you are to attack him, because he is the person who has created the nuisance.

Lord Benholme wound up:

> ...what is illegal may be put down, whenever it is a contributing cause to an injury.

The principles underlying the legal notions of nuisance seem to be clear and simple. It does not matter what the activity is, so long as it constitutes a nuisance—as Lord Wright said: 'The forms which nuisance may take are protean . . .'

It does not matter who does it, how many people are involved, or how much they contribute, as long as the end product is nuisance to others. It makes no difference whether or not negligence or malice is involved, people acting in good faith can be nuisances, and it doesn't matter whether or not they know that their activities are harming others or even whether they have the means of finding out.

The encyclopaedic view apparently taken by the law widens the debate considerably. We see that a happy, fulfilled, devoted mother, blessed with an adorable child, would be too angelic to be believed in if she did not find her infant a nuisance if it screamed inconsolably from 3 a m onwards on a night when she had gone to bed exhausted and with a splitting headache. Our nearest and dearest are nuisances to us—as we are to them—whenever they want to do things which conflict with the satisfaction of our own wishes. Part of the art of living together in co-operative groups, such as the family, is the avoidance of, or compensation for, the nuisance value of the other members, coupled with the mitigation of one's own nuisance value to them. Even a dedicated doctor with all the aids of modern science at his disposal can be a nuisance to his patient if the latter is aged, alone, in pain, and tired of it all.

A sad little case of behaviour of surpassing innocence and simplicity becoming a nuisance was reported recently.[44] A man aged 79 and his 73-year-old wife were served with a notice under the Public Health Act because they fed birds in their garden. Neighbours complained that the birds became a nuisance. The man, Mr Newman, was reported as saying:

> It's my only pleasure in life. The birds are my friends, I give them breakfast, lunch, and dinner.

His wife added:

> I look after three birds—a thrush and two blackbirds which are crippled. How can I be breaking the law?

Nevertheless council officials took a census of the birds visit-

[44] *The Guardian,* October 4, 1969.

ing the Newmans' garden and later the Town Clerk wrote to them, saying:

> Investigations show that the birds amount to a nuisance within the meaning of the Act. It is therefore necessary for me to ask you to cease this practice within seven days.

It is difficult to imagine a more innocent activity than feeding birds and if the Newmans had had a bigger garden or more remote neighbours there would have been no problem until their flock became very much larger, and it seems tragic that two people so near to the end of their years should have to be deprived of this simple pleasure. Nonetheless, huge flocks of birds in a residential area must be a considerable nuisance to others and the price has to be paid in individual liberty—that of the bird lovers or that of their neighbours.

This indicates that we must be prepared to accept that the most innocent and desirable things can be nuisances in some circumstances. If the preceding arguments are valid and the legal precedents binding then we must accept that human beings as such can be nuisances, simply by existing, and without having done anything morally or legally wrong. The question we have to decide is then not whether but in what circumstances, and these are simply when there are too many of them.

Responsibility for the population 'nuisance'

Although it will probably be agreed that if the world is already or later becomes over-populated then a nuisance is being created and damage is being done, it may be thought that it is through so long and complex a causal chain that a court might have difficulty in analysing it and apportioning responsibility. However difficult this is, it will not do for parents to argue: 'It isn't my child/family, which brought it about'; although the arithmetic underlying this argument is convincing on the face of it. A family producing as many as twenty-eight children in Britain by 1970 increases the population by 0.00005 per cent, approximately—half of a ten-thousandth of 1 per cent. It could be argued that any particular infant or indeed large family forms a totally insignificant proportion of the population as a whole. It would follow from this that the responsibility of the parents producing these 'surplus' infants must, correspondingly, be vanishingly small.

Unfortunately all populations are produced by individual couples creating individual[45] infants. Even if the globe were to be covered with a layer of human flesh fifty miles thick it would have been brought about simply by greater numbers of increasingly infinitesimal increments.

If, instead of what is actually happening, all the three billion or more surplus infants expected by the year 2000 were being produced by a small and clearly identifiable—not to say miraculously fertile—group, the citizens of Fertilia,[46] say, possibly on another planet, whose friendly and co-operative progeny overflowed throughout the world so that the result at the receiving end was exactly the same as if the surplus had continued being produced locally, somewhat different attitudes could be expected. In otherwise stationary populations, all the new competitors for space, food, shelter, raw materials, working capital, education, recreation, transport, and the rest would be identifiable as members of an outgroup, Fertilia, and all the pent-up frustration we now feel at the constantly increasing pressure of numbers would almost undoubtedly be directed against them.

If the skins of Fertilians happened to be a different colour the outcome could be cataclysmic but even without this element the situation would be explosive enough and a powerful reaction would be generated against the pathologically fertile source of the pressure. Sanctions sufficient to cure the problem, whatever they entailed, would almost certainly be forthcoming—even annihilation of Fertilia—and the world would heave a sigh of relief when the pressure was turned off, even if the price were some twinges of conscience.

At the moment we have no social mechanism, legal or otherwise, or much of a philosophy, for focusing our feelings on the source of so many of our problems and frustrations because population pressure is not generated by the carefree copulations of the Fertilians but by our own mums and dads, friends and neighbours, or—worst of all—by us in person. We cannot direct our frustrated aggression at these targets so the fuse must fizz on until something which *can* explode is reached, but however reluctant we may be

[45] The proportion of multiple births is small, about 1.3 per cent of all maternities. For details see: Benjamin, B (1968) *Health and Vital Statistics* (p 58).
[46] This name was invented by Professor J. E. Meade (see Bibliography).

to recognize responsibility in this sphere the law has set us clear precedents in others.

Who is your neighbour?

We have asked the question who is responsible for the harm done by over-population and proffered a tentative reply. We must also ask who must not be harmed and the law answers: Your Neighbour. According to Lord Atkin:

> The rule that you are to love your neighbour becomes in law, you must not injure your neighbour; and the lawyer's question, Who is my neighbour? receives a restricted reply. . . .
>
> The answer seems to be—persons who are so closely and directly affected by my act that I ought reasonably to have them in contemplation . . . when I am directing my mind to the acts or omissions . . . called into question.[47]

Whether excessive fertility injures our neighbours is a question of judgment but there appear to be very strong grounds for answering in the affirmative from the evidence of crowded classrooms and other facilities and the extra burden on ratepayers, without dwelling on the effect of problem families and the nuisance caused to neighbours in the ordinary sense of the word, let alone the danger to world peace and harmony from over-population.

Where to draw the line

We must not lose sight of a consideration on which the law relies heavily, that of commonsense, what is reasonable and practicable, having in view all the circumstances, at a particular time and place. The law would frown, as most of us would, on the conclusion that if human beings can be nuisances they should be abolished. The law is utilitarian in that it sees itself as one of the main agencies concerned with the maintenance and continuation of society and its activities will generally take those two goals for granted.

Part of the business of being reasonable and practical is taking account of considerations of 'how much?', 'where?', 'when?' and 'for what motive?' Under the law this could very reasonably take the form of judging that, on balance, pursuit of one of its main

[47] McAlister (or Donoghue) v Stevenson (see Wright, p 188).

goals—the maintenance of society—necessarily involved maintaining it about its present or some other optimum size, that increase in numbers beyond this point might well mean the destruction of society. This would have the logical implication that the flow of recruits to human society, i e its infants, is not only reasonable but necessary insofar as it compensates for those who have died, but a nuisance at least and possibly a danger if it goes beyond this.

The law would frown, as we all would, on any imputation of guilt against these extra little humans simply for existing and there would be problems in identifying *which* were the surplus individuals—they had no say in the process which created them. If justice was to be done those responsible would have to be tracked down and called on to answer for their acts, or failures to act, which had the outcome of nuisance or danger to their fellow citizens, in accordance with the classic judgment in the fifteenth century Case of Thorns.[48]

> ... though a man doth a lawful thing, yet if any damage do thereby befal another, he shall answer for it, if he could have avoided it....
>
> ... he that is damaged ought to be compensated ...

These would of course be parents—not all parents, but those who reproduced excessively, and it would be to them that education, appeals to reason and social conscience, and finally constraints if necessary, must be addressed.

Primitive societies as we are fond of styling them, have almost invariably had a legal code, or customs forming the equivalent[49] of such a code, which actually enjoined parents or at least permitted them to do whatever was necessary to prevent unwanted human beings from constituting a nuisance or danger to the tribe or nation.

Societies of high civilization in the past have had laws permitting or requiring population control through infanticide. As David Hume pointed out:

> It was Solon,[50] the most celebrated of the sages of Greece, that gave parents permission by law to kill their children.[51]

It is only modern so-called civilized nations which legislate for rights which are physically impossible of realization in the long run.

---

[48] 1466. Year Book, 6 Ed IV. 7, pl 18.
[49] See Chapter 15, Population Policies, for examples.
[50] The great Athenian lawgiver (638–558 BC).
[51] 'Of the Populousness of Ancient Nations' (an essay).

Summary

It has been argued that with respect to positive law there is no problem—if a duly constituted legislature enacts fertility controls they are good law. In the case of Divine law, only mentioned in passing, at least as far as the Bible goes, there is authority for restricting fertility.

The most important field appears to be natural law and in this there appears to be no historical basis for a right to procreate without limit. Many if not most past societies living in a sense by natural law, and with little or nothing in the way of positive law, have in fact controlled their fertility—often by extremely barbarous means. Even the Roman Catholic case against some forms of birth control, resting on the foundation of a particular interpretation of natural law, does not encourage or permit unlimited or irresponsible procreation.

It has been tentatively suggested that legislation and case law have already developed principles, precedents, and concepts which lie ready to hand for further adaptation in the field of population control, should legal controls prove necessary.

It was further and more fundamentally argued that the law has always recognized that liberty is a compromise between conflicting interests and that no group or person has ever been granted the legal power to do as he likes, with the possible exception of kings during the era of Divine Right. No one can claim absolute rights under the law, either in the field of procreation or anywhere else.

With respect to rights and duties it was argued that they are reciprocally and so intimately related as to be inseparable, we cannot have one without the other, and a great disservice is done to humanity by our incessant advocacy of the one at the expense of total neglect of the other.

Grossly oversimplifying reality but nonetheless extracting a nugget of truth we can say that in their philosophy and to a certain extent their practice in the Communist world they have many duties but few rights—a cultural element shared with Fascist movements —whereas in the West we grant ourselves numerous rights while imposing virtually no duties, a variant of anarchism. In order to generate enough survival power—let alone conditions fostering happiness and moral and spiritual emancipation of men and women—societies of the future must strike a very much more sensible balance between rights and duties. In particular, the undoubted right to procreate in appropriate circumstances must be regulated by the duty not to procreate too freely.

Another and perhaps even more basic point is that the law is one of our main means of social control, the central goal of which is survival. This means that, although many frills can be and are tolerated, it is concerned with the practical down-to-earth realities of life and, in the sphere we are concerned with in this book, the central one is the finiteness of the Earth and all its resources.

If we tackle it early and sensibly there is no reason why population control when it comes, should not be, as Thomas Aquinas put it a long time ago:

> ... An ordinance of reason for the common good, made by him who has the care of the community. ...

It could be rational, humane, moral, and democratic, and leave intact every one of the basic civil liberties listed by all the authorities.

We must clearly recognize that the law is not fixed and unchangeable, either in its form or its principles. One great authority, Mr Justice Holmes, has written:

> ... the law ... is always approaching and never reaching consistency. It is forever adopting new principles from life at one end and it always retains old ones from history at the other end, which have not yet been absorbed or sloughed off.[52]

This shows that even if the law had never been used to regulate sexual behaviour in the past there would be no overriding reason preventing its extension to this field in the future. However, since it has been almost universally used in this fashion the possible need to modify it marginally so as to regulate sexual relations differently need cause few qualms or practical problems.

Wright puts forward the general proposition:

> Everyone owes the world at large the duty of refraining from those acts that may unreasonably threaten the safety of others.[53]

The legal problem arising from this is whether excessive fertility is such an 'act'. If it is, there is little difficulty for lawyers.

As Dicey put it:

> Parliament however habitually interferes, for the public advantage, with private rights. Indeed such interference has now

---

[52] Quoted in Wright (*Op cit*) (p 151).
[53] (*Op cit*) (p 198).

(greatly to the benefit of the community) become so much a matter of course as hardly to excite remark, . . .

It is common knowledge that the law in most societies is powerful and respected enough to take away a person's property and liberty—even his life, for the greatest good of the greatest number, and there seems little reason to doubt that this awesome force could be turned towards population control if we leave it too late.

A useful incentive in the case of any new legislation involving sexual activities, for the purpose of population control, is that a *quid pro quo* can be given. A number of new sexual microfreedoms have been granted recently and quite a few more could follow, if we chose, in return for the loss of the microfreedom to procreate irresponsibly.

There is every reason to hope that this matter of excessive fertility will be settled out of court by means of education, persuasion, and financial incentives, but if the case *Homo Moderatus* v *Homo Prolificus* should ever be called before the bar of civilization there can be little doubt which way the verdict should go.

Chapter 9

The ecology of liberty

I am so besotted unto liberty that should any man forbid the access unto any one corner of the Indies I should in some sort live much discontented.

Montaigne[1]

Everyone has the right to freedom of movement and residence within the borders of his own state.

Universal Declaration of Human Rights[2]

. . . in some animals the freedom reflex is so strong that when placed in captivity they reject food, pine away and die.

I. P. Pavlov[3]

Progress be damned. All this will do will be to allow the lower classes to move around unnecessarily.

Duke of Wellington
(on seeing his first railway train)*

The four quotations at the head of this chapter reflect the fact that at least some thinkers and men of affairs have recognized that the foundation of the liberty of a mobile living creature lies in its relationship to its environment. We might call it a behaviouristic approach to liberty. It has long been universally recognized that depriving such a creature of its freedom to move about—to stretch its limbs, as we say—is one of the worst torments which can

---

[1] *Essays.*
[2] Article 13 (1).
[3] Lectures on the work of the cerebral hemispheres. In Koshtoyants, KS (1955) (ed), Pavlov, IP, *Selected Works* (p 184), Foreign Languages Publishing House, Moscow.
* I am indebted to Robert Arvill's excellent book *Man and Environment* (1967) for the Duke of Wellington quotation.

be inflicted. Imprisonment has been the basic form of punishment in the human species from time immemorial and the closer the confinement—the smaller the cell—the more severe it is recognized to be. Confinement in such a way that the prisoner cannot properly stand, sit, or lie down is still used as a form not merely of punishment, but of outright torture.

The word 'ecology' was coined by the great naturalist Haeckel.[4] It comes from the same Greek root, 'oikos'—meaning house or living place—as 'economics' and 'ekistics'[5] and it is used to describe the study of the relationships between living things and their environments, environment being understood in a wide sense to include other living creatures both of the same and other species.

If ecology is the study of the relationship between a living creature and its environment and the latter plays a vital part in its liberty then it follows that, just as there is a philosophy, psychology, sociology, and jurisprudence of liberty, so should there be an ecology of liberty.

The concept of a 'territorial' instinct associated with characteristic behaviour patterns is now well established by students of animal behaviour. Territorial animals establish a living-space for themselves—either the nuclear family or a somewhat larger group —and defend it against all trespass by members of their own species, and often by members of other species, too. Lorenz describes a classic case of a male turtle dove being practically flayed alive by a female ring dove when he put it in her 'roomy cage'.[6]

In his book, *On Aggression* (1966), Konrad Lorenz argues that in territorial creatures the aggressive urge directed against trespassers increases geometrically from the periphery of the territory to the centre and that;

> ... this increase ... is so great that it compensates for all differences ever to be found in adult ... animals of a species. (p 28)

Many studies have shown that serious abnormalities of behaviour frequently occur when animals are put too close together. Paul Leyhausen's studies on cats and other animals bear this out and he has at least a partial answer to those who argue that pathological

---

[4] (1868) *The History of Nature.*
[5] The science of human settlement.
[6] (1952) *King Solomon's Ring* (p 202).

behaviour due to overcrowding in lower animals cannot be related
to our species. He says:

> Nearly five years in prisoner-of-war camps taught me that
> overcrowded human societies reflect the symptoms of over-
> crowded wolf, cat, goat, mouse, rat or rabbit communities down
> to the last detail and that all differences are merely species-
> specific; the basic forces of social interaction ... are identical ...[7]

In 1967 Robert Ardrey wrote in his controversial book, *The
Territorial Imperative*:

> Man, ... is as much a territorial animal as ... a mocking-
> bird ...
> ... we defend the title to our land or the sovereignty of our
> country, ... for reasons no different, no less innate, no less in-
> eradicable, than do lower animals ... (p 16)
> ... it may ... be the strangest of thoughts that the bond
> between a man and the soil ... should be more powerful than his
> bond with the woman he sleeps with. ...
> ... this force ... is a portion of our evolutionary nature, a
> behaviour pattern of such survival value ... that it became fixed
> in our genetic endowment, ...
> ... it is no less essential to ... contemporary man than it was
> to those bands of small brained proto-men on the high African
> savannah millions of years ago. It is ... a force shaping our
> lives in countless unexpected ways, threatening our existence
> only to the degree that we fail to understand it. (p 18)

Another well-known animal behaviourist, Niko Tinbergen,
having argued that man displays the phenomenon of 'group' territoriality (as distinct from individual or family territoriality) wrote:

> ... we now live at a far higher density than that in which
> genetic evolution has moulded our species. This, together with
> long-distance communication, leads to far more frequent, in
> fact to continuous, intergroup contacts and so to continuous
> external provocation of aggression.[8]

Professor Wynne-Edwards, a most distinguished contributor to
this field, has pointed out that animals in the wild are not generally ill fed. He shows that their numbers are not normally con-

[7] 'The Sane Community—A Density Problem'. *Discovery*, September, 1965
and Conservation Society Reprints, No 1 (1968).
[8] 'On War and Peace in Animals and Man'. *Science*, 160, June 28, 1970.

trolled by starvation any more than by predation, violence, or disease, and presents a very good case for the thesis that the essential process of population control has been the main force behind the evolution of social organization through the mechanisms of territory and the peck-order.

Among many species of birds in the breeding season he says:

> ... each male lays a claim to an area of not less than a certain minimum size and keeps out all other males of the species: in this way a group of males will parcel out the available ground as individual territories and put a limit on crowding. ...
>
> ... Instead of competing directly for ... food ... the members compete furiously for pieces of ground, each of which then becomes the exclusive food preserve of its owner. If the standard territory is large enough to feed a family, the entire group is safe from the danger of over-taxing the food supply.[9]

Professor Wynne-Edwards disagrees with Leyhausen's view that identical principles underlie the behaviour of human beings and the lower animals, albeit in a sphere which Dr Leyhausen could not observe in his prison camp, that of reproduction. He claims there are '... two outstanding differences ...':

> In the first place, ... control of animal population is strictly automatic ...
>
> Man's fertility and population growth, on the other hand, are subject only to his conscious and deliberate behaviour. ...
>
> Primitive man, limited to the food he could get by hunting, ... evolved a system for restricting his numbers by tribal traditions and taboos ... [and] these customs, consciously or not, kept the population density nicely balanced against the feeding capacity of the hunting range ... human population, ... now shows a tendency to expand without limit ... and
>
> ... man cannot look to any natural process to restrain his rapid growth. If it ... is to be slowed down it must be by his own deliberate and socially applied efforts.[10]

It may be that Professor Wynne-Edwards is mistaken on one point. It could be that man's mechanism for controlling his numbers

---

[9] 'Population Control in Animals'. *Scientific American*, August, 1964. An abbreviated version of his monumental work *Animal Dispersion in Relation to Social Behaviour* (1962).

[10] (*Op. cit.*)

is violence and destruction. Hitler's stress on the need for *Lebensraum* was used as an excuse for wars of aggression. It is true that modern wars have done little to hamper population growth but in the past when dependence on the environment was more immediate, populations were decimated in warfare and this could be the case in future wars if we allow the world to become grossly over-populated and wars to take place in it. With the weapons of mass destruction now at hand many hundreds of millions could be destroyed in a few days, though there would also be the danger that resources would be destroyed in proportion, or even more so, leaving any survivors worse off, per capita, than before. However, weapons of mass destruction without this drawback are now becoming available, such as the cobalt bomb and chemical and biological warfare, so that war could once again redress the population balance, unless we are careful.

The case presented here does not rest on pathological togetherness of this order but on the need for restraint on fertility long before this stage is reached in order to preserve not merely a minimal biologically adequate habitat but one capable of sustaining a comfortable, free, spacious, and civilized way of life.

The ecology of liberty for domestic animals

The relationship between ecology and liberty is slowly being recognized in the field of animal husbandry with the advent of factory farming, one of the reasons for which is population pressure, though, to the best of the present writer's knowledge, no one has yet applied the term 'ecology' to it or attempted to develop a general principle or theory in this field.

Ruth Harrison, author of *Animal Machines*, and gadfly to the nation's conscience on this issue of increasing barbarity towards our domestic animals, wrote in the *Observer* recently, with reference to the Brambell Report, which—though laid on the table in Parliament in 1965—has never been debated:

> ... Basic to their recommendations for the immediate relief of suffering was their fundamental principle containing five freedoms:
>
> That an animal should have at least sufficient freedom of movement to be able without difficulty to turn around, groom itself, get up, lie down and stretch its limbs . . .[11]

[11] 'Why Animals Need Freedom to Move', October 12, 1969.

The standards it laid down had to be a compromise on what was right for the animal and what was feasible in the context of agricultural practice. But members of the committee unanimously agreed that their standards were the absolute minimum necessary to prevent actual suffering and should be put into force immediately and made mandatory. They also recommended that standards of stockmanship should be improved through education, that there should be a new Act redefining animal suffering, that there should be veterinary inspection of farms and that there should be a standing Farm Animal Welfare Advisory Committee which, like theirs, should contain nobody with a commercial interest.

... the immense value of the Brambell Report was that for the first time a government committee faced the issue of where the line should be drawn in our use of animals:

In principle, we disapprove of a degree of confinement of an animal which necessarily frustrates most of the major activities which make up its natural behaviour.

One of its members, William Thorpe, Professor of Animal Behaviour at Cambridge University, pointed out in an appendix that:

All the domestic animals which man farms are species which in the wild show a fairly highly organized social life.... This means that their mental and behavioural organization is also potentially on a high level....

Professor Thorpe said later:

All these species have evolved over millions of years of life in the wild. The genetic changes which have come about as a result of domestication are an extremely small proportion of the total genetic make up of the animal. Indeed, I doubt whether there is a single domesticated form or race or type which could not resume life in the wild if given the opportunity.

The ecology of liberty for the human animal

Thomas Hobbes put the essence of the ecology of liberty in 1651 in his great work, *Leviathan*. Here, in his chapter entitled 'On the LIBERTY of Subjects', he stated:

LIBERTY or FREEDOME signifieth (properly) *the absence of Opposition;* (by Opposition, I mean *externall Impediments of motion;*) and may be applyed no lesse to Irrationall, and Inanimate creatures, than to Rationall. For *whatsoever is so tyed, or environed, as it cannot move, but within a certain space, which space is determined by the opposition of some externall body, we say it hath not Liberty to go further.* And so of all living creatures, whilst they are imprisoned, or restrained, with walls, or chayns; and of the water whilest it is kept in by banks, or vessels, that otherwise would spread it selfe into a larger space, we use to say, they are not at Liberty, to move in such manner, as without those externall impediments they would. . . .

And according to this proper, and generally received meaning of the word, a FREEMAN, *is he, that in those things, which by his strength and wit he is able to do, is not hindered to doe what he has a will to.*[12] (First and second italics added, third original)

A modern poet has thrown another light on the same problem.

> *Some thirty inches from my nose*
> *The frontier of my Person goes,*
> *And all the untilled air between*
> *Is private* pagus *or demesne.*
> *Stranger, unless with bedroom eyes*
> *I beckon you to fraternise,*
> *Beware of rudely crossing it:*
> *I have no gun, but I can spit.*[13]

The four freedoms granted to a slave in ancient Greece when he received 'manumission', was liberated, that is, included: '. . . the right to movement according to his own choice'.[14]

In the modern world we are increasingly losing this basic right simply from the opposition of other bodies. A recent edition of *The Guardian*[15] carried two separate expressions of this from articulate literary people. First, Mr A. P. Herbert:

[12] Everyman's edition (1949) (p 110).
[13] Auden, WH, 'Prologue: The Birth of Architecture'. Quoted in Hall, ET (1969) *The Hidden Dimension* (p 107).
[14] Westermann, WL, 'Between Freedom and Slavery', *American Hist Rev* L (1945) 213–27.
[15] February 22, 1969.

> Every year it seems Man's mastery of the elements improves.
> ... But every year there is less room, less comfort, every year I
> feel more like a cow....

Second, Mrs Joy Presson Allen, the wealthy New York writer:

> I love spending money ... pictures ... furniture ... travel ...
> but most of all privacy. And it's getting to the point where the
> most expensive thing around is privacy.

Wealthy or not, literary or not, we all know these feelings only
too well, a sense of being shut in and frustrated. What the
ancients were able to grant their slaves on freeing them—freedom
of movement—we are increasingly denying to each other, even to
the privileged wealthy minority, simply by existing and making
demands on our environment.

The rich have always used their wealth to buy space and
privacy and they will be driven further and further away from the
centres of population in pursuit of these aims, perhaps, before
long, off the Earth altogether.

We need lose little sleep over the refined anguish of the pathologically affluent but as writing on the wall we would do well to
take note of it.

The German philosopher Schopenhauer is said to have likened
human beings to hedgehogs. We are drawn together for warmth,
physical and spiritual, but if we get too close we begin to feel the
spines as well as the comfort and are driven away again. My guess
would be that even if our needs in this respect were constant, which
I doubt, most of us would fail to achieve a consistent optimization of the space relationship with our fellows so that we would be
driven to oscillate. We would now draw nearer and later find ourselves thrust away again by forces inside ourselves or in the
other(s), or both. This would require the availability of 'with-
drawal-space' and have implications for the optimization of population. This philosophy of space is reflected in Sartre's play *In
Camera*, in which the character Garcin observes:

> Remember all we were told about the torture-chambers, the
> fire and brimstone. ... There's no need. ... Hell is other people.[16]

In psychological medicine pathological space relationships are
recognized under the headings 'claustrophobia' and 'agoraphobia',
morbid dread of closed and open spaces, respectively. If, as is

[16] See Browne, EM (ed) (1960) *Three European Plays* (p 191).

usual, these psychological illnesses are not totally alien to the average person but merely represent extreme or unbalanced extensions of the normal, we see that we are all agora/claustrophobic to some extent—it is a question of degree rather than of kind.

In our medical/architectural notions of hospital location and design we recognize that space is very important and we condemn the nineteenth century warehouse-like edifices used to house many of our unfortunate sick—though not strongly enough in many cases to justify actually paying for better ones. However, when a new hospital does have to be built we try to make it spacious, inside and out, setting it in pleasant grounds as well, wherever possible. This factor of space and aesthetic appeal is intuitively recognized to be an important factor in the therapeutic process.

Similarly, in our attitudes towards public parks and other open spaces, we intuitively perceive and begin to make more explicit the fact that people need breathing space. It is a source of wonder and a marvellous encouragement to the present writer that after the total war waged on the masses and the environment in Britain by the industrial revolution, parks—many of them—and some of them very large and beautiful, survive in our great conurbations.

'Proxemics'

'Territorial' behaviour in lower animals has long been studied by ethologists as we have seen, and human spatial relationships have also been studied for some time under the title 'human ecology', which, in its narrower definition, has evolved since the early part of this century as a not very respectable branch of sociology stemming from the Chicago school under Robert E. Park.

The sociological branch of human ecology, though a useful area of study, tends to be rather parochial, to concern itself almost solely with problems of urbanization, the movement of people from the rural areas into towns and the various patterns of settlement, deployment of industry and commerce, dispersion and stratification of residential districts, and so forth. Relations between city and region, between greater and lesser towns, and between towns and villages have also been studied under this same general heading, but the study of *homo sapiens* in relationship to his environment in the wider sense of the term 'ecology', such as a biologist would understand it, has largely been left out.

The term 'ekistics' was coined by the Greek architect Doxiades at a symposium at Delos in Greece in 1963, to describe what purported to be a new discipline, 'the science of human settlements', previously mentioned. This goes some way towards the development of a human ecology based on more fundamental thinking but there is a long way to go in this direction. It is no accident that at the present time a number of researchers and university departments are renewing their studies of spatial relationships in human interaction, a new discipline called 'Proxemics', having evolved.

The neologism was introduced by Edward T. Hall,[17] acknowledging his debt in passing to the anthropologist Franz Boas, who:

> Over fifty-three years ago, ... laid the foundation of the view which I hold ...
> Proxemics is the term I have coined for the interrelated observations and theories of man's use of space as a specialized elaboration of culture.

Hall breaks down the distance factor in human interaction under four headings.

1. 'Intimate distance'
2. 'Personal distance'
3. 'Social distance'
4. 'Public distance'

All of these distances he elaborates and classifies, pointing out that of course they are not separate watertight categories but shade imperceptibly into one another. Nonetheless they are characterized by typical and readily recognizable behaviour. Each distance classification is broken down into its 'close phase' and its 'far phase', the far phase of one distance shading indeterminately into the close phase of the next distance.

The close phase of 'intimate distance' is:

> ... The distance of love making and wrestling, comforting and protecting. Physical contact or the high possibility of physical involvement is uppermost in the awareness of both persons. ...
> The far phase of this distance is six to eighteen inches; the body parts:

> ... Are not easily brought into contact, but hands can reach and grasp extremities. ...

[17] (1969) *The Hidden Dimension.*

The close phase of the 'personal distance' is one-and-a-half to two-and-a-half feet, at which distance:

... One can hold or grasp the other person. ...

The far phase stretches from two-and-a-half to four feet, the distance at which we keep people at 'arms length'.

It extends:

from a point just outside easy touching distance by one person to a point where two people can touch fingers if they extend both arms. This is the limit of physical domination in the very real sense. ...

The close phase of the 'social' distance is four to seven feet, the distance at which:

Impersonal business occurs. ... People who work together tend to use close social distance. It is also a very common distance for people who are attending a casual social gathering. To stand and look down at a person at this distance has a domineering effect, as when a man talks to his secretary or receptionist.

The far phase of this distance is seven to twelve feet:

... The distance to which people move when someone says 'Stand away so that I can look at you'. Business and social discourse conducted at the far end of social distance has a more formal character than if it occurs inside the close phase. Desks in the offices of important people are large enough to hold visitors at the far phase of the social distance. ...

This distance can be used:

... To insulate or screen people from each other. This distance makes it possible for them to continue to work in the presence of another person without appearing to be rude. Receptionists in offices [being] particularly vulnerable [in this respect] ...

With respect to 'public distance' the close phase is characterized by distances of twelve to twenty-five feet.

At twelve feet an alert subject can take evasive or defensive action if threatened. The distance may even cue a vestigial but subliminal form of flight reaction. The voice is loud but not full volume. Linguists have observed that a careful choice of words, phrasing of sentences as well as grammatical or syntactic shifts occur at this distance.

The far phase of this distance is twenty-five feet or more and Hall points out:

Thirty feet is the distance which is automatically set around important public figures.

These relationships are summarized in Fig 9/1.

Fig 9/1
Socio-cultural use of physical distance

Description	Phase	
	Close	Far
1. Intimate distance	Contact	$0' - 1\frac{1}{2}'$
2. Personal distance	$1\frac{1}{2}' - 2\frac{1}{2}'$	$2\frac{1}{2}' - 4'$
3. Social distance	$4' - 7'$	$7' - 12'$
4. Public distance	$12' - 25'$	$25' - ?$

Based on data from Hall, E. T. (1966), **Op cit**

Hall points out human beings can modify the subjective and social values of physical distances by appropriate measures, including such things as customs and taboos, physical screening, even by the simple device used by the cartoonist Chick Young, the creator of 'Blondie', of arranging seats back to back so that two people physically very close to each other can engage or disengage socially with considerable freedom. He points out that shorter distances are 'sociopetal'—tending to induce social interaction, that is, while longer distances are 'sociofugal', tending to depersonalize, minimize, and finally terminate social interaction.

There is a great need for more knowledge in this critical field of human spatial relationships, and Hall's work is only one of the more interesting developments.[18]

[18] I have been privileged to see a transcript of a talk given in London by Anthony Storr which dealt with the problem of space and overcrowding from the point of view of the psychiatrist, and raised the interesting question —among others—of whether man is a 'contact' or 'non-contact' species. (To be published in 1971 by Pemberton Books under the title *Towards an Open Society*.)

A disclaimer

No attempt has been made here to work out exactly how much physical space each human being needs for a full life, let alone the minimum he can tolerate without physiological, psychological or social disaster. For this reason no consideration has been given to the well known studies, such as those of J. B. Calhoun, of apparently pathological overcrowding in rats, mice, and other small mammals.

Human beings need space not just to exist in a physiologically minimal habitat but for a full life and this seems to include an increasing amount of movement at increasing velocities as technology makes this possible.

The main variables in the ecology of liberty are numbers, space, motion, and time. Time is related to motion in two ways, firstly as an indicator of *when* a movement takes place, and secondly relating to the *rate* at which it takes place. Motion, to be fully specified must be related not only to time in both of the senses referred to but also to direction. Direction and rate together specify velocity.

In a finite three dimensional space there are an infinite number of *directions* in which motion can take place, the limits on the *rate* of individual movement are imposed by the technology, and the *total* amount of movement is determined by numbers, size of space, velocity, and organization of the system. In a finite system the amount of movement cannot expand infinitely.

For these reasons we must not allow ourselves to get bogged down in detailed considerations of just how few square inches per capita a rat community can endure before relapsing into cannibalism and exactly how few square feet per human being this represents.

These animal studies are valuable and should continue but they must not blind us to man's substantially more complicated and wider ramifying needs. It would be rather unfortunate to calculate from studies of small test groups that a human being can survive quite well with only, say twenty square feet of space, to allow the population of a nation or even the whole world to rise to a density giving each individual that amount, in consequence of the calculations, and then discover that the situation is totally different when *everyone* is in the same boat as the few in the test situation.

In the chapters following an attempt is made to indicate not the answer, but some possible ways of finding an answer to the question how much space man needs for a full life.

Summary

Despite our solicitude for the freedom of domestic animals we are slow to develop a similar logic and concern for our own species though there are small beginnings in the spheres of housing, schools, and industry—where minimal standards for floor and air-space per occupant and a few other items have been recommended. However, we can derive a modicum of comfort from a precedent in the sphere of action against cruelty. The Royal Society for the Prevention of Cruelty to [lower] Animals was founded in England in 1824, whereas the National Society for the Prevention of Cruelty to Children—still awaiting royal patronage—was not set up until 1884.[19] If the same differential concern applies we shall have more or less enforceable standards with respect to human overcrowding by 2040 or so and we must hope this will not be too late.

However, even if public opinion and government are not very quick off the mark with respect to the general ecology of liberty for the human animal, there are developments in some fields, at least, as we saw in the very brief discussion of Hall's work.

While it is clear, as this author shows, that by the use of screening coupled with subtle social norms and cunning planning of the environment, a lot can be done to optimize privacy and individual freedom with a given population density, the conclusion is inescapable that within a finite environment the process of amelioration has definite limits.

If numbers are allowed to continue increasing within a given space the public distance will gradually be telescoped into the social distance, the social into the personal and finally the personal will be crammed into the close phase of the intimate distance, the point at which privacy and individual freedom virtually disappear.

In some contexts, of course, we experience strong desires to lose our privacy and deeply desire to be and to feel as close as possible to another human being, we want to 'lose ourselves' even to the point of 'feeling at one', but this is a state which we can in the nature of things achieve—even desire to achieve—only with one or very few other people and even then only in some circumstances and for part of the time.

The prospect of being forced into this kind of physical intimacy with ever larger numbers of total strangers appals many of us and we escape from grossly overcrowded buses or tube trains with pro-

---

[19] The Liverpool Society, the pioneer in Britain, started in 1883.

found feelings of relief. The existence we must begin to picture in our mind's eye is life in a society which is, psychologically speaking, one long strap-hang in a rush-hour tube train. If this prospect is daunting, as it will be for most people, then we must look to the mechanism for preventing the situation ever arising.

The fundamental fact underlying the ecological study of human liberty is the finiteness of the Earth. In everyday language it is the age-old problem of trying to squeeze a quart into a pint pot.

Spatial liberty would be at a maximum, infinity,[20] with a world population of one person, and at a minimum, zero, at the point at which the whole surface of the Earth was covered with bodies pressed tightly against each other.[21] Spatial liberty would be optimized at some point to be decided—preferably through informed and free discussion and democratic politics—between the two extremes. Let us examine the mechanics of physical liberty under the microscope, as it were, by means of a simple game of simulation.

[20] No constraints within the confines of the Earth, i. e.

[21] After this was written a very interesting article appeared in *New Society* describing the results of some research on 'body buffer-zones' in violent and non-violent prisoners in gaol. The violent prisoners required over 300 per cent more space than the non-violent to avoid feelings of insecurity and aggression (29.3 sq ft against 7 sq ft) and their buffer zones were much larger at the back than at the front whilst those of the non-violent were symmetrical. Kinze, AF. 'Body Buffer-Zones in Violent Prisoners', *New Society* No 435, January 28, 1971.

Part 3

The freedom game

Chapter 10

The freedom game

It is possible to illustrate the basic aspects of the ecology of liberty by a simple game with a few simple rules, to be played on a board marked out in squares like a draughtboard. We can call it the 'Freedom Game'.

I do not claim that the game portrays reality in anything like its true complexity and richness but it does illustrate the central problem, the impossibility of maintaining freedom of movement—the basic microfreedom—in a fixed and finite playing space with a constantly increasing number of players.

Requisites

A board marked out in, let us say, 100 squares, with pieces equal to the number of squares.

Object of game

To get the biggest 'freedom' (of movement) score by moving your piece over the biggest number of squares with the minimum number of requests for co-operation from the other players.

Rules of the game

  i Players must move in turns, their own pieces only.
  ii Only one player can move at a time.
  iii No square may be crossed more than once during the same move.
  iv No jumping allowed.
  v When it is his turn the player must move his piece through as many squares as he can in the time allowed, counting as he

goes, gaining 10 points for every square but losing a point every time he has to ask for co-operation from another player.

vi When obstructed by another piece a player may ask its owner to move and let him through.

vii Players can please themselves whether to co-operate or not when requested, but if they agree then a player can make a profit on anything up to 9 requests for co-operation from other players in order to get his piece into just one more square. i e he gains 10 points, loses 9, and profits by 1.

viii Time limit on moves decided by players.

ix Players may change the rules if they can get everyone to agree.

Figures 10/1 to 10/8 show eight sample stages of the Freedom Game showing the effects of numbers and of spatial 'structure' as the number of players increases from 1 to 100.

Fig 10/1

In Fig 10/1 there is one player, marked ⊥, in square No 1, who obviously has a potential score of 1,000 if time permits a complete circuit.

Fig 10/2

In Fig 10/2 one more player has been added in square 100, cutting No 1's no-penalty score to 990 and maximum possible score 999. (One successful request for co-operation, $+10-1=9$.)

1	11	21	31	41	51	61	71	81	91
2	12	22	32	42	52	62	72	82	92
3	13	23	33	43	53	63	73	83	93
4	14	24	34	44	54	64	74	84	94
5	15	25	35	45	55	65	75	85	95
6	16	26	36	46	56	66	76	86	96
7	17	27	37	47	57	67	77	87	97
8	18	28	38	48	58	68	78	88	98
9	19	29	39	49	59	69	79	89	99
10	20	30	40	50	60	70	80	90	100

Fig 10/3

In this figure 9 more players have been added, making 11 now, and they are all clustered together near square 100, opposite No 1, who still has 900 possible no-penalty points, the maximum no-penalty score with this number of players.

1	11	21	31	41	51	61	71	81	91
2	12	22	32	42	52	62	72	82	92
3	13	23	33	43	53	63	73	83	93
4	14	24	34	44	54	64	74	84	94
5	15	25	35	45	55	65	75	85	95
6	16	26	36	46	56	66	76	86	96
7	17	27	37	47	57	67	77	87	97
8	18	28	38	48	58	68	78	88	98
9	19	29	39	49	59	69	79	89	99
10	20	30	40	50	60	70	80	90	100

Fig 10/4

This board shows the same number of players as the last, but this time they are all clustered around No 1, thus cutting his no-penalty score to zero. This illustrates the effect of spatial structuring.

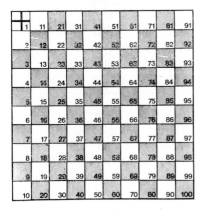

Fig 10/5

Fig 10/5 shows that even with a substantial increase in numbers, up to 50, because of the uniform distribution, No 1's no-penalty score has gone up from 0 to 20. The highest no-penalty score with this configuration is of course 40, for those away from the edge of the board.

Fig 10/6

Figure 10/6 shows the situation when the same number of players as last time, 50, are crammed together on one half of the board—No 1 again having a no-penalty score of 0, and making it very difficult for him to move at all, though it would be still worse for him if they were clustered diagonally across his 'S.E.' path.

Fig 10/7

This shows the state of play with 99 players, only square 100 being empty and only players 90 and 99 having any possibility of a no-penalty score, limited to 10 in each case.

If No 1 wanted to move to square 100, he would have to persuade No 90 or 99 to move into square 100, then 89 to move into square 90 or 99, depending on his first choice, then 79 to move into 89, say, to avoid too much repetition of alternatives, then 78 into 79, then 77 into 78, then 67 into 77, then 66 into 67, then 56 into 66, then 55 into 56, and so forth.

By this time No 1 would have cleared half his path in one direction only. He would have to carry on until the empty space was next to him, in square 3 or 11, and then repeat the whole process in reverse, until he arrived in square 100.

Even if every player granted full, rapid, and intelligent co-operation the 'journey' would be slow, complicated, and frustrating. If communications were imperfect, some players recalcitrant, some half asleep, some out to sabotage the move, some not very quick on the uptake, others stubborn, and yet others against the system —just as in real life, in fact, so that No 1 had to go via squares 71, 14, 29, and 57, say, the journey could be as long-drawn-out and complicated as you like up to the mathematically defined limit of infinity. No 1 may never make it.

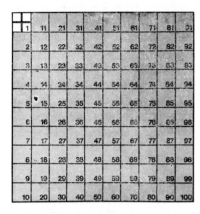

Fig 10/8

The situation on the last board was difficult enough but the addition of only one more player would make all freedom of movement disappear completely.

The only possibility of movement in this situation would be for the players to start to juggle the rules and each other in such a way that every piece could be shuffled simultaneously in a co-ordinated way.

This—if it were possible at all, which is unlikely—would require:

1. A complete, detailed, perfectly integrated, and obviously extremely complicated set of instructions for each player's 'shuffle',

2. perfect co-operation from each player—a single failure to co-operate could wreck the whole process,

3. almost certainly, central direction, via a first-class communication system.

Rewriting the rules

We have seen that as more and more players were added, the situation on the board would become increasingly complex, the direct freedom of the player would be more and more restricted and the amount of communication and co-operation required would be correspondingly increased. Penalty points lost through requests for help would begin to outweigh those gained in free movement. Scores would start to diminish so that the winner could turn out to be the one with the smallest negative score.

Long before saturation point had been reached it would have been sensible, if the basic rules permitted it, for the players to get together to arrive at some extra rules of co-operation, especially as some of their number might have adopted violent tactics, knocking pieces out of their way or attacking the other players. These rules could take the form of allocating some squares as communal spaces and agreeing that certain rows would be left free for everyone to use for purposes of communication—analogous to the 'rights of way' we have developed in society.

Conversely, if the rules were written so as to allow the most successful players to acquire more or less absolute rights over certain squares or blocks of squares, this would tend to make the whole thing less complicated though only at the expense of reducing the freedom of the other players—again something analogous to what we have in real society.

Making the game more difficult

If by some chance the original rules of the game are not difficult enough to satisfy the players we can rewrite them to any desired specification for complexity. For example, a weighting for penalty points could be introduced: 1 for the first request for co-operation, 2 for the second, and so on. However, as it would probably be quite hard enough for most players and as in real life we are constantly hoping—if not trying very hard—to *simplify* the rules, we need spend little time on this. Two possibilities, having fairly obvious analogues in real life, are worth a mention, however, removing the restriction on the number of players moving at the same instant, and/or adding an extra dimension.

i. *No restriction on moves*

When the rules say that only one player can move at a time he can see which squares are empty and plan his move ahead. If on the other hand he has no idea what the others are going to do, or when, he will be much more at their mercy. If every player could move— or at least attempt to move—as and when he chose and regardless of what the others were doing, the game would become very much more complicated and the tasks of maximizing the score and keeping track of it correspondingly more difficult—especially if the movement were to be allowed in any direction.

If the other players were moving in a predictable way—at least in predictable directions—P1 could observe them, generalize, and make predictions accordingly, but this would obviously be a very ticklish business even on a board with only 100 squares and perhaps fifty players.

Figures 10/9 to 10/16 show the effects of various kinds of movement coupled with a progressively restrictive rewriting of the rules for the purpose of maximizing capacity at the expense of freedom of movement. No attempt is made to write out full sets of rules, so that the game could actually be played, to take account of all the problems the players would face, or to chart precisely the boundary between this game and the real world. The exploration is concentrated on the two central variables, numbers and ecological freedom. Some readers may care to amuse themselves by completing a set of rules to make a game that could be played with the family.

Fig 10/9

Figure 10/9 shows the board one quarter full with 25 players and subject to rules permitting movement in 8 directions, north, south, east and west, and north-east, south-east, south-west and north-west.

This would be a very difficult situation to cope with, players would have to be very quick off the mark, and there would be many collisions.

Fig 10/10

This shows the effect of restricting movement to only 4 directions, north, south, east, and west—with the same number of players—and the situation is clearly much tidier and easier to cope with.

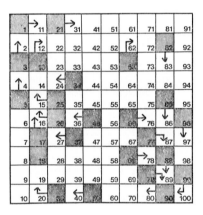

Fig 10/11

Tidying up could obviously go a good deal further and here we see the effect of restricting movement to a clockwise direction on the outer circuit and anti-clockwise on the inner circuit (keeping to the left, i e)—with movement on the rest of the board restricted to a direct line into or out of the two 'traffic lanes'.

Fig 10/12

This goes one stage further by restricting movement in the outer traffic lanes to a one-way system—clockwise round the board.

Fig 10/13

The last four diagrams show what it could be like if optimization of both capacity and movement were attempted.

This one shows that with 4 'parking lots' and two-way movement the capacity of the board would be 16 at rest plus a certain restricted number in motion at any one time, the total being kept below congestion point. Let us say 20 in motion, for the sake of argument. Total capacity now 36.

Fig 10/14

This one shows that at the expense of freedom of movement, capacity could go up to 36 in the parking areas, plus, say, 15 in motion, if a fairly comprehensive one-way system were to be introduced. Every player who is parked has freedom to move into and out of the traffic lanes without disturbing anyone else in his parking area.

Total capacity now 51.

Fig 10/15

At great cost in freedom of movement—9 players (marked X) now being hemmed in—capacity was now increased a little, to 48 in the parking area, plus, say, 12 in motion. There would have to be acceptable rules for deciding who had the middle positions from which no one can move without co-operation from his neighbours, who in turn could not move without co-operation from those in the one-way system which would be blocked while the move was taking place. Total capacity now 60.

Fig 10/16

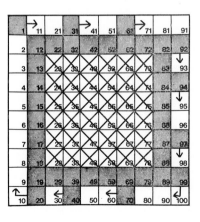

Finally, Fig 10/16 shows the ultimate in capacity, free movement having almost disappeared, with 64 players in one huge parking area and with say, 10 in movement, restricted to a single one-way lane round the outside. Thirty-six are now locked inside and unable to move without the co-operation—in some cases a great deal of co-operation—from their neighbours.

The total capacity in Fig 10/16 is now seventy-four but as soon as manoeuvring on the part of members of the outer ring of parked players begins, in order to let one of the trapped players out, the single traffic lane is blocked.

If twenty-six of the sixty-four parked players (about 40 per cent) were allowed by the rules to move out together they would fill every square in the traffic lane and all circulatory movement would have to cease.

ii.   *A new dimension*

Fairly obviously the freedom game could be played not merely in two dimensions as we have done so far, but in three. We could have not merely a single draughtboard with length and breadth but a cubic space comprised of layers of draughtboards with spaces between for the pieces to move about in, plus some means of allowing pieces to pass through intervening boards, so we have length,

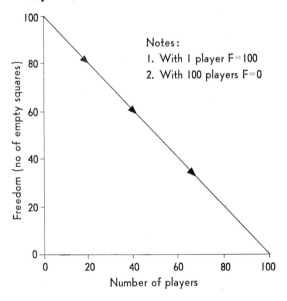

Fig 10/17

**The Freedom Game:
Decline in freedom as number of
players increases
'Simple' index**

Notes:
1. With 1 player F = 100
2. With 100 players F = 0

Fig 10/18
**The Freedom Game:
Decline in freedom as number of
players increases
'Realistic' index with cooperation**

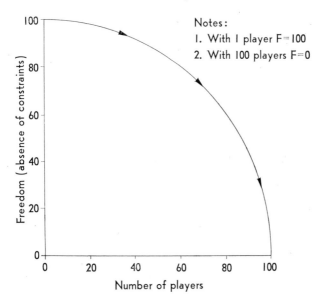

Notes:
1. With 1 player F = 100
2. With 100 players F = 0

breadth, and height—solid space in which there are a number of
'storeys' as in a building. We could then go on to fill not just the
area of one 'floor'—one of the draughtboards—but all floors until
we had filled up the total volume.

The cubic freedom game would be a vastly more complicated
one, perhaps more satisfying to egg-headed players, but it would be
based upon exactly the same sort of principles. Real society is
approaching something like this game by means of its technology
which can now carry people about not merely in one geometric
plane but in two—by means of aircraft as well as surface transport.

Even with the simplest possible rules the game would become
exceedingly complicated as the number of players rose, not just in
the mathematical sense—working out the logically possible moves
to maximize the score—but also in psychological terms, the
individual bargaining which would have to go on to negotiate extra
moves, the amount of reciprocity and the informal rules of co-

Fig 10/19

The Freedom Game:
Decline in freedom as number of
players increases
'Realistic' index with active
opposition

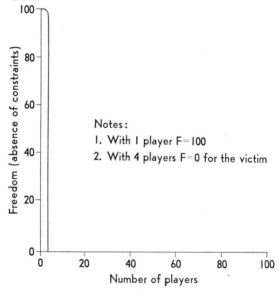

Notes:
1. With 1 player F=100
2. With 4 players F=0 for the victim

operation which developed, the sanctions against failure to carry out agreements, the amount of bloody-mindedness encountered, and so forth.

With the game deliberately made difficult by means of more complicated rules, achieving the highest possible score would require mathematical powers far beyond those of the present writer, even if full co-operation were obtained. If more than a tiny proportion of the players refused to co-operate, the combined genius of Euclid, Machiavelli, Einstein, and Botvinnik may not be adequate to the task of maximizing the score.

Figures 10/17 and 10/18 illustrate different ways of measuring number one's freedom as the number of players increases. Figure 10/17 uses the simple index of the number of empty squares, paying no attention to the practical difficulties in the way of moving between them.

Figure 10/18 is only a guess at what the 'realistic' freedom

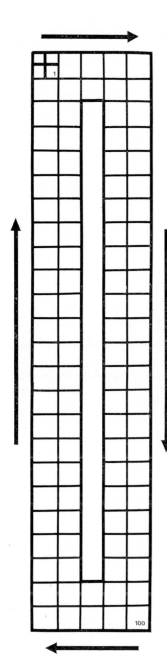

Fig 10/20

Figure 10/20 shows the freedom game taken a stage nearer reality with the 'long-board' style, the same 100 squares on a long narrow board with constraints in the form of a one-way system and a barrier down the centre line except for two communicating squares at each end. Only square number one is shown occupied but little imagination is required to picture 99 squares filled and the ensuing problems of mobility.

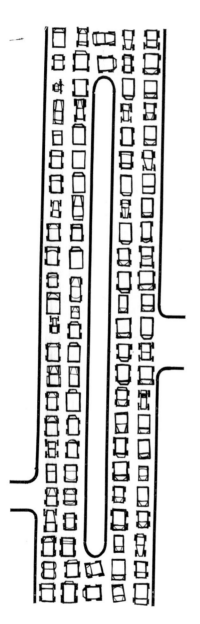

Fig 10/21

Figure 10/21 shows the game taken one stage further still, almost completely bridging the gap between fantasy and reality.

index would look like with co-operation, as measured by the practical effect on mobility of increasing numbers. The last eleven or twelve players hamper movement as much as the first eighty-nine did, a point largely borne out by experimental evidence in Chapter 12, with evidence from road traffic.

Figure 10/19 is another guess what the index would be if there was active opposition to one player which of course would involve co-operation between the others. In this case the addition of three more players could reduce number one's freedom to zero by boxing him in in a corner. (Only two more players could achieve this if only vertical and horizontal moves were allowed and the other two did not mind sacrificing their own mobility.)

Optimum vs maximum

This freedom game illustrates in an elementary fashion the problem of optimizing and maximizing desirable factors. If we maximize—valuing individual freedom of movement above all things—then the optimum number of players is one.

If we value numbers above all things and maximize capacity, the number of players would be raised to 100 at the expense of a complete disappearance of the other variable, freedom of movement.

Fig 10/22

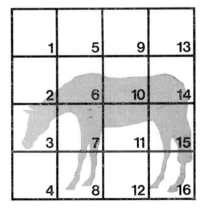

A simple way of demonstrating the disproportionate increase in complexity and difficulty of movement as the 'freedom board' is filled up is as follows.

i. Draw on paper or cardboard a square containing, say, 16 equal smaller squares for your 'board' as in Fig 10/22.

ii. Cover it with another piece of paper or card marked out in exactly the same way.

iii. Draw on the top card a design, an animal, or another picture, in such a way that only 6 of the squares are left blank.

iv. Remove the top card, cut it into its 16 squares, and temporarily discard three of the blank ones.

Fig 10/23

v. Put the 13 remaining squares on the board in random order, possibly as in Fig 10/23, and then reassemble your picture *solely by sliding the little cards about on the board*, no lifting or overlapping being allowed.

vi. Reshuffle the picture, put one of the discarded little squares back, and try again.

Fig 10/24

vii. Put another little blank square back as in Fig 10/24, and try once more.

viii. Finally, put the last square back, when it is clearly impossible to play the game any more without breaking the rules.

In some toyshops it is possible to buy this puzzle ready made—with only one blank square, of course—and it is surprising how few are able to solve it.

If we want to optimize both numbers and freedom of movement together, many solutions are possible, depending on collective values and wisdom in realizing them. A few would prefer the glorious anarchy of Fig 10/9 no doubt, while others would be tempted to go for Fig 10/15—or even 10/16—but the solutions in Figs 10/13 and 10/14 would probably appeal to the majority—on paper at least. A comfortable number and variety of players with no one hemmed in and movement not unduly restricted, even in Fig 10/16 with thirty-six players parked plus an agreed number in circulation.

The freedom game and reality

The fact that the game is a gross over-simplification of reality needs little stress, although it is true that the increasing number of people (players) viewed simply as objects does reduce human freedom to move about and increase the necessity for co-ordination and enforcement to maximize the remaining freedom. We do not all stand on squares on a large draughtboard as Alice did in some of her adventures. We do not have players moving us about unless, perhaps, as Omar Khayyam put it:

> 'Tis all a Checker-board of nights and days, Where Destiny with men for pieces plays.

Sheer size is the largest single contribution to the extra complication of the real life freedom game. We have been talking in terms of up to 100 players on a board perhaps a foot square whereas even in a small country like the United Kingdom there are 56 million people spread out over 60 million acres.

Fifty-six million players sounds a lot more than 100 players, even at face value, but the effective increase in complexity is geometric—a compound interest rather than an arithmetical growth curve. Instead of being 560,000 times more complex than the freedom game with 100 players (56 million $\div$ 100), the ratio is astronomically high.

Two further examples of real-life complication are that we really do play the game in three dimensions, and that there is no 'rotation of turns' rule restricting moves to one player at a time while all the others sit tight waiting for him to finish.

Most players in real life are free to move—or at least attempt to move—as and when they feel the urge, though society increasingly applies constraints to make us give way to each other in fairly predictable ways. Traffic lights provide a good example of the rules giving the right to make a move—not to individuals but to groups, admittedly—while others are prevented.

We can also observe certain spontaneous regularities in the behaviour of our fellow citizens which enable us to predict the future and act accordingly. We know there will be a 'rush hour' every working-day morning and evening in every conurbation and can therefore avoid it for shopping expeditions. This gives us the equivalent of a rule of the game.

If large numbers of us had helicopters, real life would be still more closely analogous to the cubic freedom game. Even without them, however, we have got to the point in all highly developed societies where our stack of draughtboards, as it were, is pretty well filled. Extremely complicated and onerous rules are now required for the 'stacking' of aircraft as they take off, move about, and try to land, but even so, the airspace of many countries is now approaching saturation point.

Many other factors make the freedom game more complicated in real life and one of them, the private property 'rule', is very important. If we allow some individuals to acquire monopoly rights over some squares this must restrict other people's freedom. If we allow these individuals to sell to others the rights to use their squares through rents, entrance fees, and the like, some of the other people's liberty would be restored, at a price, and this of course is the way our present society works.

At the other end of the spectrum we could have not private property but communality. Land could be nationalized, either in whole or in part, or taken over in some other way for communal purposes and the squares set aside for communication, recreation, and such purposes as government, organization, industry, agriculture and so forth. This again is what we do to some extent in real life because it is essential. If the allocation of land (squares in the draughtboard analogy) were to be left entirely in private hands it is difficult to see how enough communality to make the system work would be arrived at or maintained. It follows that as the number of people increases—the number of squares being fixed, of course, in real life—the greater is the demand for extra communal squares for the purposes stated—just as the supply of extra space inevitably goes down.

If the private property rule is operating and some individuals have been allowed to acquire more squares than they absolutely need, then the effective supply for communal purposes can be increased for a time simply by taking extra space away from the individual owners and there is a law of 'eminent domain'[1] which gives society precisely this power—a universal right over property required for the public good—which is being used with ever-increasing frequency. It is equally obvious both that this process is going to become much more onerous for some time and that it cannot go on indefinitely.

The two final complications added by real life are:

i. The certainty that a minority will not only not co-operate in making the rules work but will actively sabotage them—which might not happen in the game—so that society is driven to extract co-operation of a sort by coercion, or to withdraw the excessively

[1] *Dominium eminens* in legal phraseology.

recalcitrant players from the game and let them cool their heels for a time in their own private little cubes.

ii. Society retains the right to suspend, add to, rewrite, or otherwise modify the rules of the game in more or less any way at any time.

All of these differences between life and the freedom game underline the fact that it is only a pale reflection of reality but for all that it does illustrate the crux of the ecology of liberty in a finite playing space.

Let us look at the application of the game to modern Britain.

Chapter 11

The Briton's freedom game

For some minutes Alice stood without speaking, looking out in all directions over the country—and a most curious country it was. There were a number of tiny little brooks running straight across it from side to side, and the ground between was divided up into squares by a number of little green hedges, that reached from brook to brook.

Alice said at last:

'I declare it's marked out just like a large chess-board! ...

There ought to be some men moving about somewhere—and so there are! ...

It's a great huge game of chess that's being played—all over the world—'

Lewis Carroll, *Through the Looking Glass*

Let us now test the concept of an ecology of liberty in modern Britain, considering our living space as though it were set out in squares, as Alice observed, earmarked for various uses and governed by intensive 'rules', which now bear upon us more heavily and more universally every day, to ensure that they are used effectively and only for their proper purposes.

One of the major purposes for which greater and lesser squares are set aside is that of building the various structures on which modern civilization depends: housing, hospitals, schools, roads, factories, shops, administrative buildings, sewage installations, and so on. These are normally grouped together in urban areas and the process of taking over hitherto open land for these purposes is called urbanization. Let us concentrate mainly on this problem and ignore virtually all others—our inability to provide more than half of our food and many essential raw materials, for instance—however important they may be, so as to reduce the problem to its bare essentials. If we see that an impossible process is going on in one sphere—impossible in the sense that it cannot continue for much longer—then we can safely ignore the fact that impossible processes are going on in other spheres, the outcome being certain in any case.

The basis chosen for this discussion is a concise and obviously carefully thought out statement by the then Prime Minister, Mr Harold Wilson, in response to the first of a series of open letters written to him on Britain's population problem by Sir David Renton, MP. Sir David, a leading member of the Conservation Society, subsequently had the correspondence published in pamphlet form, hardly surprisingly in view of what Whitehall is said to have regarded as his distinct intellectual victory over the Prime Minister.

The first letter, in part, read as follows:

House of Commons
15th November 1966

Dear Prime Minister,

You will remember that on Thursday, 16th June, I asked you what steps were taken by HM government to predict future trends of population, to influence such trends, and to ensure that social policies are planned in accordance with a realistic and acceptable policy of controlling immigration and encouraging emigration. . . .

Sir David went on to make many of the points dealt with in this book about the United Kingdom having a very high population density, higher living standards, and consequently greater consumption of space for recreation. He stressed the great loss of land through urbanization, appended a strong plea to the government to discourage large families, among other things, and ended.

I look forward to knowing your views on these vital matters.

Yours sincerely,
David Renton

The Prime Minister replied:

From the Prime Minister   No 10 Downing Street,
                                                                              Whitehall

Dear David,

...At present only about 8 per cent of the land area of Britain is urbanized and the indications are that, if present estimates of population growth are realized, this figure will have risen only to 10 per cent by the year 2000.

Many of the most important problems in this field are in fact created by the concentration of our population in a small number of major urban areas. In my view a great deal can be done to ease the problems of a growing population by policies designed to secure a more balanced regional population growth and the government attach great importance to these. The National Plan mentioned that long-term plans are to be drawn up to provide for the increase in population. . . . Work is continuing on these, on the review of population trends and the pattern of settlement up to the year 2000, and on the examination of areas suitable for large scale development in the longer term . . . feasibility studies are to be put in hand to examine the potential for large-scale population growth on Humberside, Solentside and Tayside.

Yours sincerely,
Harold Wilson

Let us first examine what these figures mean in concrete[1] terms in the immediate future, and then consider their deeper significance when the longer view is taken.

The short-term view

Impact on land use and policy
The Guardian reported:

The Chairman of the Land Commission, Sir Henry Wells, took a strong line against the owners of 'White Land'—a planning term for land normally used for agricultural and country pursuits.

'The magnitude of the housing problem is, I am afraid, just not comprehended by the countryside.'

The plain fact was that the housing problem could not be solved without very large areas of 'White Land' being zoned

[1] In more senses than one.

and developing for housing and ancillary services.

In the South East at least 650,000 houses would have to be built in the area between the London green belt and the new developments at Milton Keynes, Northampton, Peterborough, Ipswich and South Hampshire. The siting of these houses was virtually unplanned and there was 'a clear humanitarian duty' imposed on the countryside to make land available for development. If those who control the countryside fail to recognize their duty, the Land Commission would not hesitate to put in planning applications coupled with compulsory purchase orders. . . .[2]

Impact on the Green Belt

Sir Henry Wells returned to this theme at a conference in London organized by the Federation of Registered House Builders and was reported in *The Times*[3] as follows:

TIDAL WAVE MAY HIT GREEN BELT

Sir Henry Wells, . . . gave a warning yesterday that pressure for building land would burst through on to the green belt and on to the best agricultural land like a tidal wave, if the planning machinery did not release land in areas where pressure was greatest . . . the total needed . . . [being] of the order of 36,000 acres a year over the next seven years.

This totals about 400 square miles—roughly the size of the counties of Middlesex and Rutland put together. The rate of development would almost certainly increase over the years, some authorities put it much higher already,[4] but even at this figure of 36,000 acres a year it would add over 1,700 square miles by the end of the century, about $2\frac{1}{2}$ times the county of Surrey; Suffolk plus Middlesex; Northumberland plus Huntingdonshire plus Rutland; Surrey plus County Durham; or Kent plus the Isle of Wight.

The loss of open country to towns, serious enough in its own right, is exacerbated by the fact that a disproportionate amount of the best agricultural land is used, its productivity being '. . . 70 per cent higher than the average of all enclosed farm land'.[5]

[2] October 6, 1967.

[3] November 29, 1968.

[4] Between 1960 and 1965 it amounted to 44,000 acres a year in Great Britain alone, over 20 per cent greater than Sir Henry Well's figure. See Best, RH, 'Extent of urban growth and agricultural displacement in post-war Britain', *Urban Studies*, Vol 5, No 1, February, 1968.

[5] Wibberley, GP, 'Land Scarcity in Britain', *J. of the Town Planning Institute*, April, 1967.

Not only is there this loss of good agricultural land, but many thousands of applications for development in green belts and national parks are granted each year in addition. What these add up to as a total area is not known, as no government department thinks the matter important enough to collect the relevant statistics.

Impact on existing towns

Not only will the pressure of population be felt on agricultural land, but we shall be forced into higher and higher density development in existing urban areas and in some cases this is going to mean—unless the trends change—the destruction of the character of many of our existing towns and villages, including many of our cultural treasures.

The case of Bracknell Old Town
The Guardian carried an article on this:

WHY PROMISE ON NEW TOWN HAD TO GO
Mr Crossman, the Minister of Housing and Local Government, ... who has just approved plans for the town to grow to some 60,000 people ... said in Bracknell New Town yesterday that it was 'a tragedy' that a promise to preserve the old town centre had had to be broken.

He did not like doing this, he continued, but he could not see what else could be done.... If in 1949 the town of 60,000 had been planned for, the old town centre could have been saved.... Such development must be justified by 'relieving population pressure on London....'[6]

Perhaps it is worth stressing that this promise, no doubt given and accepted in good faith was not broken by some arrogant Gauleiter acting on behalf of an authoritarian regime but by a kindly, decent, well-meaning spokesman for a democratic socialist government.

What value will promises such as these have in the future? It seems that population pressure makes inroads not only into existing urban areas and new agricultural land but into the region of trust, reliability, and respect, in politics and public affairs in general. If this continues it will become more and more a question of the most powerful groups getting what they want and the devil taking the hindmost.

[6] July 15, 1965.

Impact on the building industry

The Guardian reported:[7]

STATE OF TOTAL WAR IN THE BUILDING INDUSTRY
Britain (is) almost in a state of total war in the building industry,
Sir Donald Gibson, President of the Royal Institute of British
Architects, said at the annual luncheon of the British Precast
Concrete Federation in London yesterday.

The nation needed 40 new cities, each the size of Bristol, to
be completed at the rate of one a year.

'Those of us here are in the front line... because we have
one of the ... commodities (pre-cast concrete) that is going to be
the answer to this problem.'

He returned to a similar theme in September the following year
and was reported as follows in *The Guardian*.[8]

The number of buildings will double in Britain by the end of
the century, Sir Donald Gibson, Director General of Research
and Development at the Ministry of Public Building and Works
said ... at the opening of a school of architecture at Newcastle
University. The boom meant the reshaping of our entire
environment.... 'This is a colossal opportunity either for a more
extensive rape of Britain or to create a really beautiful Britain.
The figures ... thrown up ... [by] ... the National Economic
Plan ... call for a greater achievement by the construction
industry than is needed by any other section of our economy.'

Figure 11/1 shows the number of new town equivalents required
by the end of the century to house and supply our increasing numbers, although of course there would be room—if we permit this
huge increase to take place—for a good deal of experimentation
and variety. We could rebuild one old town upwards, at one extreme, and at the other build no new towns at all, simply scattering
small housing estates all over the country. A further possibility
would be to build the two-mile-high tower cities designed by Wilem
Frischman, each providing housing, jobs, and some of the recreation needed by a third of a million people. Yet another possibility
would be to build Soleri's 'arcologies', cities of strange geometric
shapes and an extraordinary density of population.[9]

7 April 28, 1965.
8 September 27, 1966.
9 Soleri, P (1970) *Arcology*.

Fig II/I
Building made necessary by population growth, UK 1968–2000: Equivalent numbers of existing cities or towns

Number needed		Cities or towns
Either	2 times	Greater London
or	14 times	Birmingham
or	16 times	Glasgow
or	28 times	Sheffield
or	35 times	Bristol
or	52 times	Cardiff
or	67 times	Derby
or	150 times	Cambridge
or	220 times	Bedford
or	360 times	Perth
or	1,000 times	Harwich
or	1,640 times	Caernarvon
or	5,000 times	Arundel

Notes:

1. Based on the Municipal Year Book 1970, and the Registrar General's 1968 projection

2. These figures make no allowance for:
   (a) making up the present housing backlog
   (b) replacement of obsolescent buildings
   (c) changes in design
   (d) increase in living standard

The long-term significance

In his first letter to Sir David Renton, as we saw on p 196, the Prime Minister indicated his belief that an increase in urbanization from 8 per cent in 1966 to 10 per cent in the year 2000, a mere 2 per cent, (10−8 per cent) is insignificant. Looked at a little more carefully, however the increase turns out to be really 25 per cent.

$$\frac{(10\%-8\%)}{8\%} \times 100 = \left(\frac{2\%}{8\%}\right) \times 100 = 25\%$$

Coupling this with another elementary fact, that this letter was written at the end of 1966, leaving thirty-three years to the end of the century, we see that what Mr Wilson was dismissing so airily was an increase in urbanization, that is to say building over agricultural and other rural land, of 25 per cent in less than half a lifespan. This means that in every whole lifespan the amount of rural land covered by building increases by two-thirds, in round figures, and that the urbanized area doubles about every 100 years,[10] a huge rate of increase which cannot possibly be sustained for more than a brief historical epoch. The graph in Fig 11/2 shows how the amount of urbanized land would increase if the present rate of building continues.

It starts off at the bottom left with 8 per cent of the countryside urbanized in the year 1967, goes on to Mr Wilson's 10 per cent in AD 2000, and then shows how the amount of countryside covered with buildings would increase as the years rolled by.

The horizontal scale of the graph is graduated in lifespans as well as years and we see that by the year 2340 or so, only five lifespans away, the whole of the country from John O'Groats to Lands

Fig II/2
United Kingdom:
Growth of Urbanization,
AD 1967–2340 approximately

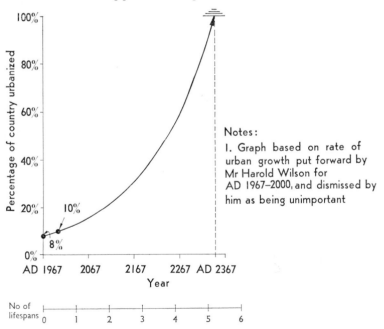

Notes:

1. Graph based on rate of urban growth put forward by Mr Harold Wilson for AD 1967–2000, and dismissed by him as being unimportant

[10] This is by no means an impossible rate. In England and Wales it doubled between 1900 and 1960.

End would be covered by buildings. By the year 2400—only one more lifespan into the future—building equivalent to an area half of the United Kingdom over again would have been built upward or over the sea to contain the increase in population, and the rate of increase itself would be increasing enormously.

England and Wales alone

If instead of the United Kingdom we take the case of England and Wales alone, the picture is far worse. By 1960 the urban area of England and Wales had reached 4 million acres, equivalent to 10.8 per cent of the total land surface, there having been a 10 per cent increase in the previous decade,[11] and a 100 per cent increase since 1900.

It has been estimated that from 1960 an additional 1,600,000 to 1,700,000 acres, around 2,600 square miles, will be required for development by the year 2000, so that the urban area then will be approaching 16 per cent of the total land surface.

This rate of increase, almost 50 per cent in forty years, means that the whole of England and Wales would be urbanized within 250 years—just over three lifespans.

The economics of space

The price of land is rising with great rapidity under the pressure of two factors, rising population and increasing per capita wealth, and it means that all activities including a land component—which is most things—are having to pay a greater and greater proportion of their income for the space they need to carry on their activities. The site values for houses and flats are rocketing, which must increase rents and mortgages in proportion, and we have already reached a situation in which many young couples will not be able to pay for their houses during their working lives because of the combination of rising costs and increased interest rates.

The lowest prices for building land in the UK are said to be in Wales and Monmouthshire where it is sometimes possible to buy building land for £1,200 an acre, going up to £18,000 in the more desirable areas. The average for Yorkshire and Humberside is in the £5,000 to £10,000 per acre range, in Bedfordshire, Essex,

[11] Equivalent to 1 per cent of the total land area of the country. See Best, R (*Op cit*).

and Hertfordshire, land is available in the £10,000 to £20,000 range, £23,000 per acre is the norm at a twenty-five-mile radius from Charing Cross, and within a five-mile radius of the same point it is £90,000 to the acre, as we have seen, with prices rising to well over a £2,000,000 per acre in the 'expensive' areas and the stratospheric level, so it is said, of £10,000,000 to the acre[12] for especially attractive sites in the City.

Open space in urban areas

In pursuit of the goal of a healthy and esthetically appealing environment, touched on in the last chapter, the County of London Development Plan, in 1951, set up an ultimate target of 7 acres of open space per 1,000 people with an immediate target of $2\frac{1}{2}$ acres per thousand.

An expert in this field, D. M. Winterbottom, has written that, in addition to $2\frac{1}{2}$ acres per 1,000 for playing fields:

A central park, in the best Victorian tradition, of some $\frac{1}{2}$ acre per thousand of the population is required, and also $\frac{1}{2}$ acre per thousand for children's play spaces ... The $2\frac{1}{2}$ acre standard should be provided in large areas of 20–25 acres serving 8–10 thousand people. This gives a total provision of $3\frac{1}{2}$ acres per thousand of population overall, which contrasts strikingly with the minimum provisions suggested by the National Playing Fields Association of 7 acres per thousand of population.

However, this writer goes on to modify these standards by drawing attention to a recent and considerable increase of emphasis on the need for open space:

... There is a growing awareness for the need of a spacious setting for a town—particularly for emphasizing the break between home and work places, and for softening the stark appearance of the vast new road structures whose provision seems to be inevitable.

As a result, it was suggested that while the physical need may only be for $3\frac{1}{2}$ acres of open space per thousand population

[12] Prices like the last mentioned seem to be the norm in very densely populated urban areas. In the centre of New York it was $400 to the square foot (£7.3 million per acre), by the mid-1960s.

within a town, the aesthetic and peripheral need is for more, probably for as much as 10 acres in all. . . .[13]

The market value of open space in towns is rising at a great rate and when society comes to realize how much capital it already has locked up in this sphere, irresistible economic forces may be let loose to bring it on the market for development, the exact opposite of the process the GLC and other authorities are engaged on, increasing the amount of open space for the rising tide of urban dwellers.

Greater London has approximately 70 square miles of parks, excluding Ministry of Works territories. At an average of, say, £50,000 an acre this represents no less than £2½ billion and the annual interest on this at a nominal 5 per cent amounts to £112 million, perhaps £65 a year for the average London family.

With the growth of 'cost benefit analysis', working mostly on the side of the angels against nuisances such as noise and pollution, it is not inconceivable that it may be turned against planners and conservationists, pointing out the enormous potential wealth which is being consumed for purposes, i e personal pleasure, which are hard to justify in economic terms, and a demand that people walking in parks must pay cash on the nail for the privilege.

If each of the London families mentioned above makes one visit per week on the average to their local park, then an economic entrance fee would be in the region of 30s, allowing a little for overheads and maintenance.

It could be argued that where the parks already exist this is an artificial calculation, that no one has bought the land at these prices and all that is required is its maintenance. However, even granting this, the GLC wants to increase its amount of open space by a factor of about three, as we have seen, and this can be achieved only by the acquisition of new land which must be paid for not only at present-day prices but at prices inflated still further by the demand created for this very purpose. In one form or another the taxpayer has got to foot the bill, if ever it is footed, that is, with costs of this order—another £5 billion or more to be found in the next few decades—our city fathers may well decide enough is enough and society will be much the poorer for it. A sad case of too many open-air lovers seeking too little open air.

[13] 'How much urban open space do we need?', *J. of the Town Planning Institute*, April, 1967.

If the GLC manages to raise its provision of open space to the levels recommended by Mr Winterbottom, 10 acres for each 1,000 persons, at a notional cost of £50,000 to the acre, its capital value will be £500,000, £500 per head. At the same nominal interest rate mentioned before, 5 per cent per annum, the annual charge would be £25 per head, about £110—£115 for the average family, or just over £2 a week unless the costs are borne by the beneficiaries only. If only one-third of the families were to use, and pay for, these improved facilities the cost would have to be three times as great, over £6 a week, ignoring overheads.

If land prices continue to rise sharply, which seems inevitable, the cost of open space will zoom even higher. In the GLC elections early in 1970, Mr Ray Thomas, a PEP economist, now of the Open University, a candidate for the 'Homes Before Roads' movement, claimed that by 1981 land in inner London will average £400,000 an acre. If his forecast is correct the cost of the park-loving family's 'open air' at the desirable level mentioned will have increased by a factor of eight to £50 a week.

The scarcity and cost of land under the pressure of excessive demand are inexorably reflected in the density of housing. In Great Britain in 1967 the average number of persons to the acre in all housing schemes was 69.2. Just under 10 per cent of all housing was in the least dense category recorded, 'below 40' persons to the acre, while about $2\frac{1}{2}$ per cent fell into the highest density category, '260 or more' to the acre.[14]

In Hong Kong, on the other hand, where the price of land has reached £9 million per acre, the latest housing schemes are working on densities of nearly 2,000 persons to the acre.[15]

The high price of land created by rising demand is leading to serious difficulties in the country as well as the urban areas. John Cherrington, the Agricultural Correspondent of *The Financial Times*, recently wrote:

> Twenty years ago, when land was £50 an acre and a 300 acre farm worth £15,000, duty on the death of the owner would have been negligible. The same farm could be worth £100,000 today on which the duty, . . . would be £25,000.

This is particularly hard on the family of an owner-occupier—

[14] HMSO *Housing Statistics; Great Britain*, No 10, July, 1968 (p 35).
[15] Reported *The Guardian*, October 5, 1968 (with photographs).

and half the farms in Britain are in this category—because his farm is valued on his death at a vacant possession price. . . .[16]

In other words, owing to this 'artificial' rise in the value of land the death duty on the farm would now be nearly twice as much as its total value when the deceased farmer bought it only twenty years ago. Few families have liquid assets of this order and these pressures mean the inevitable demise of the owner-occupier. Meanwhile we shall all have to help to pay for these inflated costs in two ways, directly in the form of higher food prices, and indirectly in the form of higher taxes to provide the state subsidies to farmers, already running at £360,000,000 a year.[17]

The Englishman's freedom game

To wind up this chapter let us combine four elements:
    (i) the notion of freedom, as expressed by Thomas Hobbes:

> . . . the absence of opposition; . . . externall impediments of motion . . . such that a person . . . is tied or environed as [he] cannot move but within a certain space, . . .

Fig II/3
The Englishman's Freedom: Decline in amount of space per head, AD 1086–2051

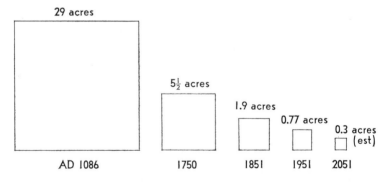

' Includes inland water

16 October 3, 1968.
17 New, 1970–71, figure.

(ii) the ecological idea of creatures in dynamic relationships with each other and their environment,

(iii) the simple geographical facts of life in England—the worst off in this respect of all the countries comprising the United Kingdom, and,

(iv) the freedom game.

Figure 11/3 shows how the size of the Englishman's square has diminished as his numbers have increased, since the time of the Domesday survey. The squares represent each Englishman's

Fig II/4

**The Englishman's Freedom:
Amount of space for each 10,000
Englishmen,
AD 1086–2000**

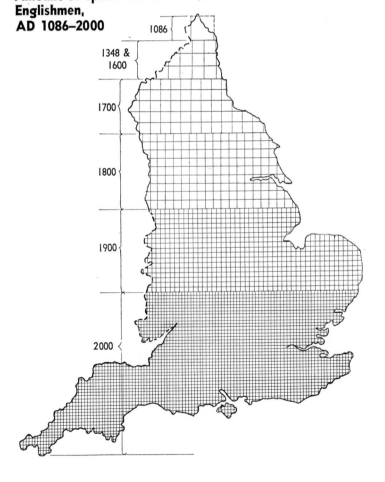

'ration' of living space, for growing food, finding a workplace, amusing himself, and all the other calls that a healthy, active person makes on his physical environment.

Figure 11/4 shows the size of the squares on the Englishman's freedom board itself—the whole country—over the same period. In this case each square represents the ration of space, not for one person as it would be too small to see, but for each 10,000 persons. The point is the same, however. The diagram shows that if past and present trends are allowed to continue much longer the Englishman will have to find some way of playing his freedom game in three dimensions in the very near future if his score is not going to drop to zero. Even in three dimensions the zero score will soon be attained if he permits his numbers to continue to increase. He cannot have his environmental cake and eat it.

Impermanence of our living platform

We have seen that the freedom game must be played on some sort of 'board', and, with the aid of Alice, considered Britain as an arena. Our strongest metaphors for reliability, permanence, and stability use many 'earthy' terms; 'terra firma', 'dry land', 'feet on the ground', 'firm as a rock', and so on, but this is possible only because of our somewhat parochial outlook. As David Hume, a man wise beyond his time, pointed out:

> There is very little ground, either from reason or observation, to conclude the world eternal or incorruptible. The continual and rapid motion of matter, the violent revolutions with which every part is agitated, the changes remarked in the heavens, the plain traces as well as tradition of a universal deluge, or general convulsion of the elements; all these prove strongly the morality of this fabric of the world; and its passage, by corruption or dissolution, from one state or order to another.[18]

Through the marvels of American technology we have seen live colour television pictures of our planet Earth and now know it for what it is, a sort of space-ship, not only finite and impermanent but, by astronomical standards, very small and rather lonely. In fact the Earth is now entering its middle age and changes appreciably as it wears and matures. There are more than a million earthquakes each year; the great continents are drifting and rotating,

[18] In an essay, 'Of the Populousness of Ancient Nations'.

the magnetic field changes and the poles wander about, and the level of the sea has gone up and down by several hundred feet[19] in part because greater and lesser quantities of water were locked up in the ice-caps and glaciers as ice-ages came and went. We have had at least four of these in recent times (geologically speaking) and no one knows whether a fifth is on its way. With our massive pollution of the atmosphere by carbon dioxide we may, through the 'greenhouse effect', raise the temperature of the Earth, melt the glaciers and again raise the sea level by at least 70 feet[20]—thereby drowning many of the world's major cities and much of its land. On the other hand our parallel pollution of the atmosphere with dust and dirt tends to lower the Earth's temperature, by scattering the sun's energy back into space, and this could start another ice age.

Nobody knows which of these tendencies will win, if either, but only a slight lowering of the Earth's temperature could trigger off a new ice-age through what engineers and cyberneticians call a 'positive feedback' process. Reflection back into space of the sun's energy could cause a slight cooling and a small increase in the extent of the polar ice-caps; these in turn would reflect back an appreciably greater amount of the sun's energy, leading to more cooling, more ice, more reflection, more cooling, more ice, . . . and so on.

Apart from these massive changes affecting the whole Earth, or large portions of it, there are local changes of considerable significance brought about by weathering—the gradual wearing away of the land through frost, rain, and wind—and coastal erosion.

We must come to appreciate that our own small piece of the Earth, Britain, 'sceptre'd'[21] though it be for the time being, is not the 'fortress'[21] Shakespeare would have had us believe.

> England, . . .
> Whose rocky shore beats back the envious siege
> Of watery Neptune, . . .[21]

In Britain we have a special problem in that our land mass is tilting in such a way that the south-east is gradually becoming submerged while the north-west is getting higher, as Fig 11/5 shows.

[19] One authority thinks sea-level may in the past have changed by more than 1,000 feet. Ref Dury, G (1966) *The Face of the Earth* (p 122).
[20] Dury (*Op cit*) (p 114). Some authorities say it would be much more.
[21] All from Richard II.11.1.

Taking London as our vantage point and looking as far into the future as we know of its past, 2,000 years of history already, we see that Roman remains found on such sites as the temple of Mithras—discovered during the construction of Bucklersbury House in 1953—are now over 6 feet below high water mark. The south-eastern counties are now some 1 to 2 feet lower than in 1850 and it seems likely that by AD 4000 all parts of London at or below 67 feet above the present sea-level will be submerged unless it is protected by massive sea walls.

Fig 11/5

Tilting Britain

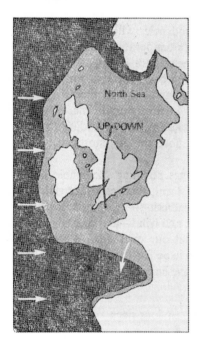
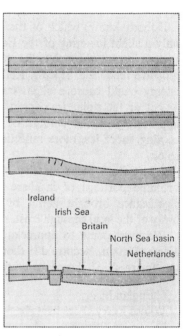

A whole province called Lionesse,[22] or Lyonesse, joining Lands End, Lizard Point, and the Scilly Isles, is said[23] to have disappeared largely in the sixth century AD and the remainder between then

[22] Referred to in *Faerie Queene*, bk vi canto ii.
[23] Willson, Beckles (undated, prob early twentieth century), *Lost England*, (Hodder and Stoughton).

and the twelfth century. Other regions are suffering rapid erosion and inundation. According to one authority[24] the 34 miles of cliffs between Bridlington and Spurn Head have worn away quicker than any other stretch of our coastline, about 83 square miles have gone since Roman times, a strip 5 to 6 feet wide disappearing every year now.

We must not look wholly on the black side, of course, already half the Dutch population lives below sea level, it is now technically feasible to build cities out to sea on the ocean shelves, and, as well as erosion and submergence, other processes forming new land are going on in some areas though it is not known whether we shall be net gainers or losers in the long run. According to Taylor and Smalley,[25] on whose writings most of this section rests, it may be that the tilt of our living platform led to the industrial revolution by causing coal to outcrop frequently and thereby provide a readily available source of energy.

It is also probable, according to Clifford Simak's exposition of the latest explanation of the succession of ice-ages—the Ewing Donn Theory—that glaciation will start again soon after the

> ... warm Atlantic waters ... get over the sill ... of the Arctic Ocean
> ... then the likelihood is that the Ice Age will continue until there is some geological change of rather massive proportions to alter the characteristics of the Arctic Ocean ...
> ... man will be forced to retreat southward as were the animals of the Pleistocene. ...

Simak points out that all this would probably take a long time and that more land would become available in the warm zone because of the recession of the oceans, nonetheless: 'The world's population will be squeezed into less living space.'[26]

This author does not consider the social implications of such massive enforced migrations but we ought at least to ponder over a situation in which an over-populated Africa, say, is invited to play host to the citizens of an over-populated Europe, possibly still of a different race,[27] for an indefinitely long period—certainly many thousands of years.

---

[24] Steers, JA (1969) *Coasts and Beaches* (p 80).
[25] 'Why Britain Tilts', *Science Journal*, Vol 5A, No 1, July, 1969.
[26] (1967) *Trilobite, Dinosaur and Man. The Earth's Story.*
[27] We may all be coffee-coloured by this time, of course.

Summary

Fortunately life in Britain has not yet reached the point at which humans and their structures consistently get in our way but there are many situations in which they do. It is now an everyday occurrence, something new in history, for human mobility to be blocked frequently and effectively simply by the presence of masses of other human beings.

Travelling in the 'rush' hour is an example of this, either on buses, tubes or other forms of public transport, or by private vehicles, as is queuing to cross the road, or get into exhibitions, places of entertainment, shops, and similar places. In some regions these conditions obtain throughout most of the working week. In shopping areas, for example, people drastically curtail each other's freedom simply by being where they are at a given time.

If numbers continued to increase this situation would become more and more the rule rather than the exception and the limiting case would be reached when the whole surface of the land not required for other essential services would be covered by human bodies, though of course, it is not argued that we shall actually reach this point.

The urbanization graph in Fig 11/2 is another example of the compound interest curve and the object of presenting it here is not to show that the United Kingdom really will be covered with buildings three or four centuries from now, but that a process which cannot possibly continue indefinitely has been started. The point is not to demonstrate that a catastrophic state of affairs will be reached by the year 2400, when urbanization *must* end because there is nothing left to urbanize, but that the process is intolerable so that it must be halted long before then. The questions can only be 'when' and 'by what means?' will this process be halted.

The problem which concerns us is not how we shall live when the whole of Britain is covered with bricks and mortar, but what will be the social processes of decision making which will halt urbanization some considerable way short of that. How will they operate, what will the alternatives be, who will choose, what will it feel like at the receiving end?

It appears that we must soon restrict both our numbers and our urge to engulf the environment in a tide of buildings even if the area we have to live on were to be fixed for all time. However, we have seen that our environment is not only not permanent but that it is changeable to the point of fickleness when viewed on a moderately long timespan.

The implication of the facts regarding the instability of our living platform is that a prudent nation will not permit its numbers to increase up to the maximum permitted by its present environment, the carrying capacity of which may diminish—despite improving technology and conservation—because of the simple fact of a diminution in its size.

Instead of thinking in terms of *terra firma* we might do better to try and see ourselves as passengers packed rather too tightly on a flimsy surfboard with an overstocked bar but little food, with no certificate of seaworthiness or pilot, and act accordingly.

In the interim the Sassenach-dominated government might do well to make friends with the Scottish nationalists ready for the day when the proportions of territory[28] are reversed and the cultural-industrial centre of the nation has been washed up from London to Glasgow.[29]

[28] At present England constitutes 57 per cent and Scotland 34 per cent of Great Britain's land area.

[29] Since this was written the 'Alice' aspect of the freedom game has been somewhat reduced by the action of the British Foreign Office in producing a working paper for the UN committee on the sea bed, which proposes that the oceans of the world shall be marked out into squares and rights of exploitation of their floors allocated by random computer techniques. Foreign and Commonwealth Office (1971), *International Regime* (mimeo).

Chapter 12

Freedom of the road

The motor car has begun to be thought of as a kind of social evil. But, in fact, it represents for most of the people of this country a tremendous breakthrough to freedom. With a motor car you can choose your leisure more adequately, you can choose where to shop and, up to a point, you can choose where to send your children to school. This is a social freedom and the people will choose freedom of mobility even if it entails pollution of the atmosphere, congestion of the city centres and all the rest of it; and it is for conscious political decision what we do with the marvellous technical advances that have been given to us.

Baroness Llewelyn-Davies of Hastoe,
speaking in the House of Lords[1]

Become one of Britain's fourteen million drivers and it would appear that you are immediately regarded as a second-class citizen—a person to be abused, restricted, regulated, taxed almost out of existence, and shackled by a thousand different laws, by-laws and regulations.

P. G. M. Gregory,
'The Plight of the Motorist'[2]

There is a certain whimsical charm in the fact that we call the period when all traffic comes to a virtual standstill the 'rush' hour, a chastening example of our seemingly ineradicable refusal to call a spade a spade. We call it the rush hour not because anybody is rushing anywhere but because a vastly increasing number of people and vehicles are trying just to crawl about in the same space. The

[1] *Hansard*, February 19, 1969 (col 855).
[2] (1968) A pamphlet published by the Conservative Political Centre.

term 'crush' hour would be very much more appropriate, were it not for the fact that the 'hour' contains anything up to 120 minutes.[3]

To anyone using our urban roads it is obvious that chaos, if not actually engulfing him at that particular instant, is only a hairsbreadth away. On other roads at other times, particularly at weekends in fine weather, at holiday times, or where sporting events draw crowds, actual chaos is common.

The BBC frequently announces traffic jams up to 20 miles long,[4] miles of motorway blocked by multiple crashes and sealed off from other road users until armadas of police-cars, AA or RAC patrols, breakdown trucks, and ambulances have cleared the wreckage, human and mechanical, convoys of mechanized morons hurtling into banks of thick fog at 50 miles an hour or more and many other neon-like examples of the writing on the wall for our 'freedom of the road'.

We all know the situation cannot continue to deteriorate at this pace and most of us know in our hearts, spokesmen for motoring interests probably excepted, that there is no possibility of dealing with the problem if the flood of cars is allowed to continue unabated. We all know our island is small, our population density very high, and that pressure on our land resources, already colossal, is increasing, and yet the relationship of all these factors to road traffic seems to be almost systematically avoided. Accordingly I shall attempt to spell out some of the more pressing problems and show that population growth is the key factor, and in case what follows sounds like a diatribe against motorists and everything to do with them perhaps I ought to mention in passing that I started my own motoring career in 1930 at the age of nine, driving a bull-nosed Morris bread-van on the private parts of its delivery round near Burton-on-Trent. I also drove, about the same time, a Sunbeam big twin combination of which the motor-cycle part had a distinct list to port. Keeping it straight almost wrenched my young arms out of their sockets. My official driving career started at the age of sixteen with a solo 350 cc side-valve New Imperial motor bike, bought for 50s, and it has continued with motor vehicles of many shapes, sizes, and vintages ever since, at present averaging a modest 12/14,000 miles a year.

[3] The length of the 'rush' hour varies directly with the size of the town.
[4] A jam 36 miles long was reported in May, 1970, more than 100 miles of road being blocked simultaneously.

For the same reason let me call on a distinguished and wholly committed representative of motoring interests to lay the foundation stone of my case, Mr A. C. Durie, Director General of the Automobile Association and Vice-chairman of the British Road Federation, with an excerpt from a paper[5] he presented at a meeting of the Insurance Institute of London:

> We are well aware of all the advantages that make the motor car the most 'beloved monster' of our time but are we equally aware of its anti-social aspects which are at last beginning to affect the public conscience? Already, those concerned with the development of this most important and revolutionary invention since the wheel are paying increased attention to such factors as noise, fumes, congestion, and accidents which on a global scale are equivalent in loss of life and injury of the greatest wars in history. . . .

> It is high time that we began to take the business of road safety seriously and realized that [we] . . . have an unmistakable responsibility to tackle this enormous social evil. Legislation against noise levels and air pollution from exhaust fumes will become an increasingly common part of any government's programme. . . .

> . . . Those of us alive in the 1980s [will] look back to the noise and stench we put up with today with a kind of stupefied amazement that we could ever have endured it.

Microfreedoms on the roads

The two quotations about motoring freedom at the head of this chapter seem to be flatly contradictory. At least they present a curious paradox. Which of them has got it right? Baroness Llewelyn-Davies or P. G. M. Gregory?

Both are right up to a point if we analyse the conflict between them in terms of the concept of microfreedoms. The Baroness is right in saying that in acquiring a motor car in our society one acquires also a 'breakthrough' from *some* constraints to *some* microfreedoms, though it may be doubted if the total is as 'tremendous' as she says.

The new owner of a motor vehicle gains the microfreedom to set off on any journey at any time, his worries about time-tables,

---

[5] *Motoring into the 1980s*, January 22, 1968, subsequently published by the AA.

connections, stations, and bus stops ceasing forthwith. He gains the microfreedom of door-to-door transport and the right to change his mind about his destination en route, he can turn off and explore somewhere that takes his fancy, stop for a meal, a nap, or a paddle in an inviting brook—even about-turn and go home. A further gain is that at little extra cost he can take with him as many people as his vehicle will hold and the same applies to luggage or other goods. If he is able and prepared to pay dearly he gains a further microfreedom to travel in great luxury and comfort.

Many microfreedoms will be gained by acquiring a motor car but all of them will be at a certain cost. The most immediate of these will be the loss of the microfreedom to spend on other things the substantial sum of cash involved. Cars already cost a good deal more than public transport, as a general rule, and are likely to cost a great deal more in the future.

What about the new car owner's microfreedoms vis-a-vis his new status as a '... person to be abused, restricted, regulated etc.?' On acquiring the new status of car owner we immediately lose many microfreedoms we possess as pedestrians alone. Our use of road space is immediately constrained—when at the wheel we are not allowed to wander about at will as we are when on foot. We have to pay a tax to use the vehicle on a public road and for insurance against third-party risks. We must qualify and pay for a driving licence and many other items—we have lost our microfreedoms to do without all of these things. People regard most of these as reasonable, up to a point; the vital question, however, is up to *what* point?

The point at which natural constraints develop and further restrictions must be applied comes earlier and earlier as numbers increase. The motorist's microfreedom to move about in his own good time as the Baroness emphasized is purely nominal. He can move from position 'A' to position 'B' only if someone is not occupying it at the time he wants to be there, and he will not even be able to get to 'B' to find whether it is occupied or not if many others want to be on the route between 'A' and 'B' at the same time.

Motoring writers often seem to sense in an essentially unconscious way the approach of the inevitable point of total saturation of our road system, if population is allowed to increase indefinitely, and lash out in a sort of Pavlovian freedom reflex to assert their 'right' to unrestricted mobility in private transport.

For instance Mr A. C. Durie, the distinguished commentator already mentioned:

> By the 1980s we shall have double the number of motor cars—
> *demanding freedom to flow . . .*[6]

There was another example in *Drive* recently:

> Too often government has operated almost in the belief that if motoring is ignored or discouraged, it will go away: that if cities are permitted to congeal with traffic . . . motorists will renounce *their entitlement to freedom of movement. . .*[7]

The final example comes from another well-known public figure, Mr James Fisher, a naturalist and Deputy Chairman of the Countryside Commission, who almost manages to state the threat realistically and then retreats before its implications, albeit in fairly good order and to a prepared position, with a rearguard action designed to drive away elementary ecological facts by appeals to courage and morality:

> Motor cars can . . . exert grave erosive pressures . . .
> [and] . . . the prospect of . . . vehicles doubling by the end of the century, if not in the next decade, is a mighty challenge, . . . for we have a warm, traditional love for the personality of our country-side.
>
> We know we have to lose some hundreds of rural square miles to the new towns, industrial developments, airports and roads. . . .
>
> But I do not foresee a clash between human and motor population on the one hand and our landscape . . . on the other, so long as we keep our nerve and listen to everyone concerned in planning. If we do, *our great grandchildren may still motor freely through Britain's green and pleasant land.*[8] (Italics added in all three quotations)

Numbers versus freedom

The relationship between the numbers of vehicles and road-space, the ecology of motor transport as we might call it, seems to be

[6] (*Op cit*).

[7] 'It's Highway Robbery', Autumn, 1969 (p 32).

[8] James Fisher, 'Taming the Big Game', *Drive*, Summer, 1969. (By 'Big Game' Mr Fisher meant cars, referring especially to those called 'Jaguars', 'Hunters', 'Gazelles', and similar names.) It is noted with regret that Mr Fisher was killed in a road accident after these words were written.

almost universally ignored; it has been overlooked even by such an astute, hard-headed, and unprejudiced commentator on motoring matters as Ian Breach of *The Guardian*.

No one seems to write much about it, possibly because it's assumed that everyone knows, but France has a road network that can surely be bettered nowhere in the world ... [and] carries a mass of traffic that seldom seems to jam ... the Routes Nationale which carry the faster moving and heavier traffic ... are often empty for poplar-avenued miles at a stretch ...[9]

It surely cannot be left out of the reckoning that the population of France is only 50 million, against Great Britain's 54.2 million, that France covers 210,000 square miles against our 89,000—giving population densities of 238 and 610 per square mile, respectively—and that France has only 26 vehicles[10] per mile of roadway against our 59. Our population density is more than two-and-a-half times as great as theirs while our roads are two-and-a-quarter[10] times as heavily loaded. It is small wonder that Britons fortunate enough to spend a holiday motoring in France can hardly believe their own eyes.[11]

In his admirable book[12] on safe driving J. E. Howard says, in a chapter called 'Roadspace: the heart of the matter':

The larger the roadspace ... the greater [the drivers'] freedom of choice.

In spite of this, however, and a thorough development of the theme in all other directions, he omits to point to the elementary fact that the individual driver's roadspace is rapidly approaching zero.

It is hard to see how the implications of the critical and painfully obvious connections (with a road system of a given size[13])

[9] *The Guardian*, October 20, 1969.
[10] Mid-1969 figures throughout, cars, goods vehicles, buses, and coaches only.
[11] Since writing the above passage I have spent a summer holiday motoring and camping in France, mainly in Brittany, and it was a revelation after fifteen years of living and driving in SE England. It felt almost like visiting another planet.
[12] (1967) *How to Drive Safely. The Art of Survival.* The Appendix by his wife, Marghanita Laski, 'The role of the navigator', will be received with heartfelt gratitude by most drivers.
[13] There are of course 'economies of scale' up to a certain point; there must be enough motorists to make it worthwhile to provide a road system.

between the number of vehicles, and the motorist's freedom can be so widely ignored. Let us spell them out by examining relationships between numbers and the individual driver's freedom in terms of speed, cost, and frustration. The four most important possible theories about the effect of numbers on these variables are as follows.

1. *No effect.* Number of vehicles makes no difference.

2. *Random effect.* Increase in numbers sometimes makes conditions better, sometimes worse, sometimes has no effect.

3. *Positive effect.* Increase in numbers improves conditions.

4. *Negative effect.* Increase in numbers makes conditions worse.

There are no other possibilities—ruling out more or less magical relationships—and it is obvious that the last theory is correct, the one we see borne out in everyday life.

The table in Fig 12/1 shows the relationship between the amount of traffic and motorists' freedom in terms of three basic micro-freedoms, plus the capacity of the system, in accordance with the only sensible theory of the four, the 'negative effect' theory. Figure

Fig 12/1
Decreases in freedom with increase in traffic: The 'negative effect' theory

Vehicles	Freedom indicators			
	Speed	Frustration	Cost	Road capacity[1]
One	Highest	Lowest	Lowest	Smallest
Small number	High	Low	Low	Small
Moderate number	Moderate	Moderate	Moderate	Moderate
Large number	Low	High	High	Large
Saturation point[2]	Very low	Very high	Very high	Largest
Over-saturation	Extremely low	Extremely high	Extremely high	Reduced from largest
Stagnation[3]	Zero	Infinite	Infinite	Zero

[1]. ' Road capacity ' means not the number of vehicles the road can contain, but the number which can get through in a given time

[2]. Defined as ' ultimate capacity ' (Qm) by the Road Research Laboratory, and equivalent to the point at which the maximum possible number of vehicles is getting through in a given time. If more **try** to get through, fewer will **succeed**

[3]. ' The term ' locking ' is often used by engineers and scientists studying traffic problems

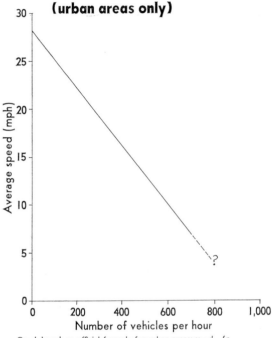

Fig 12/2

Fall in average speed with increase in traffic (urban areas only)

Graph based on official formula for urban areas: v = d − fq

Where v = actual speed
      d = desired speed (say 28 mph in urban areas)
      f = a constant based on the capacity of the road
and q = no of vehicles per hour

See Thompson, J. M., Road Research Laboratory, **Road Pricing in Central London** (1962), PRP 18

12/2 shows graphically how speed declines as numbers increase.

With pressure on road space increasing at this intolerable rate potential savings must be fully explored and put into effect where possible. Figure 12/3 shows the rapid decrease in roadspace required as speed is reduced. The Minister of Transport has already utilized this fact in his blanket limit of 70 mph, which was followed by a 20 per cent reduction[14] in accidents on the M1, for example, and the temporary limits of 50 mph in certain congested periods. A further saving in road space would be made by imposing lower

[14] HMSO *Road Research 1968* (p 88ff).

Fig 12/3

Disproportionate increase in road-space required with increase in speed

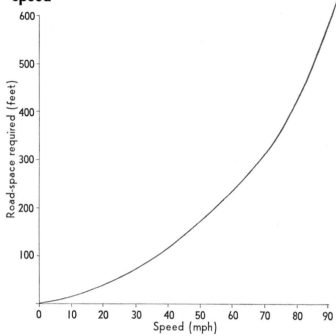

[1] Required by safe stopping distance (based on Ministry of Transport data)

limits and there will be great pressure on succeeding ministers to do this.[15]

Prevention of parking on the road is another way in which precious space may be saved. Studies on the A5 have shown that a single parked vehicle reduces the average speed of passing vehicles from 33 to 26 mph, 26 per cent.[16] It is inconceivable that we can allow much longer the microfreedom to acquire a motor vehicle and store it, as a matter of policy, on public roadspace.

Many other studies have shown that public transport uses road-space much more efficiently than private cars. Leicester's Planning

[15] Recent French experiments with speed limits have cut accidents by 40 per cent.
[16] HMSO (1965) *Research on Road Traffic* (p 426).

Officer, W. K. Smigielski, has called the motor car '...the most clumsy, uneconomic, and inconvenient form of urban transport...'[17] It covers 80 square feet of precious roadspace for an average of 1.4 occupants.

Cars carrying the same number of people as a bus occupy twelve times as much roadspace when stationary and thirty times as much roadspace when in motion.

Mr Roy Smith of London Transport has pointed out that buses entering central London form only one-sixth of the peak traffic while carrying 60 per cent of the road passengers. Cars carry only one-third while constituting 80 per cent of the traffic.

Mr Durie argued at a British Road Federation Symposium that congestion costs in London alone, caused by cars as we have seen, will be £100 million a year by 1980[18] while it was estimated in 1968 by Stephen Swingler—then Minister of State at the Ministry of Transport—that completely 'free' bus and tube services for London would cost only £70 to £80 million[19] a year.

There seem to be some pointers here for a rational use of space and wealth.

'Saturation' point

The number of motor vehicles on British roads doubled between 1956 and 1968, up to $14\frac{1}{2}$ million,[20] approximately, and we now have less space per vehicle than any other country. Numbers are expected to go on rising until we reach about 36 million by the year 2000 by which time, it is often said, 'saturation' will have been reached.

Saturation point is an ambiguous concept which needs to be used with some care. It is easy to run away with the idea that reaching saturation point about the year 2000, means that bad though the situation may be, things can't get any worse. This interpretation is wrong, and in an attempt to sound out govern-

[17] 'Fitting transport to the city', *The Municipal and Public Services J*, August 9, 1968.

[18] 'Paying For London Roads', a contribution to a British Road Federation Symposium, 'Roads in London', November 18, 1968.

[19] Reported *The Guardian*, June 19, 1968.

[20] This understates the problem as traffic is increasing quicker than the number of vehicles because individual vehicles are being used more. Between 1958 and 1968 traffic increased by 105 per cent. According to Morgan, EV, 'Economic and Financial Aspects of Road Improvements', October, 1965, '...traffic in 1980 will be nearly three times that of 1960'.

ment thinking on this topic, among other things, I wrote to the Minister of Transport on March 13, 1969, asking:

1. When and at what point is 'saturation' point in terms of the numbers of vehicles per head of the population likely to be reached?
2. What will be the residual growth of traffic due to population increase, the first saturation point having been reached?
3. When is 'saturation point' in the second sense of that term. i e saturation of the road system likely to be reached?
4. What steps are to be taken, if any, to avoid saturation point in the second sense coming about?

The reply came on June 19:

... Saturation point, in the sense of the maximum number of vehicles per head that can be expected in this country is a theoretical concept. The actual value of this level can be altered by fashion in vehicle ownership and restrictions on ownership and usage of vehicles. On the other hand it is currently believed that the vehicle ownership level will reach within 5 per cent of the current expected saturation value, calculated as 0.53 vehicles per head,[21] by the mid 1990s.

Shortening the terms to 'saturation 1', referring to the number of cars per head, and 'saturation 2' referring to the swamping of the road system, the Minister's spokesman completely ignored the latter, saturation 2, and this is fairly typical. None of us want to accept the finiteness of our environment so perhaps we cannot lay too much blame at the door of politicians.

Nevertheless the problems will not go away and my letter continued:

The public does not like facing difficult problems even of the present, let alone the future, and nobody wants to spend the amounts of money required to deal with the vast increases in traffic towards the end of the century, but I hope you will agree that this very reluctance makes it the more essential for someone somewhere to try to take the long view and work out sensible plans in the light of likely contingencies.

---

[21] This information is often given as so many persons per motor vehicle. To convert, divide 1 by the figure given. In this case 0.53 vehicles per head equals 1.9 persons per vehicle, approximately.

Considering cars[22] alone, at the moment the Americans have fewer persons for each one than any other nation. In 1962 the figures were 2.5 for the USA, 3.2 in Canada, 4.0 in Sweden, 4.7 in France, 5.2 in Great Britain, 7.3 in Italy, 264 in Japan, and 1,052 in India. It will be seen that despite the congestion on our roads Britain has quite a distance to go to catch up on the wealthy Swedes and Canadians, let alone the Americans, a nation thought by many experts to have reached saturation 1.

Of course, this prophecy could be false—people may want more cars than we expect—but insofar as it is false it will only strengthen the arguments that follow.

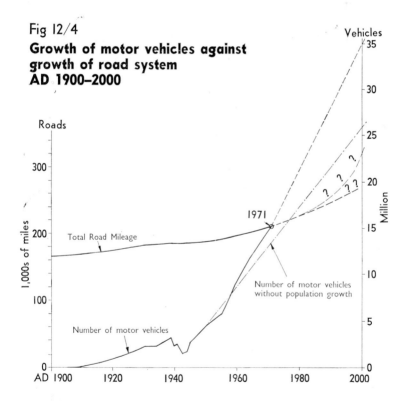

Fig 12/4

Growth of motor vehicles against growth of road system AD 1900–2000

Based on data from:

(a) British Road Federation, **Basic Road Statistics** 1968

(b) HMSO, (1968) **Highway Statistics**

(c) Correspondence with Ministry of Transport

[22] Including taxis.

Saturation 2 is a more fundamental concept, related to the number of motor vehicles—not just cars and taxis, of course—and the capacity of the environment, and it could be reached long before saturation 1. If a country has little in the way of roads, and space to build them, then long before it has as many vehicles per head as America, say, its road system could be swamped. However, even where there is plenty of roadspace for the time being, so that growth in the ownership of cars and other motor vehicles can go on until saturation 1 is attained, if the population keeps getting bigger the number of vehicles will go on increasing beyond that point, towards saturation 2.

Figures 12/4, 12/5, and 12/6 show how inexorably the roads of Britain are approaching saturation 2, and, as we see in everyday experience, the nearer we are to this point the worse is the effect

Fig 12/5
Decrease in road-space per motor vehicle: Great Britain, AD 1900–2000

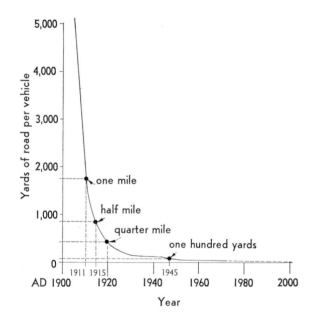

Based on data from British Road Federation, **Basic Road Statistics** 1968 pp24–5

Fig 12/6
Yards of road per vehicle, 1968
(cars, goods, buses and coaches
only)

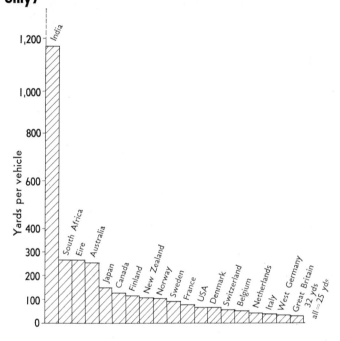

Based on British Road Federation, **Basic Road Statistics** 1969
pp14–16

of each extra vehicle. This is demonstrated indirectly by means
of a consideration of congestion costs—shown in Fig 12/11—but
meanwhile let us look at some experimental evidence produced by
the Road Research Laboratory. The experiment,[23] carried out at
Northolt airport, consisted of 'weaving' through a circuitous track
with varying traffic densities in an attempt to find out the 'ultimate
capacity' of the system, (Qm), already defined.

The ultimate capacity of the test section was 3,250 vehicles per
hour and the following figures show how disproportionate is the
increase in dislocation as saturation 2 is approached. Increasing
the flow by 100 per cent from 1,000 to 2,000 vehicles an hour

[23] Road Research Laboratory (1965) *Research On Road Traffic.*

increased the journey time for each vehicle by only 6 per cent approximately. From this point a further 50 per cent increase, from 2,000 to 3,000 an hour, raised the journey time by 44 per cent, the third 1,000 having seven and a half times more effect than the second. Raising the flow by a mere 8 per cent from this point, by only 250 vehicles an hour, up to the 'ultimate capacity' of the system (nearing saturation 2) increased the time by over 60 per cent.

The Technology Correspondent of *The Guardian* recently stated that an increment even smaller than 8 per cent can be critical:

> ...it only needs an extra 5 per cent of traffic to bring an adequately moving system to a standstill.[24]

The population effect

A vehicle population increases under the influence of two factors, growth in the human population and growth in individual income.[25] The evidence of our rapid approach to saturation 2 puts the population factor in sharp focus. There is very little we could do at present about the second factor, the increase in individual wealth; our whole philosophy is geared to rising standards of living so that saturation 1 is inevitable, even though we may come to discover that it cannot be maintained. This means that we must look very closely at population, which—if the other is inevitable—is at once the factor taking us over the last fatal leap to saturation 2 and the only one under our control.

The lower curve in Fig 12/4 and the table in Fig 12/7 show that if our population had remained stationary at the 1948 level, as the Royal Commission so earnestly desired (48.7 million for Great Britain), while living standards and per capita car ownership continued to rise at the rate actually experienced so far from the 3¾

---

[24] January 23, 1970. This is borne out by empirical studies. For example GEC-Elliot Automation Ltd, of Cologne, have written (private communication) '...traffic breakdowns occur whilst the flow...increases by 3 per cent or 5 per cent'. They add: 'One important part of GEC-Elliott Traffic Automation's Signal Plan Generation program is called density control. In case of a too high traffic demand within the controlled area, it provides "gating" at the entrances to the area, restricting the green period at certain key intersections, thus keeping traffic volume just below the saturation value and ensuring "flow conditions." '

[25] In London in 1966 only a quarter of the families with an income of £15 a week had a car, against a half of those with £25 a week.

million vehicles of 1948, and then reached saturation 1 at AD 2000, the rate of approach to saturation 2 would have been very different. Instead of $14\frac{1}{2}$ million vehicles in 1968[26] we would have had 13 million, some 10 per cent less, while in AD 2000 we would be 9 million (26 per cent) short of the forecast total of about 35 million. Putting it another way we see that, if present trends continue, population growth will have contributed about a third of the total vehicle growth between 1948 and AD 2000.[27] Or, in yet another way; the total of vehicles with population growth will be nearly 35 per cent greater than it would have been without population growth, other things being equal.

It is easy to imagine what an enormous difference to the traffic situation the absence of the 'population increment'—equal to the

Fig 12/7
Number of motor vehicles with and without population growth, Britain, 1948–2000

Year	No of vehicles (millions)		
	Without population growth	With population growth	Extra no caused by population growth
1948	3.728	–	–
1968	13*	14.446	1.5*
2000	26*	35*	9*

Note:
All asterisked figures are approximate

total vehicle population in 1961—would have made by itself, but its absence would have liberated a very large amount of capital by reducing the 'demographic investment' and enabled us to spend much more on the roads if we wanted to, so the situation could have been doubly improved.

In summary we see that saturation 1 is inevitable, that saturation 2 would have been highly probable even with a population stabilized at the number in 1948, as the Royal Commission recommended. Under the combined influence of greater individual wealth and population growth saturation 2 seems as inevitable as saturation 1, and the implication of this is that there must be an

26 3.7 persons per vehicle. (Not just cars and taxis, i e.)
27 268 per cent of the 865 per cent increase, i e.

increasing burden of control to keep the system functioning for the time being and, finally, complete control to prevent a complete stoppage.

Increase in the number of controls

The greater the number of vehicles playing the freedom game in a confined space the more they have to be controlled by one means or another to prevent their hitting each other and the boundaries of the system—not to mention ever-increasing numbers of unfortunate bystanders, as Fig 12/10 shows. The increase in control can be brought about by direct means[28]—through electro-mechanical mechanisms, probably computerized—or indirectly through a framework of law and socio-cultural norms.

Britain, the USA, and most other countries with road traffic problems are pressing ahead rapidly on both fronts and it seems likely that these trends must continue, rapidly eroding all the motorists' microfreedoms except, as far as possible, the basic ones:

(*a*) to be on the road at all, and
(*b*) to keep moving.

Let us look at the indirect means of traffic control in a little more detail. The flood of new controls needs no documentation and Michael Wolff, a London magistrate, has written:

> I have no doubt that there are too many laws in our country, and too many motoring laws. We are supposed to be a free society, but freedom means freedom to make mistakes as well as to make good. ...
>
> I would like to see our motoring laws so amended that ... the element of danger became the chief consideration and the prevention of dangerous driving ... the principal object. That would do away with literally hundreds of minor offences ...
>
> What I want above all is for the law to be respected. The present jungle of motoring laws does not command respect: let's clear it.

[28] See 'Area Traffic Control' in *Road Research 1967* and *Road Research 1968*, mentioning the 1967 central Glasgow experiment, for example. See also 'Automatic Vehicle Guidance' in the same publications. It has been estimated that automatic guidance would more than pay for its costs by savings in road investment and accidents.

From such a change in the law there could follow a change in the manner in which it is enforced. With few if any of the routine motoring offences liable to prosecution, traffic duties could be handed over to a highly mobile traffic corps, which by being allowed to enforce a law that is respected would itself earn respect.[29]

Mr A. C. Durie supported this line of argument in the paper mentioned earlier:[30]

If you allow for the permutations which can be and are used there are 2,000 laws, rules, regulations, statutes, and ordinances which the manufacturer, owner, or operator of a vehicle can infringe each time he takes, or permits to be taken, a vehicle on to the road. This is a situation bordering on the farcical and one that in the 1980s, with a vast increase in the number of motor vehicles, will become chaotic.

Mr Durie went on to argue:

I do not plead for changes in motoring law in order to permit motorists to behave as they like. The AA holds no brief for bad drivers or for persistent offenders.

I plead for a simplification of the whole structure of motoring law in the cause of the general good of the general public. Not only would the relationship between police and motorists be improved but there would be far greater good will between motorist and motorist, *and* motorist and pedestrians.

In their very proper concern with law and its enforcement neither Mr Wolff nor Mr Durie show any insight into the interaction of complex systems, such as road traffic in society, and the problems brought about by the sheer fact of size. Indeed, Mr Durie argued in favour of a large number of *new* restrictions. He recognized that drastic reorganization will have to take place and there will be much more stringent control on motoring behaviour in all sorts of ways. We shall have to be trained as motorists from the cradle upward, more or less, and he makes twenty or thirty specific suggestions for more rigorous control of drivers:

... I would like to see a more ruthless cutting out of right turns, the channelling of traffic into lanes, ... much more rigid

29 'Are our police still wonderful?' *Drive,* Spring, 1969.
30 *Motoring into the 1980s.*

enforcement of lane discipline and the improvement of direction and advanced direction signs. Included with this should be the establishment of a standard for street nameplates . . .

There must be a greater increase in one-way streets and more 'total flow' systems. . . . Greater discipline at road crossings is required. Many motorists *will* proceed into a crossing although it is perfectly obvious that the way out is not clear. More 'yellow box' systems should be employed in an attempt to educate these motorists into better habits . . . goods vehicles in the business community will operate in a 24 hours 'stretched day' to unload and load their goods outside peak commuter travel hours. . . .
. . . overhead indicators will tell a driver how fast to go to arrive at the next signal during the green—or 'go'—phase.

While Mr Durie's list of new restrictions was most impressive, as we have seen, he was not able to suggest a single candidate for abolition among the old ones, or give any hint of the sort of tidying up or streamlining which might take place.

It is interesting to see a distinguished representative of motoring interests arguing along these lines. The fundamental dichotomy between the growth of motor traffic and the possibility of living a reasonably civilized life seems to be well appreciated by him at one level and yet completely rejected at another. He is fully aware of the enormous problems that motor transport has already brought and the still greater evils in store for the future unless something little short of a miracle occurs.

If, as these two commentators would have us do, we were to abolish scores or even hundreds of regulations dealing with speed, overtaking, parking, loading, driver fitness, vehicle roadworthiness, and so forth, we would automatically introduce an enormous area of discretion into the policeman's discharge of his duties. If there were no law which said that 30 miles an hour is the limit in lighted urban areas, every policeman would have to judge the case of every car that passed him during his tour of duty and the strain on policemen, motorists, and the courts would very soon become insupportable.

This is not to say that Mr Durie's goal is impossible. Provided we accept a drastic reorganization of the whole of motoring law, which he demands, for a short time it might be feasible to go on adding new regulations and more than compensating by the repeal of existing ones but obviously this is possible, if at all, only to a certain limited degree even in theory, without considering the practical possibilities.

There cannot be any significant increase in the liberty of the individual motorist while the number of vehicles continues to increase so markedly in such a small country as Britain. The more there are the more they must be regulated. The idea that there can be some great sweeping reform transforming the situation and giving the motorist the hoped for freedom of the Shetland pony in the wild is utterly utopian.

Increase in the difficulty of enforcing traffic control

If an ever larger and more complex traffic system is allowed to evolve, and this necessitates an ever-increasing body of control measures, both formal and informal, then it is reasonable to expect an increase in the difficulty of actually enforcing those controls and this is what we find.

Some of these problems concern sheer size. For example, the BBC announced[31] in April, 1969 that the number of stolen cars is now so great that it is impossible to issue lists of their registration numbers to policemen on the beat and in patrol cars. A senior police spokesman said: '... each constable would now require a list the size of the family Bible!'

If the proportion of car thefts remains the same, obviously the absolute number of cars stolen must increase as the population increases, with the result we see above, that it progressively becomes more difficult, and eventually impossible, to track down the thieves by the means previously adopted. This means an increase in liberty for thieves and a decrease in liberty for the law-abiding citizenry.

A survey done by the School of Work Studies[32] showed that the chances of finding a vacant parking meter in Mayfair between 9 a m and 5 p m were 66:1 against, rising to 100:1 against between the hours of 11 a m and 2 p m. The chances of being caught parking on a yellow line were 15:1 against.

Ten thousand two hundred observations were made, spread over 244 meters. The results were that while in 447 cases cars were over their allotted period by as much as 30 minutes only 93 had received

[31] April 9, 1969.
[32] *The Guardian*, December 1, 1969. A follow-up survey, reported on the BBC, November 23, 1970, showed that the situation had deteriorated still further.

a 10s 'excess' ticket. Four hundred and eighty observations showed the £2 penalty was due but of these only 158 had received tickets.

The outcome of this is that it seems to be better—leaving the moral, legal, and ecological aspects aside—to take a chance on parking on the yellow line rather than waste time trying to find a vacant meter.

Of the relatively few illegal parkers in Greater London who do get tickets less than 60 per cent[33] are brought to justice. The odds against being caught and paying the penalty approach 25 to 1.

Enforcing the law here would obviously require many more staff, at greatly increased cost, substantially reduce the effective number of parking places, and further worsen relations between the public and the police. Michael Wolff, the London magistrate, wrote in the article already quoted:

> Want to see a punch-up? no need to wait until the next political demonstration. Just drop in on your friendly neighbourhood magistrate's court. . . . A big city for preference . . . when motoring cases are being heard. That is where the action is.
>
> I don't mean broken noses or policemen's helmets sent flying. Nothing unseemly like that. I mean the insidious in-fighting. . . .
>
> . . . At our busy London court I sometimes hear eighty motoring cases in a day. Week by week, case after case, I see the trust and confidence between citizen and police strained to breaking point. I believe that the conflict between the police and the motorist is one of the most disturbing factors in our troubled society today. No police force can carry out its duties without the confidence and support of the people. . . .
>
> Increasingly, motorists tend to give policemen 'a piece of their mind', especially if they reckon they've been caught anyway.
>
> Here is the conflict between police and public in general. When a case reaches the courts—and in 1967 there were nearly one and a half million motoring prosecutions—the conflict becomes intensified. All's fair in love and war and the motoring court. No holds are barred. . . . What is forgotten is that at stake is not only a man's driving licence but also the very basis on which law and order are maintained: the confidence between police and public.

The police increasingly resent the position into which this conflict with the motorist is pushing them. It is described in the

---

[33] Colin Woods, *Police Review*, March, 1969.

social survey of the 1962 Royal Commission on the Police as 'the burden of social isolation that the police feel their position carries'.

... Of nearly 6,000 complaints a year, a third arise out of the police's traffic duties. ...

Only about a quarter are likely to have any foundation, and perhaps only 10 per cent can actually be substantiated.

This pressure on the police can lead to psychological problems with tendencies to compensation, and possibly over-compensation, on their part, as Mr Wolff discussed in detail.

Road saturation and motor taxation

One of the forms that indirect control can take is fiscal measures and these can be brought to bear on either the purchase or amount of use of motor vehicles, or both.

Commenting on the Little Neddy report on the motor industry, Victor Keegan argued in *The Guardian* that by means of fiscal controls:

For seven years the Government has deliberately kept demand for new motor cars at around 1.1 million a year.

He pointed out that if the 3.5 per cent per annum growth rate in consumer expenditure is attained—a middling estimate—

... two million registrations per year would be in sight by 1974.[34]

Mr Pat Gregory, in the pamphlet mentioned earlier, wrote about motor taxation as follows:

... For years [the Road Fund] had been shamelessly plundered until we now have the situation where the taxes that the motorist pays for the doubtful privilege of being a corner-stone of the nation's economy are wholly divorced from his personal needs to continue motoring in order that, in turn, he can again continue to pay the taxes involved in his harmless, healthy pursuit.

After reading the later section on accidents the reader may be inclined to speculate just how many casualties motor vehicles would have to cause before Mr Gregory withdrew his euphoric adjectives. 'healthy' and 'harmless', quite apart from the obesity and

[34] February 2, 1970.

denegerative diseases of many motorists who deprive themselves of exercise, but his howl of protest against the alleged persecution of motorists by successive governments continues in like vein.

Although some of it is Conservative propaganda the diatribe was by no means directed solely at the then Labour administration, indeed, the first culprit mentioned in the pamphlet is Winston Churchill. As Chancellor of the Exchequer in 1909 he was the first to appropriate money from the Road Fund (£7 million), and to ordain that one-third of all revenue from motor vehicle duties on private cars should be diverted to central funds. Mr Churchill freely admitted it was a new source of revenue to the state, pointing out in 1927 that 'the coffers of the Road Fund are continually overflowing'.

To the best of my knowledge there were no 'Winston Churchill must go' stickers in those days though we can take it that feelings ran high.

The British Road Federation gave figures in 1969 showing that between January, 1968 and January, 1969 the state increased the average motorists' costs by 25 per cent on three items alone, fuel, licence duty, and purchase tax, ignoring all other items. Mr Pat Gregory claimed that in the three years from October, 1964 motor taxation increased 40.5 per cent as compared with the 9.3 per cent increase in other forms of indirect taxation.

An article in *Drive*[35] examined the true motoring costs of one of their readers, a Mr Hensher of New Malden. It turned out that his house cost him £390 and his car, a smallish three-year-old, £440. Finding that his unspectacular car cost more than his home came as something of a shock to him, as well it might.

Further financial pressure

In addition to the ever-increasing pressure through indirect taxation it is fairly certain that extra fiscal controls will have to be introduced in the near future in the form of standard tolls and/or road pricing.[36] Intensive studies are now afoot under the Ministry of Transport and other bodies to determine what sort of charges will

[35] Spring, 1969.
[36] For a very good brief introduction to this topic, see Roth, G (1967) *Paying for Roads, The Economics of Congestion.* For a brief explanation of the mechanics of charging tolls see: Beckman, MJ, 'On Optimum Tolls for Highways, Tunnels, and Bridges, in: Edie, *et al* (1967) *Vehicular Traffic Science.*

be required to slim obese demand down to fit the slender garment of supply, and find efficient means of collecting them.

What appears to be happening is that public authorities are being forced—possibly without realizing it—to use fiscal means of controlling traffic, however belatedly and ineffectively, in a desperate attempt to avoid being overwhelmed.

In a discussion of a proposal to increase the parking charges in Westminster to 3s an hour an official spokesman made this control aspect, rather than financial gain, explicit:

> It is not because we want to increase revenue, we just want to control traffic. Ideally we would like to get a meter occupancy in the West End of about 85 per cent—in other words, 1 in 7 left vacant for the arriving motorist. But we find that it is something nearer 95 per cent, which rather destroys the point of the scheme. So we have just got to discourage those who stay too long.[37]

The motoring interests are beginning to recognize this—probably only semi-consciously at this stage—and react against it. For instance, Mr Pat Gregory:

> ... yet if one dispassionately examines the deliberate anti-motoring, anti-private transport campaign that has been waged with mounting viciousness by Whitehall over the last couple of decades or so, one is led to the conclusion that the 'powers that be' regard the motorist as their enemy. Since 1964, the road user has been hit both ways with no fewer than ten separate increases in the rates of tax and three cuts in road expenditure. Is it merely a figment of the inflamed imagination seriously to suggest that a devilish cunning, subterranean plot has been propounded by the present government to drive the driver off the road? To discipline the army of private motorists into docile queues relying purely on public transport for their sole means of conveyance?
>
> Undoubtedly, this supine body of British motoring was the target selected for a malignant *coup de grace* by the Chancellor and his cohorts in the recent budget of March, 1968.

[37] Reported *The Guardian*, November 18, 1969. An earlier report (July 19, 1967) by *The Guardian's* Planning Correspondent pointed out that when meter occupancy exceeds 85 per cent. '... the streets begin to fill up with cars hunting around for a slot'.

Mr Gregory hits four more nails on the head here, all unknowingly. The first is that the motorists are an army, a vast one. The second is that armies have to be kept on a democratic leash. The third is that governments have gradually been driven to perceive us (speaking as a motorist myself) as enemies, albeit not of the government but of society as a whole—at least of a sane society.

The fourth is with the reference to the

> ... devilish cunning, subterranean plot ... to drive the driver off the road ...

Mr Gregory is again not far off the mark concerning the true reason for the mounting constraints on the motorist. Though neither 'devilish' nor 'cunning', it is to some degree 'subterranean' as it is the result of a more or less unconscious awareness that somehow or other some motorists *must* be driven off the road if the survivors, those not driven off, are to be able to continue motoring at all.

There appears to be a very close parallel between taxation on motoring and the extremely high financial disincentives to cigarette smoking, an activity causing considerable damage to individuals and to the fabric of society. In a weaker sense this might apply to alcohol, also, as the social costs of alcoholism, road accidents, and other damage to society from the consumption of alcohol become more apparent.

In a more moderate attack on this principle of fiscal control Mr A. C. Durie said:

> ... We are opposed to road pricing in the 'popular' sense of its being used as a control mechanism to limit the growth of traffic. This would be completely negative.[38]

The sad fact is that it would be irresponsible of any government to do anything about traffic legislation, in the field of taxation or anywhere else, which might reasonably be expected to increase the numbers on our roads.

Control by taxation and increased risk of accidents and injuries

Apart from its painful effects on the motorist's pocket and on the prices-wages spiral there is evidence that the use of fiscal means of control will lead to lowered standards of vehicle maintenance with a consequent increase in accidents, injuries, and deaths.

[38] 'Paying for London Roads', (*Op cit*).

An AA statement recently claimed:

> ...motorists are making the most dangerous economy of all ...skimping on servicing...there is plenty of evidence...More and more breakdowns attended by the AA patrols show a marked lack of basic maintenance, and there is a steady drop in the standard of vehicles inspected by the AA on behalf of prospective buyers....
>
> Early this year a sample of AA members was asked what they would do if their cost of motoring rose another £25 a year ...65 per cent said they would try to make some economy, and of these, 24 per cent said they would try to do their own maintenance. One car-owner in ten admitted he would skip the occasional service,...[only] 4 per cent...said they would give up motoring.
>
> These are the answers of people near the end of their tether. ...When the State burdens a section of the community to the point where they will take dangerous risks, risks which could kill, it has gone too far....[39]

Swamping of repair services

Notwithstanding the economies made by motorists under the pressure of rising costs, motor repair services seem to be overwhelmed by the demand brought by increased population and wealth. Jean and Andrew Robertson wrote in the *New Statesman*.

> There may be a clue to a worrying future for the private motorist in the report of the Little Neddy on Motor Vehicle Distribution and Repair, *Future Demand for Garage and Workshop Services* ... The Economic Development Committee, forecast that by the 1980s ... maintenance facilities will not be adequate either to service cars under present conditions or to keep up with the increasing demands made by the Ministry of Transport.[40]

Ian Breach drew attention to the manpower side following the publication of another Neddy report:[41]

> ...[this] will not be encouraging reading for those who hope for a raising of standards in repair work...
>
> One out of every four repair staff was ... an apprentice.

[39] *Drive*, Autumn, 1969 (pp 33/4).
[40] August 3, 1968.
[41] *Labour Utilization and Turnover in Garages.*

... A much higher proportion of staff (26 per cent) is below the age of 22 than the national ... average (19 per cent) ... 28 per cent of the staff leave their jobs in six months or less; and 29 per cent are discharged for one reason or another.[42]

Fully trained and experienced staff would obviously cost still more and reinforce the tendency to skimp on servicing, so that as vehicles are crowded ever more closely together—a situation putting an increasingly high premium on vehicle roadworthiness—standards in this crucial sphere will continue to decline.

What it all costs

The costs of the traffic system can be considered in many ways. We have already seen that one of the social costs is a rapidly worsening relationship between the public and the police, another is lowered standards of vehicle roadworthiness—and it must not be forgotten that there is a black as well as a red side to the balance sheet—but the main components are probably the human cost, the cost of accidents, of road space, and of congestion.

The human cost in terms of death, injury, and blighted lives is hard to measure except by means of raw statistics and Fig 12/8 shows that, bearing in mind the enormous increase in the vehicle population and the substantial increase in the human population since 1928, there has been a relative decrease in the human toll—especially with respect to deaths. Nonetheless in 1968 the overall number of casualties was more than double the 1928 figure. Every year more than ten times the population of Dover is killed or injured, and the number killed on British roads so far roughly equals the total deaths for the whole British Commonwealth and Empire in World War II[43] while the number of injured is roughly twenty-five times as great as the total of the war wounded. Two out of every 100 children born now will be killed on the roads and the rest have only a 50/50 chance of escaping injury on the roads during their lifetimes.[44]

Mr Durie wrote, in the paper quoted earlier:

I am convinced that death and injury on the road will become one of the greatest burdens of our society as we motor into the

[42] *The Guardian*, April 28, 1969.

[43] 354,000 and 475,000, respectively (see *Everyman's Encyclopaedia*).

[44] See statistics of World Health Organisation and Royal Society for the Prevention of Accidents.

1980s. Hardly a single household in the land will escape the long hand of human destruction, either by removing loved ones from the home or condemning them to live only half a life permanently shattered. . . .

Fig 12/8
Road casualties:
Great Britain, 1928–1968

Year	Killed	Injured	Total (index)
1928	6,138	164,838	100
1938	6,648	226,711	195
1948	4,513	148,842	185
1958	5,970	293,767	175
1968	6,810	342,398	204

Based on British Road Federation, **Basic Road Statistics** 1969 pp14–16

Figure 12/9 shows the steady increase in the number of casualties per road accident which is probably due to the increased intensity of road usage.

Fig 12/9
Increase in number of casualties
per accident, 1954–1966

Year	Casualties per accident
1954	1.217
55	1.236
56	1.240
57	1.252
58	1.263
59	1.277
1960	1.279
61	1.294
62	1.294
63	1.312
64	1.319
65	1.330
66	1.345
67	
68	
69	
1970	
1971	

HMSO **Road Research 1967**, p67

There are of course many more pedestrian injuries in urban than in rural areas and research has shown a definite ecological relationship between traffic flow and casualties, as Fig 12/10 illustrates.

In the developed countries as a whole about six million people are killed or injured on the roads every year.

Statistics have not long been available for the economic costs, as distinct from the human costs, of road casualties, but estimates of the figures for 1963, 1964, and 1965, were £196, £222, and £246 millions, respectively.

Fig 12/10

Increase in pedestrian casualties with increase in traffic

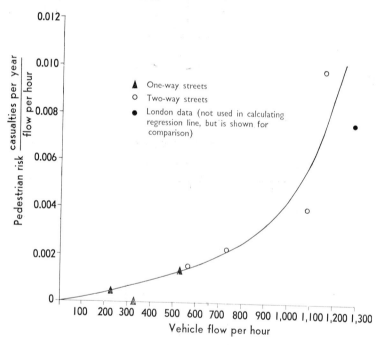

HMSO, **Road Research** 1967

The cost of existing roadspace

It is often said that the motorist is bled white. Little of what he pays in taxation is spent on the roads and society makes a handsome profit. There is another viewpoint. A distinguished economist

specializing in road use, D. J. Reynolds, who worked at the Road
Research Laboratory for many years, has written:

The case for additional road space to combat congestion is
generally assumed rather than stated, for if it is accepted that
the purpose of the road system is to accommodate satisfactorily
... [whatever] ... traffic flow that arrives on it the obvious solution to the congestion is ... expansion. ...

Like all assumptions, however, the idea ... needs to be ques-
tioned, particularly in the case of densely built up areas. ...

... The appropriate cost of the road system is usually taken
to be the annual expenditure on [its] maintenance and improvement. ... *The more normal and current cost and/or price of
an existing asset,* however, *would be its market price,* or in the
absence of a market, the current value of the road system
demanded by the traffic, assessed at the marginal costs of road
space—i e the cost (per unit area) of adding to road width. To
define the cost of the road system without including a considerable sum for the use of assets as scarce and valuable as road
space ... is unrealistic. ...

... There is fairly clear evidence that, including taxation, the
average road user pays more than the full real cost of his
journeys on rural roads which are uncongested and relatively
cheap to improve, and more important, ... *considerably less than
the true cost of his journeys on urban roads which are congested
and/or relatively expensive to construct or improve.*[45] [Italics
added]

*Excessive congestion may arise from failure to charge vehicles
the cost of the road space that they occupy, or the costs that they
impose on other road users,* or a sufficient tax to represent a
convenient expression of these values ... [Italics original]

... Assuming conservatively that one additional vehicle hour
costs ten shillings, the cost imposed on other vehicles by a single
vehicle is some 5.3 pence [2.21p] per vehicle-mile, whereas the
average fuel taxation paid by vehicles is only of the order of
1.65 pence [0.69p] per mile under congested conditions, e g a
fuel tax of 2/9 [14p] per gallon with a mean fuel consumption

[45] Very nearly half the total motor traffic is concentrated on only 5 per
cent of the road mileage, and only 10 per cent of the mileage takes two-
thirds of all traffic. A great deal of this is concentrated in urban areas and
this means that most motorists are not paying the true costs of their use
of the road system. *Highway Statistics,* HMSO, 1967.

of 20 miles per gallon. Similarly, if it is assumed that such a flow continues for a 1,000 hours in the year, the taxation paid by traffic is only some £62,000 per mile per year.

Even ignoring the maintenance costs attributable to road use by vehicles, at a rate of interest of about 5 per cent this is enough to pay the annual charges on a road with a capital value of only about £1.2 million per mile. . . . Well below the existing value of a main street, which . . . might be valued at up to £10 million per mile on the basis of a street 40 feet wide . . . [on 1961 values, i e]

. . . Both in principle and in practice, therefore, . . . the cause of excessive congestion in cities is the failure to charge road users the full cost of their journeys either in the form of the congestion they impose on other road users or in the cost of the rare road space that they occupy. If the difficult problem of charging the road user the full costs of his journeys, . . . can be overcome and the traffic flow reduced to those willing to pay [them], it is possible that the existing road space may prove adequate . . .[46]

It should be borne in mind that this writer was commenting on the situation in 1961. Since then costs have gone up very markedly, though of course motorists are paying more toward the real cost of urban roadspace.

This writer summarizes:

. . . The construction of urban motorways would be a costly and risky 'shot in the dark' which well may do little to solve urban congestion problems and lead to dangerous and irreversible ultimate effects . . .

Other authors[47] have produced detailed studies of congestion costs. For instance:

[Unless] traffic flow is so small that the interference of vehicles with each other is negligible, the presence of an extra vehicle causes delays and risks to *other* road users, so that the . . . incremental cost of a vehicle mile (to the vehicles as a whole) exceeds the . . . incremental cost (to the extra vehicle) . . .

[46] 'Urban motorways and urban congestion', *British Transport Review*, Vol VI, No 4, August/December, 1961.
[47] Beesley and Roth, 'Restraint of traffic in congested areas', *Town Planning Review*, Vol XXIII, No 3, October, 1962. Reprinted by Liverpool University Press.

Figure 12/11 shows the working of this principle in a numerical example.

The authors argue:

> ... even if all the vehicles value the journey equally, the addition of an extra 200 vehicles over the 600 so reduces the speed of *all* the vehicles that there is a net loss to the system, although the extra 200, when considering only *their own* costs and benefits, would still find the journey worthwhile. For example, the 800th vehicle would obtain a gross benefit of 3s [15p] at a cost to itself of 2.7s [13.5p], but ... impose costs of 10.9s [54.5p] on the 799 other vehicles. The result would be even more striking on the more realistic assumption that some vehicles value the journey more than others, ... and that as the flow increases the value of the journey to additional vehicles decreases.

They point out that this argument refers only to the vehicle population and the drivers. It ignores the very substantial costs imposed on others.

Fig 12/11
Increase in costs with increase in number of vehicles

No of vehicles per hour	Average speed (mph)	Costs per mile One vehicle	Costs per mile All vehicles	Net benefit from last vehicle	Extra costs added by last vehicle To last vehicle itself	Extra costs added by last vehicle To all vehicles together
199	17.622	8.17d	135/6			
200	17.600	8.18d	136/5	+ 2/1	0.01d	10.8d
399	13.222	10.89d	362/1			
400	13.200	10.91d	363/7	+ 1/6	0.02d	1/6
599	8.822	16.32d	814/9½			
600	8.800	16.36d	818/2½	− 5d	0.04d	3/5
799	4.422	32.56d	2,168/2½			
800	4.400	32.73d	2,181/9½	− 10/7	0.17d	13/7

Adapted from Beesley and Roth (1962)

Congestion is usually regarded as an unmitigated evil but it is arguable that in fact it is very useful, performing a definite social function, like the toothache which tells us we must visit the dentist. Professor Kolbuszewski has written:

> ... [congestion] ... is the mechanism of achieving stability

... it serves a useful purpose in giving a warning that the limits of road capacity are being approached.[48]

The appropriate 'dentistry' in this case appears to be fertility control.

The economic costs of congestion for the country as a whole have been variously estimated. For example, two members of the Road Research Laboratory put it at £200 million a year in 1954, about 10 per cent of the real cost of road transport and 1 per cent of the net national income.[49]

Glanville and Smeed showed in 1957[50] that the time costs of congestion increase at twice the rate of increase of traffic, other things being equal, traffic then increasing by 7 per cent per annum and congestion costs at 14 per cent.

Professor Morgan's more recent and very cautious summary[51] of the evidence concluded that congestion costs were still increasing at 14 per cent per annum, compound interest, and had reached £1,080 million by 1965. In the same report Wilfrid Andrews, Chairman of the Roads Campaign Council, states that they will have reached £2,000 million per annum by 1975, only half of what Professor Morgan's formula would give, the discrepancy largely being explained by Mr Andrews' exclusion of the value of non-working time. On Professor Morgan's basis the economic costs of congestion would be about £1,800 million in 1969, and well over £2 billion in 1970.

He also wrote, quoting official sources:

> Over 26 per cent of inter-urban traffic is using roads ... classified by the Ministry of Transport as 'severely overloaded,' i e carrying more than twice their design capacity.
>
> In urban areas the situation is still worse. As long ago as 1960, 64 per cent of urban trunk roads and 48 per cent of urban Class 1 roads were overloaded.

It seems almost certain that the situation has deteriorated since then but the Ministry of Transport has no comparable statistics for the present time.

[48] 'Transport and the Human Environment', *The Chartered Mechanical Engineer*, October, 1969.

[49] Reynolds and Wardrop, 5th International Study in Traffic Engineering, Nice, 1960.

[50] *Basic requirements for the roads of Great Britain*.

[51] (1965) *Economic and Financial Aspects of Road Improvements*, Roads Campaign Council (p 13).

Cost of new road space

In addition to the true cost of the existing road system we must consider the cost of maintaining, improving, and adding to it, which by 1968 had reached £493 million for the year.

Out of this figure about £37 million went on cleansing and administration, leaving £456 million for maintenance and improvement, a figure which will very rapidly be overshadowed if any serious attempt is made to cope with the flood of vehicles.

Wilfrid Andrews, Chairman of the Roads Campaign Council, wrote in his Foreword to Professor Morgan's report that £7,100 million must be spent on the roads by 1980 to provide '... what are scarcely more than the bare essentials ...'.

Only £683 million had been spent on new construction and major improvement by the end of 1968, however, a shortfall of some three-quarters of a £billion, on a pro rata basis, more than 50 per cent, that is.

For the future I cannot do better than quote Barbara Castle, as former Minister of Transport:

> [the money needed] ... to provide a reasonably adequate primary network by the early 1980s ... is of the order of £10,000 millions. ...
>
> Even if I were able to persuade the Government to spend on the roads throughout the 1970s at three times the rate of the next five years—and you would be prepared to do the same—we should still be spending only a quarter or a third of the estimate.[52]

Figure 12/12 shows an overall balance sheet for the public aspects of road transport. Many relevant items are normally completely ignored in working out these costs, and some are listed in Appendix B at the back of this book. For instance, administering the law to motorists; the Ministry of Transport, the Lord Chancellor's Office, and the Home Office all deny any knowledge of what this costs, but after some rumbles of indigestion the last-named produced an overall figure of £238 million in 1968/9 for 'Home and Justice'. As about two-thirds of all convictions are said to be for motoring offences it would be safe to allow £100 million a year. The Institute of Civil Engineers is said to have estimated between £50 and £250 million for item 5 ii, damage to buildings by vibration. Figures for

---

[52] Speaking to the Association of Municipal Corporations. Reported *The Guardian*, March 27, 1968.

Fig 12/12
The Balance Sheet, 1969

£ millions

Income[1]		Costs[2]	
1. Fuel tax	£969m	1. Congestion costs	£1,800m
2. Vehicle and		2. Spent on roads	£ 550m
licence duties	£400m	3. Accident costs	£ 250m
3. Purchase tax	£195m		
(say)	£1,600m	(say)	£2,600m

[1] Actual figures
[2] Author's estimates

the other items are hard to come by but it seems unlikely that they would total less than £500 million.

The psychology of liberty at the wheel

Pavlov's concept of the 'freedom-reflex' applies with especial force in the field of motoring. If it is true that we have a spontaneous urge towards physical mobility within our environment, even while restricted to Shanks's pony, it seems likely that mechanized modes of transportation will serve to reinforce it. The engine of a car or motorcycle seems to act as a freedom-amplifier and a similar effect has been produced in many other cultures, including quite primitive ones, by galloping on horseback, scudding along in canoes or sailing vessels, tobogganing, skiing, skating, and by many other means of getting about faster than nature appears to have intended.

If the foregoing is true then it could easily follow, our ecological liberty having been amplified, that any frustrations to the exercise of that liberty would also be amplified. People in crowds tend, in absence of unusual stimuli such as a cup final or a revolution, to behave in a rather sheep-like fashion, spontaneous outbursts of violence seeming rare. 'Crowd' behaviour in motor vehicles seems to be somewhat different and aggressive feelings and gestures are everyday occurrences, acts of aggression or downright violence being not at all uncommon. A relative of one of my friends, caught in a traffic jam in Italy, was stabbed to death by a neighbouring motorist with a screwdriver from the tool kit. This is an extreme example, but the feelings of drivers caught in a big traffic jam in the large conurbations of modern civilization seem to become progressively more ferocious and destructive, and it may be that a large part of this stems from a more or less suppressed fury at being the proud owner and, in psychological terms, omnipotent Führer of a machine capable of up to $1\frac{1}{2}$ miles a minute, or even more, spending most of its time trapped in a stationary mass of similar vehicles and able to cover in the average hour rather less than ten miles of ground.

Role-conflict

An important source of frustration for motorists, reinforcing that already mentioned, must be what social scientists call 'role conflict'. To explain what this means let us look very briefly at the basic social processes underlying it.

Social science and commonsense alike teach us that all societies 'socialize' their citizens from birth upward into various social roles and these can be classified as 'general' or 'particular'. The general roles are the ones we carry around with us more or less all our lives. For example, in this country we are socialized into being males or females[53]—to be English, Welsh, Scottish, or Irish, as the case might be, to be members of a particular social class, religion, and so on. All of these really basic social roles become essential parts of our individual character and are very hard to change afterwards if the occasion should ever arise.

The particular roles tend to belong to individual situations and organizations and we can put them on and take them off just as if they were items of clothing; we often say we 'wear different hats', meaning we occupy different roles. We have one social role at home, another face-to-face with our colleagues or work-mates, another for our friends, and so on. We all learn a number of parts like an actor, a 'method' actor, so that we can produce appropriate behaviour on most social occasions.

By and large these social roles dovetail into each other and fit into a coherent social structure for the very good reason that they are designed to. We have evolved social roles for a highly mechanized and mobile society and defined with quite a high degree of precision appropriate forms of behaviour. The motorist must be

[53] It is a mistake to think that the sex roles are determined by purely biological factors, as evidence from very different sex roles in other societies proves.

physically and mentally fit, skilled, of sound judgment, properly informed about the control of his vehicle and the restraints imposed upon him as a driver by road conditions and the law. He is expected to be courteous, considerate, and thoughtful into the bargain. No such role is defined for the pedestrian, who if he is prepared to take his life in his hands, can do more or less what he likes on the same roadspace.

Unfortunately, from this standpoint, people filling the roles of pedestrian and motorist are not two separate groups. Many of us occupy both at different times and in the role of pedestrian we want the microfreedom to nip across the road in the smallest of gaps between vehicles to save the bother of walking to a safe crossing place, behaviour we deplore when we are in our 'motorist' role.

Similarly, for the motorist there are a number of different roles he feels are appropriate to different forms of motoring activity. Perhaps the most obvious distinction is between the roles of the motorist-in-motion and the motorist-at-rest, i e parking, where there is a clear conflict of interest. In the role of motorist-in-motion the driver wants his way to be clear and this means preventing other drivers from cluttering it up with parked vehicles. As their microfreedom to park is increased, his microfreedom to move about is correspondingly decreased. Conversely, in his role as motorist-at-rest the driver who parks sees that his car occupies only 80 square feet or so of roadspace—he is only too aware how important his business is, it would be awkward to make this call at some other time, he tried to find a better place, and anyway he isn't going to be there very long. He really cannot see why he should have to put up with frowns or furious toots from other drivers, let alone suffer the indignity of being moved on by a policeman or booked by a traffic warden.

We all have a great capacity for switching-off when it suits us but we cannot escape from the fundamental psychological conflict produced by this situation. In our role as motorist-in-motion we see clearly that motorists parking in narrow streets, on dangerous corners, or in heavy traffic are really being selfish, unco-operative, and should not be tolerated. Though we may try very hard, we cannot forget this completely when we want to switch to the role of motorist-at-rest and park in just such places ourselves.

In busy urban areas motorists are switching from role to role with great rapidity and the ensuing burden of conflict and frustration must play an important part in the psychology of driving. We want the maximum of freedom and the minimum of constraint in each of our social roles, regardless of their incompatibility. The more freedom we have within the roles the greater must be the conflict between them, whether they are embodied in the same person or in different ones. Conversely, the less freedom we have within a role the more frustrated we feel and the more our irritation is directed against the authority causing the restraints.

'Realistic' and 'Unrealistic' conflict

Social conflict[54] is classified by social scientists under the headings 'realistic' and 'unrealistic', the first being between two or more individuals or groups over some real issue which divides them. When two children quarrel over a tricycle their conflict is realistic. There is only one tricycle and only one of them can ride it at a time. If 'A' gets it 'B' must fail, and vice versa.

Much social conflict is of this kind—where there is a limited cake, such as the gross national income, and a number of individuals or groups to share it. Bigger shares for some then mean smaller shares for others and it is often legitimate to enter into conflict—suitably circumscribed by Queensberry rules—to determine who gets what. However, a great deal of it is of the other, unrealistic, kind—often resulting from the 'displacement' of anger and frustration from some realistic conflict situation which may not be apparent to the protagonists or too painful for them to recognize and bring out into the open.

Much of the anger and frustration of motorists as expressed in the 'X must go' stickers—where 'X' is the current Minister of Transport—is unrealistic conflict. To make it realistic motorists must find their true enemy—they must look through their windscreens and into their driving mirrors and realize the 'X' must stand for 'other drivers'. The stickers ought really to read:

'Other motorists must go!'

Summary

'What shall it profit a man if he gaineth two cars but findeth it quicker to walk?'[55]

[54] See Coser, L, *Op cit.*
[55] Mr Richard Marsh, Minister of Transport, reported *The Guardian* November 24, 1969 (slightly modified by author).

As the years roll by the situation on the roads gets progressively worse and, whatever their politics, succeeding chancellors increase motoring taxes as their colleagues in Parliament and at the Ministry of Transport introduce further regulations.

It is not the fault of any government, policy, or minister that the situation is as it is. The basic cause is sheer numbers. Admittedly, road-building, reorganization, and redeployment can help the situation to some degree and many of the actions of central and local government bearing on the traffic system do improve it but, unfortunately, many of these ameliorations have to be in the form of further encroachments into existing individual microfreedoms as we have seen.

The drivers of motor vehicles are playing the freedom game on a 'board' which is not only finite but extremely limited and capable of only small increases in size even if vast sums—which show little sign of materializing—are expended. The simplest way of picturing it is to think of a 'dodgem' arena at the local fair, the more patrons and dodgems there are the slower one's progress and the greater the number of bumps. An intermediate real-life situation is provided by car parks—which all too often these days cannot admit one more vehicle—and the same basic ecological laws apply to the road system as a whole.

I have examined the concept of road saturation, broken it down into saturation 1, the per capita ownership of vehicles, and saturation 2, the saturation—at 'ultimate capacity' point—of the road system. I have argued that saturation 1 is inevitable as personal wealth increases, that saturation 2, followed by over-saturation and stagnation, is equally inevitable if population continues to increase. I have also argued that by the year 2000, other things being equal, population growth will have made the total number of vehicles 35 per cent larger than it would have been had we acted in accordance with the Royal Commission's recommendations, and that as saturation 2 approaches each extra vehicle causes appreciably more obstruction and delay than the one before until, finally, the 'nth' vehicle stops the system dead. Population is the only one of these two variables (potentially) under our control.

A motorist is free to move about only insofar as others do not want to be in the same place at the same time and this factor is not under the control of the motorist himself, the central government, or the motor licensing authorities. If the number of motorists wanting to be in the same road space at the same time increases arithmetically the complication of their relationships, actual and potential, increases geometrically and the larger must be the number of restrictions placed upon the mass of moving bodies to prevent an undue amount of accident or injury—though it is very doubtful if this goal is achieved—and to stop the system seizing up solid.

Unless the system is completely self-regulating, with virtually all motorists spontaneously learning by heart and then operating the necessary restrictions—co-operating whole-heartedly to keep things going—then it must fall to someone's lot to enforce the rules and regulations. The more traffic there is the more rules there must be and the greater is the problem of enforcement. If this trend is allowed to continue it will be hard to avert a state approaching total war developing between motorists and the police, as Mr Wolff and Mr Durie fear.

In effect I have been discussing the applicability of the concept ecology of liberty to the roads and conclude that there are three possible outcomes.

(i) The Buchanan 'solution'. To spend scores of billions of pounds in the next two or three decades to cope as far as is humanly possible with all the vehicles that appear. This is impossible in the towns, as Buchanan admitted, and in the long run impossible elsewhere, which he did not admit, as our island is finite.

(ii) Drastic measures to restrict private motoring.

(iii) Total seizure of the road system.

As outcome (i) is very unlikely, since no one intends to spend a tithe of the money and resources required, and outcome (iii) cannot be permitted, outcome (ii) is really the only possibility and this raises the question of means.

In broad terms we can control traffic directly or indirectly or both. The direct means are:

(a) physical and legal barriers, rationing schemes, and the like, or,

(b) the price mechanism, raise motoring costs until the number of those who can afford it coincides with the capacity of the system, possibly using part of the income to increase that capacity up to the optimum level in environmental terms.

The indirect means is via population control, letting people have as many cars as they want but keeping the road system from saturation 2 by controlling the number of people.

Ours is basically a capitalist society which believes in rationing scarce resources by the price mechanism. There are some partial exceptions in such fields as health and housing, but many parents believe that if they want the best education for their children they must pay heavily and opt out of the grossly overcrowded state system. The same applies to medical and dental services, living accommodation, clothing, food, and holidays, not to mention yachts, grouse moors, art collections, and the like. Most of the better quality material things of life are kept from the masses by price barriers, so solution (ii b) seems the likeliest for the time being and this will come to hedge in the private motorist more and more as Mr Gregory saw with such agonized clarity.

However, the solution which would maximize motoring macro-freedom is that which must come in any case in the long run—on other grounds if not on these—population control. Motoring organizations are in a continual state of conflict with the authorities. To make it 'realistic' conflict, in sociological terms, the true enemy would have to be faced—incessant population increase and all that it implies, and then a campaign started against the government and local authorities to reduce it to a minimum, eventually halting growth altogether, and then, possibly, in the long run, actually reducing our numbers.

No amount of railing against public scapegoats will change the facts of life and the AA and the RAC should be agitating not for utopian schemes to double, treble, or even quadruple our road space but pressing firmly for the implementation of the Family Planning Act and going as far beyond as turns out to be necessary to prevent the birth of the extra 10 million potential drivers who will otherwise be cluttering up the roads in the early 2000s.

Chapter 13

Freedom to enjoy yourself

We have entered an area of dramatic evolution in our material living progress. Living standards are rising. There is a demand for reduced working hours. More and more people are requiring greater leisure ... and the means to enjoy it. Consequently we are faced with the need for better, more abundant, and sophisticated facilities for our leisure activities.[1]

... by the end of the century people would have twice the leisure and twice the amount of money to spend on it ...[2]

As in the case of motor vehicles and roads we can use the concepts saturation 1 and saturation 2, the first being the maximum amount of leisure and amenity resources we are likely to consume per capita, and the second the saturation of the country's total capacity for providing pleasurable outlets.

A few sports are waning—or at least failing to surge ahead with all the others. Rowing, for example, seems to have reached its peak, for the time being at least, because of the enormous increase in the cost of craftsman-built boats. Lawn tennis reached its peak—as measured by the number of clubs—in 1964, after more than doubling since 1948, since when there has been a slight decline. Cycling too has lost much of its popularity, in part because more people can afford cars and in part because the roads are so much more crowded and dangerous. However, the norm is a gigantic increase because of rising wealth and population.

[1] Chairman's Foreword to Report of Sports Council, November, 1966, by Dennis Howell, MP.

[2] Mr Wilfred Burns, Chief Planner at the Ministry of Housing and Local Government, at the conference of the Institute of Park and Recreation Administration at Newcastle upon Tyne. *The Guardian* report, September 10, 1968.

Some sports require very little space, some require no extra space at all as they can be carried on in areas normally used for other purposes; people often do exercises in their bedrooms or gardens and amateur weightlifting can be practised—or at least started— in the privacy of the home.

Some sports can be practised more widely because space can be converted from other uses for the purpose—a farmer's fields can easily be turned into a golf course or sports stadium, and others such as fishing, sailing, or gliding require some more or less natural amenity. It is true that, for example, gravel pits can be flooded, stocked with fish and then used for fishing, sailing, bathing, and water-skiing but these come as mere by-products. It would not be thought practical to excavate solely for the purpose of creating an artificial lake.

Figure 13/1 shows the growth of a number of indoor sports requiring some but not a lot of extra space, although the economic costs of providing gymnasiums in urban areas can be very high.

Fig 13/1
Growth of Indoor Sports: Number of clubs

	1947	1967	Growth %
Weightlifting	180	278	55%
Badminton	1,682	2,975	77%
Squash	206	474	130%
Table Tennis	2,200	6,917	215%
Fencing	98	499	409%
Basketball	20	550	2,650%
Judo	30	1,191	3,180%

Sources: Annual reports of sports governing bodies

From the point of view of the student of the carrying capacity of an environment, the 'space-extensive'[3] sports and naturally limited outlets are more relevant and present a much greater threat. In the case of pot-holing, for example, Nature's limited supply of caves and pot-holes is already so overwhelmed that a shroud of secrecy envelops the activities of many of the clubs. A powerful code of 'ownership' and ethics is developing to prevent 'piracy', as it is called, of one club on another's territory. Digging

[3] Space-'intensive', after the economic model, sounds wrong in this context.

and exploration are coming to be regarded as the only means for getting away from the crowds but new 'pothole capacity' is obviously severely limited and it may be that this sport is already approaching saturation 2.

Climbing

Figure 13/2 shows the 325 per cent increase in the number of mountaineering clubs in Britain between 1948 and 1968 and the following quotation from an article by D. M. Rees shows what pressure on resources feels like in this sphere. In this case it is a nursery slope, Stanage Edge, a rocky outcrop in the Derbyshire Peak District, near Sheffield.

Fig 13/2
Growth in Mountaineering: Number of clubs

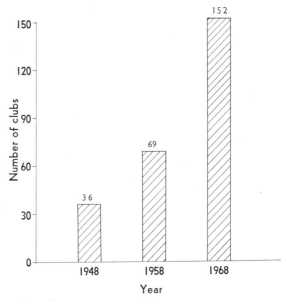

Note:
332% increase in 20 years

Source: Research Dept, Central Council for Physical Recreation

... a whole host of people, mainly young and husky with beards and jeans, students and apprentices, but also some older, seasoned and hardy souls, come to Stanage Edge every weekend. The black granite rocks are like a magnet. They swarm with enthusiasts. The road below can have as many as a hundred cars and there may be anything from 300–400 people climbing. It's a multi-coloured ant heap. Voices echo back loudly from the rock face. Ropes criss-cross the rocks like the tendrils of creepers.

Everywhere you look on Stanage Edge there are people spread-eagled on a rock face, lodged in a crevice, inching along a ledge, or just hanging at rope end in a curious taut limbo. It's a kind of climber's Blackpool ... [4]

This congestion is not confined to nursery slopes or to Britain. The Tanzanian Government announced in April, 1970 that it was introducing a rationing scheme for those wanting to climb Kilimanjaro.

Gliding

In the case of gliding, in the single decade between 1958 and 1968, while the number of clubs increased by just over 100 per cent, the number of sailplanes increased by 176 per cent, and the number of launches—the true index of the increase—went up by 390 per cent.[5]

Bowls

Figure 13/3 shows the growth of bowls—a 170 per cent increase in the number of clubs between 1927 and 1968. The entries for the National Championship increased by some 450 per cent in the same period.

Angling

Fishing is the most popular sport among adult males and probably the least class-conscious. Figure 13/4 shows how it is burgeoning and what pressure is being put on the naturally limited resources. In 1968 the National Anglers Council launched a £10,000

[4] *The Guardian*, November 28, 1968.
[5] The number of gliding *hours* probably increased some 600 per cent but the British Gliding Association frowns on this index for some reason.

Fig 13/3
Growth in Bowls:
Number of clubs

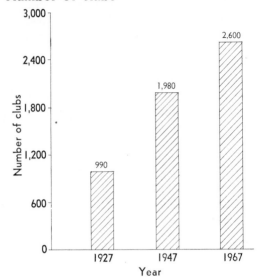

Note:
163% increase in 40 years

Source: Research Dept, Central Council for Physical Recreation

fisheries research scheme at the *Compleat Angler* at Marlow, reported[6] as being:

> ... designed to ease the frustrated life of British freshwater fishermen, a life so cramped that even Mr Dennis Howell, Minister of Sport, is prepared to concede the fact. In a message to the meeting, passed through the Sports Council's deputy chairman, Sir John Laing, he bemoaned the growing army of anglers [almost 4 million now, increasing at ... 8 per cent annually] and the shrinking number of available fisheries.

The article went on to demonstrate that the situation has got beyond the resources of private enterprise and asks for government intervention:

> Everyone concerned with fishing knows that the basis of its

[6] *The Guardian,* February 3, 1968.

success abroad is government control or sponsored fishery organizations.

... It would be a gesture for the government, through the Sports Council, to assist, [with the research project].

If the finance barrier[7] were breached much neglected and useful water could be wrested from uninterested private owners.

Here again pressure on the resources is leading to the development of marginal supplies at higher costs and only with the aid of government intervention and a consequent restriction of individual freedoms can the problem be resolved; or so it is thought.

Fig 13/4
Growth in Fishing: Number of fishing licences (rounded)

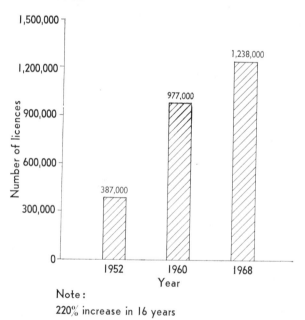

Note:
220% increase in 16 years

Source: Association of River Authorities

[7] Fishing rights on the Bourne and the Dart were sold in 1969 for £16 5s and £24 7s per yard, respectively.

Camping and Caravanning

Mr Samuel Alper, Chairman of the National Caravan Council, speaking at a press conference at the International Caravan and Camping Exhibition at Earls Court in 1968, said caravan sites are becoming increasingly hard to find in Britain and the situation is getting worse, 67,000 caravans being made in Britain in 1967 alone.

Overnight stops are fewer and worse equipped than any in Europe. . . . It is curious that the country which invented caravans is the most backward in recognizing the need to promote them.

He said that because there were so few overnight stops for Britain's 142,000 touring caravans, he had begun to negotiate with breweries to see if they could get space at the back of village pubs for parking caravans. He was also putting the same proposition to owners of filling stations and asking British Rail and the National Coal Board to rent out waste land.

It seems likely that a number of additional parking places for caravans will be found by these means but obviously the rate at which demand is increasing is soon going to saturate any possible supply.

Figure 13/5 shows the growth in camping by one of the possible indices—membership of the Camping Club of Great Britain and Northern Ireland—and it must be remembered that this particular one by no means shows the total number of campers. For example, in 1968 about half a million campers visited Forestry Commission sites alone.

A recent Fabian pamphlet describes graphically what pressure on camping facilities can be like.

The Forestry Commission opened its first organized camping site in the New Forest in mid-1964 with no advance publicity; within two days the number of campers exceeded the capacity of the camp and several hundred had to be turned away. Visitors have driven cars over paths and tracks into the very centre of the forest itself. There is much vandalism, fire fighting apparatus is destroyed, litter is left, the soil under trees is eroded by traffic so that even mature trees died. In 1965 seventeen abandoned vehicles were removed. The grazing of animals is interfered with, wildlife is driven out, flora destroyed.[8]

[8] Rubinstein, D, and Speakman, C (1969) *Leisure, transport and the countryside* (p 8).

Fig 13/5

Growth of Camping: Membership of the Camping Club of Great Britain and Northern Ireland

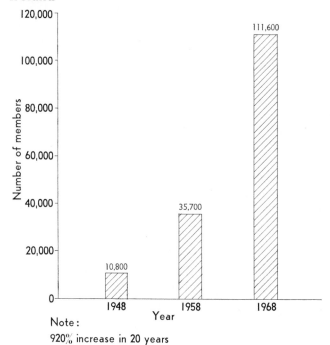

Note:

920% increase in 20 years

Source: Camping Club of Great Britain and Northern Ireland

Estimates are given for the number of visitors to the New Forest of 56,000 in 1965, rising to 190,000 by 1980, and 270,000 by AD 2000. The havoc wrought by 50,000 or so in 1964 bodes ill for the year 2000 with the five-fold torrent of visitors.

Golf

The situation is already looking dark for golfers and all the surveys show an even bleaker prospect for the future. It was reported in *The Observer* colour supplement[9] that at a number of public golf courses at weekends the queues begin to form at 4 a m and by

[9] November 11, 1967.

dawn the entire morning's allocation is taken. With respect to private clubs the situation is very little better in many parts of the country but in this case a rationing system—not allowing people to join unless there is room for them on the course—helps out.

Mr A. G. Birch, Research Officer at the Central Council for Physical Education, has pointed out that the situation is worse in the USA:

> ... it is some consolation that in America queues form at midnight on Saturday for tee-off at dawn on Sunday—private clubs have long waiting lists, even at entrance fees of $1,000.[10]

My information is that the situation is worse still in Japan. On the main island pressure on land is such that the resultant costs put membership of golf clubs completely beyond the reach of private members, excepting the very rich. Membership fees are paid by the larger business corporations as a perquisite for a few senior executives.

The Golf Development Council said, following a pilot survey of national facilities for playing golf:[11]

> (f) most of the clubs adjoining built up areas are full and have waiting lists.
> ... Public courses are used to excess and this leads to maintenance problems. In addition ... it is not unusual for players to be turned away from the public courses ... full up at the time....
> (g) *Areas in urgent need*

[Where]

> (i) population exceeds 35,000 per nine holes,
> (ii) clubs are full and have waiting lists,
> (iii) public courses (if any) subjected to excessive use,
> (iv) public courses (if any) turning players away.

In section 4 '*Conclusions*' the report went on to say the following areas are among those in urgent need.

(a) London and the home counties (34,000/9),
(b) Birmingham and Coventry (45,000/9),
(c) West Hartlepool and Middlesbrough (59,000/9),
(d) Hull (50,000/9),
(e) Dunstable and Luton (45,000/9),
(f) Bristol (36,000/9).

[10] In a paper read at the Recreational Management Conference, Loughborough University, July 9, 1968. Copy kindly supplied by the author.
[11] 'Preliminary Report on Playing Facilities' (1968). Mimeographed.

The figures in brackets indicate the number of people in the local population per nine-hole golf course or its equivalent.[12]

Golf in the northern region

A survey[13] showed that even in the north where population density is much lighter than the south and where land is more readily available and consequently a good deal cheaper, there is already a severe problem of accommodating the golfers of the present, let alone those of the future. The report said, under the heading 'Capacity':

> ... there is room on the region's courses for only 1/3 of the region's golfers at any one time. One third of the region's clubs are known to have waiting lists and they are spread roughly in proportion throughout the price range. Over 1,000 people, approximately, on waiting lists, only 120 of these on the lists of rural clubs.
>
> Only one club in eleven had any space on its course at weekends ...
>
> ... There is considerable pressure on the region's golf courses and little room for more members. Most clubs have already reached capacity and new clubs would be needed to cater for an increase in participation. (p 7)
>
> There are sufficient potential members on waiting lists alone to support two new clubs. This gives only a crude guide to pressure, as some people may appear on more than one list, but many may not even register once, despairing of their turn ever coming, and it is known that some clubs have closed their lists simply because of their inability to meet demands. (p 23)

Figure 13/6 shows the shortfall in golfing facilities expected in the north in 1981 and it must be stressed that true demand is hard to measure. Mr Birch pointed out in the same paper:

> ... Inadequacy of [golfing] facilities holds down the true level of demand ... [in the north] club membership has risen by 61 per cent in the last ten years but as many of the club lists are full this represents only part of the story ... Municipal courses near big cities are already past saturation point ... with queues form-

[12] i e an eighteen-hole course counts as two nine-holes. 35,000 persons per nine-hole course is defined as the absolute maximum tolerable.

[13] North Region Planning Board and Northern Advisory Council for Sport and Recreation. Paper No 1, Golf, Autumn, 1967.

Fig 13/6
**Shortfall in golfing facilities',
Northern England 1981**

Region	Increase already planned	Proposals for further increase	Total by 1981	Required by 1981		Shortfall	
				Lower est	Upper est	Lower est	Upper est
Tyne	3	2½	5½	14½	29	9	23½
Tees	3	1½	4½	6½	10½	2	6
Mid-Durham	– ½	2	1½	7	22	5½	20½
Rural Northumberland	½	1	1	4½	6½	3½	5½
Rural Durham and NR	½	0	1	6	11½	5	10½
Cumberland and Westmorland	2	½	2½	9	26	6½	23½
Totals	8½	7	15½	48	104½	32½	89

' Measured in 18-hole golf course units (ie a 9-hole course counts ½)

ing in the early hours of Saturday and Sunday morning, prospects are far from bright . . .

Sailing

Figure 13/7 shows the growth in sailing between 1947 and 1970 as measured by the number of clubs affiliated to the Royal Yachting Association, some 380 per cent. If the increase in individual membership over the same period is taken as the index, as in Fig 13/8, it is in the region of 12,000 per cent. Figure 13/9 shows the increase in licensed craft on the Norfolk Broads, 180 per cent in twenty years.

Huge though these increases are they do not reflect the true demand because many sailors who do not belong to affiliated clubs are not included. Even if all present sailors were included, however, the substantially increased figure would represent only a fraction of the potential demand, as the following quotation shows.

Participation in sport and physical recreation takes place among a minority of the population . . . a factor . . . often overlooked when dealing with absolute numbers of participants. For example, the Royal Yachting Association's estimates of half a million sailing enthusiasts represents only 1 per cent approximately of the population of the United Kingdom. But it represents a great demand for facilities and water. Because participation is at present confined to a small proportion of the population there is clearly the potential for considerable increase in activity; it is conceivable that the number engaging in certain sports

Fig 13/7
Growth in Sailing:
Clubs affiliated to the
Royal Yachting Association

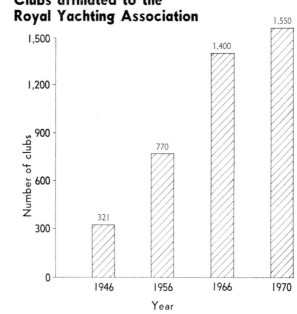

Note:

384% increase in 24 years

Source: Royal Yachting Association

and recreational activities could double or even quadruple in the near future and the effect on the provision of facilities could be dramatic.[14]

In an article in *The Guardian*[15] James Moore reported:

As the yachting boom grows apace so the question of where all the cruising boats are to be kept becomes an increasing problem. Many popular centres are said to have reached their natural saturation point,[16] while others seem likely to very soon.

[14] 'Sports Facilities'. GLC and SE Sports Council, 1968.
[15] March 9, 1968.
[16] The river Hamble in Hampshire has recently been studied by the riparian authorities who have come to the conclusion that saturation point with small craft will soon be reached. Footnote added by present author.

Fig 13/8
Growth in Sailing:
Individual membership of
Royal Yachting Association

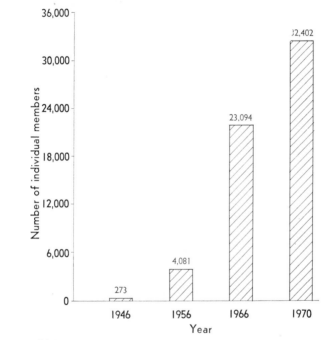

Note:
11,800% increase in 24 years
Source: Royal Yachting Association

The only solution at present seems to be the commercially run yacht harbour or marina.

There are a dozen marinas around the coasts or on inland waters already in operation with at least 50 schemes either under way or at the planning stage ...

In the imagination of keen business men, there seems to be no limit to how many we can have ... here is the universal panacea for the cramp which could stiffen joints of the boat-building industry and prevent it reaching that delectable state where cruising yachts roll off the production lines like cans of beans or washing machines ...

Fig 13/9
Norfolk Broads:
Increase in licensed craft

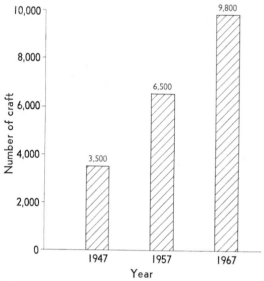

Note:
177% increase in 20 years

Source: Great Yarmouth Port and Haven Commissioners

James Moore discussed the pros and cons for marinas and said:

Where space is limited there is no doubt that a marina makes the best possible use of it and there are many additional advantages. Craft are accessible, safe from the weather and from thieves and vandals, electric power and water are handy. Repair services, spares and so on. There are ancillary services like hot water, restaurants and shops, and finally . . . the not inconsiderable social benefit which accrues from boat owners being brought into close contact with their fellows. The result is that the marina becomes a weekend recreational community.

On the debit side the author lists some weighty considerations:

Perhaps it is this very chumminess [of the marina] which causes many a yachtsman to shy away from such organizations. . . .

... Removed, too, from a would be yachtsman's curriculum are such things as pulling a dinghy over a strong flood tide, picking up a mooring in half a gale of wind, and all the other acts of seamanship which are not only essential to becoming a good sailor but part of the joy of yachting. Robbing the scene of much of its former spirit of adventure, the yacht marina is too close to the car park for many; too orderly, too well equipped with amenities they do not want, and will tempt them to spend more money than they can really afford, and too expensive.

The clash of interests: sailors versus the rest

Not only does the great increase in sailing cause congestion of the moorings and facilities required, and obstruction on the waterways, it creates an increasing amount of conflict between sailors and other would-be consumers of overlapping amenities, as the following quotation from *Drive* makes clear.

... Between the lock at Sawley and Trent lock, on the outskirts of Nottingham, the Sunday rush starts at 5.30 a m. By mid-afternoon so many people are jostling for room on the River Trent that the peace and tranquillity they seek often goes overboard.

These pictures[17] show the confusion on a one-and-a-quarter mile stretch of the river, a stretch 140 feet wide, warmed to a comfortable 77°F by a power station, shadowed by its gaunt cooling towers and fouled by a 40 per cent sewage content from 4,500,000 people.

At first light anglers tramp through the dewy grass to settle like marsh birds among the reeds and begin the rush for Sunday recreation. By 8.30 a m coaches are queuing up the lane, disgorging anglers who left Manchester, Birmingham, Derby and Leicester at dawn. They line the banks at 6 feet intervals, 2,000 long rods making the river even narrower for the 140 sailing dinghies.

At noon water traffic is at its height. Eighty-six locally hired boats pass up and down with jaunty motor cruisers on canal-crawling holidays from as far away as London and Leeds.

A dozen canoes from one of twenty clubs in the region creep in convoy close to the shore, weaving between the anglers' floats and trying to keep clear of invisible lines.

17 Not reproduced here.

Fleets of sailing dinghies from two clubs battle for favourable starting positions in a tense silence. A motor cruiser, trapped between them, goes astern, loses way, then drifts helplessly. Two dinghies collide near the bank, fishing rods are lifted, curses muttered, and a handful of maggots is thrown into a boat.

Aloof and immaculate in yachting cap and navy-blue blazer, a sailing club's officer of the day stands at the helm of a rescue launch, aptly named *Chaos*. Among sailors, a popular view of angling is 'a line with a maggot on one end and a fool at the other'. Yet it was the anglers, outnumbering sailors by ten to one, who instigated a speed limit of 6 mph upstream and 8 mph downstream thus eliminating water-skiers, and speedboats that often impaled sailing dinghies on their bows.

After nine months of negotiation four stretches of river near Trent Lock were designated for water-skiing. The Trent Power Boat and Ski Club can use any three at one time, but only after 3 p m at weekends. But the timetabling breaks down when 'pirates' appear: either anglers who don't know of the agreement and throw bottles at bona fide club skiers, or water skiers, similarly ignorant, who disturb the anglers' peace.

A bleak future of timetables and waiting lists faces the six sailing clubs, eight boat-yards and marinas, four canoe clubs which use the Trent near Nottingham—not to speak of the hundreds of people who just sit on the banks dabbling their toes.

Timetabling, new water being created by the gravel industry, and mutual toleration—these are the alternatives to survival of the fittest on the River Trent . . .[18]

The foregoing evidence points to a general overloading of our resources as noted by interested parties and journalists on the look-out for a story. All of this is interesting and relevant to the problem and its possible solution, but let us consider some more realistic forms of control before going on to examine detailed and systematic studies of pressure of demand on the Lake District.

Control by the price mechanism

As our environmental resources are not only finite but distinctly limited the price mechanism is inevitably coming to the fore in an attempt to stem the avalanche of demand in this sphere as in motoring.

[18] Andrews, M, 'Pressures On a Stretch of Water'. *Drive*, Summer, 1969.

A Sports Council Study Group Report said under 'Finance':

25. Traditionally, local authority facilities are low-priced, or free to the user. On the other hand, facilities provided by commercial organizations are commonly much more costly ... How far has this customary pattern led to public resistance to any reasonable charge for the use of 'public' facilities?

26. *A low price may mean that facilities are grossly overcrowded, with a consequent reduction in the quality of enjoyment: a member of the public cannot always buy the space he wants* (e g in a swimming pool). How far should it be made possible for him to do so? *A higher charge might achieve two objects.* Firstly, a reasonable rate of return on capital might encourage and enable an authority to provide more and better facilities, thus easing the congestion problem. Secondly, *the higher charge may of itself reduce demand and thus act as a regulator*—one possibility might be to have a variable charge, with the maximum at peak periods. How far should the price mechanisms be allowed to operate, and how far should facilities (and what kinds?) be provided without charge?[19] (Italics added)

James Moore, quoted earlier, shows—without making the point explicit—how the screw of the price mechanism is being turned on the sailors.

Yachting is already one of the most costly participant sports in terms of basic equipment. At between £5 and £7 a foot a year as a kind of average mooring charge for a seaside marina (a price dictated by the high investment necessary), keeping a 25 footer would become more a prerogative of those who seek to keep up with the Jones rather than those who will enjoy sailing for its own sake, especially when one adds sums for insurance, hauling out and launching, fitting out and repairs. . . .

If, as we are constantly told, yachting is to become our premier participant sport in the next few years and it is to be a pastime for everyman, it is essential that by one means or another ways be found to keep the ownership of craft bigger than dinghies within the financial grasp of those with modest incomes and ambitions. I cannot see how a rash of commercially owned yacht marinas will help us to do that.

[19] Report of a study group of the Research and Statistics Committee, Sports Council, 1967. (Mimeographed).

The increasing burden of the price mechanism leads inevitably to a quest for help from other members of society, via the agencies of central or local government. Mr Moore goes on, somewhat plaintively:

> ... alternatives to private commercial marinas were not easy to find. We might well have yacht harbours sponsored and financed by municipalities, as they do in the United States, though much opposition to marina development ... does seem to come from town councils.
>
> Yacht clubs, in the majority of cases, can scarcely think in terms of the finance needed. ... One hesitates to suggest embroiling the central government in yet another sphere of private interest, yet it does seem that a national plan for the development of water-sport amenities would be regarded as being of some importance.

What this author is asking for, almost certainly without realizing it, is a subsidy for sailors paid by their fellow-citizens. To the best of my knowledge the yachting fraternity has not hitherto been distinguished by its socialist principles or other manifestations of radicalism and though selective subsidies are not unacceptable in principle to many of us, the case for subsidizing this particular sport must be argued with some cogency, the more so as the golfers, gliders, football and cricket-players, campers, climbers, and many others may want to get in on the act—if they are not being heavily subsidized already.

It appears we may be in some danger of arriving at a situation in which everybody is subsidizing everybody else—or at least all sportsmen are being subsidized by all non-sportsmen—in order to camouflage the unpalatable facts of supply and demand.

Physical control

There are possibilities of control other than through the price mechanism. One of these is restriction of one sort or another, selective or total, and of course these measures are also under consideration. One of two leading spokesmen on conservation problems in Devon recently said in a BBC broadcast that he would like to post large signs on all roads into his county proclaiming 'Devon Full!'. The other said there is no problem if only we organize ourselves properly. He claimed that no one minds booking three weeks ahead for something popular in the theatre, what is wrong with doing exactly the same for, say, a picnic in the New Forest.

Mr Niall MacDermott, Minister of State, Ministry of Housing and Local Government, told a weekend conference of national parks planning authorities at Newcastle upon Tyne:

> An electronic counting machine which would ration the number of cars allowed to enter national parks had the ring of 1984 about it. . . .
>
> I reject any notion of using the national parks as a test bed for the national parking meter.

Equally he recoiled from any idea of 'rationing' the countryside.

> It would be the antithesis of everything that is meant by recreation and leisure. But unless we meet the challenge of growing demands upon the country, unless we can provide the means for people to enjoy the open air and teach them how to use them, then I suppose we have to admit the awful possibility that it could one day come to something like this.[20]

On the key issue of how we can 'meet the challenge of the growing demands upon the country...' Mr MacDermott remained silent, and the 'awful possibility' is a good deal nearer than he seemed to realize. Already the USA—a country with a population density only about one-sixteenth of ours—has introduced a central computerized booking system for camp sites.

However, rationing schemes may not be enough in some cases. The Sports Council report already mentioned asked the questions:

'How may the "carrying capacity" of a resource or facility be defined?', and:

'How can any detrimental effects arising out of excessive demand be minimized or avoided?'

It then raised the much more basic issue:

> *May it be necessary, in certain instances, to destroy some resources or ban some activities in order to accommodate a greater number of people?*
>
> *. . . may it be desirable to preserve a resource by restricting public access . . . ?*' (Italics added)

An unlikely threat here is from scientific interests, which, insofar as they impinge upon amenities and conservation at all, normally

[20] Reported *The Guardian*, October 8, 1967.

tend to be on the side of the angels. Scientists want to preserve wild life and natural habitats and on some occasions they have acted as a powerful political pressure group to preserve areas such as the Island of Aldabra threatened by the government's military plans.

However, from the general public's point of view, they can present a threat to amenities by seeking to get certain areas declared of 'special scientific interest'. An amendment proposed to the Countryside Bill, reported by *The Guardian*,[21]

> ... could have the effect of closing large areas of the Lake District to the public.
>
> Miss J. E. McInnes, ... raising the matter at a meeting of the Lake District Planning Board ... referred to a possible 'take-over bid' for Skiddaw Forest, near Keswick, by the Nature Conservancy.
>
> Mr C. Bignell, Chairman of the Board's Development Control Committee, said the amendment being considered during the House of Commons committee stage raised two vital constitutional points.
>
> The first is that if the Nature Conservancy can make a directive which results in the whole of Skiddaw Forest becoming an area of special scientific interest, we must think of the possible implications with regard to farming and the holiday enjoyment of the hills. ...
>
> The Clerk, Mr K. S. Himsworth, explained that *if the Nature Conservancy so designated a site and arrived at agreement with the owner, then that land was for ever more free from the possibility of being included in any access agreement....*
>
> *... The Nature Conservancy ... could bar the public access to this land.* [and] *... no national park authority, nor even the Minister, could do anything about it* ... (Italics added)

As the population increases so the number of scientists will increase, other things being equal. There are said to be over 100,000 naturalists already and the number of biologists, ecologists, botanists, and others interested in wild life and the countryside, requiring space for their laboratories and field studies will grow rapidly. In most cases this could only be at the expense of the supply of amenities for the general public.

Let us now look at the imminent saturation of one of our almost

[21] April 4, 1968.

priceless national assets and the physical controls now in train to ameliorate it.

The case of the Lake District

The Lake District Planning Board is charged by Section 5 (1) and 10 (1) of the National Parks and Access to the Countryside Act, 1949, with formulating proposals 'for the purpose of preserving and enhancing the natural beauty of the area ... and for the purpose of promoting their enjoyment by the public,' and must at all times have regard for these dual statutory responsibilities.

The paragraph above opens the 'Report On Traffic In the Lake District National Park',[22] published in 1965, the purpose of which is to consider:

... the traffic problems affecting the Lake District now and in the years ahead, and in particular the effects which will be caused by the increased pressure on routes into the National Park with the continued advance and link up of the National Motorway networks.

This increased pressure is developing as follows. Surveys had shown that 80 per cent of the 3,300 visitors during an average sixteen-hour day in August came from points within a three-hour radius of travel, containing a population of $15\frac{1}{4}$ million in 1960. By 1964 this population had increased to 15.8 million and the number of journeys to 4,100, a 24 per cent jump in four years.

By 1974 an additional 5.7 million, total $21\frac{1}{2}$ million, are expected in the southern and eastern sectors alone of the three-hour radius circle, and $25\frac{1}{2}$ million by 2010.

Section 5.1 of the Report, on Principal Routes, states:

Throughout the National Park many Principal Routes have traffic volumes beyond their capacity. ...

Accident records on these routes now seem to show a disproportionate increase over Class 1 routes elsewhere and this should be studied in more detail.

[22] Prepared at the request of Lake District Planning Board by the chief officers of Cumberland, Lancashire, and Westmorland County Councils. (Mimeographed.)

Section 5.2, on Secondary Routes, states:

The volume of traffic on many of the Secondary Routes is near to their capacity and they are, or will be, incapable of dealing with the average August traffic flow in a few years. Peak flows exceeding road capacity already arise, and control measures on these occasions should be implemented in the immediate future....

Accidents on Secondary Routes ... seemed to indicate *a marked tendency for accidents to occur on previously free minor roads* ... (which is *to be expected, with traffic increases and conditions developing towards saturation.*) (Italics added)

Section 7 deals with parking and the introductory paragraph points out:

... the *existing parking facilities are inadequate for the present traffic volumes and will become less capable of meeting* ... *requirements* ... (Italics added)

The report stresses that: '... cars in parks should not be obtrusive, and the park should be landscaped to suit its surroundings', and this need for unobtrusiveness is of course the limiting factor in the traffic capacity of the Lake District. It is technically possible to make space there for 100,000 or even a million cars but this could only be at the expense of the essential character of the Lake District which draws people there in the first place.

The preamble to Section 8 ends:

If no action is taken, congestion is likely to result from increasing traffic volumes to such a point that visitors will be discouraged from travelling on the roads. On road safety and amenity grounds, this congestion is undesirable and therefore the following solutions are suggested.

The principles by which traffic must be controlled had been stated earlier and these were:

4.1.1 Local traffic should be given freedom of access.
4.1.2 The character of the National Park must not be spoilt.
4.1.4 During peak traffic flows, speed is unimportant as long as blockage is prevented.

The measures to be introduced to fufil these principles as the situation steadily deteriorates were described as follows:

8.1   Solution 1   (Information and Dispersion).
8.2   Solution 2   (Flow Control of Traffic).
8.3   Solution 3   (Complete Restriction).

Solution 1 might be called the appeal to commonsense and co-operation and it is designed to operate by encouraging:

... voluntary use of alternative routes and the maximum use of car parks. This is preferable to control and restriction. Legislation, which might cause delays by public objection, could possibly be avoided.

The object would be to keep traffic flow on Secondary Routes below saturation level by advising the time at which routes approach their capacity and also indicating an alternative less congested road. This could be arranged by automatic congestion indicators or manually operated signs....

... *Discouragement to roadside parking should start as soon as there are adequate numbers of car park spaces.* Appropriate signs at entrances to the National Park may avoid the need for constant warning against parking on the roadside ... but they ... would probably require special legislation ...

It should be noted that even Solution 1, which I have called the appeal to commonsense, would require a good deal of restriction and control. 'Discouragement to roadside parking ...' means—as is made clear elsewhere in the report—that parking in other than official parks would be forbidden and the restriction enforced by traffic wardens as in the centres of our larger towns. It seems to be the thin end of the wedge, as Solution 2, 'Flow control of traffic', begins to show.

This would involve:

Control of traffic flow to keep it below saturation level. This could only be effective if all entrances and exits to the route, all car parks on the route, were controlled and their activities co-ordinated. This would require a complicated and expensive system of controls which could be simplified in certain cases if roads leading off secondary routes were restricted to local traffic only. Local traffic should be given priority at all times ...

A similar pattern of car parks would be required for this system as for Solution 1, with larger car parks ...

For [it] to be effective there must be no waiting or roadside parking unless specifically permitted. Such a system would be expensive to install, and means of financing it will have to be explored. . . . (Italics added)

The thick end of the wedge begins to show in Solution 3, 'Complete Restriction', which reads as follows:

> *Restrict all traffic, except essential local traffic,*[23] *on roads feeding away from the principal routes, and use particular types of buses* [mini-buses] *as public service vehicles.* This may make the best use of the highway capacity but may be an unpopular measure for both inhabitants and tourists, and could have an adverse effect on tourism along the secondary routes. The economics of a . . . special transport service using small vehicles may present practical difficulties. (Italics added)
>
> This type of total restriction would concentrate the main parking requirements of the Secondary Route at its connection with the Principal Route and could lead to extremely large car parks at certain places, e g Keswick and Windermere.

Section 10, the final part of the report, gives the 'Recommendations', graded and listed according to the period. The first section deals with the roads in the period 1964–1974, the second 1974 to 1984 and the third from 1984 onwards.

10.1 Roads 1964–1974
Solution 1 may satisfy this period but it may be necessary to introduce Solution 2 at certain points before 1974.
10.3 Roads 1974–1984
Solution 2 may suffice, but it may be necessary for Solution 3 to be introduced at certain points . . .
10.5 Roads 1984 onwards
Although Solution 2 may still suffice if no major changes of habit or use take place, it is likely to be necessary for Solution 3 to be introduced at further points during this period.

Although this survey was extremely valuable and showed the essence of the problems facing the Lake District—not to mention, in microcosm, the nation as a whole—it also underlined the need for further and more detailed studies and these were soon under way.

Borrowdale and the Langdales were studied in detail and a brief resumé of the latter, going right to the heart of the matter, just

[23] The definition of 'local traffic' could present problems.

how much motor traffic the area can stand without irreparable damage, is reported in the Appendix with definitions and calculations of optimum capacities.

In a circular letter to all interested parties, dated October 22, 1968, the Planning Board to the Lake District National Park referred to:

> ...a recommendation to the highway authorities that, at the present time, no measures of traffic regulation be introduced.

This was in despite of the fact that the overwhelming impression given by the letter—over four foolscap sides—is that traffic rationing cannot possibly be postponed much longer. Though regulation has been shelved for the time being in this distinctly temporizing document—a decision involving the rejection of all of the recommendations made by the Board's own officials and expert advisers —nonetheless the foundations are clearly laid for control in the fairly near future.

Destruction of 'Wilderness'

As pressure of demand rises, use of all amenities increases in proportion and quiet little spots visited only by a relatively small number of enthusiasts become more and more popular—partly because the absolute size of the minority liking wildness is increasing, partly because pressure on the more popular areas is becoming intolerable, and this leads inevitably to increasing costs and the need for control.

The reasons for this are easy to seek. If only a handful of people go to a quiet wood, a remote beach, a lonely hilltop, it doesn't matter very much if they attend to the calls of nature without the benefit of proper sanitary facilities, but as numbers increase this becomes less and less tolerable so that, beyond a certain point, it is essential in the interests of public health—without even considering the aesthetic aspects—to put in buildings with lavatories and sewage plant or main drainage but these destroy the very thing that people went for in the first place, to get away from it all.

A summer survey carried out by a team of Bristol University researchers,[24] who interviewed 5,000 people at six West Country beaches, showed that the holiday makers who go to the smaller beaches prefer them to remain wild and unspoiled and would rather

[24] Reported *The Guardian*, September 7, 1969.

do without facilities like lavatories and amusements: 75 per cent of them didn't want better road access and parking areas; 60 per cent did not want lavatories; 90 per cent did not want refreshment facilities; and 99 per cent did not want amusements to be laid on for them. As time goes on and population continues to increase the small minority—the 25 per cent in the survey who did want better road access and parking areas and the 10 per cent wanting refreshment facilities and so on—would grow larger in absolute numbers, eventually reaching the point at which it would become profitable for someone to provide commercial facilities to answer their needs and thereby destroy the amenities for the 75 per cent and the 90 per cent as these could find it hard to have their say and prevent it.

Summary

We have seen that virtually all sports and recreations are growing at an enormous rate, an expansion of several thousand per cent since the war being nothing unusual. I have argued that the concepts saturation 1 and saturation 2 apply in this field, as in motoring, although it will have become obvious to the reader that we cannot write in a tidy figure for sports saturation 1 by the year 2000, or any other deadline. Given a sufficient increase in wealth and leisure time perhaps 50 per cent of the population may want to have a boat of some kind, *plus* a glider or light aeroplane, an aqualung, a set of golf clubs, and a few other items, not to mention going in for a little tennis, weightlifting, and archery, on the side. Saturation 1 could finally be reached only when the limits of time and space were reached, it being impossible to pursue more than one sport at a time.

Once again we are playing the freedom game with our environment and extra people are constantly filling up the 'squares' we want to be in, the mooring for the dinghy, the run for the waterskis, the path up the mountain face, or, more prosaically perhaps, a quiet picnic spot or just 12 square feet of smooth sand to lie by the sea in the sun.

As the squares acquire greater scarcity value we begin to ration them more and more stringently by price and physical controls, and perhaps the best example[25] of the latter in Britain was afforded

---

[25] Since these words were written the Goyt Valley in the Derbyshire Peak District has been closed to all private motor vehicles at weekends and on public holidays. Whit Monday, 1970, was the last day of the free-for-all.

by the Lake District proposals. Even the Planning Board's solution No 1, labelled here 'an appeal to commonsense and co-operation', requires a good deal of new legislation and control, not to mention a high degree of knowledge, intelligence, and self-discipline on the part of the masses of motorists now attempting to use the area.

'Discouragement to roadside parking...' is a euphemism and means that parking anywhere except in an official car park would be forbidden, a restriction enforced by traffic wardens as in our urban areas. Traffic wardens and parking tickets in the heart of what is ostensibly a wilderness—an escape from it all—is an ominous sign to this observer at any rate. It seems to be the thin end of a very thick wedge, as solutions 2 and 3 described by the Planning Board make clear. Solution 2 requires control of:

> ...All entrances and exits...all car parks,...and their activities co-ordinated.... [requiring]...a complicated and expensive system of controls...

Solution 3 starts off, 'restrict all traffic...' the word 'restrict' again being a euphemism for 'ban'...except essential local traffic, ...and use...[mini-buses] as public service vehicles.'

If we shrink from rationing by the price mechanism amenities such as those provided by the Lake District, about the only acceptable thing left is physical control of this type.

What is essential, inevitable, even 'desirable' in the highly undesirable situations which are developing, is rigorous control by the least unacceptable means—provided only that effectiveness is guaranteed—to prevent the despoliation of priceless natural assets such as the Lake District by the ever increasing hordes of pleasure seekers.

This once more involves the loss of one microfreedom—to travel as you want, in your own private motor vehicle in order to preserve a greater microfreedom—that of others to enjoy what is left of our national assets relatively unimpeded by noise, fumes, stench, eyesores, and danger. A miserable but inevitable choice if numbers continue to increase.

Mr Moore, writing on yachting, was relating—apparently without realizing it—the sad tale that must be told with respect to all amenity resources as they become saturated with would-be consumers. At first the easily developed resources are used and there is plenty of space for everyone. Everyone can enjoy himself with little or no interference from his neighbours or from the authorities.

Later, less and less useful resources are exploited and the fun of the thing progressively diminishes as costs continue to rise. Eventually extremely marginal resources have to be pressed into use, and, finally, pressure of demand raises prices enough to lead to commercial exploitation in the worst sense of that term and the exclusion of many through the price mechanism.

This is sad enough but perhaps sadder still is the fact that, even for the few who can afford to pay prices inflated by saturation of the supply of this particular amenity, the essence of messing about in boats has disappeared.

> Gone is the privacy, so cherished, and long regarded as the pre-rogative of sailing as a sport, of lying on a mooring in mid-stream just close enough to call across to friends yet far enough away to ignore them without giving offence. It is hard to believe that such a state of affairs is condemned to extinction and that natural mooring areas have reached saturation point. Could not a little reorganization work wonders?[26]

Mr Moore's question at the end of the last quotation is so poignant that it seems almost churlish to ask what form a '... little reorganization ...' of Britain's population and coastline could take in order to transport the yachtsman back to the days when he was monarch of all he surveyed?

The countryside and our waterways cannot be made to grow with population—although the effectiveness of their use could no doubt be improved to some degree—so that rationing schemes of one sort or another must be imposed sooner or later. It is the old problem of the quart and the pint pot and if we permit numbers to increase constantly, the question is not 'whether' but 'when?' and 'how?'.

Private discussions with officials of the various bodies concerned with the provision of facilities for sport almost invariably get around to the questions of numbers and the utter impossibility of discharging their functions much longer—providing playing fields or what-ever it might be—if population continues to increase. The same is true of many groups in other spheres, road transport, planning etc. The conversation, having got this far, is almost certain to include the phrase 'of course *we* wouldn't touch it with a bargepole', 'that's completely outside our terms of reference, or 'our resources are strictly limited—we have to confine ourselves to the main task'.

[26] (*Op cit*).

Democracy works largely by means of pressure groups—one might almost define it as government *by* pressure group—and if all of the units operating in the front line of the battle between numbers and resources opt, without exception, out of any discussion of the issue they all admit in private is central to all their problems, what hope is there for finding a solution, or, in the long run, for democracy itself.

The bodies endeavouring to preserve our open spaces, ancient buildings, or coast line, to increase our roadspace to match the number of vehicles, to conserve our water supplies, prevent pollution, ensure the survival of a viable agricultural system, or to balance our imports and exports all have not only the right but the plain duty to speak out, they owe it to their fellow citizens to utter the blunt truth they admit in private and give us the benefit of their seasoned experience and best judgment about the inevitable outcome if present trends are allowed to continue. If the reason given for their present silence is lack of funds or facilities we can reasonably ask what is the cost of writing a paragraph into the annual report or a few sentences into the President's or Chairman's address to the annual conference?

The true reason for avoiding this critical topic appears to be compounded of fear of controversy and an unnecessary and unjustifiable sense of delicacy and these feelings must be overcome in defence of living democracy if for no other reason. The pressure groups must give the matter their urgent attention and then speak out before it is too late.

It may be thought ill-judged or even frivolous to have devoted a whole chapter to sports and pastimes when far weightier topics cry out for attention but the fact seems to be that in Britain we are far more concerned about our pleasures than about the empty ricebowls of the Asians. The greater part of the argumentation in this book is addressed to intelligent self-interest, not because I think self-interest is more important than selflessness or morality, but because in the present situation it seems likelier to produce appropriate action.

Appendix: the Borrowdale and Langdales studies

These[27] followed quickly on the heels of the first study mentioned in Chapter 13 and delved much more deeply into the problem.

[27] Lake District Planning Board (1968) mimeographed.

Here, in brief, are the details of the means by which the saturation capacity of the Langdales was worked out.

The Langdales consist of two valleys 'Great' and 'Little' Langdale, served by B5343 and an unclassified road respectively. There are four access points for motor traffic.

After the briefest of introductions this study immediately got to the heart of the problem, a consideration of just how much motor traffic the area could absorb without being irretrievably damaged.

2. Maximum levels of use

When considering an existing level of use in an attempt to ascertain the degree of use, an optimum use level must be fixed to act as a base for comparison. This optimum use level may be given two values:

(a) Maximum possible use; a purely physical value ignoring all factors not directly related to the use.

(b) Maximum acceptable use; a value taking regard of factors affected by the use.

In relation to the motor car and its use in the Lake District:

Case (a) above would produce the maximum number of cars it would be possible to cram on to the roads and into the car parks, with regard only to speed and space, before a complete breakdown of the system occurred.

Case (b) above would provide the maximum number it is felt could be allowed before they detract seriously from the amenities which has attracted them. It is this optimum level of use which it is proposed to use as a base.

3. Maximum acceptable use: Car-parking

In a given area there is a given amount of space for parking. The number of spaces available should never be more than is ... acceptable from the amenity point of view. Thus, the maximum acceptable parking capacity of an area will be when all spaces are fully occupied all day.[28]

4. Maximum acceptable use: Road traffic

A rough guide to the traffic capacity of a defined road pattern

---

[28] The maximum parking capacity in an eight-hour day is defined as eight times the number of parking spaces, on the assumption that each parking unit is one hour.

can be gained by taking the number of lane miles in a given system and dividing it by the minimum amount of road space a vehicle requires to allow it to pull up in safety when travelling at a given speed, this speed being the maximum safe velocity after consideration of the overall road circumstances. The roads in Langdale can be divided into two basic categories:

(a) single lane 5.3 miles,
(b) two lane 6.9 miles.

Ignoring directional flow, this gives just over 19 miles of single lane carriageway in the Langdales. It is proposed to use 15 mph as the maximum safe velocity. At this speed the average vehicle requires sixty-five feet ... to stop safely; with an average vehicle length of fifteen feet, this gives eighty feet as the minimum road space requirement for every vehicle at this speed. Dividing the 19 lane miles in the Langdales by this figure of 80 feet gives a traffic capacity of 1,254 vehicles. This is a maximum *capacity* figure, obviously the maximum *acceptable* capacity lies below this value. (Italics added)

The prime factor when assessing this lower value is to make an allowance for all cars which might be in the valley, although not actually occupying road space, so that in the unlikely event of all these vehicles wishing to move on the road at the one time, the resultant traffic would not be above the maximum possible capacity.

Therefore, it would seem reasonable to state acceptable capacity as maximum possible capacity minus the maximum number of vehicles which would be in the valley although not on the roads.

Vehicles in the valley but not occupying road space, could be made up from the following sources:

(a) Vehicles occupying available parking spaces   386
(b) Vehicles belonging to residents computed at the rate/
        head of population for rural Westmorland   140
(c) Vehicles belonging to visitors occupying caravan
        and camp site and hotel rooms, etc.   250
                                                                 ———
                                                      Total   776

Taking this figure from the maximum possible capacity figure of 1,254, the resultant free-flow acceptable figure would be 480 vehicles (approximately).

5. *Maximum acceptable use—Saturation point*

Taking incoming traffic as the critical flow, saturation point will be reached if after all available parking spaces are filled (i e 386 vehicles are parked in the valley) 480 vehicles have entered the Langdales, and there has been no reduction in the number of parked vehicles.

Parking

The Supplementary Report on Car Parking in Borrowdale said there is

... a shortfall of 190 spaces, i e a need for almost as many spaces again before an efficient parking management scheme could be undertaken.

... the maximum acceptable number of parked vehicles compatible with amenity, that could be allowed in the valleys was 386. The proposals outlined ... are aimed at ensuring that these 386 vehicle spaces are available in the Langdales in purpose made parking areas.

The success of this concept of management of parked vehicles, by the application of a maximum acceptable use, is entirely dependent upon the making of an order under section 9 of the Road Traffic Act, 1967, prohibiting all parking on a public highway, and the use of traffic wardens whose main duty would be to confine all parking to the sites provided.

A further conclusion ... is that the situation where the above scheme of management will need to be implemented will have been reached by 1973. Accordingly, it will be necessary to programme the proposed car parking works so that they are completed by this date ...

Part 4

Freedom to choose

Chapter 14

Freedom to choose:
I. Optimum populations

There's nothing, situate under heaven's eye,
But hath his bound, in earth, in sea, in sky.

William Shakespeare[1]

We have already seen that there is a connection between numbers and liberty and there appear to be fundamental general relationships in nature between the size,[2] shape, and functions of living objects and groups and it would be rather surprising if the underlying principle did not apply to whole societies.

In biology there is a relationship called 'the square cube-law'[3] which illustrates the fact that a potential Jack the Giant Killer has little to fear from a Giant ten times as big (tall) as himself, the reason being that the Giant's volume would be greater by 10^3—his weight increasing accordingly—whilst the cross-sectional area of his legs, which would have to support his weight, would be greater by only 10^2. The weight of his body in relationship to the strength of its supports would have increased 10 times. This would mean that the Giant's legs would be overstressed and would crumple. They would fail 'in compression' as engineers say.

This law is exemplified in heavy animals like the elephant whose legs appear to be disproportionately thick for its size. The heaviest

[1] *Comedy of Errors*, Act 11, Sc 1.
[2] See for example Haldane, JBS, 'On Being the Right Size'. (An essay.)
[3] For a treatment of this topic, an application in organization and management theory, and an extensive bibliography, see Haire, M (ed) (1961) *Modern Organisation Theory*.

animal of all, the whale, had to evolve in the water as the number and size of legs it would require with such a huge bulk and weight would be something of a problem to articulate and control.

Another example is in the evolution of human types in the extremes of temperature we find on the Earth. In colder climates the evolution tends to be towards shorter and fatter individuals and in the hotter climates to longer and thinner.[4] The reason for this is that the shorter fatter body has a smaller outside area with respect to its volume, giving reduced heat loss for a given mass, the opposite applying to the taller thinner people who have a relatively great area of body surface as compared to body mass and therefore radiate more heat and keep more comfortable in a hot climate.

The same principle applies to the construction of atomic bombs. The explosive material in an atomic bomb is manufactured and placed in the bomb in 'sub-critical' masses, two halves, I believe, each half having a volume to surface-area ratio lower than the critical value. At the moment of detonation the two halves are forced together by an explosion of some conventional material, at which point the critical ratio of volume to surface area suddenly changes, making the mass of fissile material explode.

Meaning of 'optimum'

The word *optimum* comes from the Latin word *optimus* which means 'the best'. Now for precisely the same reasons for which it was argued earlier that 'liberty' means virtually nothing without qualification—we must look very carefully at the notions 'optimum' or 'best' when applied to a population. We have to ask best for what, best for whom, best how, when, where, and why? We must not forget to ask in addition 'how does our society decide these questions—*who* decides, and by what social mechanism?'

Once these questions have been asked it has become obvious that no simple answers are forthcoming. Does this mean that finding answers is impossible? Surely not, difficult though it may be we have not only to attempt the task but to succeed, however tentatively, otherwise natural mechanisms of the future will optimize the human population as it optimizes others, on the basis of simple physical, chemical, and biological criteria, an equation containing no symbol for liberty or any other cultural values.

[4] See Barnett, A (1961) *The Human Species* (p 147 and plates 14 and 15).

Nature—and it is a mistake to think of nature as a single entity, perhaps we ought to repeat nature with a little 'n' or, better still, talk not of nature as a single entity at all but of 'natural processes' —which though apparently blind and purposeless must nonetheless operate within the physical laws of the universe in such a way as to come to some kind of tentative and shifting synthesis or balance. The variables written, in effect, into these 'equations' by natural processes, would be the amounts of physical space, sustenance— which means in physical terms energy and mass—the quantity and kinds of toxic substances produced by the life processes, and the regenerative capacity of the environment.

These basic physical processes would be operating through biological mechanisms and, in the case of some living things, psychological mechanisms which might produce further constraints as density increases. For example, it seems likely that stress, aggression, and violence will increase and this would be one of the factors entering into nature's population optimum.

A population optimized by these mechanisms would have very little to recommend it to any civilized human being—even an uncivilized one, come to that—and humanity must surely think in terms of writing social, cultural, and spiritual variables into the optimum population equation in addition to the others listed.

Optimum size of small groups

A modern basic test in social psychology[5] gives a good brief review of the literature on the effects of group size on task performance by the groups.

> Seashore (1954) measured the cohesiveness of 228 work groups in a large factory ... and found that smaller groups ... were, on the average, more cohesive than large groups ...
>
> ... [and] ... numerous studies show that low group cohesiveness goes with voluntary absenteeism, which may be regarded as an indication of dissatisfaction. ...
>
> Miller (1950) found larger conference groups to be more disruptive than smaller groups. 'Sense of belongingness' in these conference groups correlated minus 0.44 with group size. And lack of opportunity to talk, which correlated highly with group size (r—0.80), was associated with feelings of frustration.

[5] Krech, Crutchfield, and Ballachey (1962) *Individual in Society.*

Hare found that ... five-person groups [of scouts] arrived at a significantly higher level of consensus after discussion than did the twelve-person groups.

Slater (1958) examined some correlates of group size in a sample of 24 'creative' groups ranging in size from two to seven members ...' after four meetings to discuss human relations problems.

Members of the five-man groups expressed complete satisfaction, no one reporting that he felt his group was too large or too small. Members of groups larger than five persons reported that they felt their groups were disorderly and wasted time, and the members were too pushy, aggressive, and competitive. Some of ... [them] ... asked for more central control ... others grumbled about the high-handed way some of the members dominated the discussion.

The members of groups smaller than five persons complained only that their groups were too small. ...

These various studies ... consistently point to the same conclusion; people tend to be happier in smaller groups. ...

The authors go on, however, to qualify any intuitive leaps one may be tempted to make from small groups to large societies:

... we must ... be cautious in extrapolating this finding from groups to *organizations*. ...

They continue:

Bales and his associates (1951), Stephan and Mishler (1952), and others have suggested ... that as the size of the group increases the most frequent contributor assumes a more and more prominent role in the discussion. The bigger the group, the greater the gap in the amount of participation between the most frequent contributor and the other members of the group. ... Moreover, the number of persons in a group who contribute less than their proportionate share goes up as the size of the group expands ...

Carter and his co-workers (1951a) ... 'concluded' ... in the larger groups only the more forceful individuals are able to express their abilities and ideas, since the amount of freedom in the situation is not sufficient to accommodate all the group members.

... The correlation between authoritarianism and leadership

behaviour was found to increase as the size of the group rose ...

Hemphill (1950) also found '... that in the larger groups the demands upon the leader were greater and leader-centred behaviour was tolerated more by the members.'

Marriott (1949) ... found a negative correlation between output and group size, groups of less than ten producing 7 per cent more per man than groups of more than thirty. This result ... may be due to the fact that the group bonus scheme under which his groups worked becomes ineffective for large groups.

Worthy (1950) has reported ... that both worker satisfaction and operating efficiency tend to decrease with increase in the size of administration units ... Though the authors qualify this by saying 'there is ... surprisingly little convincing research evidence that small work groups have a higher output per man than large ones.

The joint authors summarize as follows:

It appears probable, that, for any given task there is an optimum group size for maximum effectiveness. The optimum size will be a function of the complexity of the task and the degree of heterogeneity of available members in the abilities and skills required by the task. The more complex the task and the more homogeneous the available members, the larger the optimum size. ... Large groups have difficulty organizing themselves for effective work and constraints upon participation are experienced with increase in size. To sum up, Thelen (1940) proposed that a group should ideally be the smallest possible that contains all the skills required for the accomplishment of the tasks of the group.

Size versus efficiency. A tug-o-war team

A simple but profound study showed that increasing the size of a tug-o-war team progressively reduced its efficiency.

The experimental set up was as follows. Instead of having two tug-o-war teams pulling against each other the experimenter had a single team pulling against an instrument so that the group's effort could be measured. Figure 14/1 shows the results of changing the size of the team from one up to eight in stages. As each new member of the team was added, although the total pull went up, the extra contribution went down, as did the average pull of the whole team. The graph shows the relationships between total, average, and 'marginal' pulls (of each succeeding new member of the team).

This, incidentally, is an example of 'diminishing returns'. Increasing the size of the team from one to eight increases the total pull exerted from 63 to only 248 kilogrammes. In other words an eightfold increase in the size of the team is accompanied by less than a fourfold increase in the total pull; the last member contributing, effectively, only 1 kilogramme (0.4 per cent) to the total effort of the team.

Fig 14/1
Tug-o'-War team:
Decline in efficiency with
increase in size

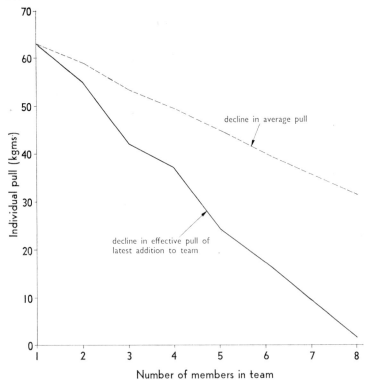

Based on data from: Moede, W., (1927)
Experimentelle Massenpsychologie
Summarized in Klein, J. (1956) **The Study of Groups**, p3

Optimum size of societies. Ideas of the ancients

It is hardly surprising that ideas on such an important topic as the optimization of population have been in circulation since ancient times. Hippodamus,[6] the first town planner, who laid out the Piraeus, specified the ideal city (the basis of the city state) as having a population of 10,000 souls divided into three classes—one of artisans, one of farmers, and a third of professional soldiers for defence. He divided the land similarly into three parts, sacred, public, and private; the first to maintain the established worship of the gods, the second to support the military, and the third to serve as property for the agricultural class. Plato thought the ideal city state would have 5,040 citizens proper, giving an overall population of about 60,000.[7]

Aristotle, putting first things first, started off with a consideration of what societies are for. In his chapter 'A' 'Political Aims and Educational Principles' (Book VII),[8] he starts off as follows;

1. *The most desirable life*
No proper enquiry into the ideal constitution is possible unless we have first determined what is the most desirable way of life. The ideal constitution must remain uncertain so long as this question is unanswered; for it is only reasonable to expect that in the normal course of events, those will lead the best life who live under the best form of government permitted by their circumstances ... First, therefore, we must ask, which is the most generally desirable life, and secondly whether or not the same life is best both for states and for individuals.

If an ideal state is one in which desired values are optimized and population is an essential part of any state, as Aristotle says, then in order to realize the ideal state the population must itself be optimized. Aristotle himself certainly thought this; let us now see what he thought about optimum populations.

2. *The ideal State Described*
(A) POPULATION AND TERRITORY

... (1) First among the materials required by the statesman is a body of human beings, whose quantity and quality he will have to consider, as well as the area and topographical features

---

6 Reported by Aristotle in *Politics*.

7 *Laws*, Bk. V (p 737/8).

8 Politics.

of the country they are to inhabit. Most people think that a state in order to be happy must be great; but even if they are right, they take no account of what is meant by 'great' and 'small' with reference to a state. They judge its size by the number of inhabitants instead of by the more truthful yardstick of capacity. A state, like an individual, has a function to fulfil; and that state which is best equipped to carry out its task must be reckoned the greatest, in the sense in which Hippocrates might be described as greater than someone taller than himself....

...A state...composed of too few members is not (as a state is by definition) self-sufficing. One that is composed of too many is self-sufficing with regard to mere necessaries, as a barbarian tribe might be; but it is not a *state*, since it is incapable of true constitutional government. Who can be general of such an enormous multitude? or who will give it orders, unless he has the voice of Stentor?

...we know from experience that it is difficult, if not quite impossible, for a very populous state to insure general obedience to law; all those which are now reputed to be well governed have limited populations.

In the eighteenth century Jean Jacques Rousseau reiterated the same point:

As nature has set bounds to the stature of a well-made man, and outside those limits, makes nothing but giants or dwarfs, similarly, for the constitution of a State to be at its best, it is possible to fix limits that will make it neither too large for good government, nor too small for self-maintenance. In every body politic there is a maximum strength which it cannot exceed and which it only loses by increasing in size. Every extension of the social tie means its relaxation; and, generally speaking, a small state is stronger in proportion than a great one.[9]

It will encourage those who hope to see our population optimized to find exactly the same arguments still being put forward by contemporary social scientists. For example, F. Cottrell in his original work on the relationship between the supply of energy and the structure and function of social systems:

There seem to be limits on the size of the effective social unit: beyond a certain point organization cannot be made comprehen-

[9] (1762) *The Social Contract,* Everyman's edition (p 37).

sible enough for succeeding generations to learn to operate it. It thus appears that large units such as the USSR, the British Commonwealth, and perhaps the United States have reached the point where any technological gains to be derived from an increase in size would be outweighed by the increased costs of creating and maintaining the necessary social, political and legal controls. Assuming that these organizations are big enough to maintain their military defence, enlargement would weaken rather than strengthen them.[10]

Of course, the writings of great men and other scholars dò not necessarily prove a point but at least they give us substantial food for thought, and there is much more evidence from other sources.

Maximum as optimum

The traditional Christian idea of an optimum population is that of the maximum; the slogan: 'Be fruitful and multiply, and replenish the earth', is repeated twice in the book of Genesis. It is a pity that a devastating analysis made by Harold Cox[11] has not been more widely read.

...Most of those who quoted it,...[or]...heard it...seemed to have assumed that it settled the moral question for all times. A more striking illustration of the power of mere words over human minds it would be hard to find.

...Even the words themselves, if critically examined suggest that the instruction to be fruitful and multiply is not applicable to all times. The persons to whom this command was given were told 'to replenish the earth'. How then does [it] stand when the earth has been replenished?

...If the command is a universal injunction, as the persons who quote it invariably imply, its application extends to all men and women. Yet, in defiance of this command, the Roman Catholic Church has established a celibate priesthood for men and nunneries for celibate women...who it regards...as being peculiarly holy persons, although the vows they take involve direct disobedience to the divine command to be fruitful and multiply....

[10] Cottrell, F (1955) *Energy and Society* (p 164). See also Deutsch, K, 'Nature of International Society', Ch in *Conflict in Society* (1966), CIBA Foundation Symposium.
[11] (1922) *The Problem of Population.*

Colin Clark, the distinguished Roman Catholic apologist, has taken this line about as far as it can go. In his ponderous work *Population Growth and Land Use*, he refrains from discussing optimization of population at all. The word 'optimum' does not appear in the index—an extraordinary omission (neither do the key concepts, 'carrying capacity', 'birth control', 'family planning', and 'population control'). Nonetheless he does seem to imply a kind of optimization of population, equating it with the biggest one possible, and this he works out in terms of the minimum amount of land required to grow the food to keep a human being in reasonable health.

> ... We then come to the interesting conclusion that the full support of one person requires the continuous cultivation of an area no larger than 27 square metres.[12]

Relating this to his acceptance of the maximum possible cultivable area[13] of the world (with 'large additional capital expenditure and new methods') of 9.33 billion hectares,[14] and performing a simple division sum we arrive at an optimum population for the earth of:

$$\frac{9.33 \text{ billion hectares}}{27 \text{ square metres per person}} = 346 \text{ billion people}$$

The figure which Clark takes here, 9.33 billion hectares, as he himself admits:

> ... approaches the 13.6 billion hectares of the Earth's surface (excluding tundra and lands of perpetual frost).

The world's present agricultural area totals 4.01 billion hectares[15] and Clark's 'optimum' would require this to be more than doubled, a gigantic feat of technology, social organization, and capital utilization, to support a population—at something above the bare physiological minimum—100 times the 1967 world total.[16]

---

[12] (p 157).
[13] After Malin (1965).
[14] 1 hectare = 2.471 acres (1 sq mile = 260 hectares, approx.).
[15] 1.43 b arable + 2.58 b grazing.
[16] Professor Fremlin has beaten even this with one of his now famous *reductios*; 12,000 million million in 800 years' time, with further growth halted by the 'heat barrier'. See 'How Many People Can The World Support', *New Scientist*, **24** (pp 285–7) and Conservation Society Reprints, Vol 1, 1968.

It is hardly surprising that Dr Clark did not include a chapter on material resources and living-space.

However, in the sphere of fertility and population, as in others—perhaps fortunately—the Bible is somewhat ambiguous and scriptural authority can be found for the restriction of numbers as well as for increasing and multiplying.

> But woe to them that are with child, and to them that give suck. . . .[17]

> But Jesus turning unto them said, Daughters of Jerusalem, weep not for me, but weep for yourselves, and for your children.
> For, behold, the days are coming, in which they shall say, Blessed are the barren, and the wombs that never bare, and the paps which never gave suck.[18]

It is also possible to find a precursor of the modern eugenicist's and conservationist's motto, Quality before Quantity!

> Desire not a multitude of unprofitable children, neither delight in ungodly sons.
> Though they multiply, rejoice not in them, except the fear of the Lord be with them.[19]

The technical meaning of 'optimum population'

A good technical definition of 'optimum population' is given by Gould and Kolb:[20]

> . . . the . . . population size or density at which the value of some . . . normatively selected variable is maximized.

The variable normally selected is the per capita income, as it is simple to understand and measure. Economists generally shy away not only from other normatively selected variables but from the optimum concept itself, on the grounds that it is too complicated and controversial to have any practical value. Nonetheless economists frequently lay down the law about the economic benefits of large and ever-increasing populations in total disregard of other factors, including important economic variables such as congestion-

[17] St Mark, xiii, 17.
[18] St Luke, xxiii, 28–9.
[19] Ecclesiasticus, xvi.
[20] (1964) *Dictionary of the Social Sciences.*

costs and shortage of raw materials—even the finiteness of the environment and therefore the supply of land, let alone aesthetic and psychological factors, and we must view their arguments with a beady eye.

'Critical population density'

For his Presidential Address to the British Association for the Advancement of Science, meeting in Nottingham in August, 1966, Sir Joseph Hutchinson chose the title 'Land and Human Populations'. The key concept in his discourse was that of 'critical population density' (developed by William Allan[21]) which he defined as

> ... The maximum population density that can be supported by a given agricultural system without progressive deterioration of the land.

He pointed out that the author of the concept was concerned with subsistence farming in an agricultural community but goes on to say:

> ... the concept can be usefully applied much more widely than this. It is characteristic of our biological environment that we can for a limited period exploit it in excess of its real productive capacity, and only after a lapse of time is it apparent that we have initiated in it a progressive decline. We have spent working capital as well as income, and when the capital has been depleted the income falls ... that the degeneration of the environment is a real problem, and may lead to an almost irreversible decline in productivity, is evident from the present state of the Mediterranean land after six or so millenia of over-cutting, over-grazing, and over-cultivation, and from the present state of heaths and moors in Britain for which we have evidence ... that they once carried a forest cover.

This concept of 'critical population' is relevant in all human communities. It is in the natural course of events that a developing community should service its development first by bringing into use its unused resources. There comes a time, however, when all the readily available resources have been brought in. At this point of time, the population density has reached the critical level, and the choices before the community lie between the

21 (1965) *The African Husbandman.*

over-exploitation of resources to the long-term detriment of the system, the planning of new systems of resource use that are both more conservative of resources and more productive of real income, and population control. . . .

The history of population growth and the agricultural exploitation of the land in this country is one of alternation between the first two of these choices culminating in the position we have reached in the last decade, of an abundance of farm produce, even though the growth of our population continues unchecked. Our present food supply position might lead us to the complacent conclusion that we have now learned how to match with increasing supplies our ever increasing needs. The historical evidence is against such a conclusion. . . . Current assessments of our need, . . . indicate that our present abundance may not be long continued. . . .

. . . We have come to the point where the future well being of our people depends upon our undertaking now to control the size of our population.[22]

Three choices for Britain

Professor J. H. Fremlin has worked out the implications of three greatly differing values for the optimum population for Britain[23], at 1; 30; and 1,000 million, respectively. If your ideal is:

. . . living between a pub and a bingo-hall over a fish and chip shop and opposite a department store then 1,000 millions is probably too small . . .

despite the fact that electricity would be vastly cheaper and intellectual life stimulating, with:

. . . several Newtons and Shakespeares, Jane Austens and Constables . . . alive at the same time. . . .

With 30 millions:

. . . the housing problem would disappear . . . and increase mobility and hence freedom . . . far more families would have their own gardens—school classes would be smaller . . . it would

[22] Broadcast by the BBC and printed in *The Listener,* September 1, 1966. Also in *Advancement of Science,* September, 1966.
[23] 'An optimum population for Britain', *New Scientist,* December 21, 1967. Also Conservation Society Reprints No 2 (1969).

be perfectly practicable to grow all our own food ... without battery hens or calves ... [and] an individual motor vehicle for every adult would be perfectly practicable outside the central areas of the larger towns.

With an optimum of one million:

> ... the advantages would be far more specialized and the disadvantages more numerous ... although ... there would be room for every adult to have his own helicopter, ...

Professor Fremlin plumps for the 30 million optimum himself and his arguments in both directions from that point—though well worth reading—are really reductions to absurdity.

The standard technical definition of an optimum population is inadequate for practical purposes as there is no single variable which should be maximized at the expense of all others, unless it be some extremely complex notion like the 'standard of living' or 'quality of life'—going far beyond mere per capita income because of the inclusion of such factors as peace, health, space, comfort, and aesthetic fulfilment. What we must do is choose the most important factors in our value-system and then realize the total 'mix' as far as possible with as clear and flexible an understanding as may be achieved of the interaction of the various components, especially of the key fact that very often more of component 'x' means less of component 'y'.

Individual liberty could be the single variable maximized, provided we accept that it is extremely complex, the sum of all microfreedoms, that is. To optimize individual liberty we would have to break it down into its component microfreedoms and see how far these reinforce or interfere with each other and carefully arrange matters so that the largest quantity of the best mix is created.

The Optimum Population Symposium

In September, 1969 a symposium on the topic, 'The Optimum Population for Britain', sponsored by the Institute of Biology, was held at the Royal Geographical Society in London, the proceedings being published subsequently.[24]

Twelve papers were contributed by a wide range of experts in biology, demography, economics, sociology, and other disciplines

[24] Taylor, LR (ed) (1970) *The Optimum Population For Britain.*

but despite the impressive range of learning displayed, the strongest impression made on this observer was the difficulty most academics seem to have in calling a spade a spade, let alone rolling up their sleeves, picking it up and using it to clear away the pile of obstacles in the way of commitment and effective social action.

Of the thirteen contributors (one paper was jointly presented by Lady Medawar and Madeleine Simms), ten were academics, all of whom were British except two, Professor Paul Ehrlich of Stanford University and M. M. R. Freeman of the Memorial University of Newfoundland. Of the eight British academics three ignored the optimum concept and population control, three rejected both, one was equivocal, and only one—the animal ecologist from Imperial College, T. R. E. Southwood—accepted the need for control and discussed the possible contribution of his discipline towards the estimation and realization of an optimum population.

Both of the foreign guests accepted unequivocally the need for population control—Ehrlich the biologist very forcefully indeed. Freeman regretted the almost complete avoidance of population facts and problems by his fellow anthropologists and gave a thorough review of the problems and literature. Ehrlich pessimistically concluded:

> I would be less than honest if I expressed the conviction that such a change will occur. If I were a gambler, I would take even money that England will not exist in the year 2000, and give 10 to 1 that the life of the average Briton would be of distinctly lower quality than it is today.[25]

The three authors of the two papers presented by non-academics all took the same starting point—expressed by Mr Douglas Houghton, MP, in his paper, 'The Legislation Barrier'—as follows:

> (a) the absolute necessity for population limitation. (p 117)

Medawar and Simms added to a similar statement the words:

> ... if a civilized way of life is to be possible in the next century.[26]

In addition to those expressing outright support for population control two other British scholars present, Sir Alan Parkes and Kenneth Mellanby are known sympathizers and the only sociologist present, Geoffrey Hawthorne, comes very close to it at times in his public utterances.

[25] (p 161).   [26] pp 117 and 131, respectively.

In the face of this substantial academic majority for a seat on the fence it is striking indeed that when Sir David Renton, MP, chairing the final session, took a straw vote on two questions the answers were almost unanimously of the opposite opinion, nearly all[27] answering the following two questions in the affirmative:

1. Is it possible to give a reasonable meaning to the concept 'optimum population'?, and

2. Has Britain already passed the optimum point?

The pioneering spirit of Dr Taylor of the Rothamsted Experimental Station, who organized this symposium, is greatly to be welcomed and it is to be hoped that academics of many different disciplines will soon be getting together again to discuss these issues in greater detail. However, unless our scholars are prepared to put their heads on the chopping block by committing themselves to definite views—or at least procedures for eliciting answers to our huge and baffling problems—it will be left to public-spirited citizens to do the best they can alone, a sad state of affairs.

Dr Taylor's admirably committed and cogent Introduction provides a very sound starting point for the next phase.

An optimum population should seek to maximize:

1. the vigour and potential of individuals;
2. the currently acceptable pattern of social organization;
3. the realization of cultural goals which were listed as moral, political, and aesthetic standards;
4. real output per head.

it should minimize:

1. pollution;
2. nutritional and
3. social stress.

To do this it must be less than the carrying capacity of the environment and hence *capable of being indefinitely maintained* (Italics original).

Optimizing liberty

If what we want to do is to optimize human joy and fulfilment— one might say joy through fulfilment—one of the means to this noble end would surely be the optimization of liberty. We need

[27] About 90 per cent.

to create a system in which every individual is free to pursue as far as possible, without harming others, the things that *he* regards as desirable, which give *him* satisfaction in the light of *his* own unique genetic inheritance, social conditioning, and self-development up to that point. We need to create a system in which all get what they need and give to society what they are able to give.

Perfect freedom, perfect understanding, perfect individual development, this would be the ideal, but we must come back to earth with a bump to look at the practical possibilities. What has been described is a state of anarchy in which nobody rules anyone else so that everybody can do as he pleases. But as anarchy does not seem viable, at least at present, a distinction must be made between what is advocated as an ideal and what is practicable.

It seems highly probable that in the foreseeable future if there were to be perfect freedom, a significant minority, at least, would abuse it. Some individuals, owing to the quirks of their genetic and social inheritance and moral illiteracy can fulfil themselves only through becoming Napoleons, if not of war, then of crime, politics, or culture, and as soon as they arise the liberties of the others, the non-Napoleons, are restricted.

This would be incompatible with the goal of the system, maximum liberty, and means that there must be enough constraint to prevent the kinds of fulfilment that some dominant individuals seek, from interfering too much with the freedoms of the rest. This means that constraints have to be introduced up to the minimum degree necessary to optimize liberty within the system. The minimum amount could be found out only in practice by trying out different sorts of constraints in different conditions to see what it was at that particular time and place and the control-system should be flexible. Constraints should be kept constantly under review so that new ones would be introduced should they become really necessary and, equally important, old ones could be removed wherever possible.

Freedom for women, (i) women in general

Many of the attitudes which support the present craft system of training and discrimination against women common to both employers and trade unionists are deeply ingrained in the life of the country. Prejudice against women is manifest at all levels of management as well as on the shop floor.

This quotation is not a historic relic from the earlier part of the industrial revolution but from paragraph 359 of the Report of the Royal Commission on Trade Unions and Employers' Associations, published in June, 1968.

Mrs Shirley Williams, Minister for Higher Education, pointed out in a speech in London that whereas in the Soviet Union one engineer in three was a woman, in France, one in twenty-eight, only one in five hundred was the figure for Britain.

This is hardly surprising as our women receive much lower standards of education, on the whole. If we consider the eighteen-year-olds in 1964, 45 per cent of the boys were receiving some formal education against only 26 per cent of the girls. Even where girls are receiving higher education they suffer from serious inadequacies in laboratories and other equipment in teaching for science and mathematics in the girls' schools. There is even a Ministry of Education bulletin (2nd ed 1954) recommending less laboratory space for girls' schools.

According to the Fabian pamphlet *Equality for Women* this discrimination percolates throughout the whole of our society, especially in the field of remuneration.

> Most women workers are subject to a double discrimination. Not only do they have difficulty in getting training, skilled jobs and promotion, but their pay is grossly below that of men doing comparable work. The ending of discrimination and the introduction of equal pay are interlocked.[28]

The pamphlet points out that over a third of the British labour force consists of women and that it is estimated that as few as one in ten are receiving equal pay for equal work.

If liberty in the system is to be optimized then women in the system must be as free as men, no more and no less. Both must be liberated from oppressive pressures in their environment. This is essential from a moral point of view—it is *unjust* that women should be discriminated against, from a social and economic point of view—so that they may make their maximum contribution to the cultural, industrial, and commercial life of the nation and consequently its prosperity, and because liberation from prejudices confining them to kitchen and nursery will tend to decrease their fertility.

If society prevents women from expressing themselves freely

28 Rendel, M, *et al* (1968).

through most of the channels open to men then pressure is applied to them to fulfil themselves through motherhood. Equality of the sexes is an essential part of a democratic and humane programme of population control.

Freedom for women, (ii) wives in particular

In a devastating article called 'The Unplanned Children'[29] Pauline Shapiro demonstrated that there is a long way to go if wives are to be freed of unreasonable demands and behaviour inflicted on them by their husbands. Mrs Shapiro was describing a case-study she made between 1950 and 1959 and it is to be hoped that some of the horrifying practices she describes will have disappeared by now. However, social change tends to be slow and it would be surprising if this study is not representative of what still goes on in many families. The study was designed to compare a group of 'satisfactory' large families as against 'problem' families. But the records turned out to be too complex to make an overall assessment possible and the study was able to take into account only the central variable, 'mothers coping' or 'mothers not coping' in accordance with their physical and personal care of their children.

> The 'copers' were affectionate mothers whose children were cleaned, clothed, fed, and kept under reasonable control in a manner that would not bring them to the notice of children's social agencies. The 'non-copers' varied in their affection but were alike in their lack of control of their children and the squalor of home conditions which brought them to the notice of numerous social agencies.
>
> ... It proved impossible ... to divide the families into only two groups: a small intermediate category was needed which we have called 'transitional'.

The 128 records retained for analysis yielded 55 coping, 51 non-coping and 22 transitionals. The families were selected through the maternity and welfare child service of Birmingham's health department and all had at least five children of school age or under, some of them being very much larger. Hardly any of these mothers wanted such large families and the reasons why they had them were many and varied, one however was the sheer beastliness of their

[29] *New Society*, November 1, 1962. Pauline Shapiro is Lecturer and Tutor, Child Service Course, University of Birmingham.

treatment by their husbands who insisted on their 'rights' without any regard whatever for the needs of the woman or the existing children, let alone any social criteria. Mrs Shapiro gives a number of case histories to illustrate her points.

The first is the case of the Foxes, both parents 34 years old with nine children ranging from twelve down to a few months. The children had been born yearly except for an interval of four years between the first and second child while Mr Fox was abroad in the army. Material standards were low and there were affectionate family relationships but these latter were

> ... deteriorating chiefly because of the burden of so many children and the wife's fear of further pregnancies. Though Mrs Fox told the student that she thought four children was a nice size for a family, she began (unsuccessfully) to try to terminate her pregnancies after she had had two children. Her guilty feelings about these desperate attempts were reinforced by her sister's comments that her boy's naughtiness was 'God's punishment for trying to kill them'. After the birth of the sixth child she begged the doctor to arrange for her to be sterilized, but there were no grounds for doing so ...

> ... As she began to recover from her ninth confinement Mrs Fox sought desperately for other remedies. She put the year-old child to sleep between her husband and herself. ...

> ... She asked her husband to take precautions 'But he is quite adamant in his refusal'.

This particular husband did not object to his wife's use of family planning devices, had she been able to bring herself to go through the routine of visiting the Family Planning Clinic and doing all that they said—she was in fact rather embarrassed about all this—but personally he would do nothing whatever to help her in her dire need.

The ignorance, pettiness, selfishness, and downright brutality of many of the husbands in this survey is almost beyond belief. One of them was reported by the interviewer as saying he likes '... having so many children as long as they don't inconvenience him'.

Another one, Mr Lawrence, having seen more of the birth of his last child is now '... in favour of having no more'.

Yet another, Mr Mills, had stayed at home one day to look after the children, after which he cried: 'Never again! and no more children.'

For the most part the men regard it as their wives' concern.

It is essential to bear in mind that all of these families had at least five children and it is hard to imagine the degree of callous self-centredness which these men must have displayed to have fathered families of this size without developing any awareness of what is involved in child-bearing or rearing. Most of them, even the ones who were affectionate towards their wives, seemed to regard them as little more than a combination of concubine and skivvy. Surely it is an outrage in an allegedly civilized society that women should be treated in this fashion, with all that it implies for their status and for the care and welfare of the offspring carelessly fathered on them by these brutish males.

Freedom from unwanted children. Family planning services in Britain

The optimization of liberty requires that individual couples shall be free not to have children they do not want and society should be free from the burdens these often impose. This in turn means that family planning services shall be freely available to everyone. People who really ought to know better often testily dismiss this problem and say:

> Anyone who really wants to get help with family planning matters can, the resources are there, it's simply a question of making the effort.

In Britain there is no law, Church, or coherent body of public opinion which prevents birth control, there are shops that sell the appropriate equipment, advertisements in newspapers, and so on. How then can it be argued that family planning is not available?

The answer lies in the distinction often made between theory and practice, between 'formal' and 'informal' organization, in the language of the sociologist. In the formal sense it is strictly true that anyone who wants to use birth control techniques can get the necessary information and appliances. It is one thing for an educated, well-organized, comfortably off, middle-class couple—accustomed to manipulating their environment rather than being manipulated by it—to get the necessary help with family planning. It is quite another for a mother of three or more small children, not too well off, having an unsympathetic or downright hostile husband, with no relatives or friends nearby to look after the children while she goes to the clinic, and living in the area of one of the vast majority of local authorities failing to provide adequate family planning services, to have access to family planning facilities. On paper both have the same access to the appropriate information, goods, and services.

Figure 14/2 shows the provision of family planning services by local health authorities in England and Wales up to July 30, 1968, more than a year after the National Health Service (Family Planning) Act was passed. We see that less than 17 per cent are providing a full service—and even a 'full' service leaves much to be desired. Over 63 per cent provide a restricted service and nearly

Fig 14/2
Provision of Family Planning Services by local health authorities in England and Wales

	No of authorities	%
No action	39	19
Restricted service	129	$63\frac{1}{2}$
Full service	34	$16\frac{1}{2}$
No information	2	1
	204	100

Following on from National Health Service (Family Planning) Act 1967. Supplement to **Family Planning**, October 1968

20 per cent have taken no action at all following the new Act. Over 65,000 married women are said to have family doctors who refuse to discuss birth control with them in any circumstances, and there are an estimated 100,000 abortions a year, half of them illegal even now.

In these circumstances it is a travesty of the truth to argue that family planning services are readily available and insofar as they are not then serious inroads are made into the freedom of unwilling parents—not to mention hundreds of thousands of infants born unwanted, as we saw in Chapter 4, and destined to a life lacking in love and care.

Freedom from the dictates of fashion

In addition to providing full and free access to the latest techniques of family planning as a matter of right we must see that there are no social pressures on the childless to become parents against their wishes or in spite of difficult circumstances. If people are pushed into having children they would not otherwise have had their freedom has thereby been diminished, whether this pressure was applied by the state or through public opinion. Michael Humphrey, lecturer in Mental Health at Bristol University has described the results of a survey[30] he carried out on childless couples, making the point that there are what one might perhaps call 'legitimate' pressures on childless couples to have children:

> ... children are a passport to other homes, and unless ... parents *choose* to isolate themselves ... The childless couple, in contrast, can rapidly become alienated from the fertile masses unless they make special efforts to counteract this danger. And where both partners are working full-time (as is commonly the case) there is less chance of building up friendships in the locality. The theoretical solution is for couples to seek out their own kind, but unfortunately childlessness does not draw people together in the same way that parenthood can. Indeed, the hypersensitive couple may not want to associate with couples in the same plight.

He then deals with what could be called 'illegitimate' pressures towards parenthood:

> ... childlessness is a matter of widespread curiosity. ... the childless couple draw attention to themselves in the same way as other minority groups ... we are all irritated, fascinated or mystified by what we cannot understand ...
> ... the childless couple may be suspected of incompetence. Doubts may be even raised about the consummation of their marriage.
> ... many of the women ... were acutely sensitive about their childlessness. ...
> ... Social difficulties were frequently mentioned, and one woman went so far as to declare ' .. you are social outcasts ...'

[30] 'The Enigma of Childlessness', *New Society*, March 13, 1969, pp 399/402. Based on his book (1969) *The Hostage Seekers*.

...Only half of the women reported that their relatives had been sympathetic, and the other half met with lack of awareness if not envy and distrust.

...Wounding insinuations...were recalled by almost three women in four and produced considerable distress in more than a quarter...

It is encouraging that the unpleasant, indeed sometimes malignant, pressures put on these childless couples did not wreck their married lives, although they obviously caused a great deal of stress at one stage or another, but surely pressures like these are unjustifiable. People should be free as far as possible to have or not to have children, just as they choose; and if they decide not to, or for biological or psychological reasons beyond their control they are infecund they should be permitted to live with their condition as best they can without insidious suggestions from the outside that they are lacking in moral qualities or sexual potency.

If individual liberty is to be maximized one of the things which must be removed, in addition to the persecution of individual childless couples already dealt with, is the dictation of fashion—sometimes deliberately manipulated by commercial interests—for large families.

Katharine Whitehorn headed her *Observer* column on one occasion: 'Fecund to a Fault'.[31] She gave further evidence supporting Michael Humphrey's findings and pointed also to the force of habit and custom:

> Every time one reads of a mother leaving her baby with a minder who keeps three babies in their prams in a dark shed; or a film world mother who comes into the nursery only to have rows with an ever-changing stream of nannies, one always asks: 'Why on earth did they ever have children at all?' The answer usually is that it simply didn't occur to them not to; and the fact that it still doesn't, in an over-crowded island liberally sprinkled with contraceptives, seems odd enough to stand investigation....
>
> ...I would like to see it considered more immoral to have a baby 'to save a marriage' than to go for a divorce...

Gillian Tindall returned to this theme in an article called 'Talk-

[31] April 18, 1965.

ing about the family cult'[32] and stressed the cult of both the family and fatherhood among intellectuals and professional people:

> ... a young, healthy intelligent couple, should, in defiance of the world population problem, have a number of children fairly close in age.

In an article called, 'The Fashion for Families',[33] Elizabeth Still, a researcher in this field, wrote:

> It is no longer true that the lower down the social scale and the less educated people are, the more children they have. The inverse relationship between social class and family size which has been a feature of western societies for the last century, seems to be disappearing fast ...
>
> The general census figures of 1961 confirm the impression that more people in the professional classes are having more children. ...
>
> In the 1920s and 1930s the typical professional or upper middle-class couple had one or two children. Today, four has become an increasingly fashionable number.

Mrs Still points out that the increase in the size of the professional family, 0.26, in the ten years since 1961 '... is exactly the same as the decrease in the unskilled manual labourer's family in the same period'. So we see that there are trends operating in the opposite directions in the different social strata. However if it is true that the higher social classes tend to set the fashions later to be emulated by the lower social classes this process could go into reverse and make it the general fashion to have larger families once more. It is very significant that '... 52 per cent of the husbands and 51 per cent of the wives came from ... one or two child families'.

Mrs Still points out that her survey is not representative of the population as a whole as it was based upon the replies of 460 *Observer* readers, all of whose families '... consisted, as requested, of four or more children, actual or firmly intended', so in its qualitative aspects the survey can be no more than a straw in the wind. However, the evidence from the census is clear enough and indications from other sources reinforce the likelihood that there is an increasingly dominant fashion towards larger families which

[32] *The Guardian,* June 20, 1967.
[33] *New Society,* June 8, 1967.

could have very unfortunate effects from the national point of view.

The Royal family in Britain has been exploited as a rather unfortunate precedent with regard to family size and some of the glossy women's magazines have advocated the fashionability of sex, family life in general, and large families in particular. The lengths to which journalistic licence can go are well illustrated by the article reproduced on the next page, 'The Status Symbol of the 4-Baby Family', by Monica Furlong.[34]

If liberty is to be maximized then people must be freed from insidious pressures such as these which suggest, subtly and unsubtly by turn, that people who don't have, or don't want a large family, are selfish materialists lacking in human warmth, spontaneity, and sociability.

Freedom from religious persecution

The study by Mrs Shapiro referred to earlier shows that families generally and women in particular are by no means free from religious persecution even in this day and age. Mrs Shapiro said:

> ... Attitudes to family size among these Catholic families varied from devout acceptance, weary resignation or revulsion to fear of the condemnation of priests, Catholic neighbours or, occasionally, a strong rebuttal. 'The priests,' said Mrs Forman, 'can keep out of our bedroom.' For a number there was acute conflict between the tenets of their religion and their need to do something about their too rapidly increasing families, a conflict greatly exacerbated when sterilization or attendance at a family planning clinic was advised by the doctor on account of the wife's ill-health. Some of the most acute marital disharmony was found in such situations, whether or not the medical advice was followed. One example will serve to illustrate the unhappiness resulting from such conflict.
>
> As the Weavers are Catholic it was extremely difficult for them to accept the obstetrician's advice that Mrs Weaver should get help from the family planning clinic. Mr Weaver finally agreed only because of the strong medical reasons. The priest told him that it was 'better for his wife to be dead than damned'. The family doctor, also a Catholic, was extremely critical and

[34] *Daily Mail*, August 18, 1963.

The Status Symbol of the 4-BABY FAMILY

BY MONICA FURLONG

TAKE a look around when you do your weekend shopping today. And as you pick your way through the prams and pushcarts you will realise what has happened.

The three- and four-children families h a v e become popular again.

They are almost a new status symbol in a materialistic world. And there is a tendency to take an immense pride in family life.

Success

IN Fleet, Hampshire, last year they were producing babies at a rate faster than 24 per thousand people, an achievement which strikes me as the most hopeful I've heard for ages, along with the rising national birth rate.

It is, I believe, part of a nation-wide new trend (well, newish—nothing to do with having babies is new), a trend which, thank God, is prepared to snap its fingers at bombs, radiation and more insidious dangers such as smog.

It is, I think, a middle-class movement, which is why it is so noticeable in a town like Fleet, full of successful commuters and scientists working on local projects.

But one can see it busily at work in the New Towns and in the comfortable suburbs up and down the country.

In the '30's professional people and the more prosperous middle-class couples tended to "plan" two children, to feel it was "advanced" to plan their family and to look down on the "working-class mother with her large brood."

Nowadays the roles have been changed and it is the middle-class mother who is likely to be surrounded by the patter of tiny feet and the accompanying symphony of bangs, crashes and cries.

Why do people want more children?

According to many of the critics and the moralists who are always taking whacks at our society, we are all mad on acquiring things, gadgets and devices which, by sheer cost, give status.

Why, then, should we dream of going in for anything as expensive as a child when, for the same money, we might get at least within hailing distance of the Joneses?

Mr. Reginald Pestell, of the Marriage Guidance Council, has been observing this growth of the family, this desire by younger parents to have three or four children.

"There is a resurgence of pride in the family," he says. "What I have found is that the majority of young couples have decided views on the pattern of their married life and how many children they want. Most of them like to think of three babies, but four is becoming a popular number."

Security

MR. PESTELL'S researches would indicate that in the '30's family growth in the middle classes was restricted by the economic situation.

"The middle-class wife at that time scientifically restricted the growth of the family," he suggests. "It is likely that the working-class wife of that time was a little more haphazard.

"Today economics still govern family life, but younger parents can see full employment and hopes of security which were unknown in the '30's. Then a middle-class young man very often could not afford to get married until he was about 30—by which time he might be able to establish himself and support a girl of his own class in the way of life to which she had been accustomed.

"These late marriages meant that many couples restricted their families, thinking it would not be fair to be 50 years old when a third or fourth child arrived.

"If the housing situation could be eased, I am certain that the population would increase even more and that the desire for larger families would spread even more rapidly."

Searching

IN my own London, middle-class suburb, an estate agent confirms this. He is besieged with inquiries for four- and five-bedroomed houses. A few years ago he could not get rid of them. Now the new families are demanding them.

If the new larger family is to be regarded as a status symbol, what a healthy one!

And how much more heartwarming than some dreary mechanical invention which demands nothing (except money) and is rapidly outmoded by some more stunning model.

If we are proud of our children and our family life, then this, though it has its dangers, is a great deal better than being proud about something lifeless, dumb and uncreative. Children, after all, are bound to teach us something about life and what it is for.

One's heart warms to the people of Fleet—all these proud mothers and fathers—in a way that it never warms to a line of cars or a window full of washing machines.

'no longer thinks well of them' because the wife has attended a family planning clinic, although he knew it was dangerous for her to have another child. . . .

The Selbys relied on a book written by a Catholic doctor, but this had 'let them down', the mother said, on three occasions, as the first three children had all been conceived in the 'safe period' . . .

. . . Mrs Andrews had three stepchildren by her husband's first marriage, and, at the time of the student's first visit, four young children of her own. Before her marriage she had been in a sanatorium for tuberculosis and was still delicate. She confided in the student that her nine months baby was a 'mistake', and that she was anxious not to have more children but, being Catholic, she could only use 'the safe period'. By the time a social worker visited her two years later, another baby had been born. . . .

. . . It is clear . . . that the rhythm method would have been beyond the capacity and control of many of these parents. The necessary restraint and planning are qualities markedly absent from one or both parents in the non-coping category and from some in the transitional category. Apart from the obvious difficulties of poor intelligence and fecklessness, the lack of co-operation and physical demands of many of the husbands would have rendered the method ineffective.

The Casey family will serve to illustrate this problem. The parents had both emigrated from Ireland, were practising Catholics, and began their married life with several strengths. The father was hard working; the mother, originally devoted to her children, began by maintaining the good standards that she had been used to in her own childhood in spite of the difficulties of poor housing and a rapidly increasing family. By the time that the student visited this family, six young children had been born in eight years, the mother was suffering from hyper-tension and was in an acutely nervous state. Yet the father insisted on sexual intercourse whenever he wished and was never deterred by his wife's fears of pregnancy; he had even insisted on intercourse half an hour after she returned from hospital with her sixth baby. Some solution other than the rhythm method was needed in these circumstances. Other methods had been suggested —contraceptives for the wife or sterilization. Neither were acceptable to the husband who refused to allow his wife to use con-

traceptives and had given only grudging consent to an arrange-
ment for sterilization. On account of her poor physical state and
deteriorating mental condition arrangements had in fact been
made for sterilization while she was in hospital after her sixth
confinement. Mrs Casey told the student that a Catholic nurse
informed the priest who had come to the hospital and he dis-
suaded her from having the operation. Her conflict was now
extreme: when she thought she might be pregnant she abandoned
all her fears of priest, husband, and Catholic neighbours, but as
soon as she found she was not pregnant she gave up the thoughts
of plans not sanctioned by her church and resumed her self-
questioning. The student commented: 'The religious question is
really the crux of her problems'.

If there ever should be a Day of Judgment some of these
Roman Catholic priests, doctors, and nurses may find they have a
lot to answer for, having pursued their primitive sexual dogmas
with little thought for humanity, love, sympathy, kindness, tolerance, or understanding. A democratic society must surely ask itself
sooner or later, whether it can tolerate what amounts almost to a
conspiracy on the part of small minorities to undermine the laws
of the land permitting family planning, including voluntary
sterilization and abortion where the medical and social indications
are suitable. Few of us would want to see Roman Catholic doctors
or nurses compelled to carry out abortions or perform other acts
against their consciences but they in turn must refrain from per-
secuting their fellows, including their co-religionists.

Freedom to invent our own future

Dennis Gabor, the eminent physicist, has argued in a book called
Inventing the Future that we must accept freedom in the fullest
sense of the term, taking on the freedom for and responsibility of
creating our own future deliberately, rather than waiting for it to
happen to us. He might agree that a slightly more consistent title
would have been 'Inventing a Future', or 'Inventing Futures'. The
title chosen has an unfortunate carry-over from old ideas that *the*
future is one thing, or set of things, which is coming regardless of
human volition. '*A*' future or '*futures*', the amended title, suggests
that different possibilities are open to us, with which Dennis
Gabor would certainly agree.

The question which immediately arises is, can we accept, can we use, can we live with a massive dose of new freedom to take hold of the future of humanity and shape it deliberately, if flexibly, firmly, if sensitively, confidently, if with humility? This is really the crunch, we prate endlessly about freedom and individual liberty but how much of it do we really want? How much of it can we really take? The answer to both questions, unfortunately, seems to be very little. Much of our talk about freedom is a smoke screen put up to avoid really facing the issues of being free, or at least of becoming free and acting accordingly. Perhaps the twin great tasks of the future are to make free those who are still suffering from an old fashioned lack of freedom under authoritarian regimes of one kind or another, but also to make those who already are, or who think themselves free, into *really* free individuals in a free society, choosing for themselves, acting spontaneously rather than merely *re*-acting to events in their environment, without leading them into the simple-minded trap of thinking that they can 'conquer' nature and mould the world to do their will. As Bacon pointed out a long time ago: 'Man may command nature, but only by obeying her'.

A genuine desire to maximize individual liberty requires open-mindedness, a long view, and a realistic analysis of the human condition so that we do not grant to ourselves freedoms in the short run which will destroy more or greater freedoms in the long run. In particular we have to weigh the ultimate cost in liberty of allowing to continue indefinitely the present freedom to breed *ad lib*. Not only would the automatic loss of other freedoms be heavy in its own right but the cost in liberty of the control measures needed to start society back on the path to sanity and survival might be truly exhorbitant.

Summary

We have very briefly examined some of the relationships between size, shape, and efficiency in groups, as assessed by differing criteria, and found that 'small' groups are generally best when made as small as possible. We have rejected the identification of an optimum population with a maximum size of population, together with the technical definition of an optimum population as one in which a single factor—chosen on the basis of judgment or opinion —is maximized, and put forward some of the objections to the usual choice of economists, per capita income, if the single variable optimum is insisted on.

We have seen that the idea that there are right and wrong sizes for things is not only fundamental in biology but has shown an extraordinary tenacity in the thought of our intellectual forbears, with respect to social systems also, persisting unmodified to the present day.

The idea that bigger populations always give greater economies of scale and are therefore economically beneficial has already been rejected in Chapter 7 and the concept 'critical population density' was put forward here as an absolute limit on population growth, a limit we would do well to avoid.

Professor Fremlin's tongue-in-cheek selection of optima was mentioned briefly to stress the central point, the one he is making, incidentally, that the problem is one of choice, we must choose an optimum and work towards it or choose not to choose and let the population and the environment fight it out between them.

With regard to optimizing the world population—apart from noting in passing that H. G. Wells thought that 300 million,[35] one twelfth of what we have in 1970, was about the maximum that could be sustained if everyone was to develop his potentialities to the full—all that we can hope at the moment is that each individual nation will soon start to optimize its own population, having some regard to its neighbours and the world situation. In the long run we must hope that a democratic world authority will optimize the population of the Earth and its space environs with somewhat less parochial terms of reference than individual nations are wont to have.

It is no part of the purpose of this chapter to lay down the law about an optimum population for Britain, the world, or anywhere else. My own intuitive choice for the United Kingdom—for what it is worth—would probably be somewhere between those put forward by Professor Fremlin, 30 million, and Professor Hutchinson, 40 million—it would certainly be a good deal below the present level, though, if we set out to practise conservation and ecologically informed self-management in real earnest, a population at this or an even higher level might yet be compatible with a very much more satisfactory way of life than we now have. No, the point of this section, indeed of the whole book, is not to dogmatize

[35] Huxley, in *Brave New World*, put it at 2 billion.

about the answer but merely to pose the question and urge that as a society we ought very soon to set about coming to a decision.

Optimizing a population is a political matter and in a democracy it should be decided by democratic politics. Our political parties and other pressure groups, interested individuals, intellectuals, writers, theologians, philosophers, social, biological and physical scientists, poets, cavemen, obscurantists and fanatics should all participate in the great debate of what our society ought to be like and how many people are needed in order to bring it about.[36]

If we decide individual liberty is what we prize most—and many worse answers could be proposed—then there is no reason why this should not be the variable '... normatively chosen...' for maximization as we have seen. From the point of view of the economist liberty may be regarded as a 'welfare indicator' along with income, health, and housing, and it simply is not adequate to the majestic task of maximizing liberty to discuss it in black or white, all or none, yes or no, terms—a far more subtle and realistic approach is a prerequisite of a fruitful debate which is itself a prerequisite of a satisfactory outcome. We must discuss *particular* freedoms and constraints in the greatest detail, following their ramifications through the complicated web of social relations. We must recognize unequivocally that if we continue to increase in numbers—to take two of the issues discussed in some detail earlier —we cannot possibly have the microfreedoms to continue:

(i) to have unrestricted car ownership and use;

(ii) to have unrestricted access to the Lake District and other amenity areas.

We have to co-operate in order to produce individual liberty and the profit gained thereby is to some extent counter-balanced by the loss of some previously existing microfreedom(s), if only the microfreedom not to co-operate.

[36] See the concept of the 'quasi-optimum' suggested in Appendix B.

Chapter 15

Freedom to choose:
II. Population policies

What steps does Her Majesty's Government propose to take to control natural population growth, in the light of the Registrar General's forecast that on present trends the population of England and Wales will grow by 18.5 million in the next 36 years?

Christopher Rowland, MP

None.[1]

Charles Loughlin,
Parliamentary Secretary for the Ministry of Health

Of course, it is a long time yet from the moment when any government would be right to take up any position on these matters.[2]

Lord Kennet

It is impossible for policy in its effects as distinct from its intentions to be 'neutral' on this matter since over a wide range of affairs policy and administration have a continuous influence on the trend of family size.[3]

What future ages will probably find one of the more inexplicable things about twentieth century 'scientific' man is his naive

---

[1] Written Question and Reply. *Hansard*, April 30, 1965.
[2] Lord Kennet. *Hansard*, Lords, February 19, 1969 (col 836).
[3] Report of the Royal Commission on Population (1949) Cmnd. 7695 (para 654).

belief that large, complex, and wealthy societies pressing more and more heavily upon the resources of their finite environment could hope to survive without comprehensive, realistic, and rigorously enforced population policies.

Our belief that we can not only get by but positively thrive with an occasional more or less random prod at population problems in the form of poverty, land use, housing, education, and the rest, will seem as quaint to them as the ancients' belief in a flat Earth seems to us, the more so as a large number of past societies —including very many that we are pleased to style 'primitive'— have been fully aware of this need and had social policies producing the necessary outcome, a balance—if only a rough one—between population and resources at a given time.

The intellectuals, theologians, historians, philosophers[4] and the rest, at lest from the time of the Old Testament onward, have almost invariably commented on these facts—more or less in passing as they were so obvious—and their implications for practical, orderly, and effective government.

William Graham Sumner, the pioneer anthropologist, pointed this out in his classic *Folkways*:

> ... *It is certain that very early in the history of human society ... the evils of overpopulation, were perceived as facts, and policies were instinctively adopted to protect the adults.* The facts caused pain, and the acts resolved upon to avoid it were very summary, and were adopted with very little reasoning. Abortion and infanticide protected the society, unless its situation with respect to neighbours was such that war and pestilence kept down the numbers and made children valuable for war. The numbers present, therefore, ... constituted one of the life conditions ... subject to constant variation, ... in regard to which the sanctions of wise action are prompt and severe. (Italics added)

Sumner describes the means adopted to carry out population policies:

> Abortion and infanticide are ... the earliest efforts of men to ward off the burden of children and the evils of over-population by specific devices of an immediate and brutal character. The ... burden of children differs greatly with the life conditions of

---

[4] The views of the early Christians and Aristotle were mentioned under 'optimum' population.

groups, and with the stage of the arts by which men cope with the struggle for existence ...

On the stage of pastoral-nomadic life, or wherever else horde life existed, it appears that numerous offspring were regarded as a blessing and child-rearing, in the horde, was not felt as a burden. It was in the life of the narrower family, whatever its form, that children came to be felt as a burden, so that 'progress' caused abortion and infanticide ...

... Abortion and infanticide are primary and violent acts of self-defence by the parents against famine, disease, and the other calamities of over-population, which increase with the number which each man or woman has got to provide for... The customs begin in a primary response to pain and strife ... become ritual acts, and are made sacred whenever they are brought into connection with societal welfare. ...

Sumner gives numerous cases of these practices:

The Papuans on Geelvink Bay, New Guinea, say that 'children are a burden. We become tired of them, they destroy us'. The women practise abortion to such an extent that the rate of increase of the population is very small and in some places there is a lack of women. Throughout Dutch New Guinea the women will not rear more than two or three children each ...

The people of Nukuoro are all of good physique, large, and well-formed. They have a food supply in excess of their wants and are well nourished. The population has decreased in recent years, by reason of the killing of children before or after birth ...

The Australians[5] practise infanticide almost universally ...

Conditions made wandering a necessity ... [and] a woman could not carry two children. Therefore, if she had one who could not yet march, and bore another, the latter was killed. One or both twins were killed ... One reporter says that the fate of a child depended much on the condition the country was in at the time (drought, etc), and the prospect of the mother's rearing it satisfactorily. Sickly and imperfect children were killed because they would require very great care ... Very rarely were more than four children of one woman allowed to grow up ...

Men killed half-white children [but] all authorities agreed that

[5] He was writing at the turn of the century and was referring to the aboriginals.

if children were spared at birth they were treated with great affection.

And so it goes on, page after page of practices both brutal and grotesque to the modern mind, but, as Sumner stresses, these have not been confined to primitive societies. He reminds us that in Plato's Republic the ideal was put forward that men over fifty-five and women over forty should not procreate citizens. By abortion or infanticide the offspring of such persons should be removed from the social scene. Aristotle also thought that imperfect children should be killed off and that numbers in general should be limited. 'If parents exceeded the prescribed number, abortion should be employed.' (*Politics*)

Later Sumner says:

> The Greeks regarded infanticide as the necessary and simply proper way to deal with a problem which could not be avoided.

His central point in this regard is expressed as follows:

> ... Abortion and infanticide are especially interesting because they show how early in the history of civilization the burden of children became so heavy that parents began to shirk it, and also because they show the rise of a population policy, which is one of the most important programmes of practical expediency which any society ever can adopt ...

Sumner shows that population control operated at both ends of the age span and points out that cultures can be classified under two headings according to typical attitudes found towards the elderly. In one set of mores the teaching and usages inculcate conventional respect for the aged, who are therefore 'arbitrarily' preserved for their wisdom and counsel, perhaps also sometimes out of affection and sympathy.

In the other the aged are regarded as 'societal burdens', which waste the strength of society, already inadequate for its tasks.

Sumner points out that where the culture does not inculcate respect for the aged:

> ... they are forced to die, either by their own hands or those of their relatives. It is very far from being true that the first of these policies is practised by people higher up in civilization than those who practise the second. The people in the lower civilization profit more by the wisdom and the counsel of the

aged than those in higher civilization, and are educated by this experience to respect and value the aged. . . .

. . . the custom of killing the old, especially one's parents, is very antipathetic to us . . . [but] . . . for nomadic people, the custom is necessary. The old drop out by the way and die from exhaustion. To kill them is only equivalent, and perhaps kinder. If an enemy is pursuing, the necessity is more acute. All this enters into the life conditions so primarily that the custom is a part of the life policy; it is so understood and acquiesced in. The old sometimes request it from life weariness, or from devotion to the welfare of the group.

A few of Sumner's scores of examples show how widespread this policy has been and how brutal were some of the methods used to carry it out.

. . . The Hudson's Bay Eskimo strangle the old who are dependent on others for their food, or leave them to perish when the camp is moved. They [sometimes] move in order to get rid of burdensome old people without executing them . . .

Many tribes in Brazil kill the old because they were a burden and they could no longer enjoy war, hunting, and feasting. The Tupis sometimes killed a sick man and ate the corpse, if the Shaman said that he could not get well. The Tobas, a Guykuru tribe in Paraguay, bury the old alive. The old, from pain and decrepitude often beg for death. Women execute the homicide . . .

In West Victoria the old are strangled by a relative deputed for the purpose and the body is burned. One reason given is that, in cases of attack by an enemy, the old would be captured and tortured to death. The victims often beg for delay, but always in vain. The Melanesians buried alive the sick and old. It is certain that, when this was done, there was generally a kindness intended. Even when the younger hastened the end for selfish reasons, the sick and aged acquiesced. They often begged to be put out of their misery.

Sumner quotes another authority, Holub, as saying there was:

. . . a great cliff from which some South African tribes cast the old when tired of caring for them.

. . . In the Niger Protectorate the old and useless are killed. The bodies are smoked and pulverized and the powder is made into little balls with water and corn. The balls are dried and kept to be used as food. The Somali exploit the old in work to the last point, and then cast them out to die of hunger ... The aged of the Chuckches demand, as a right, to be put to death. Life is so hard and food so scarce that they are indifferent to death, and the acquiescence of the victim is described as complete and willing ... an old man of that tribe ... was put to death at his own request by relatives who thought that they performed a sacred obligation. The Yakuts formerly had a similar custom, the old man begging his children to despatch him.

Sumner quotes other cases in which the elderly are killed—not on the face of it for reasons of population control, but for others, where nonetheless the customs would have the effect of controlling population. One of his authorities, Gomme, quotes

> ... a fifteenth century MS of a Parsifal episode in which the hero congratulates himself that he is not like the men in Wales ...
> '... where sons pull their fathers out of bed and kill them to save the disgrace of their dying in bed.'
> He also cites mention of the 'holy mawle' which (they fancy) hung behind the church door, and which, when the father was 70, the son might fetch to knock his father on the head as effete and of no more use.

Sumner mentions a case where this mode of population control was introduced to meet an unusual situation. In Iceland, in a time of famine:

> ... it was decided by solemn resolution that all the old and unproductive should be killed. That determination was part of a system of legislation by which, in that country, the society was protected against superfluous and dependent members.

Sumner winds up this section on a rather happier note:

> Later, when greater power in the struggle for existence was won the infants and the old were spared, and the old customs were forgotten. Then they came to be regarded with horror, and the mores protected the infants and the old.

Mary Douglas, in an address to the Association of British Zoolog-ists, (see 'Population Control in Primitive Groups', *Brit. J. Sociol*, 17, 1966), has given an account of some of the varied forms of population control still practised, for instance, that of the Pelly Bay Eskimos '... who regularly kill off a proportion of their female babies...', the Rendille, camel herders of the Kenyan highlands. who:

> ... postpone the age of marriage of women, send numbers of their women to be married to polygamists in the next tribe, kill off boys born on Wednesdays or... after the next eldest son is old enough to have been circumcised...

The Tikopia, studied by the famous anthropologist Raymond Firth, '... used abortion, contraception, infanticide, and suicidal migration...'

The fourth group which she studied is perhaps the most interesting because it is a highly successful, wealthy, and sophisticated élite—not unlike those of Western cultures; these people, the Nambudiri Brahmins

> ... belong to one of the richest land-owning castes in southern India. They are... very exclusive... and... to maintain their social and economic advantage they avoid dividing their estates, but allow only the oldest son to inherit and administer it on behalf of his brothers...

> For each married couple only one son and one daughter are likely to be allowed to marry. The other sons console themselves with women of another caste, but the daughters are kept all their lives in the strictest seclusion.
> ... such a ruthless course must presumably be justified by the value of the prize,... a social and economic hegemony.

One of these methods practised by the Rendille, postponing marriage, is still in use in Eire and was at one time practised in England as the recent studies[6] in 'family reconstitution'—notably of the parish of Colyton, in East Devon—have shown. Here fertility was regulated by this means in accordance with the fluctuating of fortunes of a mainly agricultural economy.

The former Hindu rite of suttee, burning a dead man's living widows on his funeral pyre, was a very effective curb on their subsequent fertility and the Roman Catholic insistence on chastity

---

[6] Wrigley, EA, 'Family limitation in Pre-Industrial England', *The Economic History Review*, XIX, 1966. Reprinted in Drake, M (ed) (1969) *Population in Industrialization.*

for both priests and nuns must have had quite an effect on population growth over the centuries.[7]

The point of quoting W. G. Sumner at length on the barbarous forms of population control used by earlier societies—by no means all of them primitive, as we have seen—is not to advocate the resumption of such measures. It is to underline the extremes to which *homo sapiens* has gone in pursuit of the essential goal of the population-environment balance, and to raise the question whether he is liable to sink to these depths again if the problem is allowed to get out of hand. There is no evidence that our species has evolved to a more elevated plane since Aristotle's day, or to suggest that in life-and-death situations our level of behaviour[8] would be any higher now than it was then. Cruelty to children and/or the old is the norm in some societies and even in those where kindness is expected there are very many individual exceptions. Modern man shows his savage propensity for cruelty and destruction in war, politics, racial persecution, and religion, and there seems little reason to doubt that ruthless destruction of surplus infants, the sick, and the old could become acceptable again if pressure on resources becomes too great.

If and when there is a swing away from the at present probably unduly high proportion of our medical resources expended on the aged sick,[9] it could easily go too far and take us dangerously close to the barbarities of the not too distant past.

Sumner's evidence adds substance to the already weighty arguments for controlling numbers early and by humane means to prevent the possibility of irresistible pressures towards barbarism arising later.

Under the heading 'Population Policy' Sumner argues with massive and elemental commonsense the case for fitting the population to the culture, technology, and environment of the time—a

---

[7] The Vatican announcement (reported in the press, September 7, 1970) that lay women may have themselves consecrated as virgins will act in the same direction.

[8] According to one writer, even in eighteenth century England:
'...unwanted babies were often thrown on to the rubbish heaps beside the roads to die of exposure and starvation'.
It was the frequency of the sight which led Thomas Coram to set up his foundling hospitals. Barron, E, 'Thomas Coram, the man who saved children'. *The Lady*, January 25, 1968.

[9] More than three times as much per capita for the over sixty-fives as compared with the under sixty-fives. See Office of Health Economics (1968) *Old Age* (p 26).

refreshing comparison with the fantasy of our modern age that any number of people can be fed and supplied regardless of conditions of time and space. Writing just after the turn of the century, he said:

> ... at the present moment, the most civilized states do not know whether to stimulate or restrict population; whether to encourage immigration or not; whether immigration is an evil or a blessing; whether to tax bachelors or married men. These questions are discussed as if absolute answers to them were possible, independently of differences in life conditions. ...

The general approach must be flexibility coupled with firmness. If an environment is under-populated or over-populated as indicated by the failure to optimize the values most desired by the society occupying it, then action must be taken to increase or decrease numbers, as the case might be. If it was arguable in Sumner's day that governments did not really know whether or not to 'stimulate' population—although the briefest of backward looks ought to have shown the writing on the wall even then—there can be little doubt what most governments ought to be doing now. It may be that Australians and Canadians and a few other peoples would lead fuller lives in the long run if there were more of them. but countries in this situation are in a very small minority nowadays and the world as a whole—if not over-populated already—certainly will be in less than one lifespan unless something drastic happens.

Population policy in Britain

The short answer to a question about Britain's population policy is that there is not and never has been one in anything like the sense stipulated by Sumner. There has been concern about population from time to time, enquiries concerning it, and legislation touching on certain aspects, but never a consideration of the problems in the round, let alone a coherent or comprehensive policy orientated towards the essential goal, an ecological balance, a 'steady-state' in the cyberneticians's terminology, involving a population and an environment in harmony with each other *over the long term*.

In 1949 the Royal Commission on Population strongly recommended a policy of continuous population review, at least, with the implication that the government should act firmly as and when necessary. Indeed it would be strange if in a climate of opinion accepting the obvious necessity for government intervention to hold the ring in virtually all important social and economic spheres that population, the foundation stone of all social activities, were to be the only one left to *laissez faire*.

Those who think it should be left to private enterprise—that the state has no right to intervene in this sphere—must search their minds and consciences as to what their attitude would be if population, left completely to its own devices, started to decline. Would they still be certain that population is nothing to do with government and must be allowed to disappear if that seems to be its spontaneous tendency?

Not many would accept this possibility and those few individuals who do are the only ones who can consistently argue that governments must not attempt to control trends when they point to over-population rather than under-population.

The Royal Commission

The main recommendations of the Royal Commission in 1949 were as follows:

1. *Importance of population question*

   The industrial progress, the standard of living and security of the British people, the development and cohesion of the British Commonwealth, the influence of British ideas, traditions and institutions throughout the world may all be affected subtly but powerfully by demographic changes. (para 255)

2. *Implications for government and society*

   It is impossible for policy, ... to be neutral, ... in this matter ... (para 654. See beginning of this chapter for full quotation.)

   Our enquiry has convinced us that the relation between the trend of family size and community outlook and policies is peculiarly close, and underlying all our recommendations is our concern to have this fact recognized so that in all relevant branches of policy and administration the population factor will be taken into account. (para 687)

3. *Need for constant population review*

We recommend that the Lord President of the Council should be made responsible for a continuous watch over population movements and their bearing on national policies. (paras 607, 611, and 685)

4. *Population studies*

After a number of criticisms of population studies and related statistical services the Commission advised against setting up:

a new and separate organization for population research [provided] a means could be found of bringing this subject within the scope of an existing body concerned with related fields of research. We think this might be done through the Inter-departmental Committee on Social and Economic Research ... (para 603)

5. *Education*

An educational effort is needed to spread throughout the community some understanding of the broad facts of the population trend and its consequences. (para 680)

Preparation for family life ... should be given a more prominent place in the educational system ... [and] achieved by a wide development of sex education in schools ... (etc) (para 681)

In addition to these fundamental points the Commission made a number of recommendations on specific aspects of public policy. For example:

1. *Immigration*

The prospect of '... continuing pressure to bring in immigrants to make good shortages [of manpower] in particular occupations ... we regard as ... undesirable ... because ... the sources of supply of suitable immigrants are meagre and the capacity of a fully established society like ours to absorb immigrants of alien race and religion is limited ..., para 648) (Other reasons were given, too.)

2. *Equality for women*

Public policy, . . should assume that women will take an

increasing part in the cultural and economic life of the community ... (para 657)

3. *Family welfare*

Measures to promote family welfare and particularly to reduce the inequalities in material circumstances are fully justified on grounds of equity and social welfare, ... (para 657)

4. *Family planning*

... giving ... advice on contraception to married persons ... should be accepted as a duty of the National Health Service, and existing restrictions on giving such advice by public authority clinics should be removed ... (para 667)

These recommendations have been virtually ignored by all the parties and successive governments and in the intervening twenty-one years our population has grown by some 6 million (12 per cent). It looks like increasing by another 12 million by the year 2000, a 36 per cent increase in half a century.

The position today

Despite the ignorance, indifference, and neglect of the parties and governments since the Royal Commission there are straws in the wind which give some grounds for hope. Awareness of the terrible truths of the population explosion on the world scene, the effects of increasing pressure on our limited resources, of poverty, pollution, hunger, and violence, is slowly percolating through our national conscience and we are beginning to sense the possibility that, perhaps, not all is well on our tidy little island. Until very recently the usual response to any suggestion that Britain is or may soon be over-populated was incredulity or ridicule, but individuals are beginning to sit up and take notice and pressure groups are forming—such as the Conservation Society[10]—to urge the nation and somewhat laggardly governments to take action. However snail-like, things are beginning to move and those who have been

[10] This is the only body in the United Kingdom, in the field of conservation or any other, which has a population policy. Anyone who wishes to take constructive action after reading this book may care to join. S. G. Lawrence, Hon Sec, 21 Hanyards Lane, Cuffley, Potters Bar, Herts.

working in this field for some years are very much more hopeful for the future.

The political parties and population problems

Though the Labour Party has twice debated birth control, in 1927 and 1940 (the Conservative Party not at all), to the best of the present writer's knowledge—though it must be borne in mind it is hard to prove a negative case—none of the parties have displayed any interest in problems of population control at home or abroad. The only problems discussed have been in the sphere of aid to the developing countries.

The only exception to this generally negative situation is the Labour Party Conference of 1966,[11] during which one of the party's old war horses, Mr Tom Braddock of Wimbledon, speaking for a composite resolution (No 20) urging the provision of family planning services under the National Health Service, argued as follows:

> Comrades, it is now forty-two years since our women's annual conference passed a resolution of this sort, and nothing has been done. . . .
>
> We must realize that most of our political problems such as health, education, etc cannot be effectively dealt with simply because the numbers of our people are always outgrowing our manpower and resources. . . .
>
> Comrades, until this population problem is solved there is little hope of any real progress in human affairs or of avoiding great international disputes and wars as a result of increasing population. . . .

Mr Braddock's was a lonely voice.

[11] NB. (i) An urgent plea for all forms of birth control to be made available under the National Health Service was made at the Annual Conference of Labour Women at Hastings in June, 1970. (ii) At the Labour Party Annual Conference at Blackpool in September the following resolution, No 200, from the Honiton Branch, was proposed:

'This Conference is alarmed at the steady growth of Britain's population and the inexorable pressure on land and living space that results from it. It is concerned at the worsening ratio of earners to dependants in our society, and at the high capital cost of providing for a quarter of a million additional people every year.

It calls on the National Executive Committee to accept as a matter of urgency the need for a population policy, and to press for the setting up of a permanent agency to study the effect of economic and social policies on population growth.'

The all-party motion on the population problem

If the political parties proper have done virtually nothing about Britain's population problem this is probably more to do with the timidity or inertia of the hierarchies, possibly reinforced by apathy in the constituencies, than to the lack of concern of the rank and file of MPs, as the all-party motion, indicates.

In February, 1968 Sir David Renton, Mr Douglas Houghton, Dr Winstanley, the Earl of Dalkeith, Dr Shirley Summerskill, and Mr Edwin Brooks put their names to the following motion with the hope of securing the signatures of more than half of the members of parliament, a target figure of 316.

> That this House noting that England itself, rivals Holland and Taiwan as the most densely populated territory in the world. apart from small island and city states, and that the population of the United Kingdom is likely to increase by a third from 55 to 73 million[12] by the end of the century, calls upon Her Majesty's Government to establish permanent and adequate machinery for examining the difficulties to which such population growth will give rise and for giving early warning to parliament of such difficulties and to advise what steps should be taken to overcome them well in advance of crisis point.

By the time that parliament re-assembled on October 14 the motion had been signed by no less than 321 members of parliament of all parties, well over the target figure, and it must be borne in mind that probably 130 of the 630 MPs cannot sign motions of this kind, according to tradition, as they are office-holders in the government or their equivalents in the opposition.

Bearing in mind the quite extraordinary success of this all-party motion and the fact that a recent public opinion poll[13] showed that 46 per cent thought that the population problem was the greatest one facing our society in the future, one is driven to wonder what our governments are waiting for. It is very hard to avoid the conclusion that under the Labour government the personal predilections or fears of Mr Wilson himself were the main stumbling block. He wrote a book, published in 1953, called *War on Want* in which the words 'birth control' did not appear—let alone population control—and a number of commentators have raised the question

---

[12] The latest projection is lower, as we have seen.
[13] *Sunday Times*, February, 1970

whether there may not be a connection between this systematic fighting shy of population facts and the situation in his constituency which contains a large number of Irish Roman Catholics. On the other hand it could be that he really believed that bigger populations are always better populations, which he always seemed to imply in his comments on this topic in the House of Commons, as in his correspondence with Sir David Renton, quoted earlier.

Whatever the reason we must hope that as Leader of the Opposition one of his colleagues will persuade him to re-read the 'World Leaders' Declaration on Population', which he signed as Prime Minister, presented at the United Nations on Human Rights Day, December, 1967, and which contains the words—repeated by our Ambassador to the United Nations, Lord Caradon, with warm approval:

> *We believe* that the population problem must be recognized as a principal element in long-range national planning if governments are to achieve their economic goals and fulfil the aspirations of their peoples.
>
> *We believe* that lasting and meaningful peace will depend to a considerable measure upon how the challenge of population growth is met.

It also contained the words, written by Secretary General, U Thant:

> We bear an immense responsibility for the quality of human life in future generations.

and a contribution by Dr Turbay-Ayala, the Colombian Ambassador:

> To take thought for a population policy is today the imperative duty of every statesman. The outworn principle that governing a country involves peopling it must give way today to the principle that governing entails family planning and the control of over-population.

We must also hope that the present Conservative administration will heed these words and make population one of its main concerns.

The Douglas Houghton controversy

Mr Douglas Houghton, Chairman of the Parliamentary Labour

Party, said in a speech at the opening of the Sociological Research Foundation in London:

> Just as marriage and divorce is not a purely personal and private matter; just as abortion isn't either, so the procreation of children is not a purely private matter . . .
> Already large families are a form of social irresponsibility. Shortly they will be regarded as a form of social delinquency . . . [but at present we see] . . .
> . . . shilly shallying and objections . . . to providing an advisory service on contraceptive methods . . . from local health authorities . . .[14]

The next day all hell was let loose, Mr Houghton was attacked from all sides. Mr Des Wilson, Director of the Shelter Campaign, said he was appalled at Mr Houghton's inflammatory language. Mr Lynes of the Child Poverty Action Group said the speech was shockingly irresponsible for a politician of Mr Houghton's seniority, and six Labour back benchers tabled a motion:

> . . . Deploring and regretting . . . Mr Houghton's remark.
> . . . as an affront to family life and to the mothers who have contributed to the greatness of our country in both peace and war.

It is interesting to observe that two of the protesting Labour MPs are from Liverpool, a predominantly Catholic area, while another is from Bootle a hop, skip and a jump away and dominated by the same influence. A fourth came from another Catholic area, the Gorbals in Glasgow. It is not necessary to know the religious allegiance of the other two protesting MPs to see the powerful and unreasonable influence the extremist Roman Catholic tail has on the Labour dog. Three of these MPs threatened to resign from the Labour Party and the then Prime Minister felt obliged to assure them that Mr Houghton's views on large families:

> . . . Do not in any sense represent the views or policy of Her Majesty's government, nor are they in any way Party policy.

Six other Labour MPs led by Mrs Reneé Short, MP for Wolverhampton NE, congratulated Mr Houghton on his 'sensible speech' indicating the dangers facing Britain from its population explosion, and went on to call for an extension of the Family Planning Act

[14] Reported *The Guardian*, July 3, 1968.

and its operation through government initiative.[15] Though this also made the news it had nothing like the impact of the equal number of Roman Catholic protestors and it seems quite obvious that extremist Roman Catholic pressure operates in a rather sinister fashion to stifle debate on population problems and birth control within the political parties, especially the Labour Party, which for some years before the last election, through duly constituted processes, provided us with our government.

The moderate Catholics, of whom there are very many—the vast majority practising 'illicit' forms of birth control—increasingly convinced that the stand of their Church on population and birth control is immoral if not disastrous, seem always to be swamped by the shrill minority of diehards. Both Labour and Conservative parties and their leaders would do well to cringe a little less and debate these matters of critical public concern much more freely.

Secret population committee

Perhaps, after all, governments are beginning to see the light on Britain's population problems because Mr Wilson set up a secret committee to study them, probably some time in 1968. The present writer was able to discover this by a small amount of the most elementary detective work and disclose it in a lecture at the House of Commons in July, 1969, attended by both public and press, coupled with a protest against secrecy in this sphere. The news fell flat on both this occasion and at another lecture,[16] at the University of York in September, but a repetition during discussion of the papers contributed to the Institute of Biology's Symposium on an Optimum Population for Britain[17] appeared to lead to some action.

After brief corroboratory interviews with representatives of the press this information was publicized in the subsequent issues of *Nature*, *New Scientist*, and *The Observer*, and only a few weeks later the problems of population and ecological balance in Britain were turned over to the Parliamentary Select Committee on Science and Technology in a blaze of publicity. Whether the secret committee was wound up at the same time was not made clear but the

[15] Reported *The Guardian*, July 3, 4, 5, 9, 10, 12, 13, 1968.
[16] The inaugural lecture at the 17th Annual Conference of the Rationalist Press, since reprinted in *Planners versus People*, Pemberton Books (1970).
[17] London, September, 1969. Proceedings published by Academic Press, 1970 (ed) Taylor, LR.

population problem is now edging towards where it has always belonged, the political arena. We must all be informed, concerned, and consulted, as is proper in a democracy, and if our government will not lead us we must kindly, gently, but firmly lead it. As Dean Acheson is said to have remarked when he was US Secretary of State, reformulating a point made by Plato long ago: 'Policies do not trickle down, they well up.'

Future governments and population control

It seems unlikely that the Liberals will form a government in the near future so we need mention only the Labour and Conservative parties, and neither of these has given any consideration to population control as an aspect of party policy. There are a number of striking individual exceptions as we have seen but whichever party had gained office after the last election it would have had to start, *as a party*, more or less from scratch on this issue, although certain measures started by the last Labour administration[18] will aid the Conservative government, if it wants to be aided, that is.

The Conservatives are hampered with respect to population control by the fact that they still have a strong emotional attachment to the idea of *laissez faire*—though they would never dream of applying it to the farmers, for example—and because they are conservative. Population control sounds a radical social innovation and their immediate reaction will tend to be against it. On the other hand, perhaps the most active single person in parliament on Britain's population problem has been a Conservative, Sir David Renton, and a large number of his colleagues signed the joint motion initiated by him. It might be a far cry, however, from Her Majesty's Government, or Opposition, to the committees of the constituency parties and the Annual Conference. However, Conservatives might draw considerable comfort from the fact—not at all widely known, apparently even amongst demographers and historians—that a tax was imposed in England in 1695 on marriages, births, and deaths. It seems to have been suggested by a similar tax in Holland and was secured by means of a register kept in every parish. The amount of the tax varied according to the social class. For example, poor people paid 2s (10p) for births, 2s 6d (12½p) for marriages, and 4s (20p) for burials. A 'gentleman'

---

[18] A study of Britain's family planning services by the government Social Survey was announced on March 20, 1970.

paid an extra pound in each case while a duke paid amounts vary-ing between £25 and £50.[19]

These taxes were repealed in 1706 because the annual yield after the first years was thought to be too small. Another attempt was made in 1783, when a tax on the registry of burials, marriages, and deaths was again introduced. This was repealed only one year later, however, as it was acknowledged:

> ... To have an injurious operation as regards the morals of the people.

Mr Douglas Houghton[20] has been extremely active on these issues, as his controversial speech illustrated, and it seems very probable that he would have gone further and faster had it not been for the ties of his allegiance to the government in office until recently. Other radical MPs have also done a lot of good in the general area of population problems, notably Mr Edwin Brooks on the family planning front and Mr David Steel on abortion law reform, two very solid victories for the population control move-ment.

Nonetheless, population control is especially difficult medicine for socialists to swallow because the twin pillars of their thought, social engineering for a better future and the labour theory of value —plus a dash of utopianism—are centred on people. As F. Cottrell has written:

> The Romantic Socialist [is] taken in by Marx's cavalier hand-ling of the 'law of diminishing returns.' ... If more Socialists will only take a look at the cost of unlimited population growth they are more likely to achieve their goals than by this utopian conception that since labour produces everything there can never be a shortage due to too many people.[21]

In an attempt to provoke the Labour movement into some con-cern I wrote an article called 'Socialism versus the Population Explosion' for the *New Statesman* in 1964. This appeared some six months later, the title amended to 'The Population Explosion'

[19] Dowell (1965) *History of Taxation and Taxes in England*, Vol. 2 (p 453). I am indebted to Mrs Cynthia Blezard for unearthing this fact for me. See also the medieval Scottish marriage tax, *merchet*, p 344f.

[20] Douglas Houghton's valuable contribution to the Optimum Population Symposium, 'The Legislation Barrier' should be read by anyone interested in the formulation or execution of practical population policies.

[21] Private communication.

without my knowledge or consent, thus destroying its essential point—the *versus* part—and caused not the slightest ripple apart from a letter in support from the Labour MP referred to at the head of this chapter, Christopher Rowland.

My opinion of the challenge to the Labour movement has not changed significantly since 1964 when it was described as follows:

> A socialist movement is committed to tackling, as near the source as possible, and removing or ameliorating anything causing poverty, injustice or degradation of men in any way. Explosive population growth has caused and will cause more of these than all past wars and tyrannies put together. Numbers have to be restricted now or very soon and it is the duty of a forward-looking movement to initiate the necessary measures earlier than parties which act only when they are forced to.
>
> What is needed is something hard for socialists even to envisage, let alone bring about: a restrictionist philosophy in the field of reproduction—with all this means in the denial of basic instincts, sex, love of children, and so much else that is warm, generous and expansive—coupled with an expansionist philosophy in the field of production and distribution of all the other good things of life.
>
> Preventing people having as many children as they want is so repellent to most of us that the idea of a humanitarian party doing it first will appear outrageous, if not ludicrous. Unfortunately, however, this is just what is needed on precisely the same principle as that used to prevent the antisocial minority from driving on the right. Socialists are convinced that their ethic, coupled with modern knowledge, can bring leisure and fulfilment to everybody, but the stark facts of population growth mean that unless something really drastic is done soon, far from entering the Golden Age we shall find that this was it and humanity has passed on.[22]

Elements of a realistic policy

Bearing in mind that population is a political question if the argument here is correct, and that 'politics is the art of the possible', as Clausewitz is said to have remarked, we must determine the goal

[22] *New Statesman,* April 30, 1965. Reprinted in Conservation Society Reprints, No. 1.

to which policy is to be directed. Commonsense and systems theory alike tell us that it is impossible to maximize more than one variable at a time excepting those tied to each other in some way. If our goal is the maximum number of human beings the environment can possibly sustain this will require one policy, if we want to optimize income per capita this will necessitate another, if individual liberty is the variable to be maximized this will call for yet a third. F. Cottrell has stated it forcefully:

> ... securing the largest possible population and ... a higher material standard of living are mutually exclusive objectives.[23]

As this book is about population and liberty let us assume that individual liberty is what we want most of. This will mean that we require a policy giving minimum restraints; restrictions would be allowable only where they produce greater, or at least equivalent liberties elsewhere in the system. We can then say, as a general principle: constraints must be kept as few as possible *consistent with the attainment of the essential goals of the system*. If this is so it is useful to think of a sliding scale of constraints varying from those which are barely noticeable to those reaching the ultimate in brutality of impact. Let us try to list them under five main headings in order of severity.

First, the *psychological*. This would consist of an appeal to the mind, rationality, and sense of responsibility, through education and information.

Second, the *social*. This could be made to work through social pressures, through propaganda, and through the breaking down of no longer tenable customs and social norms.

Third, the *economic*. This would operate through financial measures which could be classified under three sub-headings:

i. Progressive removal of positive incentives to fertility such as family allowances, income tax relief, and free education.

ii. Progressive introduction of positive *dis*-incentives to fertility, negative family allowances, that is, taxes on fertility, very high fees for marriage licences, and so on.

iii. Progressive introduction of negative incentives, the payment of non-fertility bonuses. It would be hard to work out exactly what the figure is but it would be surprising if in Britain we couldn't afford to pay every woman at risk for childbearing £20 a year not

[23] (1955) *Energy and Society* (p 143).

to get pregnant[24] *and* show a handsome profit for the taxpayer into the bargain.[25]

Fourth, the *political/legal*. Rationing systems for family size, laws regulating fertility, penalties, fines, imprisonment for violations, etc.

Fifth, the *physical*. Compulsory birth control, possibly by means of semi-permanent implantations or chemical additives to the diet, seizure and destruction of illegally conceived infants, sterilization or even execution of illegal parents, and so on.

The libertarian's heart will sink further and further into his boots as his eyes scan the foregoing list but the logic of the facts is inexorable. If the first-level constraints fail to operate we must switch to the second, if that fails we must switch to the third, and so on until eventually we wind up at the bottom, back in the situation depicted so graphically by Sumner.

There is a further possibility, not mentioned so far: we can decide that these control mechanisms are so inhuman that the system must be allowed to take its own course regardless of where that might lead. We might wind up in a world filled with poverty, famine, disease, and violence as a result of inexorable natural processes, but at least we wouldn't have done this particular unethical thing, controlling fertility, to each other on the way. I have heard this point put forward quite seriously by an intelligent and sensitive observer and Dennis Gabor has written:

> My Roman Catholic friends gave me this answer to my worries about the future: 'Let the population expand to its natural limits. Life will then remain a worthwhile game, in which the daily bread will be a daily victory.'[26]

It is hard to avoid speculating how many of Professor Gabor's Roman Catholic friends ever had to worry where next year's

[24] Dr Aubrey Manning of Edinburgh University has said it would pay Britain to offer a £500 bounty to encourage people to be sterilized. *Daily Telegraph*, January 7, 1970, *Journal of Fertility Control,* and *The Ecologist*, **1**, No 1, July, 1970.

[25] For detailed administrative proposals see:

(*a*) Berelson, B, 'Beyond Family Planning'. In *Studies in Family Planning,* No 38, February, 1969. The Population Council. A condensed version appeared in *Science* at the same time.

(*b*) Taylor, CE, 'Five Stages in a Practical Population Policy'. *International Development Review*, X, No 4.

[26] (1963) *Inventing the Future* (p 69).

luxuries were coming from, let alone a crust for tomorrow, and what sort of rules their little game would have.

The dimensions of the control problem in England and Wales

The 1968 balance-sheet

In England and Wales in 1968 nearly 71 per cent of all legitimate live births to women married once only (totalling 732,000 approximately) were either first or second children, leaving 29 per cent as third, fourth, and so on, up to 15+.

If we define a large family as one with four or more children then $6\frac{1}{2}$ per cent (over 47,000) of all live births were into existing large families, and a further 7 per cent (over 51,000) converted small families into large ones. Adding these together we get $13\frac{1}{2}$ per cent of legitimate live births—totalling nearly 99,000—into existing or new large families of women married once only.

In addition there were nearly 70,000 illegitimate births and a further 17,000 born to women married more than once. If we take the same proportion of the last figure, $13\frac{1}{2}$ per cent of 17,000, as being born into or creating large families we get 2,300, giving a grand total as follows:

Live births into 'large families' (women married once only)	99,000
Do (women married more than once)	2,300
Illegitimate births	70,000
Total (rounded)	171,000

The total number of live births was 820,000 and the number of deaths 577,000, both rounded, giving a natural increase of 243,000. If we subtract from this the 'extra' children born into large families and the illegitimates—171,000, as we have seen—the surplus is reduced to 72,000 (243,000−171,000).

This is to say that if nobody with three or more children already had produced another and that no illegitimate births had occurred we would have had only 72,000 births above the number required for a stationary population. Sixteen per cent of all births (131,000) were to mothers aged twenty and under and if we can somehow persuade women to start their families later this would be an appreciable help in reducing the overall birth rate. If only 15 per

cent of live births into families with one child or none were unwanted and could have been prevented, this would have more than
covered the 72,000 and left us with a slight deficit.

It must be stressed that this balance-sheet is for England and
Wales only—comparable figures for the United Kingdom as a
whole not being readily available—but it does give an insight into
the size of the problem, which turns out to be quite manageable.
If those at present liking large families were to content themselves
with three children—plus any adoptions they are able to make (the
supply of adoptive children would more or less dry up if illegitimacy
were to be prevented)—and we were to more or less abolish illegitimacy, the problem would be solved.

The rearguard action

There is always a battle over the introduction of new social controls, however essential—just as many social changes are resisted—
and this often continues long after they are firmly institutionalized
and generally accepted. We need have little doubt that the barons
thought it an outrage when their age-old *jus primae noctis* was
challenged and in at least one case[27] of legislative abolition compensation had to be paid to them, by the groom, for the loss of
their microfreedom to deflower the bride.

Three examples from recent history, of particular relevance to
population questions, should suffice to make the point.

(i) *The microfreedom not to be numbered*

It was obvious to thinking people by the middle of the eighteenth
century that it had become necessary for the government to know
quite whom and what it was governing. However, when a proposal
for a census was presented to the Commons in 1753 for

> ... taking and registering an annual account of the total num-
> ber of the people and of the total number of marriages, births
> and deaths ...

a substantial number of MPs thought it an intolerable intrusion
into the Englishman's liberty, as this extract from the speech of
Mr William Thornton, MP for York, shows:

[27] By Malcolm the III of Scotland (d 1093). This later turned into a
marriage tax called *merchet* or *mercheta mulierum*. Everyman's Encyclopaedia.

... I did not believe that there was any set of men, or indeed, any individual of the human species, so presumptuous and so abandoned as to make the proposal we have just heard—I hold this project to be totally subversive of the last remains of English liberty—the addition of a few words will make it the most effectual engine of rapacity and oppression that was ever waged against an innocent people. . . .[28]

As a matter of fact the Bill was carried by a comfortable majority in the Commons but the Lords at least agreed with this spirited not to say fiery defence of individual liberty and threw it out. Nearly half a century elapsed before the measure was accepted and the first census taken (in 1801).

It seems highly probable that the publication of Malthus' first draft of his great *Essay on the Principle of Population*, in 1798, had a lot to do with it, although Sir John Sinclair's monumental 21 volume *Statistical Account of Scotland*, appearing in the 1790s, must have done a lot to prepare the ground.

Perhaps filling in the census form once every ten years is a bit of a nuisance but the idea that it is a fundamental invasion of individual liberty is preposterous to the modern mind.

(ii) *The microfreedom to maltreat your children*

A good deal less than a century ago parents in Britain and America had the right under the law—as many Arabs still have—to do practically what they liked with their children. They could thrash them within an inch of their lives, burn them, scald them, whip them, beat them with chains, lumps of wood, or pieces of iron and no one could say them nay. It was a 'natural right' to do what they wanted with their children in the privacy of their home. A story told at the Jubilee Annual Meeting of the NSPCC in 1934 illustrates this.

A missionary visiting a dying German immigrant woman in a dilapidated tenement house in the Hell's Kitchen district of New York was asked by the woman to try to help the child next door who was most violently beaten day after day.

The missionary promised to do what she could but when she called . . . a powerfully built, loutish man answered the door and

[28] Quoted Caradoc Jones, D, *Social Surveys* (probably early 1950s), also, somewhat differently, in Glass and Blacker (1938) *Population and Fertility* (p 40).

met her enquiries with torrents of abuse and threats of violence. She approached the police, magistrates, heads of charitable institutions, and prominent private citizens, only to be told with somewhat varying degrees of sympathy and understanding that the law did not permit any official intervention in the case and that parents had a right to chastise their children.

Finally she decided to call on Henry Bergh, the founder of the New York society for the prevention of cruelty to animals, and to seek his aid. Bergh, together with a lawyer friend, searched the statute books for some law which would justify the rescue of the child, only to find that while animals enjoyed legal protection children did not. This fruitless search did not daunt them and they decided to act as though the child were an animal. Officers of their society removed her, seized the scissors with which her head and body had been beaten and gashed, and brought her, wrapped in a horse blanket, before Justice Lawrence of the Supreme Court.

Many of those ... in court were much moved when they saw the child's condition and the court had no hesitation in convicting her adoptive parents and sending them to prison. The case thoroughly aroused the general public and a society was formed to protect the children of the city from cruelty and neglect and to waken public sympathy to their sufferings.

Meanwhile events were moving in England, but the difficulties to be surmounted in educating public opinion and in persuading parliament to pass the necessary enactments were so formidable that even the great Lord Shaftesbury wrote to an enquirer:

> The evils you state are enormous and indisputable, but they are of so private, internal and domestic a character as to be beyond the reach of legislation, and the subject indeed, will not, I think, be entertained in either house of parliament.

However public opinion did not rest and in 1883 the Liverpool Society for the Prevention of Cruelty to Children was formed which dealt with 211 cases during the remainder of that year.

> The first case to attract public attention was that of a girl named Helen Harrecan whose father had punched her in the face with his clenched fist, ... he was arrested and in court the child's black eyes and swollen face told their own tale so eloquently that he was sentenced to three months' imprisonment. To modern

ears this sounds a mild sentence but to contemporaries it was astonishing. The reporters in court could not believe their ears. What, punish a man for hitting his own child! In his own house! Many newspapers published the sentence with a great variety of comment.[29]

From that time on the Society's affairs prospered but only at the expense of what had hitherto been regarded as a sacred right of parents. The microfreedoms of parents were reduced but the microfreedoms of children, freedom from brutality and persecution, was correspondingly increased. Surely society as a whole gained greatly in liberty, dignity, and stature from the abolition of this long-standing parental freedom.

(iii) *Microfreedoms in the coal industry*

Until about the middle of the nineteenth century employers had the microfreedom to employ women and small children in inhuman conditions in industry, including down coal mines, and the women and children themselves had the microfreedom to go and work there for a pittance. When the Ashley Bill was passsed in 1842 to prevent miners from sending their children down the pits, Lord Londonderry, nicknamed 'the friend of the miners', stood up for the freedom of the individual against the state. Lord Londonderry declared it was:

> ... a most unjustified interference with their rights as parents.

The young miners—down to the age of four or so—were, he said,

> ... generally cheerful and contented, modelling figures of animals and men in clay, etc.[30]

Londonderry thought the prohibition on sending women down the pit was also unjustified. He argued that certain coal seams were too steep or too thin to work with ponies, therefore it was essential to make use of women and he stoutly defended the freedom of the employers and employees to perpetuate this state of affairs.

There are many other examples of resistance to new social controls evolving with increasing social awareness and moral sensitivity, improvements in the standard of living, the demands

---

[29] Allen, A and Morton A (1961) *This is Your Child* (pp 15–18).
[30] Challinor, R, and Ripley (1969) *The Miners' Association*.

of technology, and, perhaps above all things, the increase in numbers and the complexity of the social organization needed to deal with it. If numbers and complexity are to be allowed to go on increasing we must get used to the idea of an endless torrent of new restrictions simply to permit the system to retain its viability for a few more decades, though, of course, the potentialities of this approach are strictly limited, and a dead end—if not catastrophe—must be reached soon.

The only alternative to this prospect is to forego those microfreedoms which, being exercised in the short run, make inroads into other and more important microfreedoms in the long run, in other words to exercise prudence and self-restraint.

HRH the Duke of Edinburgh has made population control the supreme test of our intelligence:

> ... one could argue that as starvation has always controlled population there is nothing to worry about. Just let nature take its course. I don't believe any decent human being ... could possibly accept this argument. No matter how hopeless it may seem we can't give up without a struggle. We make so many ... claims for ourselves as beings with superior intelligence ... that *I think the least we can do* is to *prove it by controlling our numbers and standard of existence* deliberately and willingly.[31] (Italics added)

Summary

I have argued that population control has been much more normal than abnormal throughout the greater part of human history, the exceptions mainly being in environments which were harsh enough to control numbers automatically. We are living in a unique epoch when the carrying capacity of the environment is markedly though of course only temporarily expanding. In a very short time numbers must stop growing anyway because of the finiteness of the environment and it is argued that we should stop it growing earlier by means of a policy of control. A policy must have a goal and this should be a population optimum decided in the public arena of open democratic discussions—aided by expert advice based on sound science and research—along with all other important issues.

---

[31] Address to sixth formers, Freedom From Hunger Campaign, November 26, 1964. Transcript kindly supplied by Buckingham Palace.

However, though it is argued that population is a political issue it must be stressed that it is at the same time 'above' politics in the party sense; it should be a non-party issue as foreign policy, agricultural support, and others are said to be.

I have argued that none of the parties have population policies worthy of the name and though this is obviously a limitation in one sense, it is a positive virtue in another. Because none of them are entrenched behind the party-line it should be so much easier for them to get together, quietly at first, and begin to hammer out constructive and common policies for the greater benefit of themselves and our society.

Of course there will be objections, as there always are whenever essential reforms are mooted—the rearguard will put up a great fight—but surely the public as a whole is now ready to embrace this topic in debate and gradually come to accept the inevitability of a stabilized population and whatever measures are needed to bring it about.

Many and perhaps the majority of 'primitive' cultures have had customs requiring prospective husbands—and therefore fathers—to prove their manhood by slaying an enemy in battle, acquiring a human head,[32] making a canoe, or collecting cowrie shells, a thousand dolphin's teeth, or several cattle as bride-price. All of these social institutions placed stress on duties as well as rights, on competence, maturity, and social responsibility, and we might well consider re-adopting some of them. A few of the traditional mechanisms might appear somewhat ill adapted to the present day and consequently benefit from a little modernization; for example instead of human heads a young man might collect a couple of 'O' levels, a lease on a flat, or even enough wealth to put a 20 per cent deposit on a house and furnish it, on top of which he could be required to pass a medical examination—both physical and psychological—and, along with his prospective bride if the sexes are to receive equality of treatment, a test of his domestic skills.

At the moment the only qualifications required of prospective parents are the abilities to stumble across and recognize a partner of the opposite sex, find a tolerably private place, and deposit or receive semen in the appropriate anatomical niche. Nothing else is

[32] Not long ago it was reported of the Naga: '... the girls ceaselessly mock the youths until they have taken some heads: a youth may give his sweetheart as many proofs as he like, but she will not look at him until he shows her a head.' A double-acting population control. Molz (1909). Quoted in Krzywicki, L (1934) *Primitive Society and its Vital Statistics* (p 110).

required, not love, conscience, care, goodwill, or the most elementary urge or capacity to tend to the needs of self, partner, or offspring. Population control is often opposed on the grounds of the sanctity of human life but what a sublime contempt for life and the individual spirit is displayed by a society living according to such values.

If 56 million is not an optimum population in 1970, would 112 million be enough in six generations' time, 224 million eleven generations from now, or a billion about ten generations further on, in the early 2500s? If we cannot decide for the time being what is the *size* of an optimum population, can we not at least agree that its optimum *rate of growth* is zero?

The nation must choose and act, populations do not optimize themselves, unless mere survival is the criterion, the problem will not go away but will steadily get worse unless we pluck up our courage and do what is necessary now.

As Sumner said:

> ... population has always presented, as it now does, a problem of policy. That group interests are involved ... is unquestionable ... A sound population policy, according to the best knowledge we have, would be the real solution of a number of the most serious evils ...
>
> *It is a problem of the last degree of simplicity and reality,— a problem of a task and the strength to perform it, of an expenditure and the means to meet it.*[33] (Italics added)

Very briefly; a population policy must do whatever turns out to be necessary in the long run in order to achieve the goal of a stationary population. And this leaves us with three choices.

1. Early, rational, humane, and democratic policies.

2. Late, possibly still rational but certainly undemocratic and inhumane policies, and:

3. Latest, not a policy at all, strictly, opting out and letting nature take over through starvation, disease, and violence.

If this is a correct formulation of the problem there is little doubt which policy *homo sapiens* ought to choose in the rapidly shortening time left at his disposal.

The overriding stress in population policies of the future must be on the development of an almost majestic sense of responsibility in parenthood, based on a deep awareness of the awe-inspiring

[33] (*Op cit*).

potentiality for good and evil of the act of creating another human being, a sentient creature who in his brief span must learn to live, love, laugh, cry, and die.[34]

[34] Since this was written the Liberal Party has expressed great interest in these problems and I have it from Mrs S. Robson, the President, that a standing committee is to be set up. The Liberal Party could easily put Britain in its debt by becoming the spearhead of a really systematic attack on the problem.

Chapter 16

Freedom to choose:
III. Freedom from fatalism

If the present trend continues there will be another 1,000 million mouths to feed by 1980—and of course the trend will continue unless something cataclysmic stops it; the trouble is that the 'population explosion' (even the phrase is abstract) remains a 'problem' to be worried over by Governments and public-spirited people, the individual still seems helpless before it. *The Guardian* editorial.[1]

The quotation from *The Guardian* at the head of this chapter illustrates only too well a frame of mind which must be combated by all fair means—perhaps the issue is important enough to legitimate unfair means, too. This attitude is not peculiar to the population problem of course—or social problems in general—it can be found in almost any sphere of human activity, and though its effect is insidious and corrosive, most of us seem to be infected by it to some degree. Some of the most highly gifted and dynamic individuals sometimes find their will to succeed in a particular endeavour contested every inch of the way by what can only be called the 'will to fail', to fail by giving up the struggle to succeed. World-beating athletes have been heard to say that the biggest single factor preventing higher achievement on their part—running a four-minute mile or whatever it might be—has been this insidious internal sabotaging mechanism not to make the extra effort. We see this only too often in everyday life, people adopting a fatalistic attitude

[1] September 23, 1964.

which prevents them from even attempting to find a solution to a personal problem. It is not for nothing that sloth is one of the seven deadly sins.

This is extremely puzzling. There are biological analogies—though not very close—for example, the rabbit's alleged propensity to squat immobile when facing certain death from a stoat, or, at night, from an approaching car. Running *might* help in both cases and is certainly better than just sitting there. 'Freezing' is obviously useful in very well camouflaged creatures in their natural habitat, but otherwise it seems to be an evolutionary imperfection. Perhaps it is related to *Thanatos*, the 'Death Wish' of the Freudians but, either way, it is very hard to understand the biological function of such a mechanism—or to answer the question why it has not been selected out during the long evolutionary process, as one would have guessed that from a biological point of view pessimism is disfunctional and optimism functional—a positive help in enabling a species to survive.

Fatalism and the self-fulfilling prophecy

However—whatever its origins and biological function—we are landed with pessimism as a practical problem here and now, and 'practical' means that something can and must be done about it.

Illustrating this point is made easier by the use of the concept of the 'self-fulfilling prophecy'[2]—beliefs which though originally false, tend to bring about the state of affairs thought to exist, simply by being believed and acted upon.

Both optimism and pessimism fall into this category. It is fairly obvious that if a person is pessimistic, i e he believes that a certain course of action is bound to fail or has only a small chance of succeeding he will in general make less effort to ensure success. This is not true of all of us—there are some individuals who believe that however hopeless a cause, if it is worthy they will have a try and at the very least go down fighting. They will comfort themselves with the thought—and hope other people will agree—'Well, at least I tried.' In the present writer's judgment this is unusual, it is more common for people to be less energetic and constructive the less optimistic they are about the success of a possible course of action.

This has an almost inevitable outcome; pessimism produces less

[2] See Merton, R (1967) *Social Theory and Social Structure*.

action, less action produces less result, the pessimists—seeing the smaller result—see therein a justification for their original attitude and make even less effort, thereby producing still smaller results, and so forth, until action ceases altogether and the original pessimistic prophecy comes true.

This argument, that failure to act or to act vigorously enough where the mood of the actor is pessimistic, tends to produce failure, might be taken to imply in this context—where we are discussing self-fulfilling prophecies—that optimism will always bring home the bacon. This is obviously untrue, as King Canute is said to have found out. All that is being argued here is that constructive optimism is *more likely to bring about the desired result* than pessimism. The kind of optimism being discussed here is not the fatuous variety—'the Lord will provide' and that scientists and technologists can find answers to *all* our problems and feed the human population no matter how large it gets or how quickly. The sort of optimism referred to is that which would emerge from —or perhaps prompt—an internal dialogue going something like this:

> The situation is extremely difficult, perhaps it is already too late to prevent a major catastrophe, through world famine, for example. Perhaps my/our action will not be what is required. Perhaps, even though it is the right sort of thing it will be totally ineffective. Perhaps, even if effective on its own terms, its impact on so huge, complex and difficult a problem will be insignificant. Nonetheless, *if* I/we make the effort then the outcome *might* be satisfactory and constructive and it might also encourage others to join in. If I *don't* make the effort the outcome can *only* be negative.

Individual and group action

Armed with this kind of philosophy and a working knowledge of the dynamics of belief/action systems, an individual can make what appears to him a constructive effort either all by himself or with the aid of other like-minded people, and try to develop co-operative group action—as we do for virtually all our social purposes—and, of course, it might be possible to capitalize existing co-operative groups and bend them to the new task. There is no reason why an individual should try to make an impact on the population problem

—or indeed any other social problem—as an individual, if he feels inadequate to the task. One of the unique factors in the make up of *homo sapiens*—raising him far above the level of the other animals—is his sociability, his radically superior capacity for building up complex social organizations capable of carrying out purposes unimaginably remote from the potential of any individual or small group, witness the American moon walks. Our marvellous means of collecting and storing knowledge, communicating, and organizing provide a huge 'amplifier', as it were, for individual or group resolution and it is manifestly absurd to get bogged down with the idea that anything the individual cannot do, cannot be done.

However, having stressed the superior efficacy of group action, it is necessary to emphasize that great feats can be performed by individuals—not only without organized group support—but often in the face of tenacious opposition by powerful groups. History is full of examples of individuals who have changed its course by insisting that their answer was the right one; from Jesus via Galileo, Marx, Hitler, and Einstein down to Ralph Nader, who took on single-handed the gigantic American motor industry[3] and forced it to climb down—in spite of a massive smear campaign mounted against him by the industry—and accept much higher standards of engineering design and safety.

Individuals can produce profound changes in social systems—though co-operative groups are more likely to succeed—but neither groups nor individuals can achieve anything unless they believe their goals are potentially attainable.

Pessimistic propaganda

An example of this kind of thinking—in this case used as a means of evading discussion of the adoption of modern forms of birth control—was provided by Father Arthur McCormack[4] a Roman Catholic expert on population problems, who argued in response to an article preceding his in the same journal ('Fewer Children or Disaster', by Dr Jivraj Mehta, High Commissioner for India).

If a population policy uses funds or energies diverted from constructive work; if it gives the impression that birth control is

[3] Its turnover is bigger than most national budgets.
[4] 'Why I disagree with Dr Mehta', Oxfam Bulletin No 9, Spring, 1965.

cea, without stressing that so far it has been a costly ailure; ... then talk of a population control policy can do a lot of harm. ...

... The failures in Puerto Rico, in India and the disastrous results of Japan's efforts in this regard have caused the real experts to be very chary. There is no evidence that a developing country can make ... any kind of success ... of a birth control programme.

... The 'Pill' is neither safe enough nor cheap enough for the underdeveloped countries to consider it; other methods have been tried and failed.

Father McCormack does not mention that the '... disastrous results of Japan's efforts ...' led to a 50 per cent reduction in the birth rate in 10 years after the passing of the Eugenics Protection Act of 1948, so he very clearly has curious standards of success and failure. His whole article is a good example of the logic-chopping evasiveness of many Roman Catholic intellectuals favouring the officials stand on birth control.

Father McCormack is really opposed to modern forms of birth control—all of them—for dogmatic religious reasons, as he is in a sense entitled to be, but instead of coming out and saying this openly he tries to dismiss them on the grounds of their ineffectiveness. The whole point is that the more effective they are the more he and people like him oppose them.

'Success' versus 'failure', a paradox

We can throw some light on this question of failure and success with the paradoxical statement that, on the one hand, population control has already failed, but that, on the other hand, its success is inevitable. How can these two contradictory statements be reconciled?

Failure

Population control has failed in the sense that—in the opinion of all informed observers—there have always been too many people in the world for the resources contemporarily available. This is as true of the present day as of all past ages but it is worse now because—world population being so much larger—the absolute *number* in need is much bigger even if it constitutes a smaller *proportion* of the total. It seems likely that at least 40 per cent of the world's 1970 population suffers from hunger or malnutrition and this means over 1,400 million in want—an enormous number, nearly three times the world's population when the population explosion started three centuries ago. From this point of view population control has failed miserably throughout man's history so far and is failing now by a calamitously large margin.

Success

On the other side we can say that whatever is essential will, in the long run, come about. It is obvious that on a finite Earth with—for all practical purposes—finite space environs, some mechanism must bring population growth to a stop sooner or later.

Meanwhile anything which minimizes the scale of the problem and reduces the sum of human pain must be regarded as partial success. Let us look at some evidence.

Success of population control programmes

(i) *Pakistan*

At the request of the Government of Pakistan, a joint United Nations–World Health Organization Advisory Mission was formed to make a mid-term evaluation of the Pakistan national family planning programme. It was organized by the UN Population Division in association with WHO under the Technical Assistance Programme of the UN.

The report of this body said:

> The basic objective of the programme is to reduce the birth rate from its present estimated level of about 50 per thousand to 40 per thousand by 1970 . . . an ambitious target, . . . nothing comparable has been achieved by government action in any large country with a mostly illiterate population. It is hoped to achieve this target by inducing one-fourth of the fertile population to adopt the regular practice of contraception. . . .

After only two and a half years of operation for the population control programme, the Secretary, Family Planning, reports:

> . . . [I am] confident that this goal can be attained, . . . nearly 2.4 million couples are actively practising family planning out of a target of 5 million by 1970 . . . as a conservative estimate . . .

the participation of 2.4 million couples entails the prevention of 600,000 births per annum, about three-fifths of the objective of preventing about one million births per annum by 1970...

This conclusion was supported by an independent survey which said that the reduction in births brought about through the population control programme is:

... about 50 per cent of the reduction needed to achieve the plan's objective in 1970.[5]

(ii) Taiwan (Formosa)

A significant success has also been attained with population control in Taiwan as the graph in Fig 16/1 shows. Fertility was declining rapidly anyway from the very high crude birth rate of about 45 per thousand in 1954, but the introduction of a population control programme in 1963 increased this decline in fertility by no less than 135 per cent,[6] a very substantial result by any criterion.

Of course in Taiwan—as in Pakistan and most of the other poor countries—there is a very long way to go indeed before fertility is brought down to the level desired and great efforts must be made to reduce it still further. However, this should not by any means be allowed to blind us to the very substantial successes which have been made with relatively limited resources and against substantial opposition from the Roman Catholic Church and other obstructionist bodies.

(iii) An international programme of control

In 1966 the US Population Council mounted an international postpartum birth control programme in twenty-five hospitals spread over fifteen countries.[7] Figure 16/2 shows the results of the campaign as measured in terms of the number of 'acceptors', 'direct' and 'indirect', of birth control advice and appliances, over 101,000 in twelve months.

The report states that:

Each hospital survey showed that the non-acceptors ... [had] ... a higher incidence of pregnancy at six months post-

---

[5] *Studies in Family Planning*, No 40, April, 1969. The Population Council, USA.

[6] $\dfrac{5\cdot4\% - 2\cdot3\%}{2\cdot3\%} = \dfrac{3\cdot1\%}{2\cdot3\%} = 135\%$ inc in rate of decline.

[7] Chile, Hong-Kong, India, Iran, Japan, Mexico, Pakistan, Philippines, Puerto Rico, Singapore, Thailand, Turkey, UAR, Venezuela, and USA.

Fig 16/1

Taiwan: Fertility Decline before and after establishment of Family Planning Programme in 1963

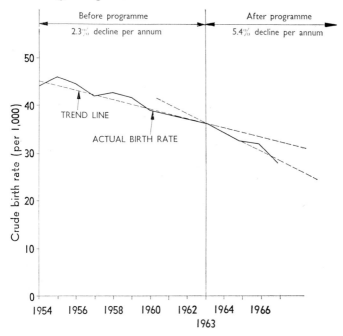

Source: Studies in Family Planning, No 41, April 1969

partum than those who had accepted family planning . . . *in the 2,109 non-acceptors . . . one in fourteen thought she was currently pregnant* . . . [*whilst*] *of 1,930 acceptors, only one in eighty-four thought she was.* . . . In other words there is *a six-fold difference in pregnancy rates* at six months . . .[8] (Italics added)

A recent UN report[9] pointed out that in the world as a whole policies of population control are already well advanced. India was said to be the first[10] country to adopt an official family planning policy, in 1952; Pakistan followed in 1955, since when many others have followed, the world total now being in the region of thirty.

The report states that '. . . in all countries with a population

[8] *Studies in Family Planning*, No 22, August, 1967.
[9] *Report on World Population Situation*, UN, 1969.
[10] Japan passed her 'Eugenics Protection Act' in 1948.

Fig 16/2

Cumulative number of direct and indirect Acceptors by months of activity

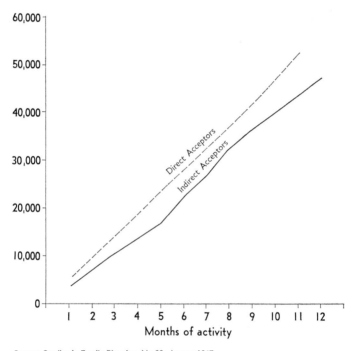

Months of activity

Source: **Studies in Family Planning**, No 22, August 1967

exceeding 100 million, family planning is being promoted by government agencies', and notes that in 1969 Yugoslavia became the first developed nation to adopt a policy of population control.

Of course most of these are policies of control in the weaker sense of that word—the encouragement of voluntary birth control —but if the reports are to be believed China has gone a good deal further in public exhortations—strongly backed by the fear of Party disapproval—to marry late and have fewer children and the others will probably have to move much further in this direction in the near future.[11]

[11] The World Bank made its first loan to help a national population control policy in mid-1970, in this case $2 million to Jamaica. *UN Population Newsletter*, No 9, June 1970 (p 18).

Scale of the problem

Two further points seem worth making in this context. The first is that people sometimes feel a problem is simply too big to be tackled, that its scale is Herculean, quite beyond the scope of mortal man—*The Guardian* editorial implies this without actually saying so. This is not the same thing as a feeling that a problem is approaching *inexorably*, that it is part of the natural order which nothing can stop, although the two often go together, the size of a problem itself provoking the feeling that its progress is inexorable. But who can say until society's best efforts have been bent towards a solution, without success, that a problem is too big? How much too big would the problem of curing most of the world's killing diseases have seemed in the earlier part of this century—bringing life-expectancies all over the Earth up to somewhere near the biological maximum? It would have seemed a fantastic task.

As late as 1944, when radicals were writing such books as *Death Pays a Dividend*, it seemed a mere pipedream to think that the arms trade could be brought under government control. The idea of preventing individual capitalists and middlemen from making and selling arms to the highest bidder—often playing off rival nations one against the other in the process—seemed utterly utopian. Yet, after a good deal less than half a lifespan, it has become accepted in the main that irresponsible individuals cannot scatter armaments around as and when they see fit.

Of course, there are still some individual armaments dealers, especially in the secondhand market, and even though governments are now mainly in control, we can see there is still a good way to go before a really responsible control of the manufacture and sale of armaments is achieved. Nonetheless, there has been a great step forward, one which seemed almost impossibly remote as recently as the early 1940s.

Summary

This corrosive fatalism—this 'Will of Allah' approach exemplified in the newspaper editorial quoted at the head of the chapter

> ... and of course the trend will continue unless something cataclysmic stops it; ...

is not merely unnecessary and inappropriate but positively harmful. *The Guardian* makes a signal contribution to our society and perpetuates many great principles, it has already helped a lot in this sphere and could go on to make a unique contribution to the solution of the population problem. *Guardian* readers, at least, could be kept better informed than the general public by giving the issue more stress in the news columns and editorials, by keeping more closely in touch with developments—especially by giving prominence to population returns, pressure on land, road space, and other resources—and by inviting outside experts at intervals to contribute stimulating articles. It could do a lot to encourage the spread of a responsible attitude among journalists towards the population problem as one of the greatest threats humanity has had to face, and make clear that *The Guardian* at least thinks that slipshod, evasive, ill-informed, and often downright misleading articles on this topic such as we all too frequently see should not be tolerated by a responsible body of professional men. It could also exhort the political parties, the government, and the United Nations to take constructive action.

This stunned withdrawal from tackling the population problem is even less acceptable from *The Guardian*—with its tradition of northern blunt speaking—than from most of our great newspapers. If the editor of *The Guardian* feels there is a problem here requiring a drastic solution—and he certainly seems to feel this—then surely he has a responsibility to deploy the solid intellectual and moral resources of his great organ of public opinion in an attempt to provide one. I hope it does not sound as though *The Guardian* is being pilloried, this certainly is not intended, but I think we can exhort it to exhort its readers on this great public issue as it does on others. We cannot very well apply higher standards of morality to the staff of *The Guardian* than to other informed and intelligent people. We are all in the same boat and carry responsibility in direct proportion to our capacity to understand and act, but the staff of the great newspapers carry an extra share of civic responsibility because of the influence they have on the informed and serious minded section of the public.

The only people exempted from the necessity for action are those, who, having made a thorough and honest attempt to understand the facts of population growth, have come to the conclusion that they do not constitute a problem. These have no responsibility to act in this way of course, but the rest of us cannot escape. What is there to prevent all of us becoming '. . . public spirited people . . .' such as the editor of *The Guardian* wrote about?

People who feel they have a particularly difficult moral problem over this issue include some of those who have innocently produced a largish family—especially if it was without specifically wanting to—and only later come to realize the awful inexorability of the population problem. These sometimes feel guilty about their past actions and become morally 'tongue-tied', as it were, about coming to terms with it and committing themselves to what they now see only too clearly is necessary, stabilization of the population in the near future, even if it means that fewer others will be able to do what they have done—have a large family.

However, just as we condemn retroactive legislation, so must we refrain from retrospective moral condemnation—self-condemnation included. We cannot blame ourselves or others for acts which not only could not be seen to be damaging at the time—except perhaps by a handful of long-sighted experts—but which might well have appeared absolutely positive, wholesome, generous, expansive, loving, and biologically 'right'—perhaps even in the national interest.[12]

We, in Britain, are supposed to be a nation of empiricists—we are supposed to be practical people—we don't believe too much in theory, but any statement such as:

> The world population problem is too big/too inevitable/too far advanced for any social action to bring under control

is itself a theory and should accordingly be rejected by the hard headed practical man. Theories should be put to the test of experience at the very least, we cannot know until we have tried whether or not the population problem is susceptible of a social solution. As a practical people, we have no option but to make the effort and see that we can achieve.

Finally, it must be stressed again that any impact whatsoever on the problem constitutes partial success. In that sense we can see it is impossible to fail, unless the word 'failure' is given the totally unjustifiable connotation, 'anything short of 100 per cent success'.

---

[12] The apparently substantial minority of middle-class people who feel they have a duty to produce a large brood to keep their end up against the great unwashed are perhaps on shakier moral ground and might need a little extra persuasion.

We shall be setting out to tackle this great task knowing not that we are bound to fail but that we are bound to succeed.

Anything which can be done to ameliorate human suffering during and after the transitional stage is a net gain. If the question is not *whether or not* but *by how much* we succeed, we see that we have a much more tractable immediate problem facing us, one in which the degree of success will be determined by the amount of effort we put in. We see further that there is no inherent or overriding reason why the effort put in should not be extremely large, giving the reasonable likelihood of an extremely large pay-off.

Surely the only humane, intelligent and moral commitment is to roll our sleeves up and have a go at this admittedly colossal problem, knowing that the worst possible outcome is a success which is only partial.

Summary and reflections

Summary of the main argument

1. The facts of population increase, both in the world as a whole and in Britain, prove that if we take the long view—even over one or two lifespans—an impossible process is going on. Even infinitesimal growth is impossible in the long run and increases of the present order must halt in the very near future—regardless of things like food production and per capita income—because of the finiteness of the Earth and—for all practical purposes—the universe.

2. If growth must stop we have to ask ourselves when and by what means? Shall we allow the age-old natural checks to operate; starvation, disease, and violence, or shall we readjust our social controls so as to balance birth rates with the lowered death rates we all want to have and to extend.

3. If we are disposed to consider the approach via social control rather than physical or biological control we must accept:

(i) that population growth itself is probably the greatest single threat to individual liberty.

(ii) that liberty must be analysed with care and defined with precision before any meaningful discussion can take place.

(iii) that social control is the friend rather than the enemy of liberty.

4. A means of handling the debate on liberty versus control is proposed:

Liberty = Macrofreedom = the sum of all microfreedoms, where the microfreedoms are specified—or at least specifiable—in some detail so that we can have solid practical discussions on real issues rather than harangues based on slogans, nostalgia, or pipedreams.

$$L = Mf = \Sigma_0^n mf$$

5. The concept of an optimum population was discussed and the point made that it is impossible to maximize two or more variables together unless they are tied to each other, which is not normally the case. It is impossible to maximize at the same time the number of people, the standard of living, and individual liberty. It is necessary to choose one at the expense of the others.

Of course it is impossible to *optimize* two or more variables together if optimization is taken to mean maximizing the value of factors 'a' and 'b', say, *having regard to the need to preserve to a certain degree factors 'c', 'd', 'e'*, and so on.

This is what we must do. Decide how many people can be reconciled with our most desired notions of wealth and liberty—though if we regard individual liberty as of overriding importance we can maximize that—and then set about realizing our goal in practice.

6. A case was presented for regarding freedom of movement in physical space as possibly the most important microfreedom humans can have—one we are in danger of losing—and for treating it as the central variable in the optimum equation.

Hence an ecology of liberty was proposed, together with the simplifying concept of the freedom game played against the environment.

7. Examples of the freedom game were given in two critical areas of behaviour—on the roads and in the sphere of leisure pursuits—demonstrating that the number of players is already very near to saturation point.

8. Population policy was discussed, stressing that population is a political problem which must be discussed, along with all other contentious issues, in the market place and the lobbies, that politics is the art of the possible, that democratic governments cannot be expected to do very much about this issue, any more than any other, without being pushed by articulate and insistent public opinion.

Particular methods of controlling population were touched on and the central point made that societies are goal-seeking systems pursuing a hierarchy of goals at the top of which are normally the goals of *survival and preservation of essential identity*. Sooner or later these goals can continue to be realized (only) via the 'instrumental' goal of a stationary population, which must be formulated, accepted, and realized by *whatever means turn out to be necessary*. The sooner we start the more likely it is that the means will be democratic, rational, and humane. If we fail, chaos must ensue.

9. Some of the statements about liberty by lawyers were examined which led to the view that the basic principles of law appear to be capable of adaptation to fertility control without radical changes. Legal experts personally concerned with the population problem are invited to take up these preliminary explorations and give the problem the rigorous treatment it seems to deserve.

10. It was finally argued that to pursue a policy of optimization within a framework of law a further instrumental goal must be freedom from fatalism—we must not allow ourselves to be mesmerized by the sheer immensity of the problems, or by prejudice or inertia. We must not pretend that we are landed with an inevitable state of affairs—avoiding 'bad faith', that is, in Sartre's terms —and go on to realize our 'freedom *for*', as Fromm put it, or to '*invent*' our own future in the words of Dennis Gabor.

Summary of the ecology of liberty

Putting together the two sets of facts discussed in chapters 6 and 7, the tendency of some microfreedoms to *in*crease as numbers increase (because the numbers of people with like minds or similar needs will also tend to increase and make it possible to separate out more and more individualistic activities), and the constant *de*crease in freedom to move about from the sheer growth in the number of bodies—to put it at its most basic level—not to mention the huge increase in bureaucratic control. Once again there is a clash between microfreedoms, the problem is not whether 'FREEDOM' is present or absent, but *what kinds of microfreedoms* are present or absent, and to what degree.

This leads us to a quest for a scale of values by which we can measure the value of one microfreedom against another and brings us once more to the concept of an optimum population in which the most desirable microfreedoms are realized most and the least desirable microfreedoms least. We must reduce some microfreedoms in order to maximize others.

In the analogy of the freedom game this would mean halting the growth in the number of players at some point short of total congestion of the board so that the microfreedom of the players to keep on playing, and, playing, to keep on scoring, is not increasingly hampered and finally reduced to zero.

Britain has pioneered a code of basic freedoms for domestic animals—the five basic 'ecological' freedoms being, as Ruth Harrison pointed out:

> Sufficient freedom of movement to be able without difficulty to turn round, groom itself, get up, lie down and stretch its limbs.

Might it be reasonable to hope that we shall now pioneer a similar code for that other domesticated animal, *homo sapiens*? If we are consistent, radical, and bold enough to carry these principles forward into a code of practice for human beings in their natural and man made habitats it is to be hoped that the definitions of the basic minimal space for an individual human to live, move, breathe, and have his being will be somewhat more liberal. Being able to stand up, lie down, turn round and stretch your limbs is very much better than nothing, it is true, as many political prisoners could testify, but there is no inherent reason why the minimal dimensions of mobility should not be greatly increased, nor yet any great difficulty in extending these basic principles to include such microfreedoms as:

1. Freedom from excessive supervision, co-ordination, co-operation, or control of your physical activities in any field whatever.

2. Freedom to walk in urban areas without undue danger of being run over or suffering excessively from noise or air pollution.

3. Freedom to own and enjoy a house and a modest amount of property without undue risk of its amenities being ruined and its economic value diminished by developments due to population pressure, with *full* compensation paid by those who cause the damage when your privacy and enjoyment are invaded for really inescapable reasons.

4. Freedom to reach open countryside in not more than one hour's travel.

5. Freedom to walk in the country at two miles per hour without meeting other human beings more frequently than once every thirty minutes on the average.

6. Freedom to find 'wilderness', in which human beings are rare, in not more than four hour's travelling time.

7. Freedom to own and drive a private motor vehicle on public roads without being brought to a halt by other vehicles, traffic controls, road works, pedestrians or other obstructions for more than five minutes in every hour, on the average.

8. Freedom to use the nearest municipal swimming bath without queuing more than five minutes to get in or find a cubicle to change in, or more than one collision per length as you swim.

9. Freedom to fish from any pier with not less than 2 yards between yourself and your nearest neighbours, or along the coast or banks of rivers and reservoirs with at least 20 yards between you and your neighbours.

10. Freedom to play football, rugby, squash, cricket, tennis, bowls, or any sport that takes your fancy without undue travelling, cost, delay, or interference.

11. Freedom to play golf without having to queue up from the small hours of the morning or excessive cost or undue pressures from golfers to get a move on.

12. Freedom to sail a dinghy or other small sailing vessel in our coastal waters and estuaries without danger of collisions or entanglement of rigging.

13. Freedom to learn to climb on nursery slopes without danger of people treading on your fingers, dislodging rocks on to your head, tangling your safety line or otherwise causing danger, inconvenience, or loss of pleasure to you, and the same for climbing once you have graduated, etc etc.

This baker's dozen of microfreedoms dreamed up on the spur of the moment is obviously arbitrary and merely offered as a possible line of thought. It is clear that the more restricted they were the larger the number of people who could be accommodated within a particular eco-system at a particular time. It is equally clear that for a time increases in certain basic microfreedoms could be reconciled with increasing numbers—this is not in dispute. What is disputed is the simple-minded idea that ever-increasing numbers are reconcilable with a given code of human dignity and freedom if only we are prepared to put our backs into the necessary organization and financing of resources. Continuously increasing numbers cannot be reconciled with *any* code of human freedom, however minimal its provisions may be—the infinite cannot go into the finite. Eventually the microfreedoms to stand up, stretch your arms out, and turn round would disappear beneath the weight of numbers, literally.

The principles underlying this analysis are very simple. In any system not already over-populated a code of practice for human dignity and freedom can be realized by activities directed towards and operating upon the environment, both natural and man made. Beyond the critical point, however, when over-population sets in, the code can be realized only by activities directed towards and operating upon the population to be accommodated within the environment. From this point on either the code or the increase in numbers must be sacrificed, they cannot co-exist. If the code be subjected to the death of a thousand cuts—which is happening at this moment—progressively reducing human freedom, eventually the point will be reached at which it disappears completely. Numbers must finally stop increasing anyway, because the environment —the basis of the ecology of liberty—would simply be choked solid with human flesh. It might please some to observe that the last microfreedom to disappear was that of procreation *ad lib* but this could hardly provide lasting comfort.

If this is so it doesn't seem too unreasonable to define the code of human freedom in such a way that it prevents its own ultimate destruction.

Favourable factors

1. Until 1930 the whole population of the world would have been able to stand on the Isle of Wight. It could still be crammed into any English county, excepting the three smallest, provided it left all its belongings behind.

If space was equally shared, each world citizen in AD 2000 would still have about eighteen and a half acres of the Earth's surface; thirteen acres (71 per cent) of this would be ocean, it is true, but it is likely that some humans will be able to live on and possibly even under the sea. This would compensate to some extent for the fact that of the remaining five and a half acres (29 per cent) over four acres (20 per cent) would be desert, rock, and ice, leaving the 9 per cent, about one-and-two-thirds acres, to live and work on, to grow food, and to amuse himself.

2. Everyone has to die sometime and if everyone died more or less simultaneously all population problems would disappear, except in the eyes of those who think an Earth without human beings would be unnatural. Even these people might be satisfied to reflect, en route for the happy hunting grounds, that evolutionary

processes freed from the obtuse, illiberal, and ham-fisted interference of our species would gain a new impetus and might do far better than *homo sapiens* next time.

If only a fifth or so of the world's population—suitably distributed, of course—were to die prematurely, the world would gain a substantial respite. It might be enabled to get its social structure modernized and its economy through the crucial 'take off' stage, as England did after the great plagues of the fourteenth century, and reconstruct its demographic policies so as to avoid further crises of over-population.

3. We have seen a good deal already of the extraordinary achievements—though sometimes for evil—of scientists and technologists when they have been given substantial resources for experimentation, change, and production. We can reasonably hope that the future will produce still greater scientific marvels and cultural systems more adapted to sorting the technological wheat from the chaff and utilizing it quicker and better, which, if we are lucky, will give us a quarter to half a life span to get the population problem under control.

4. Insofar as the inevitable population control involves drastic changes in the prevailing climate of thought and related forms of behaviour, however pessimistic we are about the difficulty of introducing them in the short run we can derive comfort for the long run from even a superficial perusal of studies of human behaviour. These demonstrate that virtually every biologically possible form of behaviour has been not only tolerated but positively required in some culture or other at some time or other. No universal taboo has yet been discovered and what we define as the crimes or abominations of fratricide, patricide, matricide, infanticide, incest, cannibalism, and many others have been not only acceptable but the sacred duties of some peoples.

Many of these 'unthinkables' have seen service as mechanisms of population control and if other cultures have in the past been able to accept measures like these with equanimity surely we can put up with a bit of civilized rationing if voluntary means should fail.

5. The advanced countries of the world are already well on the way to reducing the birth rate typical of the greater part of man's evolutionary history—perhaps fifty births per thousand per annum —towards the target figure for a stationary population with high life-expectancy. This is about fourteen per thousand per annum

and in Britain we are nine-tenths of the way there, we require only the smallest extra effort, comparatively speaking, to achieve the goal.

The era of self-control

We might summarize the trends described in the section on the 'rearguard action' by saying that *homo sapiens* is entering the epoch of self-control. Throughout past history it has been possible for human beings to grab what they could, when they could, and how they could, and then throw away what they didn't want, without much thought for the consequences. The environment has been big, bounteous, and resilient enough for this to go on without massive disruption or too painful consequences except for local minorities now and then.

However, mankind has now arrived at a situation in which this is no longer possible. In all sorts of ways we now have appetites and capacities for satisfying them—or at least trying to—which are incompatible with the survival not only of individuals or local communities but of the world system. It is not for nothing that the expression 'doomsday' is back in everyday use.

For example, humanity has now stacked up sufficient weapons of destruction in the Soviet Union and the USA to destroy itself totally, together with its material resources. Severe and permanent restraint will have to be used to prevent these horrendous stockpiles being used up and, practically speaking, putting an end to humanity. Similarly, in the field of chemical and biological warfare there is now a sufficient potential for the better part of the human race to be wiped out very quickly and efficiently with small quantities[1] of highly toxic substances or virulent strains of bacteria. Here again, restraint will have to be used to prevent these frightful weapons from being liberated.

In the more personal sphere of life we have the motor car which bids fair to become one of the most lethal developments in the whole human armoury as we saw in the chapter on 'Freedom of the Road'. Severe restraint will have to be exercised in order to prevent things getting completely out of hand in the very near future. More personally still, in the richer societies we now have many symptoms of over-indulgence. The first of these is again related to the motor car—millions of people are now so reliant on their cars that they

[1] Six ounces of botulinous toxin is enough to kill everyone in the USA.

suffer from degenerative diseases and live worse and die earlier than they need because they do not get enough exercise.

Smoking is becoming a serious problem in most societies because of the amount of bronchitis and lung cancer it causes and about the only way to tackle this democratically—beyond banning cigarette advertising and compelling manufacturers to point out the health hazard on the packet, as the Americans have done—is by encouraging self-restraint.

By the same token we must avoid over-indulgence in the prices, profits and wages that our powerful pressure groups are able to squeeze out of their fellows, and, finally, in stretching the earth's capacity to absorb insult from pollution and in consuming its irreplaceable raw materials.

The same applies to eating. Obesity is a problem in most, probably all, of the better-off countries—not to mention the well-to-do in poor countries. About half the population of Britain is said to be overweight by the Food Education Society, and evidence from the USA shows that men 20 per cent or more overweight have 31 per cent greater mortality than those of normal weight. Those who have been overweight and returned to a more appropriate level by means of dieting appreciably increase their longevity.[2]

Alcoholism is a marginal case—this again is a serious problem in all developed societies but if it be a true disease, such as influenza, then clearly the sufferer is not abusing his liberty and can hardly be expected to take any responsibility for his condition.[3] However, if there is an element of choice in this—whether one puts oneself on the slippery slope towards alcoholism or not—then to that extent it also is a question of self-restraint. In other words it is now possible for *homo sapiens* to blast, poison, smoke, gorge, or guzzle himself into an early grave—either individually or en masse—and the only way to prevent this is by the exercise of intelligent self-restraint.

It seems obvious that the foregoing logic applies to the population problem, also. Now that man has cured his killing diseases—or at least got them severely in check—he can, paradoxically, easily breed himself into an early grave, if not in the literal sense of death, at least into a ferocious, animal-like existence in the

[2] For a good brief summary see: OHE (1969), *Obesity and Disease.*
[3] There is a community in the USA which bases its apparently very successful therapy on an enforced recognition by the patient that he is responsible for his condition. See Sugarman, B, 'Daytop Village', *New Society*, April 13, 1967.

burial place of all that is civilized and worthwhile. Restraint is needed here just as much as in the fields of atomic, chemical, and biological warfare—probably more so. The H-bombs may never go off, the chemical and biological weapons may never be loosed but the population bomb is ticking away inexorably the whole time. It can be checked only by self-restraint, either spontaneously on the part of a sufficient number of individuals, or by means of society as a whole developing the necessary constraints upon its members. It is a restraint which must come soon, bear equitably on society, and remain operative indefinitely into the future, perhaps the greatest self-restraint of them all.

One of the great difficulties—and it may turn out to be a tragedy —is that population problems have become so entangled with racial issues and nationalism that they cannot be appraised coolly with the result that appropriate measures are even less likely to be adopted. Radicals of both left and right tend to oppose population control—even birth control—with a white hot passion and those on the left frequently associate it with imperialism, fascism—even genocide.

Population has been associated with power from time immemorial and this belief persists even today when firepower is much more significant than manpower and when firepower may increase more rapidly with a stationary population than with one which is expanding. The reason for this is that the demographic investment is liberated for other purposes which could be, if desired, investment in military technology.

When a suggestion was made in the Rhodesian Parliament in 1966 that a family planning campaign should be sponsored within the African community, leading Africans—according to John Worrall, reporting for *The Guardian*:

> ... reacted like angry hornets ... many thought ... it was all a devilish white plot to destroy the African race and ensure white supremacy for ever.
>
> African MPs ... described birth control variously and violently as manslaughter, legalized murder, abortion, and un-Christian.[4]

The black Rhodesian birth rate is extremely high ... the population having increased by more than ten times in the last fifty years— and almost undoubtedy they would be much better off, economic-

4 March 11, 1966.

ally speaking, if their fertility was reduced; even a dedicated black nationalist government and economy could not hope to manage with this rate of increase. On the other hand their burgeoning numbers are a threat to the economy as a whole, especially under the policy of sanctions, and to white supremacy, so that their white oppressors may be driven to ever-increasing extremism in both governmental and social spheres.

Even though black Rhodesians might be much better off economically—and perhaps socially and politically as well—if their numbers were smaller, it is a lot to expect of them to agree to curtail their natural increase significantly—let alone stabilize their population—under the repression of the existing white regime. They will be driven to cut off their noses to spite their faces in an attempt to generate as soon as possible the pressure necessary for the inevitable and explosive shattering of white domination and winning elementary rights of citizenship in their own country. Only when that day comes, perhaps, will the enormity of the crime committed by the white Rhodesians and the folly of the British government which permitted it, become apparent.

Somewhat similar considerations apply in the United States of America where a sane demographic policy can never take root until the folly of racialism is utterly abolished.

What should be the attitude of anyone concerning himself with the study of mankind or with his future? It may be that the biologically correct answer is to opt out and make no attempt to prevent *homo sapiens* from destroying himself, which he is obviously well on the way towards doing, merely keeping impeccable scientific records of the actual mode of his demise in as complete, imperishable and communicable a manner as possible for the benefit of any posterity there may be, in the form of visitors from other worlds or of his evolutionary successor, another sentient and, one hopes, less blindly destructive species.

On the other hand it could be argued, paraphrasing a remark of the potential Conservative statesman, Mr R. A. Butler, on a celebrated occasion, that *homo sapiens* is the best hominid we have, so that it behoves those of his numbers who concern themselves with the behaviour and possible future of the species to do the best they can with him.

Cultural elements are playing an increasingly large part in the evolutionary process and all those who study the evolution, behaviour, and potential of their species—including themselves, of course—attempting to legislate for his future by means of a display of facts, theories, and exhortation, the scientists, satirists, moralists, and intellectuals in general, are part and parcel of it.

The implication of this is that students of human behaviour should throw themselves into the struggle to make sure that man has a future with renewed vigour, dedication, and insight. Social scientists, at present guilty of an almost universal abnegation of responsibility in Britain, should surely be in the vanguard in this struggle, not merely to preserve the species from destruction, but to develop its potential to the highest level.

The compassionate student of human behaviour can rest assured that in the long run—barring accidental or wanton destruction of the species—whatever is essential will by definition be brought about. He can then throw himself into the struggle to introduce the necessary changes as quickly and painlessly as possible knowing that he must succeed in his task, at least to some degree, if only he can help to minimize suffering during the stages of transition. The problems are huge, complex, and frightening enough in all conscience but despair is useless while constructive, energetic, realistic optimism can only help to win the day.

The great problem facing humanity—and this is especially poignant for reformers, revolutionaries, socialists, improvers in general —is to evolve a philosophy of life which is expansionist with respect to every good thing in life (things which need not necessarily be reflected in the gross national product) while becoming restrictionist in those spheres in which self-indulgence is becoming catastrophic. We must become restrictionist in this basic area of reproduction while retaining—even developing—our love of life and concern for people, we must become responsible without turning into narrow gutted killjoys, become socially aware without becoming busybodies, and community-minded while at the same time developing our individuality to the full. This is the dilemma and there is no escaping it.

This most difficult synthesis can, must, and will be achieved—if only in the long run—but the sooner we start, the better.

The slogan 'give me microfreedoms a, b, d, l, p, s, and z, or give me death!' may not be as inspiring as the original but it should be much more useful in working towards a viable balance between freedom and restraint.

It may appear selfish or parochial of me to have dwelt almost exclusively on Britain's population problems—especially as I have devoted a whole chapter to motoring problems and another to the impending saturation of our amenity resources—when people are suffering from starvation and violence caused or exacerbated by population pressure. My reasons are fourfold: first that the world's population problems have been widely canvassed already; secondly that our own population problems are usually glossed over; thirdly that we are generally more concerned with our personal problems than with other peoples—even though they may be far worse off—and fourthly that people in countries with more immediate problems are not going to listen to our propaganda about population control unless we show we mean business by practising it ourselves. Population control, like charity, should begin at home.

Homo sapiens is far too inclined to preen himself in smug self-satisfaction when he contemplates the range of environmental tolerance and variety of human types and activities but the very adaptability which permits them may itself become pathological.

If man adapts himself in the short run to things which are likely or even certain to ensure his demise in the long run—things such as environmental pollution or to social systems seeking a never-ending increase in the lethality of their stockpiles of atomic and other weapons—then his adaptability will have turned out to be a snare and a delusion. It may be more prudent in some circumstances to decline to adapt to a new mode of existence and insist on retaining the old. Ecological chains of cause and effect can be very long and of the utmost complexity. Our understanding of the mechanisms involved is primitive, to say the least. There are substantial 'lags', an engineer would say, in our control system relating to the environment and the 'biological backlash'[5] to use a term coined by Gerald Leach, can be dramatic as we have seen in the cases of Thalidomide and DDT, to name only two of many examples.

In an attempt to provide an all embracing and coherent argument I have had to skim many fields of learning. I know that the operative word is 'skim' and I present the results in all humility and with the knowledge that experts in the various fields touched on—philosophy, ecology, sociology, economics, psychology, politics, demography, jurisprudence, ethics, biology, traffic studies, sport and others—can point to books I haven't read, the arguments I have overlooked, the authorities I fail to quote, and failures to

[5] The title of a series of four documentaries on the BBC Third Programme in March, 1967. To be reprinted by the Conservation Society.

understand or to make obvious inferences and deductions from the data which *is* presented.

In writing these last few words I am only too well aware how much my thesis needs another five years or more of steadfast application. Meanwhile, however, the world cries out for a moral and rational basis for population control—the social climate has changed out of all recognition since I started five years ago—and I hope this book will help to create a stimulus to trigger off the great debate. I ask only that readers' criticism—as tough as you know how to make them—will be constructive. Where I have failed will others please go on and try to do better.

I have struggled long and hard with the notion of liberty and written very many pages about it, most of which went to the waste-paper basket, but in spite of all that I am not at all sure I have hit the right note and I think a quotation from a modern poet might help to add the missing dimension—to evoke the right timbre— to clothe a somewhat bare logical and factual skeleton with the essential flesh of humanity, spirituality, love, or whatever word or quality you may choose. Paul Potts, a writer of almost transcendental sincerity, simplicity, and innocence, wrote in his recent and remarkable work, *To Keep a Promise*:

> *Freedom is a certain graceful reverence for the rights and needs of other people.*[6]

I cannot help feeling that people who dogmatically refuse to discuss the control of fertility and rigidly insist on their 'right' to do whatever they like in this critical realm of reproduction, have not yet awoken to this sensitivity and concern for their fellow citizens. It is greatly to be hoped that rapidly developing mass societies do not dull this sense still further.

The last word can safely be left with the much-maligned Malthus:

> ... On the whole, therefore, though our future prospects respecting the mitigation of the evils arising from the principle of population may not be so bright as we could wish, yet they are far from being entirely disheartening, and by no means preclude the gradual and progressive improvement in human society which, before the late wild speculations on this subject, was the object of rational expectation ...

[6] (1970) (p 117/8).

It would indeed be a melancholy reflection that, while the views of physical science are daily enlarging, so as scarcely to be bounded by the most distant horizon, the science of moral and political philosophy should be confined within such narrow limits, or at best be so feeble in its influence, as to be unable to counteract the obstacles to human happiness arising from a single cause,

... however formidable these obstacles may have appeared in some parts of this work, it is hoped that the general result of the inquiry is such as not to make us give up the improvement of human society in despair. The partial good which seems to be attainable is worthy of all our exertions.[7]

7 Malthus, Vol 2, pp 261–2.

Bibliography

AA. 'It's Highway Robbery', *Drive*, Autumn, 1969.

Actuary's Department (Govt). 'Projecting the Population of the United Kingdom'. *Economic Trends*, No 139, May, 1965.

Adler, JH. 'Poverty Amidst Wealth'. BBC 3rd Prog. March 10, 1969

Allan, W. See Hutchinson.

Allen and Morton. (1961) *This is Your Child*.

Alper, S. (1968) Earls Court Press Conference.

Andreski, I. 'The Baby as Dictator', *New Society*, March 30, 1967.

Andreski, SL. (*a*) (1966) *Parasitism and Subversion*.

—— (*b*) (1968) *The African Predicament*.

Andrews, M. 'Pressures On a Stretch of Water'. *Drive*, Summer, 1969.

Andrews, W. See Vernon.

Annual Abstract of Statistics. Various.

Anon, MP. Letter.

Anon, reviewer of Clark. (1967) *The Economist*, July 15, 1967.

Aquinas, St Thomas. See Rickaby.

Ardrey, R. (1967) *The Territorial Imperative*.

Aristotle, *Politics*.

Association of River Authorities, Annual Reports.

Auden, WH. Prologue: *The Birth of Architecture*.

Barnard, C. (1938) *The Functions of the Executive*.

Barnett, A. (1961) *The Human Species*.

Barron, E. Thomas Coram. 'The Man who saved Children.' *The Lady*, January 25, 1968.

Beckman. See Edie.

Beesley and Roth. 'Restraint of traffic in congested areas.' *Town Planning Rev.* Vol. XXIII. No 3, October, 1962. Reprinted by Liverpool University Press.

Bell, *et al.* (1965) *Textbook of Physiology and Biochemistry*.

Benjamin, B. (1968) *Health and Vital Statistics*.

Bentham, J. (See p131f *Works* (1843) Vol II.

Berelson, B. 'Beyond Family Planning'. *Studies in Family Planning*, No 38, February, 1969.

Best, RH. 'Extent of urban growth and agricultural displacement in post-war Britain'. *Urban Studies*, Vol 5, No 1, February, 1968.

Bible (*a*) II Samuel 24. 2–8.

    (*b*) Genesis xiii.

    (*c*) Ecclesiastes, Ch 3.

    (*d*) St Mark xiii, 17.

    (*e*) St Luke xxiii, 28–9.

    (*f*) Ecclesiasticus, xvi.

Birch, AG. (1968) *Paper to the Recreation Management Conference.* Mimeo.

Blackham, HJ. (ed.). (1971) *Towards an Open Society.*

Blackstone, Sir W. (1765–9) *Commentaries on the Laws of England.*

Boas, F. See Hall.

Bonar, J. (1966) *Malthus and His Work.*

Braddock, T. (1966) Labour Party Annual Conference.

Brambell Committee. (1965) Report.

Breach, I. (*a*) *The Guardian*, April 28, 1969.

—— (*b*) *The Guardian*, April 28, 1969.

British Road Federation. (1968 and 1969) *Basic Road Statistics.* (Pub. annually).

Brook, C. 'The Cost Effectiveness of Family Planning'. *Family Planning Miscellany*, July, 1968.

Brooks, E. MP. See Renton.

Browne, EM. (ed.) (1960) *Three European Plays.*

Burke, E. Quotation.

Burns, W. *The Guardian*, September 10, 1968.

Caradoc-Jones. (Undated 1950s?) *Social Surveys.*

Caradon, Lord. See World Leaders.

Carroll, L. (1872) *Through the Looking Glass.*

Carr-Saunders, Sir A. (1922) *The Population Problem.*

Case of Thorns. (1466) See Wright.

Castle, B. *The Guardian*, March 27, 1968.

Cattel. See Krech.

Challinor and Ripley. (1969) *The Miners Association.*

Chambers, H and D 'Hard to Place', *Listener* March 4, 1971.

Chambers, JD, and Mingay, GE. (1966) *The Agricultural Revolution* 1750–1880.

Cherrington, J. *Financial Times*, October 3, 1968.

CIBA Foundation. (1966) *Nature of International Society.*

Cipolla, C. (1962) *Economic History of World Population.*

Clark, C. (*a*) (1967) *Population Growth and Land Use.*

—— (*b*) Do 'Population and Freedom Grow Together?' *Fortune Magazine*, December, 1960.

Coale, AJ. See Hauser.

Connell, KM. (1950) *The Population of Ireland.*

Cooley, CH. (1964) *Human Nature and the Social Order.*

Coser, L. (1956) *The Functions of Social Conflict.*

Coser and Rosenberg, (eds.) (1964) *Sociological Theory.*

Cottrell, F. (*a*) (1955) *Energy and Society.*

—— (*b*) (1966) *The Future of Freedom.*

Cox, H. (1922) *The Problem of Population.*

Cox, PR. (1959) *Demography.*

Cranston, M. (1953) *Freedom. A New Analysis.*

Crossman, R. 'Why Promise on New Town Had to Go'. *The Guardian*, July 5, 1965.

Darwin, C. (1859) *Origin of Species.*

Deevey, ES. 'The Human Population. *Sc Amer*, September 1960.

Demeny. See Ohlin.

Desmond, A. See Mudd.

Deutsch, K. See CIBA.

Dicey, AV. (1902) *The Law of the Constitution.*

Dictionary of Economics, Everyman's (1965).

Douglas, M. 'Population control in primitive groups'. *Brit J. Sociol* 17, 1966.

Dowell, S. (1965) *History of Taxation and Taxes in England*, Vol 2.

Drake, M. (ed.) (1969) *Population in Industrialization.*

Duke of Buccleuch v Cowen (1866). See Wright.

Durant, W. (1935) *Our Oriental Heritage.*

Durie, AC. (*a*) (1967) *Paying for London Roads.*

—— (*b*) (1968) *Motoring into the 1980s.*

Durkheim, E. (*a*) (1951) *Suicide.*

—— (*b*) (1964) *The Division of Labour in Society.*

Dury, G. (1966) *The Face of the Earth.*

Ebling, FJ. (ed.) (1969) *Biology and Ethics.*

Economic and Social Council of the UN. Statement on poverty and population control, *UN Population Newsletter* No 8, March, 1970.

Edie, *et al.* (1967) *Vehicular Traffic Science.*

Edinburgh, Duke of. (1964) Address to Freedom From Hunger Campaign. Transcript.

Elliot, H. (1917) *Herbert Spencer*.

Encyclopaedia, Everyman's. (1949–50.)

Enke and Zind. 'Effect of fewer births on average income'. *Journal of Biosocial Science 1* No 1, January, 1969.

Eversley, D. (*a*) 'Is Britain being threatened by overpopulation?' 1 and 2. *The Listener*, July 20 and 27, 1967.

—— (*b*) Letter. *The Listener*, August 3, 1967.

Fabian Society. See Rendel.

Family Planning Organization. October, 1968.

Findlay, G. (1936) *Miscegenation*.

Finer, H. (1950) *The Theory and Practice of Modern Government*.

Fisher, J. 'Taming the Big Game'. *Drive*, Summer, 1969.

Foreign and Commonwealth Office (1971) *International Regime* (mimeo).

Franklin, B. (1751) *An Essay on the Increase of Mankind*.

Fraser and Watson 'Family Planning—A Myth?' *The Practitioner*, 201, August, 1968.

Frazer, Sir J. (1950) *The Golden Bough*.

Fremlin, JH. (*a*) 'How Many People Can the World Support?' *New Scientist*, October 29, 1964, and Conservation Society Reprints, No 1, 1968.

—— (*b*) 'An Optimum population for Britain'. *New Scientist*, December 21, 1967, and CS Reprints No 2, 1969.

French National Assembly. (1793/95) *Declaration of the Rights of Man and of Citizens*.

Frere, S. (1967) *Britannia, A History of Roman Britain*.

Fromm, E. (1942) *The Fear of Freedom*.

Furlong, M. 'The Status Symbol of the 4 BABY FAMILY'. *Daily Mail*, August 18, 1963.

Gabor, D. (1963) *Inventing the Future*.

Gallie, WB. (1952) *Pierce and Pragmatism*.

GEC-Elliot Automation. (1970) Letter.

General Assembly of the UN. (*a*) (1948) *Universal Declaration of Human Rights*.

—— (*b*) (1969) Statement on parents' rights.

Gibson, Sir D. (*a*) 'State of Total War in Building Industry'. *The Guardian*, April 28, 1965.

—— (*b*) 'No of buildings'. *The Guardian*, September 27, 1966.

Glass and Blacker. (1938) *Population and Fertility*.

GLC and SE Sports Council. (1968) *Sports Facilities*.

Golf Development Council. (1968) *Preliminary Report on Playing Facilities.*

Gomme. See Sumner.

Gould and Kolb. (1964) *Dictionary of the Social Sciences.*

Great Yarmouth Port and Haven Commissioners. Reports.

Green, F. See Gabor.

Gregory, PGM. (1968) *The Plight of the Motorist* (Pamphlet).

Haeckel, EH. (1868) *The History of Nature.*

Haire, M. (ed.) (1961) *Modern Organisation Theory.*

Haldane, JBS. 'On Being the Right Size'. Chapter in *Possible Worlds and Other Papers* (1928).

Hall, ET. (1969) *The Hidden Dimension.*

Hardin, H. (*a*) 'The Tragedy of the Commons'. *Science*, December 13, 1968.

—— (*b*) Quotation, *The Guardian*, September 22, 1969.

Haney, LM. (1921) *History of Economic Thought.*

Hansard. Entered under name of speaker.

Hare. See Krech.

Harrison, R. 'Why Animals Need Freedom to Move'. *Observer,* October 12, 1969.

Hart, HLA. (1962) *Law, Liberty and Morality.*

Hauser, MP. (ed.) (1963) *The Population Dilemma.*

Hayek, FA. (1960) *The Constitution of Liberty.*

Hegel. (1812) *Logik.*

Heenan, Dr. BBC Home Service. December, 1963. (Notes.)

Hiller. See Coser.

Hippodamus. See Aristotle.

HMSO. *Annual Abstract of Statistics,* various.

HMSO. (1949) *Report of the Royal Commission on Population.*

HMSO. (1965) *Research on Road Traffic.*

HMSO. (1967) *Circumstances of Families.*

HMSO. (1967) *Highway Statistics.*

HMSO. (1967) *Road Research.*

HMSO. (1967) *Sexual Offences Act.*

HMSO. (1967) *Administration of the Wage-Stop.*

HMSO. (1968) *Housing Statistics: Gt. Britain.* No 10, July, 1968.

HMSO. (1968) *Road Research.*

HMSO. (1968) *Report of Royal Commission on Trade Unions and Employers Associations.*

Hobbes, T. (1551) *Leviathan.*

Hodge and Sons v Anglo American Oil. (1922).

Hoskins, WG. (1959) *Local History in England.*

Houghton, D. (*a*) Speech. *The Guardian*, July 3, 1969.

—— (*b*) see Taylor, LR.

Howard, JE. (1967) *How to Drive Safely. The Art of Survival.*

Howe, GM. (1970) *National Atlas of Disease Mortality.*

Howell, D. (1966) Report of Sports Council.

Hoyle, F. (1963) *A Contradiction in the Argument of Malthus.*

Hughes, DR. (1964) Letter to *The Times*, April 21, 1964.

Hume, D. (1741–42) 'Of the Populousness of Ancient Nations'. *Essays Literary, Moral and Political.*

Humphrey, M. 'The Enigma of Childlessness'. *New Society*, March 13, 1969.

Hutchinson, Sir J. (*a*) 'Land and Human Populations', *The Listener.* September 1, 1966.

—— (*b*) (1969) *Population and Food Supply.*

Huxley, A. (1946) *Brave New World.*

Inge, WR. (1949) *The End of An Age.*

Institute of Biology. See Taylor.

Jones, CD. (Undated. 1950s?) *Social Surveys.*

Kant, I. (1781) *Critique of Pure Reason.*

Keegan, V. *The Guardian*, February 2, 1970.

Kennet, Lord. *Hansard*, February 19, 1969.

Khayyam, O. (11th–12th century) *Rubaiyat.*

Kinze, AF. 'Body Buffer Zones in Violent Prisoners'. *New Society* No 435, January 28, 1971.

Klein, J. (1956) *The Study of Groups.*

Knowles, LCA. (1947) *Industrial and Commercial Revolutions.*

Kohr, L. 'Critical Size'. *Resurgence*, July/August, 1967.

Kolbuszewski, J. 'Transport and the Human Environment'. *The Chartered Mechanical Engineer.* October, 1969.

Koshtoyants, KS. (ed.) (1955) *Pavlov, IP, Selected Works.*

Kuznets. See Robinson, EAG.

Krzywicki, L. (1934) *Primitive Society and its Vital Statistics.*

Labour Party Conference. (1970) Resolution.

Lake District Planning Board, (*a*) (1965) *Report on Traffic in the Lake District National Park.*

—— (*b*) (1967) *Detailed Studies of Borrowdale and the Langdales.* Mimeo.

—— (*c*) (1967) *Supplementary Report on Car Parking in Borrowdale.* Mimeo.

—— (*d*) (1968) Circular letter. *Traffic in the Lake District.* Mimeo.

Lambton v. Mellish and Cox (1894). See Wright.

LCC. (1951) County of London Development Plan.

Leach, G. Biological Backlash. Series of four programmes broadcast in March, 1967. BBC 3rd Programme.

Leger, Cardinal. *Oxfam Bulletin*, Spring, 1965.

Lenin. Quotation.

Leyhausen, P. 'The Sane Community—a Density Problem'. *Discovery*, September, 1965, and Reprints, No 1, 1968.

Llewelyn-Davies, Baroness. *Hansard*. February 19, 1969.

Locke, J. (1690) *Second Treatise of Civil Government.*

Lotka, A. (1956) *Elements of Mathematical Biology.*

Lorenz, K. (*a*) (1952) *King Solomon's Ring.*

—— (*b*) (1966) *On Aggression.*

Loughlin, C. Parliamentary Answer. See Rowland.

Lovelace, R. (17th century) *To Althea From Prison.*

MacDermott, N. Speech. *The Guardian*, October 8, 1967.

McAlister (or Donoghue) v. Stevenson. See Wright.

McArthur, N. 'The Demography of Primitive Populations'. *Science*, February 20, 1970.

McCormack, Father A. 'Why I disagree with Dr Mehta'. *Oxfam Bulletin*. No 9, Spring, 1965.

McNamara, R. Speech in Quebec, May 18, 1966.

Malinowski. (*a*) (1947) *Freedom and Civilisation.*

—— (*b*) See Coser.

Mallinson, R. 'Property Market'. *The Guardian*, October 17, 1968.

Malthus, T. (1798) *An Essay on Population.*

Manning, AD. *Daily Telegraph*, January 7, 1970.

Mao Tse Tung. *Thoughts.*

Marsh, R. *The Guardian*, November 24, 1969.

Mazzini, J. (1907) (tr.) *The Duties of Man.*

Meade, JE. 'Population Explosion, The Standard of Living and Social Conflict'. CS Reprints No II.

Mehta, Dr J. 'Fewer Children or Disaster'. *Oxfam Bulletin*, No 9. Spring, 1965.

Merton, R. (1967) *Social Theory and Social Structure.*

Michels, R. (1915) *Political Parties.*

Miller. See Krech.

Milton. (17th century) Sonnet XII.

Mingay, JE. See Chambers.

Ministry of Transport. Letter. June 19, 1969.

Mishan, EJ. (1967) *The Costs of Economic Growth.*

Mitrany, D. (1954) *Food and Freedom.*

Moede. See Klein.

Montaigne. (1580/88) *Essays.*

Montefiori, Canon Hugh. Speech. Anglican Church Assembly, February, 1970.

Montesquieu. See Inge.

Moore, J. *The Guardian,* March 9, 1965.

Morgan, EV. (1965) *Economic and Financial Aspects of Road Improvements.*

Morris, D. (1967) *The Naked Ape.*

Mudd, S. (1964) *The Population Crisis and the Use of World Rescources.*

Municipal Year Book. (1970).

Nature. 'Note on thermoluminescence'. 219, 442, August 3, 1968.

NEDC. (*a*) (1968) *Future Demand For Garage and Workshop Services.*

NEDC. (*b*) (1969) *Labour Utilisation and Turnover in Garages.*

North Region Planning Board and Northern Advisory Council for Sport and Recreation. (1967) Paper No 1, Golf.

Norwich, Bishop of. See Montefiori.

Office of Health Economics (OHE). (*a*) (1968) *Old Age.*

—— (*b*) (1969) *Obesity and Disease.*

Ohlin, G. (1967) *Population Control and Economic Development.*

Oxborn, PG. (1954) *The Concise Law Dictionary* (4th ed.).

Paine, T. (1791) *Rights of Man.*

Parkes, AS. See Ebling.

Parsons, J. (*a*) 'The Population Explosion'. *New Statesman,* April 30, 1965, and Conservation Society Reprints No 1, 1968.

—— (*b*) 'Population v. Liberty'. In *Planners v. People* (1970) (Pamphlet).

Pavlov, IP. See Koshtoyants.

Pemberton Publishing Co. (1971) *Towards an Open Society.* (Proc. BHA Seminar.)

Pennock, JR. See Gould and Kolb.

PEP. (1955) *World Population and Resources.*

Plato, Laws. Also see Gould and Kolb.

Pope Urban II. See Hutchinson.

Pope John XXIII. (1961) *Mater et Magistra.*

Pope Paul VI (1967) *Populorum Progressio.*

Pope Pius XI. (1930) *Casti connubii.*

The Population Council. *Studies in Family Planning*, No 41, April, 1969.

The Population Council. *Studies in Family Planning*, No 22, August, 1967.

Potts, Dr M. *Conservation Society Newsletter*, February, 1969. *Reports on Population/Family Planning*, No 5, July, 1970.

Potts, P. (1970) *To Keep a Promise*.

Presser, HB. 'Voluntary Sterilization. A World View'. *Reports on Population/Family Planning*, No 5, July, 1970.

Proudfoot, VB. 'Experiments in archeology'. *Science Journal*, November, 1967.

Raab and Selznick. (1959) *Major Social Problems*.

Read v. Lyons and Co Ltd. (1947) See Wright.

Rees, DM. *The Guardian*, September 28, 1968.

Reich, W. (1942) *The function of the Orgasm*.

Rendel, M. (1968) *Equality for Women*.

Renton, Sir D. (*a*) (*et al*) (1968) All Party Motion on Population.

—— (*b*) (1967) Correspondence with Harold Wilson, Prime Minister.

Reynolds, DJ. 'Urban motorways and urban congestion'. *British Transport Review*, Vol VI, No 4, August/December, 1961.

Richard, I. MP. Letter.

Rickaby, J. (1892) *Aquinas Ethicus*.

Riesman, *et al*. (1950) *The Lonely Crowd*.

Road Research Laboratory. Report LR 291.

Robertson, J and A. *New Statesman*, August 3, 1968.

Robertson, JM. (1912) *The Evolution of States*.

Robinson, EAG. (ed.) (1963) *Economic Consequences of the Size of Nations*.

Roth, G. (1967) *Paying for Roads, The Economics of Congestion*.

Roucek, JS. (ed.) (1961) *Readings in Contemporary American Sociology*.

Rousseau, JJ. (*a*) (1762) *The Social Contract*.

—— (*b*) 'The State of Law'. Unfinished essay in Everyman's Edition of *The Social Contract*.

Rowland, CR. MP. Parliamentary Question. *Hansard*, April 30, 1965.

Royal Commission on Population. (1949) Report. Cmnd. 7695.

Royal Commission on Trade Unions and Employers Associations. (1968) Report.

Rubinstein and Speakman. (1969) *Leisure, transport and the country-side*.

Runes, DD. (Undated, 1950s) *Dictionary of Philosophy.*
Russell, JC. (1948) *British Medieval Population.*
R.Y.A. Yearbooks.
Sandford, J. (1967) *Cathy Come Home.* Also BBC TV.
Sandler, B. *The Guardian,* April 13, 1965.
Sartre, J-P. See Browne.
Sauvy, A. (1961) *Fertility and Survival.*
Shettles, *The Guardian,* April 6, 1970.
Seashore. See Krech.
Sedleigh-Denfield v. O'Callaghan. (1940) See Wright.
Seward, G. (1946) *Sex and Society.*
Sex Offences Act. (1967).
Shakespeare, W. (*a*) *Comedy of Errors.*
—— (*b*) *Richard II.*
Shapiro, P. 'The Unplanned Children'. *New Society,* November 1,
    1962.
Shorter Oxford Dictionary. (1959.)
Simak, C. (1967) *Trilobite, Dinosaur, and Man. The Earth's Story.*
Sinclair, Sir J. (1790s) *Statistical Account of Scotland.*
Slater. See Krech.
Smigielski, WK. 'Fitting Transport to the City'. *The Municipal and
    Public Services* J., August 9, 1968.
Snow, Lord. *The Guardian,* September 8, 1970.
Soleri, P. (1970) *Arcology.*
Sollins and Belsky, 'Reports on Population'. *Family Planning* No 4,
    June, 1970.
Solon. See Hume.
Sorokin, P. (1957) *Social and Cultural Dynamics.*
Spenser, E. (1589/96) *Faerie Queene.*
Spinoza, B. (1677) *Ethics.*
Sports Council. *Report of Research and Statistics Committee.* Mimeo.
Stamp, LD. (1955) *Man and the Land.*
Steers, JA. (1969) *Coasts and Beaches.*
Stewart, Sir J. (1767) *Principles of Political Economy.*
St John Stevas, N. 'A Roman Catholic View of Population Control'.
    Law and Contemporary Problems. XXV, No 3, Summer, 1960.
Still, E. 'The Fashion For Families'. *New Society,* June 8, 1967.
Storr, A. See Pemberton Publishing Co.
Street, H. (1966) *Freedom, the Individual and the Law.*
Sugarman, B. 'Daytop Village'. *New Society,* April 13, 1967.
Summerskill, Dr S, MP. See Renton, (*a*).

Sumner, G. (1906) *Folkways.*

Swingler, S. 'Free London Transport'. *The Guardian*, June 19, 1968.

Taylor, CE. 'Five Stages in a Practical Population Policy'. *International Development Review*, *X*, No 4.

Taylor, LR. (ed) (1970) *The Optimum Population for Britain.*

Taylor and Smalley. 'Why Britain Tilts'. *Science Journal*, July, 1969.

Thoday. See Hutchinson, Sir J.

Thomlinson, R. (1967) *Demographic Problems.*

Thompson, EP. (ed.) (1970) *Warwick University, Ltd.*

Thompson, JM. (1962) *Road Pricing in Central London.*

Thorpe, W. See Brambell Report.

Thorpe v. Brumfitt. (1873). See Wright.

Tinbergen, N. 'On War and Peace in Animals and Man'. *Science Journal*, June, 1967.

Tindall, G. 'Talking about the family cult'. *The Guardian*, June 20, 1967.

Titmuss, RM. 'Trading in Human Capital'. *Science*, June, 1967.

Trudeau, P. Speech. *FAO Review*, Ceres, Vol 1, No 5, September/October, 1968.

Turbay-Ayela, Dr. See World Leaders' *Declaration on Population.*

UN (*a*) (1948) *Universal Declaration of Human Rights.*

UN (*b*) (1969) *Report on World Population Situation.*

UN Association of the USA. (1969) World Population.

U Thant (*a*) *International Planned Parenthood Federation News*, No 168, February, 1968.

—— (*b*) See World Leaders' *Declaration on Population.*

Vickers, Sir G. 'The End of free fall'. *The Listener*, October 28, 1965.

Watts, M. 'Letter to Editor', *The Listener*, July 27, 1967.

Wells, Sir H. (*a*) *The Guardian*, October 6, 1967.

—— (*b*) *The Times*, November 24, 1969.

Westermann, WL. 'Between Freedom and Slavery'. *American History Rev. L.* (1945) 213–27.

Whitehorn, K. 'Fecund to a Fault', *Observer*, April 18, 1965.

Wibberley, GP. 'Land Scarcity in Britain', *J. of the Town Planning Institute*, April, 1967.

Wilson, H. (*a*) (1953) *War on Want.*

—— (*b*) Correspondence with Sir D. Renton.

Willson, Beckles (Undated, *c.* 1900) *Lost England.*

Winstanley, Dr, MP. See Renton.

Winterbottom, DM. 'How much urban space do we need?' *J. of the Town Planning Institute*, April, 1967.

Wolff, KH. See Roucek.

Wolff, M. 'Are our police still wonderful?' *Drive*, Spring, 1969.

Woods, C. *Police Review*, March, 1969.

World Bank. *UN Population Newsletter*, No 9, June, 1970.

World Leaders' *Declaration on Population*. (1967). (Pamphlet.)

World Health Organisation. (*a*) *Epidemiological and vital Statistics Report*, Vol V, No 4, April, 1952. (Pamphlet.)

World Health Organisation. (*b*) *Accident Statistics*.

Wright, CA. (1963) *Cases On The Law Of Torts*.

Wrigley, EA. See Drake.

Wolff, KH. (1950) *The Sociology of Georg Simmel*.

Wrong, D. 'The Oversocialised Conception of Man'. *American Sociology Rev*. XXVI. pp. 184–193. Reprinted in Coser and Rosenberg (1964).

Wynne Edwards. (*a*) (1962) *Animal Dispersion in Relation to Social Behaviour*.

—— (*b*) 'Population Control in Animals'. *Sc. Amer.*, August, 1964.

Young, M. 'An anti-natal policy: rewards for smaller families'. *What*, Autumn, 1969.

Zaidan, GC. 'Population Growth and Economic Development'. *Studies in Family Planning*, No 42, May, 1969.

Unattributed extracts from mass media:

BBC. 36 mile traffic jam. May, 1970.

BBC. Stolen cars. April 9, 1969.

Drive. Motoring freedom. Autumn, 1969.

Drive. Cost of car and house. Spring, 1969.

Drive. Skimping on servicing. Autumn, 1969.

The Guardian. Editorial on Royal Family size. March 11, 1964.

The Guardian. Municipal brothels. July 7, 10 and 19, 1967.

The Guardian. Zanzibar brides. October 11, 1969.

The Guardian. Warwick University, March 3, 1970.

The Guardian. Case of the old couple and the birds. October 4, 1969.

The Guardian. Literati on privacy and space. February 22, 1969.

The Guardian. Land prices in Hong Kong. October 5, 1968.

The Guardian. Effect of saturating road vehicles. January 23, 1970.

The Guardian. Parking meter studies. December 1, 1969.

The Guardian. Parking meter occupancy. July 19, 1967.

The Guardian. Parking meter and control. November 18, 1969.

The Guardian. Angling. February 3, 1968.

The Guardian. Scientific 'take over' of amenity areas. April 4, 1968.
The Guardian. Preference for 'wilderness'. September 7, 1969.
The Guardian. Douglas Houghton controversy. July 3, 4, 5, 9, 12 and 13, 1969.
The Guardian. Population explosion editorial. September 23, 1964.
The Guardian. Rhodesian birth control. March 11, 1966.
Daily Herald. On Royal Family size. September 7, 1963.
Observer. Golf queues. November 11, 1967.
Sunday Times. Opinion poll. February 1, 1970.

Thanks are due to the following publishers for permission to reprint extracts.

Butterworths. Wright, *Cases on the Law of Torts*
Cambridge University Press. Cox, *Demography*
Jonathan Cape. Morris, *The Naked Ape*
Dover Publications. Sumner, *Folkways.*
Harper and Row. Raab and Selznick, *Major Social Problems.*
Harvard University Press. Barnard, *The Functions of the Executive.*
Macmillan. Robinson, *Economic Consequences of the Size of Nations.*
McGraw Hill. Krech, *et al., Individual in Society.*
New Society, the weekly review of the social sciences, 128 Long Acre, London, WC2.
Shapiro, 'The Unwanted Children'.
Routledge and Kegan Paul. Fromm, *Fear of Freedom.*
University of New Mexico Press. Russell, *British Medieval Population.*

Full references in Bibliography.

Appendix A

Hidden Costs of Road Transport

1   Routine policing of the roads   £?

2   Controlling motoring offences and crime:
    i) apprehending and bringing to trial   £?
    ii) Trial proper   £?
    iii) Carrying out sentences   £?

3   Cost of government relating to road transport:
    i) Ministry of Transport   £?
    ii) Share of Parliament   £?
    iii) Miscellaneous   £?

4   Costs of Road Research:
    i) Road Research Laboratory   £?
    ii) Universities and elsewhere   £?

5   Damage to property:
    i) destruction of property for roadworks   £?
    ii) damage by vibration, etc.   £?
    iii) damage by atmospheric pollution   £?
    iv) costs of noise   £?
    v) losses on sale because of traffic nuisance   £?

6   Loss to economy through investment in private transport
    (less appropriate sum for increased investment in public
    transport) instead of equivalent investment in capital
    and consumer goods.   £?

7   Health costs other than through road accidents   £?

8   Cost of providing free or subsidized parking space   £?

Appendix B

**First report of the Parliamentary Select Committee on Science and
Technology*. Population of the United Kingdom.
A brief note.**

This report appeared during the proof stage of this book and I
can deal with it only briefly here.

The summary contains seven or eight specific suggestions for
dealing with Britain's population problem, stemming mainly from
the recommendations of the Royal Commission Report in 1949,
and including . . . setting up, as an integral and permanent part
of the machinery of government, a Special Office directly responsible
to the Prime Minister . . . including the duty . . . 'To coordinate and
improve the study of the United Kingdom and World population
trends . . . and their consequences' and 'To publicize the effects of
population levels and their consequences . . .'

Having said;
> *'We are convinced of the need to act 20 years in advance in
> order to influence a trend in population figures.* (Para 29, p ix
> Itals orig).

The authors go on to '. . . . finish up with a formulation of resounding ambiguity,' according to the Times editorial on the day
of publication.
> *"The Government must act to prevent the consequences of
> population growth becoming intolerable.* (p x, Itals orig).

One way of making the consequences tolerable is to prevent them
altogether by preventing the population growth which causes them
and the other is to intensify the struggle to compensate as they
inexorably mount up. The Committee gives no hint which of these
interpretations it favours but it is only fair to them to draw attention
to the extraordinary evasiveness of most of the expert 'establishment' witnesses. At one point Mr David Price remarked, in a
discussion of an optimum population for Britain;

> All our witnesses, . . . even those advocating . . . an optimum
> population, . . . have been remarkably reluctant to come out on
> this point . . . This is somewhat frustrating for a Select Committee.
> (para 903).

Perhaps we might help to liberate politicians from the constraints
imposed by this somewhat fastidious reluctance on the part of
academics to express an informed and considered judgment in the
absence of a universal proof or a widespread consensus, by airing
the concept of the 'quasi-optimum' population, defined as follows:

* See p 337.

'A population size which is reasonably acceptable to a democratic society and which the environment can sustain as far into the future as can be foreseen.'

The authors were also disturbed by the;

. . . lack of urgency in Government Departments . . . the complacent view expressed by many of the departmental witnesses, . . . (and the fact that) . . . no appreciation of the new figures for population growth has yet been made. (para 29, p ix).

The *raison d'etre* of this book, individual liberty as an allegedly irremovable obstacle to population control, crops up several times (eg. Professor Glass, para 774) and Mr Airey Neave, the Chairman, told television interviewers after publication of the report that the Committee could not countenance any interference with the family's right to make its own decisions on reproduction.**

However, Sir David Renton's memorandum did touch on the theme of the ecology of liberty, 'The higher the density the less the freedom.' (p 230).

This report is a tremendous step forward . . . the population skeleton has been brought out of the democracy's closet and there are only two further steps to take—though still rather large ones . . . First we must recognize that liberty and control are not necessarily opposed to each other and that in pursuit of an unavoidable goal— in this case a stationary population—whatever turns out to be necessary in the long run has to be done. Secondly we must get on with it.

Beyond a certain point in population growth the measures required to optimize fertility restrict individual liberty less than the measures which would be required to cope with unrestrained growth. Hence macrofreedom, the sum of our microfreedoms, will be enhanced by an effective policy of fertility control.

** See also *Guardian* report, May 19, 1971 (p 1).

Name Index

Subject Index